INDUSTRY AND INEQUALITY

INDUSTRY AND INEQUALITY

The social anthropology of Indian labour

MARK HOLMSTRÖM
University of East Anglia, Norwich

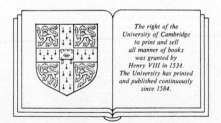

The right of the
University of Cambridge
to print and sell
all manner of books
was granted by
Henry VIII in 1534.
The University has printed
and published continuously
since 1584.

CAMBRIDGE UNIVERSITY PRESS

CAMBRIDGE

LONDON   NEW YORK   NEW ROCHELLE
MELBOURNE   SYDNEY

Published by the Press Syndicate of the University of Cambridge
The Pitt Building, Trumpington Street, Cambridge CB2 IRP
32 East 57th Street, New York, NY 10022, USA
296 Beaconsfield Parade, Middle Park, Melbourne 3206, Australia

© Cambridge University Press 1984

First published 1984

Printed in Great Britain at the University Press, Cambridge

Library of Congress catalogue card number: 84-7065

British Library Cataloguing in Publication Data
Holmström, Mark
Industry and inequality.
1. India—Industries   2. India—Social
conditions—1947–
I. Title
306'.36'0954   HC435.2
ISBN 0 521 26745 5 hard covers

FOR LAKSHMI

Contents

Acknowledgements

The people this book is about are my collaborators, not just my subject matter. Industrial workers of many kinds – educated and uneducated, with permanent or temporary jobs or no job at all, from different social origins and parts of India, as well as employers in small firms and managers in large ones, took time and trouble to answer my questions and to introduce me to their friends. They gave me hospitality, good company and often their warm open friendship. If they read or hear about this book (as some of them will) I hope they will feel I have presented their view of their own situation fairly, with my own criticisms but without distorting or reducing their story. I cannot name them all here, partly because they told me many things in confidence.

My closest collaborator, and the one to whom I owe most of all, is Lalit Deshpande of Bombay University. He showed me what to look for in my own fieldwork, criticized and discussed my ideas, and most generously allowed me not only to draw on his Bombay labour market study (commissioned by the World Bank, and initiated jointly by him and by T.S. Papola) but also to make my own tables, using the filled-in questionnaires for that study. This book, and especially the chapter on labour markets, could not have been written without him.

Others who helped me – academics, trade unionists, writers, journalists and friends – include Raymond Apthorpe, Anil Awachat, André Béteille, Deepak Bhalerao, Jan Breman, the British Council in New Delhi, C.T. David, John Harriss, Ravi Jain, Heather Joshi, Kumar Ketkar, T.N. Madan, the National Labour Institute, M.N. Panini, Sandeep Pendse, Enid Perlin, David Pocock, V.L.S. Prakasa Rao, E.A. Ramaswamy, Uma Ramaswamy, Satish Saberwal, Narayan Sheth, Hilary Standing, Hein Streefkerk, V.K. Tewari, D. Thankappan and Peter Waterman. I thank all of them, and many who are not on the list.

The Social Science Research Council paid the cost of the fieldwork and gave me a free hand: the strong views expressed or implied in this book are entirely my own. Jawaharlal Nehru University provided a base and friends to discuss and criticize my work; and my own university – East Anglia – gave me time and facilities to prepare for the fieldwork to write this book. My greatest personal debt is to my wife and daughters, who spent a year with me in India.

University of East Anglia   M.H.
Norwich

On the spelling of Indian words

Except for a few common spellings (like Brahman, Tamil), Indian words are spelt here in a new way (as in *South Indian factory workers*, Holmström 1976:xi). The common transliteration uses diacritical marks (as in ḍhūṇḍhnā) which are hard to print or type, blur the outline of words, and are easily left out: the result is a poor guide to pronunciation. A simple, practical, but accurate transliteration – like the new Chinese Pinyin – would be useful for many purposes. Though the method is used only for a few words in this book, I describe it here as I hope it will catch on.

Every phoneme is expressed by a single letter or a digraph, as in English. This requires one extra sign, a prime sign (′). It can be written or typed as an apostrophe, and any well-designed substitute would do (in *South Indian factory workers* I used a raised point ·). It is written as a separate letter, not an accent.

This sign makes the preceding vowel nasal (mai′ huu′) or the preceding consonant(s) retroflex (mand′al, Krisn′a). Long vowels are doubled (but in languages like Hindi, e o are always long). Other digraphs include sh for the palatal sibilant (not the retroflex sibilant, often written sh or ṣ); n can stand for ng, ny according to context; c and ch are like English ch (but Tamil c is often like s). Unnecessary letters are left out (kiaa not kiyaa).

Hindi (Devanagari) alphabet:
a aa i ii u uu ri e ai a′ ah
k kh g gh n(ng-)[1] c ch j jh n(ny) t′ t′h d′ d′h n′
t th d dh n p ph b bh m y r l v sh s′ s h
Dotted consonants: q kh′ g′ z r′ r′h f

Tamil alphabet:
a aa i ii u uu e ee ai o oo au q
k/g[2] n(ng-) c/j n(ny) t′/d′ n′ t/d n p/b m y r l v zh l′ r′ n
Grantha letters: j s′ s h ks′

---

[1] The longer forms in brackets are used only when the context requires them.
[2] The voiced forms after nasals, or between vowels (where they may become fricatives), or in borrowed words.

I

Introduction

This book is an attempt to develop an anthropology of industrial work in India, and an anthropological approach to a problem, the economic 'dualism' which is said to be characteristic of India and other industrializing countries.

Thus Robert MacNamara, President of the World Bank, said of the cities in developing countries:

> Economic dualism is widespread. Two sectors coexist side by side. One is the organized, modern, formal sector, characterized by capital-intensive technology, relatively high wages, large-scale operations, and corporate or governmental organization.
>
> The other is the unorganized, traditional, informal sector – economic units with the reverse characteristics: labour-intensive, small-scale operations, using traditional methods, and providing modest earnings to the individual or family owner.
>
> In the modern sector, wages are usually protected by labour legislation and trade union activity; in the informal sector, there is easier entry, but less job security and lower earnings.
>
> (MacNamara 1975:21)

This implies there are two classes of people very differently placed: a lucky minority working in the protected modern sector, and the majority outside it.

Certainly one's first impressions of a city like Bombay bear this out. There seems to be an obvious contrast between the modern sector of factories, offices and large business houses, and the labour-intensive unregulated small firms which offer a living but little security to many of the urban poor.

What are the real differences and relations between these two kinds of Indian workers? On the one hand, there are workers with permanent jobs in the so-called 'organized sector' factories which come under the Factories Act, laws on job security, social security, union recognition etc.; on the other, unorganized sector workers in small workshops not covered by the Factories Act, or working in larger firms but without the same legal and union protection, because they are regarded as temporary or casual or contract workers. What do these differences mean to the people concerned – how do they see their own social world and act in it? And why do these differences exist: is 'dualism', the coexistence of two separate economic sectors, a useful or a misleading concept for thinking about and explaining the very different situations in which these people find themselves?

The anthropology of industrial work

Here I use 'industry' to mean modern powered manufacturing industry: an arbitrary narrow definition, which is useful shorthand if one remembers that agriculture – by which most Indians live – is an industry like any other except that it needs more space and, like many industries, is usually organized in small family units. Modern powered industry, and conditions in towns where it is usually carried on, make obvious differences to people's lives; but one should not exaggerate these differences to the point of contrasting 'traditional' peasant society with a profoundly different urban-industrial society. This is a myth.

By (social) anthropology I mean the attempt to account for the varieties of human action and experience, starting from the axiom that men by nature are alike everywhere, but culture and circumstances make them different. To the extent that their actions can be explained at all, we must assume they act rationally, that is they act on beliefs about the facts of the situation (beliefs which may be true or false) to achieve ends or values which can be found out. Many beliefs are not private, but are worked out in society. They are organized into belief systems or ideologies, which combine judgments of fact and value, which have some logical consistency and which serve (usually implicitly) to explain the world and to justify actions.

The best method of explaining action is that of interpretive sociology: reconstructing the situation and motives of typical actors to give a picture of their world and the logic of their actions which is consistent with what they think and say, and which gives the best available causal explanation of what they are seen to do. But it is not enough to show how people act on the beliefs they have: especially in a fast-changing situation, we must also try to show how they come to hold and change these beliefs: for example, how their social position and interests may give them strong motives to work out a belief system which is logically closed, and which suppresses or explains away awkward facts. But we shall fall into the same trap ourselves if we reduce other people's world view deterministically, explain it away and exclude the possibility that their unfamiliar view of the facts may be right.

The attempt to develop an anthropology of industrial work, then, involves matching industrial workers' thinking to their actions and to their situation, especially those aspects of their situation which are rather arbitrarily labelled 'economic'. Because of the great size and complexity of the structures to be understood, this means combining the usual methods of social anthropology – living with small groups of people, entering into their thought and close observation of what they do – with a larger view of economic, technical and political developments: moving to and fro between different kinds of events – in the economy, in people's minds and elsewhere – which have to be studied on different scales, sometimes using the language and methods of other disciplines like economics.

There are of course several 'anthropological' studies of Indian industrial life already, some of them very good.[1] But even some excellent studies like Sheth's *Social framework of an Indian factory* have tended to avoid the problem of relating small-scale to large-scale events. Instead they have taken the wider situation as given and concentrated on the factory or neighbourhood as a more or less closed system of relations, like the 'little community' or 'face-to-face community' of many village studies.

> It is arguable that a functionalist and positivist bias had led rural anthropologists to look for closed and balanced systems of relations (sanctions and rewards etc.) and then to invent theories of 'social change' to cope with extraneous facts which could not be fitted into the model (as if there could be a sociology which is *not* a theory of social change). The shortcomings of this approach are less obvious (though not less real) when one is dealing with physically isolated rural communities. In cities there are only networks of relations, overlapping groups, conflicts not only of obligations but of ideals and ideas: a more open, dialectical approach (which would also explain the facts of rural life better) is the *only* way to make sense of urban society.
>
> (Holmström 1976:7)

This passage is from my book *South Indian factory workers*, to which this is a sequel. In that book I tried to develop an anthropology of industrial work which could take account of large scale economic and

---

[1] In particular, Sheth 1968a, *Social framework of an Indian factory*; Kapadia and Pillai 1972, *Industrialization and rural society*; Lynch 1969, *The politics of untouchability*; Lambert 1963, *Workers, factories and social change*; Niehoff 1959, *Factory workers in India*; E.A. Ramaswamy 1977, *The worker and his union*; Saberwal 1976, *Mobile men*; A.R. Desai and Pillai 1972, *Profile of an Indian slum*.

political forces, while approaching social reality simultaneously from the other side: the lives and problems of particular people observed and questioned in small groups, and the ideas and value-loaded categories they use to make sense of their experience. The point is to show not just the interactions between events on different scales, but between facts of different orders of reality: between people's thoughts, and the material conditions of their lives; between the human reality I have seen and experienced, and the level of analysis, explanation and generalization. This understanding of the interactions between circumstances, thought and action, if we can get it, should not only give better explanations of why things are as they are: it should also suggest the direction in which they are moving, the likely consequences of new initiatives, and some possibilities which are open to choice.

The background to this study

South Indian factory workers is a study of the careers and thinking of workers in four modern engineering factories in the industrial city of Bangalore. These factories – two in the private sector, two in the public sector – are not only in the 'organized sector' covered by the Factories Act and social security legislation, but have skilled, relatively well-paid workers, and strong unions which are able at least to maintain the real value of wages and to protect members against arbitrary dismissal. Though I had access to many kinds of information – statistical and historical studies of Bangalore's industry and population, my own close knowledge of the place from doctoral fieldwork in an urban village (Holmström 1969, 1971, 1972), interviews with managements and union officials and factual information in the files which managements keep on their work force – I spent most of my time making detailed case studies of 104 workers, whom I generally met in their homes, among their families and friends, in 1971.

Bangalore is an old city which experienced a remarkable industrial expansion after the Second World War; and although there are some very large factories dating from the nineteenth and early twentieth centuries, where the work force have little education and conditions are often poor, a large part of the city's population are employed in the newer organized sector factories, with modern capital-intensive technology, good conditions and strong unions. There are of course many more employed in small workshops which serve these big firms, and in shops and services and construction.

My interest was in how people get into the organized sector, what happens to them afterwards, what relations they have with people outside the organized sector, how they see their situation and whether they are right.

These 'organized sector' workers were always conscious of the difference between their own situation and that of the much larger number employed in unorganized sector workshops, or outside manufacturing industry. Sometimes they talked about this difference directly; more often it coloured what they said about their own careers and their relations with other kinds of people, including relatives. If I asked them about it, they would explain or perhaps justify the difference in various ways depending on their personal experience and background, and their moral beliefs and political ideologies. This mental map which most of them had, of society divided into a fortunate minority with permanent organized sector jobs and the rest, is on the whole a good and true reflection of the reality of Indian society as I see it.

> They tend to see factory work as a citadel of security and relative prosperity, which it is: it offers regular work and promotion and predictable rewards, as against the chaos and terrifying dangers of life outside. For everyone inside the citadel, there is a regiment outside trying to scale the walls . . . Once inside the citadel, a man can look round for alternatives, if he wants.
>
> (Holmström 1976:137)

The important thing is to get into the citadel – and to get in young, since with rising educational standards for recruitment the big firms take their pick of young men, and if you miss your chance around the age of twenty you may never get another. Once you are in you can look forward to semi-automatic slow promotion, or faster promotion if you are able to learn a skilled trade, or you can look for a better job in another factory; but never move forward without a secure job to fall back on. Very few do what many dream of doing, which is to move out and set up their own business.

Writing that book, I developed a theory which is deliberately oversimplified but which did seem to explain many things about contemporary Indian society, especially but not only in towns. The theory is that there are two kinds of people in India: those inside the citadel – people with permanent jobs in factories or offices or government service, or with enough property to give them the same security – and those outside. Almost everyone outside is trying to get in, if possible with the help of relatives or friends inside. Everyone inside is trying, first, to stay in; and secondly – a long way second – to improve his position. Security comes first. The citadel wall, the contrast between safety inside and cut-throat competition outside, is at the back of everyone's mind, or at least the minds of everyone inside and many who think they have a chance of getting in; and this explains much of their behaviour.

This study takes up problems raised in that book, especially about the relations between permanent organized sector workers and others. *South Indian factory workers* was written from the point of view of workers inside the citadel. Of course I knew many people working outside organized sector industry, then and in my previous fieldwork in Bangalore; but I saw that to make another case study of small groups of unorganized sector workers, to be compared point by point with the organized sector workers I knew, would not be practical, because these unorganized sector workers by definition do not come together in convenient large units like a factory, where I could make contact with them; any sample I could manage would be arbitrary, because organized sector factory workers all over India are fairly alike but the others certainly are not; and it would be an opportunity missed to develop an anthropology which could cope with large-scale economic structures without leaving out of account the lived experience of particular identifiable people.

Thus I decided to focus, not on the unorganized sector in itself, but on the boundary, the citadel wall, the relations between the two 'sectors'; and to study these relations systematically on several levels: the people's experience and thinking; their social origins, and the labour market for people of different origins; their relations with kin and other workers, inside and outside the organized sector; economic and technical links between large and small firms; the consequences of changing technologies; and the economic and political setting.

The 'unorganized sector' is a residual category, comprising everyone except permanent organized sector workers. There is of course another distinction within the unorganized sector, a boundary which is more shadowy but of the greatest importance: between workers in some kind of manufacturing employment, however insecure, and the vaster mass of small peasants and labourers in the country, or the urban sub-proletariat – casual construction workers, pavement-dwellers, the unemployed and underemployed and all those who live by petty services on the fringes of the industrial economy and often of the law.

To make the project more manageable I have concentrated mainly, not exclusively, on the boundary between the organized and unorganized sectors in manufacturing industry – on differences, conflicts and complementarities – without forgetting the abyss which separates even casual labourers in small workshops from the mass of the very poor.

I have also concentrated on industries which meet two conditions: strong and traceable links between large and small firms, or between the employment of labour on organized and unorganized sector terms; and some prospects for future growth in employment. Thus I paid more attention to the engineering and metal working, chemical, plastic, electrical and electronic industries than to traditional cottage industries, or to stagnant or declining industries like cotton textiles and jute.

Questions about the organized sector 'citadel'

This book deals with three kinds of questions:

1. Is it true that organized sector workers have secure employment and much better living conditions and chances than other workers? If so (and the answer is probably yes), is it sensible to think of organized sector workers as a privileged enclave or élite in a dual economy? How sharp is the boundary between the organized and unorganized sectors? Who shares the benefits of organized sector employment, and who is excluded?

2. If organized sector workers are generally better off, is that inevitable at this stage of industrialization? Or is it true that the *whole* organized sector – owners, managers, workers and unions – are privileged at the expense of the whole unorganized sector, so that the more labour-intensive unorganized sector is prevented from realizing its potential for employment and production; and that these unorganized workers, like peasants and others outside manufacturing industry, get the backwash of industrialization not the benefits? To put it another way: should we say organized sector workers are relatively well off *and* unorganized sector workers are badly off, or organized sector workers are well off *because* the others are badly off? And the same question again, about all industrial workers compared with the rest of Indian society.

3. Do organized and unorganized sector workers think and act as if it were a dual economy: for example, do they think of themselves as two classes, living in separate social worlds, with distinct or even conflicting interests? Is the term 'working class', as it is often applied to both kinds of workers, any more than political and journalistic rhetoric? What do the different conditions of life and work, in the two sectors, mean for the rest of these people's lives and for their relations with others?

All these are aspects of one problem, the relations between organized and unorganized sector labour: seen from outside, 'objectively', as these relations appear to an observer with access to information about the economy, the labour market etc. (the first and second sets of questions); and seen from inside, from the points of view of the workers themselves, to the extent that their ideas can be found out by talking to them and observing what they do.

The fieldwork

The distinctive feature of this method of research is the attempt to relate first-hand observation and questioning (my own, and that of other research workers) systematically to research and discussion on the structure of the national economy; and so to develop an anthropology adequate to a complex industrial society. The broad question in the last section had to be broken down into more specific questions, about industrial workers' situation and their consciousness of it, which this combination of methods could answer: for example, questions about the original formation of an industrial work force in India, and how its character changed when small-scale industries emerged as a distinct 'unorganized sector' after the Second World War; about the technical and economic relations between large and small firms; or about organized sector workers' attitudes towards those employed in small workshops and towards agricultural labourers.

I hesitated to embark on such an ambitious project: but on a preliminary visit to India in September 1975, to discuss this and alternative plans, people whose judgment I respect told me that a study of this kind was needed and feasible; and it seemed to follow naturally from my earlier local studies in Bangalore. Especially in the fieldwork for *South Indian factory workers*, I had learned how to follow up chains of introductions and to talk to all kinds of industrial workers, generally in their homes. Though my training as a social anthropologist emphasized intensive local fieldwork, I saw that something more large-scale and interdisciplinary was needed, with the scope and sweep of the great monographs on caste, written when caste was the central problem in the anthropology of India.

I went back to India in August 1976 and spent thirteen months there, based at Jawaharlal Nehru University, New Delhi, but travelling about the country for fieldwork and shorter visits to industrial towns. My family lived in New Delhi until we went south in May 1977.

I decided to do relatively long pieces of fieldwork in Bombay and Bangalore, the cities I knew best, where I could use union and other contacts to get introductions to unorganized sector workers outside the unions, and then to follow up these chains of introductions from one person to another; to make shorter visits to other places to find written material and references; to visit research institutes, firms and government and union offices; and to get some idea of the realities of industrial life. This took me to Calcutta, Ahmedabad, Ludhiana, Poona, Kanpur, Faridabad, Ranchi, Hyderabad, Madras and Trivandrum. I had three spells of fieldwork in Bombay, which has been more extensively studied than any other industrial city in India, and where I collected published and unpublished material from institutions like the Tata Institute of Social Sciences, from trade associations and journalists.

At Bombay University Lalit Deshpande was engaged with T.S. Papola on a study of the Bombay labour market, commissioned by the World Bank (Deshpande 1979). Investigators took questionnaires to three samples of workers in the city: factory workers, workers in small establishments (in the 'unorganized sector') and casual workers. Nothing on this scale had been done before. When I arrived in India, Deshpande and Papola were working on their report to the World Bank; and with extraordinary generosity, they allowed me not only to photocopy their draft report, but also to use the completed questionnaire forms to tabulate information not used in their own study. I employed assistants to make tables, using simple handwritten cards, which made it possible to compare organized sector factory workers with workers in similar occupations (turner, unskilled labourer etc.) employed in small manufacturing establishments. These tables, as well as the tables in the main Bombay labour market study, are a valuable statistical check on some of my findings: they show, for example, that the difference between incomes for each consumption unit (or adult equivalent) in families of workers in the two samples is much less than the enormous difference in their individual earnings. This confirmed my opinion, based on other studies and my own impressions, that many unorganized sector workers live with better-paid relatives, and that organized sector workers' pay is spread thin among many dependants.

In Bombay I visited firms of different sizes, especially in the newer industries with prospects for expansion: automobile ancillaries, engineering and metal working, plastics, pharmaceuticals and fine chemicals and electronics. I asked managements about their work force and how it was recruited; and about links between their firms and others, getting addresses and introductions. Thus I was able to go up and down a chain of firms, for example from a firm which makes whole vehicles to medium-sized ancillaries with long-term contracts for parts; smaller engineering or plastic firms which take smaller orders, which have to change their product more often and which try to diversify their markets if they can; and very small firms with high mortality, dependent on irregular job orders, in the new multi-storied 'industrial estates' which – unlike the official industrial estates – are really industrial slums, where wages are below the legal minimum, working conditions are bad and workers are laid off if orders are short or if they join unions. I made similar studies of linkages in electronics and to some extent in the chemical and pharmaceutical industry. One link is always with the engineering industries and toolroom trades, which all factories need.

I had introductions to the leaders of several unions. They spoke to me at length, and very freely, about the situation of non-union workers in the unorganized sector, organized sector employees' attitudes towards these workers, and the industrial and political situation. I hoped to meet ordinary union members who could then introduce others – relatives, neighbours or acquaintances – working in the unorganized sector or looking for jobs; but until my last spell of fieldwork in Bombay I found this much harder than I expected. Union members introduced other factory workers, whom I visited in their homes whenever I could. Although many unorganized sector workers live with better-paid relatives, some of my contacts lived in areas where there were few unorganized sector workers and had little contact with them; or they introduced relatives or friends employed in small workshops, but the new contacts had no colleagues to whom they could conveniently take me: the chain of introductions stopped there. Unorganized sector workers – unlike the Bangalore factory workers I knew – change jobs often and travel all over the city seeking work in distant places; they found it hard to understand the point of my work (which I explained in Hindi, Bombay's lingua franca), and their contacts outside their own families are less stable. Yet I was able to form a fairly consistent picture of some aspects of working life, especially recruitment, and mobility between jobs or the lack of it. I should stress that I was not looking for a statistically random sample, but for first-hand experience of a certain social world which would allow me to check and evaluate other studies, and for workers' own accounts of their careers and thinking.

Thus although I tried to get unorganized sector workers I met to introduce their friends and neighbours in the slums where most of them live, I did not get the same network of acquaintances or local contacts I had found among the more settled organized sector workers of Bangalore. This caused me to spend more time than I intended interviewing the owners and managers of small firms: I learned a great deal about linkages between firms and about technology, but my intention was to study industrial workers' world as they saw it rather than to make yet another study of 'entrepreneurship' (not that there is anything wrong with studying entrepreneurship, except that the attention given to the subject suggests a certain bias: the idea that development depends on entrepreneurship, the critical missing ingredient which must be added or stimulated).

Of course the situation was abnormal. In July 1975 the Prime Minister, Mrs Indira Gandhi, had declared a State of Emergency, suspended civil liberties, effectively banned strikes and imprisoned many of her opponents. The 'Emergency' made it difficult to follow up some contacts, and forced me and my informants to be careful in what we said, where we met and so forth. If this was a heavy burden in the first part of my work, I reaped the benefit when, early in 1977, Mrs Gandhi announced that elections would be held in March of that year. The Emergency was relaxed in February, and some of the people detained were released from prison. This made it possible not only for opposition parties to campaign, but also for trade unions unsympathetic to the ruling Congress Party to press their demands with a vigour which had not been seen since the Emergency was imposed. In March 1977, after several astonishing political developments, the ruling Congress Party was defeated by the newly formed

Janata Party in an electoral landslide which engulfed all northern India as well as Bombay city. As soon as the election results were announced, the Emergency was lifted, the remaining prisoners were released and most curbs on the press and union activity were removed. I was in Bombay throughout the election period.

In particular, the movement to demand payment of the legal minimum wages in Maharashtra State (of which Bombay is the capital) had been gathering force until the Emergency checked it. This movement marked a new stage in joint action by some unions and by non-union workers employed in small engineering units. It started again in February 1977 in the run-up to the election; I knew many of the people actively involved, and had first-hand accounts of the movement as well as press-cuttings. In my final fieldwork in Bombay, I went almost every day to a suburban office of one of these unions. I sat there talking to anyone who had time for me, making appointments to meet them again at their houses; or going out with militants to visit union members in small firms, to meetings, strikes and demonstrations.

I spent over two months in Bangalore after the election: my first visit for nearly six years. I followed up old contacts through factory workers and unions, and made new ones, especially in smaller factories in industrial estates and back streets. Here too I found it hard to meet unorganized sector workers in their homes: it was easier to meet workers from the smaller organized sector factories, when they came to union offices in connection with agitations for higher wages and bonus, or against closures and layoffs. I also visited many of the smaller firms and spoke to managers or owners (I already knew a great deal about the larger Bangalore factories); and I gathered information about the technical and economic links, not only between small firms and the large, mainly government-owned firms which dominate Bangalore's industrial economy, but also between the very small firms themselves, especially in one part of the city. I was fortunate to have access to another study in progress: a detailed socio-economic survey, based mainly on a random sample of 2000 households in Bangalore city, carried out at the Institute for Social and Economic Change, Bangalore, and giving detailed information on incomes, household size and composition and social mobility.

The main practical problems of my research were the difficulty of meeting unorganized sector workers for long detailed interviews, and the lack of other intensive anthropological studies of urban life, especially of industrial workers. This forced me to rely more than I intended on secondary written material, statistics, and accounts of industrial workers' lives and thinking taken at second hand from union officials, employers, journalists etc. Yet without such an ambitious goal before me – an anthropology adequate to a complex industrial society – I would not have met and talked to as many industrial workers as I did. The alternative of making a single long micro-study would have deprived me of the chance to travel around India, gathering information about the economy as well as about workers' lives, and seeking out many kinds of people whose experience and ideas were relevant to my work.

It is now several years since I did the fieldwork. Although many things have changed (partly, perhaps, because of more realistic official policies towards large and small industries), I do not think this affects the validity of my argument or the present relevance of the main conclusions.[2] Any ethnographic study draws general conclusions from a detailed report of the situation at one time and place – often much more so than in this book, which includes a history of the 'unorganized sector' in India to complement the many available ones of factory industry, and much material on towns other than Bombay and Bangalore where I did most of my own fieldwork. For example, I need to give details of labour legislation as it was at the time, so that you can follow the attempts of some employers to evade it and of some unions to enforce it. The general argument is about the effects of labour legislation which applies to some workers but not to others, and whether this puts one group in a permanently privileged position or, on the contrary, shows the others the sort of concessions they might win for themselves. *Mutatis mutandis*, one often hears similar arguments about other industrial countries, and this book is meant to be relevant to these general arguments as well as to India.

The debate about dualism

Has India a dual economy, in which 'organized sector' employers and permanent workers are privileged at the expense of the industrial unorganized sector and the rural masses? Not just better off, but privileged. If so, why is this and how could it be changed?

This debate is mainly about 'objective' economic conditions: not

---

[2] Inflation, of course, has changed the value of money. Wages and prices normally refer to 1976–7.

about whether people think themselves privileged or deprived, about class consciousness or the lack of it. But clearly the arguments are based on strong views about class relations and about justice.

In India these are no longer matters of debate only among academics and experts. When I was doing the fieldwork for this study in 1976–7, questions about the place of small-scale industries, about appropriate technology and whether industrial workers were unfairly privileged were becoming political issues, the subject of politicians' speeches, topics widely discussed in the press and among the literate public, including some of the urban working class. An account of the debate must cover Indian public opinion as well as the more abstract technical and international arguments.

There are several distinct issues which are often confused in a blanket advocacy of small industries against large ones, and of appropriate or intermediate technology against modern imported technology: McNamara's report (p. 1, above) is an example. It is useful to identify strands in the debate, arguments which are sometimes brought together and which start from different assumptions.

1. *Capital intensity.* The commonest argument is that larger units use modern technology which is capital-intensive. Since capital is scarce and labour abundant, this leads to growing unemployment. Traditional craftsmen lose their markets; small firms, using labour-intensive if not traditional methods, cannot offer enough alternative employment because they cannot compete with the large firms. This was Gandhi's case against the widespread use of modern western technology: a case taken up most forcefully by E.F. Schumacher (1974) and then by the Intermediate Technology Development Group, the International Labour Office, the World Bank and Indian public opinion, especially in the Janata Party.

Since modern capital-intensive technology displaces labour, it should not be used at all, or only to the smallest practical extent (the argument of Gandhi, Illich and the more extreme late gandhians[3]). Instead of blindly imitating western methods – for reasons of prestige

---

[3] Thus Charan Singh, one of the chief founders of the Janata Party who became Home Minister in 1977, told a Gandhi Peace Foundation seminar on gandhian economic and national planning that 'it was foolish for the government to take over sick textile mills. The plea given was that jobs of textile workers had to be saved, but these very jobs had originally been created at the cost of many more jobs in the handloom sector' (*Times of India*, 20 June 1977).

or ignorance – countries like India should develop appropriate technology, operated entirely or mainly in small dispersed units. This would increase employment, make for a fairer distribution of wealth, stop the drift to the cities and leave traditional ways of life intact.

Alternatively, it is inevitable that the 'modern' and 'traditional' sectors should coexist, but public policy should redress the balance between them by strengthening the linkages between large firms with modern technology and small firms with more traditional technology, and the desirable multiplier and spread effects, for the benefit of both sectors and the nation. The result will be higher employment; more production at less cost; a thriving market for agricultural products, for wage goods and services; and all-round economic development. Instead of being a 'zero-sum game' where the modern sector's gains are the traditional sector's losses, true economic development will be a 'positive-sum game' where all players can gain. This requires discrimination in favour of the traditional sector, at least until it is able to stand on its own feet: the modern sector can look after itself.

Thus the ILO mission to Kenya advocated strong action to remove the constraints on the informal or unorganized sector, and to increase the formal sector's demands for goods produced in the informal sector (International Labour Office, 1972). If small firms cannot beat the large ones, they can join them. Successive Indian governments, acting especially through the Small Industries Service Institutes, have tried to encourage the growth of small-scale ancillaries to large firms, or to find organized sector markets for the small firms' products, especially in the engineering industry. And whether or not one believes in putting constraints on large firms, it is clearly sensible to remove constraints on small ones and to foster a healthy complementary division of labour by helping those developing small units which need it most.

But is the argument about *technology* or about *size*? It is a truth (almost) universally acknowledged that capital-intensive technology and large units go together, so that an argument against one is an argument against the other. Capital-intensive technology requires large units for its efficient use; and large units choose capital-intensive methods, both for economic reasons – for example, because unions keep labour costs high – and perhaps for prestige or in imitation of foreign companies. Small is beautiful because it means more employment. This is the main justification for giving special help to *small*

firms ('small industries' in the official jargon) and preventing large
firms from expanding their production of things that small firms
could make.

Now this assumption should be examined.[4] Are existing small units
generally more capital-intensive than small ones? Clearly they are, if
one compares large modern factories with small establishments using
traditional methods, like those of handloom weavers and village
craftsmen: but the right comparison is between modern factories and
the vast number of small firms closely linked to the large sector for
their inputs and outputs (on the difference between the modern and
traditional small-scale sectors, and the links between 'modern' large
and small firms, see Kurien 1978). There is no practical possibility
that the 'traditional' small sector (with the very doubtful exception of
handloom weaving) could supply even the existing demand for mass
consumption goods, agricultural inputs etc. Any technology which
could be considered 'appropriate' to India's present needs must
involve more complex machinery and higher investments than these
traditional crafts. 'Alternative technology' (as 'appropriate technology' was originally called) is not a real option, though complementary technologies are. This may have implications for the type
of economic linkages between large and small firms, but not directly
or necessarily, unless technology dictates unit size or vice versa. I
suggest in this book that existing small firms are often as capital-
intensive as large ones, sometimes more so. Dhar and Lydall may well
be right:

> Within the modern sector of manufacturing industry . . . available evidence
> suggests that small factories use more capital *and* more labour per unit of
> output than larger factories . . . From the point of view of saving capital,
> medium or large multi-shift factories give the best results, and small factories
> usually the worst. There is, therefore, no general case for promoting small
> modern factories on these grounds.   (1961:84–5)

In some branches, like the new chemical industries, it is doubtful
whether the contrast between capital- and labour-intensive is of
much use, since one of the main inputs is the skill of a few well-paid
graduates.

Even if it were shown that large firms and capital-intensive

---

[4] A number of economists have done so, using evidence from India (Dhar and Lydall 1961;
Sandesara 1969; Subrahmanian and Kashyap 1975; Turnham 1971; Gaiha and Moman-
mad 1975; Sutcliffe 1971), but their criticisms have not had much effect on the received
wisdom, on international aid-giving agencies or on national policies. For a discussion of this
issue, see pp. 156ff below.

technology generally go together, is there any reason why they must? Or would changes in economic policy – or a different political organization of society – make it possible to combine economies of scale with efficient labour-intensive production methods? This question about possibilities rather than present facts goes beyond the scope of this book. Yet there are organizations which mobilize large amounts of labour with cheap simple technology, in India and elsewhere; just as, in countries where labour is scarce and even in India, very small units employ advanced technology.

2. *An aristocracy of labour*. Another part of the argument – and the part most relevant to my sociological purpose – is not directly about technology, but about the link between unit size and the workers' economic condition: the idea that large units, unlike small ones, lead to a privileged aristocracy of labour; and that these units are kept in being not from economic necessity, but because of political pressures from this labour aristocracy and their allies. Organized sector workers enjoy much higher wages than unorganized workers with the same skills; or, simply by being in the organized sector, they have chances to acquire valuable skills which cannot be learned in small firms. Above all, organized sector workers have security and unorganized sector workers have none. Two things perpetuate these differences: unions, which are strong in the organized sector but weak or absent in small firms; and labour legislation, which covers only the organized sector and is effective only in the larger firms.

Thus H. and V. Joshi argue in *Surplus labour and the city: a study of Bombay* (1976a) that 'the authorities have to revise their image of the unorganized sector as a motley collection of riff-raff with little productive potential' (:156–7). The unorganized sector could provide employment to a much larger number, satisfy the needs of the masses more cheaply and efficiently and produce for export if it were not held back by a structure of regulations and policies which may serve the needs of a small group with vested interests. If so this privileged group includes organized sector employers, workers and unionists.

> Whether or not there are economic explanations for the earnings differentials, the question does arise of the social relevance of a situation where a small minority of often over-qualified people secure a few relatively privileged positions when large numbers are totally excluded. The intellectual climate is also important. Radical and vocal public opinion tends to support Organized industrial workers, ignoring the Unorganized workers in industry and agriculture who are much worse off.   (:103)

Thus radical opinion – academics, journalists, middle-class supporters of left-wing parties – draws the class line in the wrong place,
between employers and workers; but a fair economic policy would
benefit unorganized sector workers and employers at the expense of
organized sector workers and employers.[5]

Similar arguments are that unions force wages to unrealistically
high levels, forcing employers to raise costs in a protected market and
to buy labour-saving machinery; that labour legislation (especially
on job security) ties employers' hands and inhibits growth of
production and employment; that organized sector workers can
afford to educate their children better, and can find them jobs, so that
the privileged class of organized sector workers continues from
generation to generation and loses touch with the masses.

A left-wing version is this: the conquests of the organized working
class must be defended as a necessary condition for extending higher
minimum wages and legal protection to other groups. The organized
sector, and especially their unions, should be the spearhead of the
working class; but too often they neglect this duty, and can be bought
over by the employers when their immediate economic demands are
met. Thus they become a self-perpetuating labour aristocracy, with
middle-class life styles and aspirations. Instead of giving a lead to the
unorganized masses, they delay the growth of militant working-class
consciousness.

3. *Urbanization.* If capital-intensive technology and large units go
together, they are also said to lead to overconcentration of people and
of employment opportunities in *towns*. This leads to slums, social
breakdown and crime.[6] It impoverishes the countryside, takes away
gifted people and puts the rural masses at a disadvantage. Industry and
population should be dispersed, if possible to the villages, otherwise to
smaller towns. This line of argument goes back to Gandhi, and the
idealization of the Indian village community in contrast to the
corruption and misery of city life.[7]

---

[5] Heather Joshi asks me to make it clear that she and Vijay Joshi never fully subscribed to the
view I criticize. Whether they subscribe to it or not, the case is set out with admirable clarity
and persuasive argument in their book. For a discussion of both sides of the question, and
specially of the difficulties of drawing boundaries round sectors, see Heather Joshi 1980.

[6] 'Industrialization had created slums in the cities and led to an exodus from rural to urban
areas. This had led to a collapse of all old values.' Charan Singh, quoted in *Times of India*, 20
June 1977.

[7] 'I do not know if a vast country like India, with her millions of people having four months of
enforced idleness on their hands, can afford to have large-scale industries and yet live a life of
tolerable comfort. Large-scale, centralized industries in India, except such industries as
cannot possibly be carried on in villages, must mean starvation of millions, unless honourable
employment is found for the displaced millions' (Gandhi 1948:42).

There are three propositions here: large units lead to greater urban concentration than many small ones employing the same number of people; those who move to towns are worse off than they would be otherwise; and the 'drift to the cities' is bad for the majority who remain in rural areas (for a critical discussion of all three propositions, see Ashish Bose 1970, 1973; Dhar and Lydall 1961; Jakobson and Prakash 1967; Lubell 1974; Sovani 1966). The first and second are doubtful (as I hope to show) but the third is harder to dispose of. Thus Lipton argues that Indian planning has ignored the needs of agriculture, and this is a result of

> . . . *urban bias* in the Indian system of economic reward, political power, education, and intellectual preference . . . Policies on employment and nutrition, both of which have tended to worsen both resource use and rural–urban inequality, are typical consequences of the 'grand alliance' of big farmers, urban employers, and industrial employees. (1968:84)

This is not an argument for stopping migration or urban development:

> the remedy is not to confine the artificial advantages of city life to the present beneficiaries by rendering urbanisation difficult, but to remove the arbitrarily assigned advantages that render urbanisation artificially attractive: to neutralise the pricing, investment, educational, medical and other policies that are currently transferring income from villages to towns, and encouraging the ablest villagers to follow . . . Urbanisation could be needed both for low-cost industrialisation and rising levels of administrative capability. The case for small-scale and rural industry often smacks of special pleading.
> (Lipton 1977:220–1)

This is a strong persuasive argument. It implies that a *class*, which is both urban and rural and includes organized sector workers, is privileged at the expense of the urban poor, but especially of the much larger and poorer masses in the villages.[8] If it is an argument about class relations, then the rural–urban difference is not important in itself: any policy which could successfully transfer resources from rich to poor would transfer more resources to the villages, where most of the poor live.

Lipton's argument is open to three main criticisms: he has drawn the class lines in the wrong place, because organized sector workers may be better off than unorganized sector workers but their long-term class interests converge; the division of interests into urban and rural confuses the issue; and it is not true that Indian planning has

---

[8] 'Migration transforms the rural poor into urban poor and the rural rich into urban rich . . . The segmentation of an urban labour market begins in the villages' (Deshpande 1979:116, 151).

neglected agriculture and the countryside. A large part of the few available resources has been channelled into agriculture, giving an impetus both to the 'green revolution' and to the increasing polarization of rural class interests. Some of the expenditure on rural welfare has gone into the pockets of the rural rich whose interests, as Lipton says, lie with the urban rich.

4. *Pollution.* Another argument against modern production methods, and against industrial towns, is that they pollute the environment more than traditional methods, and use up the world's stock of limited resources (Meadows *et al.* 1972; Schumacher 1974). As I have suggested (Holmström 1976:146) this may be partly true, but would be more acceptable if it were not so obviously a case of the rich countries pulling up the industrial ladder behind them.

5. *Alienation.* Then it is said that modern production methods not only deprive the masses of useful employment, but dehumanize those who do get employment, destroying the natural rhythms of agriculture and handicraft work. The worker becomes 'alienated'. Besides, in smaller units – even if the technology is not traditional – the relations between workers and employers are closer, more human and less exploitative than in larger firms. Small firms mean happier workers, less tension, and less danger of unrest:

> Small firms using labour-intensive methods have several advantages for developing countries. They can be managed successfully by the personal supervision of the owner, without the need for sophisticated control procedures or a complex hierarchy of authority . . . The hours of work can be more flexible and the interpersonal relationship less formal.
>
> (Marsden 1973:327–8)

M.M. Mehta (1968:31) lists among the advantages of small-scale industries 'closer relations between the employers and workers and a greater identity of interests'; Schumacher sees small units as instruments for the humanization of work, where 'Social legislation and trade union vigilance can protect the employee. Even autocratic control is no serious problem in small-scale enterprise which, led by a working proprietor, has almost a family character' (1974:221).

Yet the *Report* of the National Commission on Labour (1969:424–5 and elsewhere) describes the exploitation and insecurity of labour in the small-scale sector, the poor working conditions and widespread evasion of the few labour laws that apply to small firms, and the weakness of unions. Dhar and Lydall (1961:24) question the view 'that in small enterprises there is less of a gap, economically and socially, between a worker and his employer than in large enterprises', and 'that there is less "exploitation" in small firms'. Kapadia and Pillai (1972:177) say farm workers want factory jobs, not only for pay and security but because of 'the dislike to serve the traditional employer with whom the employee's relations are heavily grounded on personal lines'. The employers can call the workers to do odd jobs at any time, while in the factory, '"Eight hours of work, and you are free" – this was a typical answer.' Women would rather be construction labourers than domestic servants, since working for 'an organization or an impersonal employer' frees them from the drudgery and servility of domestic work. (Contrast Schumacher 1974:47: 'Women, on the whole, do not need an "outside" job, and the large-scale employment of women in offices or factories would be considered a sign of serious economic failure' in Schumacher's favoured 'Buddhist economics'.)

6. *Concentration of wealth.* Small units not only call forth reserves of entrepreneurial and management skills which would otherwise be wasted, but prevent the concentration of wealth and the growth of monopolies. A flourishing class of small businessmen, in close personal touch with their employees, are a check on the polarization of society into rich and poor; 'the existence of a large number of independent self-employed persons is a guarantee of the maintenance of democratic institutions, an obstacle to the dominance of trade unions, and a barrier to communism' (from Dhar and Lydall 1961:24, who report this view but do not agree with it). Since these are the people – small industrialists, traders and contractors – who form the backbone of the local organization of the strongest parties, it is not hard to see the political appeal of this idea.

7. *Luxuries for the rich.* H. and V. Joshi hold that large firms make the *wrong products*, mainly luxuries for the rich:

> The privately-owned part of the organized sector typically contains large manufacturing firms operating in oligopolistic markets sheltered from foreign competition by high tariffs and quantitative restrictions, selling their products mainly to middle and upper income groups. The unorganized sector contains a very large number of small producers operating on narrow margins in highly competitive product markets, selling a variety of goods and services. Its products are sold mainly to low income groups (though there are obvious and significant exceptions such as domestic service). (1976a:44–5)

Similar arguments are that the organized sector is only interested in supplying lucrative urban markets, not in stimulating the healthy growth of small firms which could complement the large ones in supplying mass consumption goods cheaply:[9] there is little multiplier effect, since the large firms use the weaker unorganized sector only on grossly unequal terms. Given its head, the unorganized sector could not only supply and stimulate mass markets in India and similar countries, but could develop its great potential for export of cheap manufactured goods, handicrafts etc. (Hone 1974). Some protection is necessary, but a policy of import substitution at all costs entrenches the rich, penalizes the consumer, inhibits industrial growth and prevents the healthier alternative of an export-led boom.

Now it is true that many Indian firms are sheltered from foreign competition – and from competition with each other – by tariffs, quotas etc., at the consumers' expense. But these restrictions benefit the small firms as much as the large: in some cases more, as when product lines are reserved for the small-scale sector. It is also true that the 'terms of trade' between large and small firms are often (not always) very unequal. But if a disproportionate amount of resources and work are devoted to making goods which only the upper and middle classes can afford, it is not clear that this is more true of large firms than of small ones. Some consumer goods for the rich (like cars) can only be made or at least assembled in large factories; but this is not true, for example, of some electronic and electrical goods, or of the components and half-finished goods the small firms make for the large. On the other hand, what effective mass demand exists for manufactured goods can be and often is supplied more cheaply and efficiently by large firms. The nature of the product is not an important dividing line between the two sectors. There are differentiated markets, but no simple dual market corresponding to the two parts of a dual economy and society:

> There is no question of a rift in production or labour relations on the basis of which the urban system can be broken down into two sectors. It is rather a continuum in which border-lines between the composite parts are drawn almost arbitrarily and are also difficult to locate in the actual situation.
>
> (Breman 1976:1874)

---

[9] 'Mr Swamy [Subramaniam Swamy, an economist and Janata Party politician] felt that the unemployment problem could be solved only by setting up small industrial units all over the country as in Japan and not by constructing big factories as in the USA and the Soviet Union . . .

Mr Swamy said that if consumer goods were manufactured by small units, the price would be low. A radio which cost Rs 200 when made in a big factory would cost no more than Rs 20 if made in a small unit' (*The Statesman*, 17 April 1977).

8. *Links in a chain of exploitation.* Others take the same line of criticism further, and argue that the organized and unorganized (or formal and informal) sectors of urban industry are merely links in a chain of relations of exploitation, stretching from the multinational companies with their political allies in rich countries, down to the poorest of the rural poor (Frank 1969; Leys 1975:18 f.). Foreign investment and aid, the import of inappropriate technology, dependence on trade with rich countries and the building up of an indigenous bourgeoisie and managerial class with expensive tastes are means by which the dominant foreign interests extract surplus in varying degrees from everyone lower down the chain. Of course, the relation between organized and unorganized sector firms is exploitative: unorganized sector workers are used as a reserve army of cheap labour whose survival is subsidized by their families involved in subsistence agriculture,[10] and some better-paid workers may collude in this exploitation; but to isolate these two links in a longer chain is to miss the point and to delay remedial action. Developing countries should free themselves from foreign firms and governments, and from their dependence on exports to finance unnecessary imports. They should aim at separate or collective self-sufficiency, and should plan their economies to meet the basic needs of their own peoples. The benefits of import substitution outweigh the costs: foreign penetration delays the healthy growth of a national bourgeoisie, who can (in the more radical version) be controlled or swept away when the time comes.

9. *Against the consumer society.* One last argument – radical in a different way – is against industrialism itself, except of the simplest kind. India should give up the vain attempt to imitate the 'west', whose happiness is an illusion. Western affluence and the 'consumer society', even if they were attainable in India, are false ideals and morally corrupting. Indians should content themselves with a modest self-sufficiency, a simple frugal life of duty, co-operation, and spiritual rather than social equality. They should return to the traditional values of the 'village republic', purged of imperfections like untouchability. This is Gandhi's argument:

---

[10] See the Report of the 1929 Royal Commission on Labour in India: 'where contact is retained with the village, there is usually some kind of home to fall back upon should the need arise. The villages have hitherto provided a measure of insurance against the effects of the various changes which may reduce, interrupt or destroy the earning capacity of the worker . . . The village is an infinitely better place than the city for the young and the aged, the sick, the maimed and the exhausted, the unemployed and the unemployable' (Royal Commission 1931a:19; cf. Engels, in Marx and Engels 1962:553).

Pandit Nehru wants industrialization because he thinks that, if it is socialized, it would be free from the evils of capitalism. My own view is that the evils are inherent in industrialism and no amount of socialization can eradicate them.

(Gandhi, writing in Harijan, 29 Sept. 1940)

Society based on non-violence can only consist of groups settled in villages in which voluntary co-operation is the condition of dignified and peaceful existence . . . The nearest approach to civilization based on non-violence is the erstwhile village republic of India.

(Gandhi, quoted in Tinker, 1963:155)

I do not believe that industrialization is necessary in any case for any country. It is much less so for India. Indeed, I believe that Independent India can only discharge her duty towards a groaning world by adopting a simple but ennobled life by developing her thousands of cottages and living at peace with the world. High thinking is inconsistent with complicated material life based on high speed imposed on us by Mammon worship. All the graces of life are possible only when we learn the art of living nobly.

(Gandhi, in Harijan, 1 Sept. 1946)

The same argument has been taken up abroad by writers like Illich; and though the label 'gandhian' is used rather promiscuously, this side of Gandhi's thought has enjoyed a revival among Indian intellectuals and politicians. When the president of the Association of Indian Engineering Industries outlined proposals to create jobs in villages by setting up workshops, repair shops and small industries, 'Mr Desai [the Prime Minister] replied that his conception of village industries was somewhat different. He wanted cottage industries with an investment of a few thousand rupees at the most and extremely simple technology which could be grasped by the villager. Larger investments would not result in the cottage industries which alone could keep village life intact.' He admitted that the country also needed heavy industry, to obtain economies of scale; but 'the country had been affected too much by Western values. He did not personally look forward to affluence in the Western sense. He wanted that every person should be happy and content with his work, emoluments and daily pattern of life' (*Times of India*, 21 April 1977).

The point of this book is to throw light on these questions about the structure of the Indian economy and labour market (including prospects for future industrial development, and how Indian industry came to be divided into two 'sectors' in the first place); and on questions of another kind, more accessible to the methods of social anthropology, about how the people live and think, their plans, careers and disappointments, who they help and depend on, how they see their economic situation, how this understanding affects or explains their actions, whether it is realistic, and how they change their views when they encounter hard realities they had not expected.

2

Industrial labour in India

The 'dual economy' – or at least the sharp division of the work force into those employed in the organized and unorganized sectors – is fairly new, dating from the great expansion of Indian manufacturing industry since Independence and especially since 1960. But this 'dualism' has its roots in the older pre-industrial society, and in the history of the 'industrial' work force since its nineteenth-century beginnings.

This chapter gives a critical survey of some historical studies of the industrial work force and of industrial towns, especially but not only as these studies point to the later emergence of the unorganized sector as a distinct part of manufacturing industry, and a separate class of 'unorganized' casual or temporary workers in organized sector firms. These changes were the result of several things: increasingly complex technology, requiring an educated work force with special skills; labour legislation; union pressures; and organized sector workers' changing assumptions about work, about the career as a line leading somewhere rather than a random succession of jobs, and about social status and the dignity of labour.[1]

Reading the historical material, we should go beyond the common idea that 'western' technology necessarily involves the import of a whole package of institutions and attitudes – the package labelled 'westernization'. But still this technology was brought to India with at least some of the forms of organization, and assumptions about work and industrial relations, which were then current in the west, particularly in Britain; and with a form of western free market capitalism, distorted in the special conditions of colonial rule.

I said (p. 2) I would use 'industry' to mean modern powered manufacturing industry. This is what most people mean when they

---

[1] On these ideas (especially a 'career' in relation to the rest of a person's life) see Holmström 1976.

talk of industry and industrial labour. But what is special about 'industrial' labour, and how does it differ from other kinds of work?

Consider some of the things that are said to distinguish modern industry in a country like India: imported technology using inanimate sources of power; high productivity, making possible higher living standards for some and perhaps eventually for all, higher profits and wages, new products which change living habits and accumulation of wealth and capital on a previously impossible scale; a type of work organization, which is believed to require a hierarchy of command staffed by professional managers, innovation by entrepreneurs, institutions for raising risk capital and a framework of contract and commercial law; a working environment which imposes a new discipline, regular timekeeping, much repetitive work and attention to detail; a larger scale of organization, whether of the individual firm or interdependent firms, leading to the concentration of the work force in vast cities; perhaps a new class consciousness, cutting across older loyalties; and so on.

Older studies of Indian industrial labour stress the inevitable consequences of introducing new technologies: their impact on a stable traditional society, and on institutions like the village, caste and joint family, which were assumed to have existed almost unchanged for centuries until they suffered the shock of contact with industrialism; migration from villages, and the growth of new industrial and commercial cities like Bombay, Calcutta and Madras, very different from the older cities which were the centres of Indian civilization. Clearly the new technology's impact could not be separated from that of colonial rule, the new systems of law, administration and education and the dominant position of the British community in India. Some writers justified colonial rule and praised its achievements; some (like Marx) did so with many qualifications, as a necessary stage in India's emergence from feudal darkness; some condemned it outright. The idea of a package of changes, 'westernization', the inevitable impact of the dynamic west on a static society, seemed obvious not only to foreign writers but to many Indians.

But how did modern powered industry really change traditional working habits and ideas about work? And more generally, how far did industry cause necessary changes in Indian society, in power relations between groups, and the ways people thought about their own society? There are two dangers: of assuming change where it has not happened; and assuming the 'traditional' society was unchanging, so that any change must be the effect of outside forces.

Though much writing on the history of Indian industrial labour makes these largely discredited assumptions about the import of a package of institutions and attitudes into a static society (the process called 'westernization', or now more commonly 'modernization'), it also contains a mass of useful descriptive material on industrial workers' recruitment, migration and living conditions; and some of the early studies were inspired by a humane imaginative concern for the welfare of the Indian masses, and specially of industrial workers and city-dwellers.

Given this idea of a great transition, partly completed, from one stage or ideal type of society to another, from a pre-industrial to a modern urban-industrial society, the writers who described or speculated about industrialization stressed different aspects of it. Foreign writers, and some Indians, wanted to find the formula for successful industrialization, the ingredients missing from the traditional society which must be added to make India an industrial country: entrepreneurship, efficient management, changes in social values, 'achievement-orientation' or a committed labour force. The problem of supplying the missing ingredient or ingredients was believed to be common to non-industrial countries which lagged behind, at various points, on the great highway of development marked out by the west and Japan.

Indian scholars, in particular, approached the same problem in a more historical way: not simply as one of identifying the missing ingredients needed to turn any traditional society into an industrial one, but as a specific problem in India's economic history with urgent practical implications for the present: why did India fail to have an industrial revolution at the same time as the west, especially Britain? After all, India had long-established trade routes between kingdoms and with the world outside, traditional manufactures, exports especially of fine cloth, communities of craftsmen with diverse skills who often formed the core of the later industrial work force, merchant classes with their own banking system and letters of credit, raw materials (especially coal and iron ore, unlike Japan) and large reserves of gold and treasure which could have financed imports of machinery and new skills.

One answer is Weber's: Hindu beliefs and values, especially caste which is inseparable from Hinduism, prevented the emergence of 'modern' capitalism with its ceaseless quest for innovation and new markets. Not that Hindus are more other-worldly: on the contrary, Hindus of all castes can be as acquisitive, energetic and ruthless as anyone else, and Hindu society puts a very high value on wealth. But in spite of the growth of an early form of capitalism in India, and a developed guild organization in the cities, restrictions on contact between castes prevented the merchants and artisans from coming together as a self-confident adaptable class confronting the nobility and priesthood, as they did in Europe; and although the belief in ritual pollution could be circumvented when it was inconvenient, it prevented change of occupation and rapid adaptation to new demands. The belief in karma or rebirth, and the web of customs and ritual duties which bound the Hindu at every point in his life, led to a 'traditionalist' attitude and a suspicion of all change even more rigid than in medieval Christianity.

> Indian justice developed numerous forms which could have served capitalistic purposes as easily and well as corresponding institutions in our own medieval law. The autonomy of the merchant stratum in law-making was at least equivalent to that of our own medieval merchants. Indian handicrafts and occupational specialization were highly developed. From the standpoint of possible capitalistic development, the acquisitiveness of Indians of all strata left little to be desired and nowhere is to be found so little antichrematism and such high evaluation of wealth. Yet modern capitalism did not develop indigenously before or during the English rule. It was taken over as a finished artifact without autonomous beginnings. Here we shall inquire as to the manner in which Indian religion, as one factor among many, may have prevented capitalistic development (in the occidental sense).
>
> (Weber 1958:4, cf. pp. 111ff)

Weber's argument here is much weaker than in his masterpiece, *The protestant ethic and the spirit of capitalism* (1930), partly because his material on India (like Marx's) was suspect and inadequate; but as with *The protestant ethic* one should not confuse Weber's own arguments with the crude oversimplification of them by writers who lack both his subtlety of thought and his wide learning, and who see the psychological conditions for capitalist entrepreneurship as the only means of economic development (like Kapp 1963). A more moderate argument on the same lines is in Mishra 1962. Singer, who has the advantage of fieldwork, suggests that Weber was wrong in his view that the 'law of ritual' dominated Indian society and made economic progress difficult ('Industrial leadership, the Hindu ethic, and the spirit of socialism' in Singer 1972:272ff).

The answer more favoured by Indians is that wealth which could have been invested in industrialization was looted by the British; traditional industries, especially textiles, were killed off by free trade and cheap imports, mainly from Britain; and the subsequent industrialization was distorted in the interests of the British economy and British firms in India (just as the vast railway system was laid out to meet the needs of imperial administration and the import–export trade, rather than trade between regions of India). Bagchi (1972) puts the case fairly, and with a mass of evidence, in perhaps the best account of Indian industrialization in this period:

> The interests of Indian business or of Indian economic development inevitably received a low priority in the imperial scheme, and could be sacrificed in order to safeguard the other interests involved in the preservation and smooth working of the system . . . The alternative explanations [of India's backwardness before 1918] that are often encountered in the literature generally ignore the facts of the exploitative relationship of Britain with India and of the relationship of racial dominance between Europeans (particularly British nationals) and Indians, fostered and maintained by the British rulers. Professor Habakkuk [1955:158], for example, writes: 'The contrast of Japan with India is certainly one which requires explanation, since India had many of the basic conditions of industrialization – a merchant class, banking and transport facilities, considerable production for the market – and perhaps in this case difference in character and quality of the native entrepreneurs was the decisive factor' . . . The emergence of Indian entrepreneurship in most parts of India was systematically discouraged by the political, administrative and financial arrangements maintained by the British rulers, and in the few cases before 1914 in which 'native' entrepreneurship had emerged, it was no less enterprising or interested in industry than were British businessmen in India. If anything, Indians showed a greater degree of courage, since they did not have many of the tangible advantages that British businessmen enjoyed because of their birth.
>
> (:423)

Nor, he says, is there evidence of a shortage of capital in relation to the demand for investment in the period.

More recently, it is argued that the same pattern of distorted development and exploitation by foreign interests was continued after Independence by the multinationals and their allies in Indian big business. Thus industrialization did not simply fail to happen: it was prevented.

Indian marxists lay more stress on this aspect of British rule than on Marx's own writings about India. Marx saw pre-colonial India as a country of self-contained village communities, governed by rigid ancient custom, and preyed upon from time to time by despotic unstable kingdoms which, however, gave the villages irrigation, wells and public works: a function he believed the British had neglected. Since the coming of British rule, India's agriculture had decayed and its small-town textile industries had been destroyed by imports. Yet the brutal exposure of the Indian economy to laissez-faire capitalism was necessary and progressive, for British rule had 'dissolved these small, semi-barbarian, semi-civilized communities by blowing up their economic bases, and thus produced the greatest and, to speak the truth, the only *social* revolution ever heard of in Asia' (Marx 1959:479–80). This was 'sickening . . . to human feeling', yet it was for the best, since

> these idyllic village communities . . . had always been the solid foundation of Oriental despotism . . . they restrained the human mind within the smallest possible compass, making it the unresisting tool of superstition, enslaving it beneath traditional rules, depriving it of all grandeur and historical energies . . . England, it is true, in causing a social revolution in Hindustan, was actuated only by the vilest interests, and was stupid in her manner of enforcing them. But that is not the question. The question is: Can mankind fulfil its destiny without a fundamental revolution in the social state of Asia? If not, whatever have been the crimes of England, she was the unconscious tool of history in bringing about that revolution.[2] (:480–1)

So much for the past. India failed to have an industrial revolution when the west and Japan did. But can India catch up with them, and if so how? For if India is now having an industrial revolution, it seems incomplete. India is already in the world league of major industrial powers, an exporter of sophisticated manufactured goods, of technological skills and consultants, and a base for its own multinational companies. Yet living standards are abysmally low, and even those who benefit directly from industrial employment are poor by world standards. Are these just the proverbial 'miseries of industrialization', a stage that must be passed through? Is India locked into a system of domestic and international exploitation that makes any real advance impossible until the system is broken, perhaps by a revolutionary convulsion? Or has India missed its chance for good? Fashionable writers, including many in rich western countries, hold that it is impossible that today's poor countries should ever reach the standard of living the west and Japan now take for granted – an absurd, destructive and possibly immoral goal to aim at. Other

[2] Daniel Thorner (1966) discusses Marx's changing ideas about India and shows how he later abandoned the idea that the Indian village, as the type of the Asiatic mode of production, pointed to the origins of later forms of European society.

Indians read their economic and social history to answer these practical questions: to find a way out.

The beginnings: caste and the division of labour

India, like England, was already 'industrial' in the eighteenth century, with diverse manufactures, commerce and skills. It is no more possible to take that century as a pre-industrial baseline, a time before change, in India's case than in England's. Here we are concerned with the differences which the introduction of modern powered industry made to a society which was already complex and changing, especially under the impact of foreign rule; and with the formation of the new factory labour force. From which social groups were people drawn into it and how? Were they town or country people? What work were they doing already, and how did the new division of labour differ from what went before?

The traditional form which the division of labour took in India, as everyone knows, was caste. But one should be clear about what this means – in particular, about the difference between caste ideology and practice – or there is a danger of drawing too simple a picture of a change from a society where birth determines occupation to a more mobile society where it does not, and where status is achieved not ascribed. In a caste theory which most people probably believed in, and many still do, everyone is born with an aptitude for a kind of work which is in his nature, his dharma. The different kinds of work, the lowest as well as the highest, are all necessary to a social organism that is part of a universal organism, which is also God. Even if we, with our limited view, cannot see the need for a certain kind of work, or if one role seems to conflict with another, it must serve some purpose. The equilibrium of the whole would be upset if any work were not done.

This is the most thoroughgoing functionalist theory ever devised. The model of society is of a system where the roles of each caste, sex and age group are in balance with each other, with technology and with nature; and the common values, constantly renewed by ritual, myth and social control, remind individuals of their roles and maintain the balance. Each caste serves the others for traditional but unequal rewards. There is no competition, and everyone is secure.

Obviously this is just ideology, a way of justifying a certain distribution of power and wealth; in particular, the so-called jajmaani system of relations between dominant agricultural castes and the specialist castes which serve them for customary rewards,[3] or similar traditional relations in the towns (Pocock 1960). In theory, 'Each [caste] serves the others. Each in turn is master. Each in turn is servant' (Wiser 1936:xxi). Gandhi believed this reciprocity had once existed in villages and could be restored. Wiser admits that the system is not 'symmetrical' – some give much more than they get. Leach argues that those at the bottom had the best of the bargain, because in pre-colonial times status and security were polarized, and the lowest castes had almost total security.

> In a class system, social status and economic security go together – the higher the greater; in contrast, in a caste society, status and security are polarized . . . In a class society the 'people at the bottom' are those who have been forced there by the ruthless processes of economic competition; their counterparts in a caste society are members of some closely organized kinship group who regard it as their privileged right to carry out a task from which all other members of the total society are rigorously excluded . . . The low castes suffer economically not because they are low *castes* but because present conditions have turned them into an unemployed working-*class*. (Leach 1962:6)

This is simply wrong: Dharma Kumar (1965) has shown that there was a large class of landless labourers in south India before the nineteenth century, and even those who were attached to a master could expect little from him unless he had work for them. Evidence from other parts of India shows there were many migrant wage labourers, often travelling long distances (Das Gupta 1976).

Nor can we assume that craftsmen or other specialists (like barbers or washermen) were insulated from market or population pressures. Villages were deserted in times of war, famine or disease. In better times, enterprising petty chieftains were granted land by their lords – or seized it themselves – and had to offer favourable terms to attract not only farmers, but a full range of dependent castes from Brahman priests to 'Untouchable' labourers. There are strong reasons to suspect that families of doubtful caste origins took advantage of the new opportunities and invented their own 'traditional' caste occupations, as they continued to do until recently (Srinivas 1966:42–4). The more sophisticated urban craftsmen, catering to the court and the merchants, were of course more exposed to fluctuations of fashion and their patrons' fortunes.

[3] The classical account is Wiser (1936). 'Jajmaani' (my spelling) has this sense only in some Hindi-speaking areas, but the system or something like it is found all over India, and the word has come into general use because of Wiser's book.

Caste ideology could be reconciled with some competition and changes in occupation, though in theory everyone had a caste occupation which it was a sin to change, because only a minority worked in really castebound occupations. Hereditary specialization and interdependence are bound up with ideas of purity and pollution: the high-caste person is polluted by close contact with low castes or by doing their work, and also by the gross biological processes of everyday life. The true jajmaani relations are between families belonging to locally dominant cultivating castes (often with military traditions) and families whose caste specialization is either to confer and renew purity (Brahmans) or to remove it (Barbers, Washermen and Sweepers)[4]: one high caste and several low ones, whose ritual duties at weddings and festivals are as important as the practical business of shaving or washing clothes. Pocock calls them 'the true, or religious specialists' (1962:95): 'true specialization for certain important castes derives from the basic opposition of purity and impurity and only by extension of this idea can other castes be said to be "specialized"' (:82). Artisan castes can be fitted in with some difficulty, according to the purity of the materials they work with (leather is very polluting, iron more pollutable than gold). But agriculture and trade – the main sources of wealth – are not really covered at all; because although certain castes are traditionally farmers or traders (Pocock calls this 'ascribed specialization'), these occupations have always been open in practice to anyone with the means to engage in them, including artisans, religious specialists, and Untouchables: not completely open, because of traditional restrictions like the ban on high castes trading in leather, or the rule that a Brahman may not handle the plough himself because it injures life, *unless he has no other means of subsistence* (see Bouglé 1971:160). Louis Dumont (1970:96) says agriculture 'is a religiously neutral occupation for the majority of castes (though there is a prejudice amongst high castes against using the plough in person), and is respectable from the non-religious point of view. Anyone who has direct or indirect access to the land – the important point – will see no disadvantage in profiting from it in any way open to him.'

This is not a small loophole, but one big enough to let most of the population through while keeping intact the image of a society where every kind of work is the 'privileged right' of a hereditary group. A

---

[4] I follow the convention of using initial capitals for castes named after traditional occupations, lower case for the occupations themselves: thus all barbers (by trade) are Barbers (by caste) but not all Barbers are barbers.

more realistic picture of pre-industrial India is of a set of closely linked dominant minorities (feudal, military, landowning and priestly), a fringe of clients (including Untouchable farm labourers) who got some security and other advantages from jajmaani relations with the dominant groups, and another class of landless labourers whose exploitation was less well disguised by the ideology of caste interdependence.

> Material transfers between the different social groups are inadequately documented, or recorded only to be confused with the *jajmani* which is only a relationship of clientship affecting a relatively weak portion of the population.
> (Meillassoux 1973:99)

But Meillassoux goes to the opposite extreme from Leach when he says the concept of caste should be 'legitimately' applied only to 'certain distinctive sections close to what we define here as "client"', limited in number' (:109) – not to outcastes or depressed castes (Untouchables) 'although they were in a majority' (which was not true in most places). One cannot ignore the people's own concept so completely, especially when there is ample evidence that the lower castes did and do divide their social world into castes, and shared some variant of upper-caste ideology. (Moffat 1975, 1979). This may be 'false consciousness', but it is a fact.

In theory the ranking of castes was fixed from the world's beginning. In practice it was often uncertain (except at the extremes – Brahmans at the top, polluting low castes and Untouchables at the bottom) and flexible. Local caste groups, or splinter groups of families which came to marry only each other, acquired wealth from agriculture, trade or new crafts and manufactures. They translated this rise in economic status into social status, without admitting it but without deceiving anyone else, in a society which was more competitive and mobile than it seemed to be (see Bagchi 1972:93 on the fallacy that peasants have traditional value systems and rigid social structures, which prevent them from seeing or taking opportunities to make money). Castes and sub-castes took alternative prestigious names, and claimed they 'really' (i.e. originally) belonged to a higher caste, from which they had fallen because of some sin, like taking up a low occupation from economic necessity – which may even, occasionally, have been true.[5] They adopted high-caste customs, like vegetarianism or the ban on widow remarriage, as a way

---

[5] 'A rise in status is never admitted but simply considered as a return to a former status' (Pocock 1955:72). For instances, see Pocock 1972 and Silverberg 1968

to claim high status – it is no sin for a low caste to eat meat (Srinivas 1952 and 1962 introduced the term 'sanskritization' for this imitation of high-caste customs). Above all, they persuaded Brahmans to serve at their weddings and domestic ceremonies (Srinivas 1966:32), or to give a more complete prestigious service (1962:45–6). A caste's chances of getting its high rank recognized by other powerful castes depended mainly on economic and political power: yet the ideology, by giving the humblest Brahman precedence over the most powerful prince or warrior, denied that wealth or power – or anything except one's inherited nature – could ever justify high-caste status; and this mobility within the caste system is traditional in the sense that it has been regular practice for a long time.

Although caste ideology has its own logic, and caused people to act or not to act in certain ways, in many situations it is more useful to think of caste as the people's way of coding and thinking about economic class differences, which barely disguised competition for resources and power; not the only way perhaps, since the Indian masses have and probably had alternative categories based directly on economic differences, and more like western uses of 'class' (see Béteille 1970a, esp. p. 138, quoted in Holmström 1976:123; and Béteille 1969).

But if caste is a disguise for economic differences, it is an effective one. If people divided up their social world into castes, the system could accommodate many kinds of change and manipulation, but within limits set by deep-rooted ideas about pollution, heredity and interdependence. Wealth and power could often be turned into status, but not always or automatically.

Two things altered the old division of labour and relations between classes: imperialism, and powered industry which developed later and more slowly. These opened up new economic opportunities for some groups and weakened others. They also exposed Indians – starting with the upper and middle classes – to foreign ideas which, however, were a mixed bag not a consistent whole: imperialism, nationalism, evangelical Christianity, atheism, positivism, liberalism, socialism, marxism, 'management' and even theosophy which is a western version of Hinduism (Pocock 1958).

Industrialization and the old society

How should we relate contemporary Indian society to the pre-'industrial' and pre-colonial society?

It is no longer possible to see empire and industry as a single package – of institutions, techniques and imported ideas – which upset a stable agricultural society with its rigid social structure and unquestioned value system. Industrialization need not mean following a well-trodden 'western' path. In India's case, at least, we know too much about the older society; and this idea of a transition to a modern society is not of much use in explaining what happened to the society or where it is going now.

We might see pre-colonial India as a society seething with unresolved tensions and contradictions, which could be contained by an apparently rigid social structure and common values only for as long as economic opportunities were scarce and were monopolized by entrenched powerful groups. The marxist idea of a 'feudal society' is one version of this. Another is in Morris' article (1960a), which demolishes a whole set of received assumptions. One of these is the idealization of country life, which comes from the tendency to place

> rural and urban life in sharp contrast and to treat the traditional rural system as a holistic institutional arrangement, entirely consistent within itself and capable of disruption only from outside. It is true that the Indian village system has persisted for many centuries, but it has also been riddled with internal tensions and centrifugal tendencies. This suggests that it has been maintained by the absence of alternatives. When alternative opportunities appear and are bulwarked by legal institutions that make them real opportunities, the village system reveals its internal contradictions and is threatened by collapse from inside. (:186)

> The general tendency in India to view the world as without material opportunity has been the ideological reflection of close observation and conformity to fact. (:189)

This 'stability', very often, was not even a successful balancing act, but a myth. Opportunities did occur, and were taken, by peasants, craftsmen and traders. Ideology could only follow one step behind, patching up the ravages of ruthless competition for wealth and power. Caste mobility, which is well documented, reflected real mobility between classes. Colonial rule and then 'industry' created wider opportunities, and new values made it less important to turn wealth into caste status; but this was simply taking further some tendencies which were already there. This may be an exaggeration, but the evidence does suggest it was true at some times and places.

Whichever of these two views is more generally true, we know enough to trace continuities between pre-'industrial' India and the present industrializing society. In the pre-colonial cities, and in the countryside until recently, dominant groups with property and security supported a wide range of clients or dependants, often bound to them by 'jajmaani' relations. Outside the circle were other groups who could claim no special relationship with the dominant groups, and who had only their unskilled labour power to sell: a real proletariat, whose existence has often been denied. 'Untouchables' included people inside and outside the circle. It is tempting to draw an analogy with the present relations between employers, secure organized sector workers, a fringe of unorganized sector or 'temporary' industrial workers, and wandering casual labourers.

How far do the inequalities in the present industrial work force reflect pre-industrial ones? The question is important because people from a particular caste or area or religion are often found in large numbers in one industry or firm or skill, for historical reasons. Members of one group first entered a line of work because they had some special skill; or because of local accidents, as when young men from dominant groups saw a good opportunity and took it, or when people from the poorest groups were forced by sheer need to take work which no one else would do. Employers continued to recruit people from the same origins, or workers brought in their relatives and friends; and these people came to have a partial monopoly of jobs which now – with increasing unemployment and higher wages – may seem more attractive to others.

Morris writes: 'While industrialism generally increases mobility and engenders consciousness of opportunity, in the absence of universal compulsory education in India industrialism has tended to perpetuate traditional social inequalities' (1960a:190). This was true of those occupations which required education, or were seen as desirable from the beginning; but there were other kinds of industrial employment which also, or only, attracted the poor and illiterate, especially the lower castes; and those who got into these occupations early sometimes managed to educate their children for better jobs.

To the extent it is true that the same groups (castes etc.) which had security and other advantages before continued to have them in the industrial society, is this because they were in industry from the beginning, say from the nineteenth or early twentieth centuries? Or did they join later, when they could use their education and connexions to get scarce jobs in technically advanced industries which required a different kind of work force?

The rest of this chapter is a brief guide to some of the writings on industrialization in India, especially as these throw light on the divisions in Indian society now.

The first powered industries, and where their labour came from

Although India for millenia has been a traditionally organized agricultural
society, this has been a very intricate and sophisticated one, characterized by a
complex division of labor and the employment of extensive skills, many of
which were transferable to the new industrial pattern. In other words, when
modern institutions began to invade India in the nineteenth century, they did
not take root in an environment entirely unprepared for them. The elements of
literacy for a modern bureaucracy existed, a sophisticated system of banking
and commerce was in operation, and there was a substantial tradition of
artisanship. As new industries slowly grew during the late nineteenth and
twentieth centuries, they found that the ground had been partly prepared.
The construction of the cotton mills in Bombay and of the steel mills in
Jamshedpur depended in large measure on the reservoir of fitter and rigger
talent that derived from the traditional shipbuilding industry of Surat. By the
late nineteenth century much traditional iron-working skill had found its way
into the railway workshops, and from the railways this modernized skill
ultimately was drafted into private industry, as at Jamshedpur.

(Morris 1960a:186–7)

Morris has argued at more length (1965) that these early factories
had much less trouble in finding both skilled and unskilled labour
than is often supposed. When specific skills were in short supply, there
were people trained in traditional crafts who could learn them, or
literate adaptable workers. But the mass of workers in these early
industries were unskilled and mainly illiterate, and were in abundant
supply almost everywhere. Where they were not, as at Jamshedpur in
a remote tribal area, people travelled long distances to take work.
Employers' complaints of a labour shortage, and of an unstable
undisciplined work force constantly returning to the villages, are not
justified by records and statistics. Where there was high labour
turnover, as in the Bombay cotton mills, this was the result of poor
management and working conditions. Workers left for better pay,
and kept up their village ties as their only security.

But if the ground had been prepared for the growth of modern
industry, some of it had then been cut away by the devastating first
impact of colonialism, which hit India just at the time when the
imperial power itself was industrializing. Modern industry came to
India as a result of colonial rule, but not a result originally intended
by the colonial rulers and not until after a delay which had a serious
and perhaps disastrous effect on industry when it finally came.

Gadgil (1971) describes the wide range of industries in pre-colonial
India. The largest urban industries made luxury goods, especially
fine cloth, for the upper classes. They were hit by the decline of the

Indian courts and by imports, but lingered on for some time – with debased artistic standards – supplying Europeans in India, and the export trade in 'oriental' curios and certain lines like the famous Kashmiri shawls. Village industries included the work of artisans, country weavers making coarse cloth, potters and goldsmiths. Similar craftsmen working for a wider market, but better organized, lived in the towns. Urban craftsmen, like the brass and copper smiths, might make artistic wares for the rich as well as common utensils. There was also a third group of mainly localized industries:

> The group included the iron-smelters of Mysore, Chota Nagpur, Central Provinces and other places, the saltpetre worker, the bangle-maker, and the general worker in glass, also the paper-maker, etc. . . . A good many required special knowledge on the part of the workers. In many, organized working was necessary on account of the peculiarities of processes and other reasons . . . Some [industries], such as iron-smelting, were industrially very important, and their products used to find their way all over the country. The methods employed were generally crude and uneconomical, but the products, as in the case of Mysore steel, were sometimes of a very high quality. But all these miscellaneous industries were already dying out. An unwise tariff and the discovery of Chili nitrates gave a serious shock to the saltpetre industry; the iron-smelting industry was suffering from the great rise in the price of charcoal – due to the reservation of forests and the extension of railways – and the competition of imported pig-iron. The glass and paper industries were also succumbing under the pressure of imported goods. Thus the opening up of the country was resulting in the killing of all indigenous industries.
>
> (Gadgil 1971:46)

For many of these industries, there was no direct transition to modern powered industry as there was in Europe. The business of the East India Company was trade not manufacture, and the old industries were almost destroyed by free trade and cheap imports two or three generations before the new ones were established. Many craftsmen were ruined.[6] Rural artisans, at least, must have turned to agriculture, farming their own land if they had any, or as tenants or landless labourers.

> This compulsory back-to-the-land movement of artisans and craftsmen led to an ever-growing disproportion between agriculture and industry; agriculture became more and more the sole business of the people because of the lack of occupations and wealth-producing activities . . . India became progressively

[6] 'What were all these scores of millions, who had so far been engaged in industry and manufacture, to do now? . . . They could die, of course . . . They did die in tens of millions. The English Governor-General of India, Lord Bentinck, reported in 1834 that "the misery hardly finds a parallel in the history of commerce. The bones of the cotton weavers are bleaching the plains of India"' (Nehru 1956:298).

ruralized . . . In the middle of the nineteenth century about fifty-five per cent
of the population is said to have been dependent on agriculture; recently this
proportion was estimated to be seventy-four per cent. (This is a pre-war
figure). (Nehru 1956:298)

The craft industries of India were not gradually replaced by factories. Having
lost his trade the artisan was forced back to the land; it was only two or three
generations later that industries grew up in Indian cities. Thus the city workers
of modern India did not come out of the ranks of artisans, but were comprised
mostly of the landless peasants or agricultural labourers.
(M.N. Roy, quoted in Revri 1972:10)

But Morris thinks it is not clear that large numbers of craftsmen were
forced to become landless labourers in the nineteenth century:

It is possible that the growth of population and the absence of any
substantial increase of urban occupations did increase relative land pressure. I
stress the uncertainty of the growth of landless labor because we know virtually
nothing about the changing character of economic activity in the critical
period 1850–1914. The decline of traditional activities was being offset by the
rise of new occupations, even in the rural sector. For example, D. and A.
Thorner, *Land and Labour in India* (. . . 1962), pp. 70–81, have shown how weak
are the assumptions regarding the 'de-industrialization' of India. See D.R.
Gadgil, *The Industrial Evolution of India* (1971) who also suggests that the
orthodox view cannot be uncritically accepted. It is even possible that the
notion that traditional handicrafts were destroyed in the nineteenth century is
not in accord with the real situation.
(Morris 1965:41)

Daniel and Alice Thorner cast doubt on the Census figures, since
families involved in several activities were arbitrarily classified as
engaged only in one kind of manufacture, or in agriculture or trade.

If, indeed, a major shift from industry to agriculture ever occurred during
British rule in India, it might have happened some time between 1815 and
1880. But we do not have the kind of data which would allow us to say with
any assurance whether or not this actually took place . . . At best, a plausible
inference from our figures is that whatever new employment [after 1881] was
created by the introduction of textile mills, rice dehusking plants, and other
modern industrial establishments may have been roughly offset by an
equivalent falling off in handicrafts. The conclusion forced upon us by the
census occupational data is that the industrial distribution of the Indian
working force from 1881 to 1931 stood still.
(1962:77)

Yet many of the old crafts survived. Blacksmiths and carpenters, in
villages and towns, continued to find repair work as well as a market
for their own products, and adopted new techniques in their family

businesses. They remained available for skilled factory employment, from the 1850s up to the present, like the ship fitters and riggers Morris refers to, or the traditional iron-workers who went into the railway workshops. Or they became industrial entrepreneurs when conditions were ripe, like the remarkable Sikh Ramgarhia caste, originally carpenters (Saberwal 1976). Those families of handloom weavers who survived the first shock of Lancashire imports continued to supply a limited market until some of them were rescued after Independence, first by official encouragement and subsidies, then by new western markets for 'ethnic' clothes and fabrics. The skill and traditions of these tightly organized castes were not lost: again, some adopted more modern technologies like the powerloom in their family firms, or became industrial entrepreneurs (see Singer 1960, 'Changing craft traditions in India'; Singer 1972:272ff; and Baldwin 1959:202–7 on the career of D.R. Madhava Krishnaiya, a handloom weaver's son).

But this was much later. Cotton, jute, railways and coal mines were the first 'modern' industries in India; and almost the only ones, from the 1850s when they effectively began until the Tata steel works opened in 1911 at Jamshedpur:

> The decade 1850–1860 stands out sharply in the industrial development of India as one in which the first successful jute and cotton mills were established, the coal fields were connected by rail to the port city of Calcutta, and the beginning of a rapid expansion of rail lines throughout India took place. Unlike countries moving into an industrial revolution, however, this was not the beginning of a diversified industrial growth, but both a beginning and an ending; for not until a century later, with the coming of independence, did India again move towards an active broadening of her industrial base.
> (Myers 1958:14. Chapter II of this book gives a useful brief history)

The jute mills, concentrated around Calcutta, were controlled by British firms and managed by British staff as were the railways – by far the largest 'industrial' employers – which were heavily subsidized by the British Government of India, for military purpose as well as those of trade, administration and famine relief. Only the cotton mills, mainly in western India around Bombay and Ahmedabad, were more often controlled by Indian businessmen, especially of the Parsi religion. Other industries, like paper and the engineering industries which used skills developed in the railway workshops, grew at a very modest pace.

The First World War caused a severe shortage of shipping space to Europe. It cut India off from European markets, and:

The war revealed . . . how utterly dependent India was on manufactured goods from England and the rest of Europe, even for her most essential needs – electrical and agricultural plant, accessories for her growing industries and even such simple things as screws and bolts and nails. Everything seemed to be lacking in India – capital, skilled labour, and expert management and industrial experience – everything, except an unrivalled opportunity for development. The absence of imports of manufactured goods created conditions similar to those which would have developed under a policy of high tariffs, while the demands of the Government alone were sufficient as an incentive to industrial growth. And as the war dragged its course, revenue considerations compelled the Government to increase its customs duties to an enormous extent. (Shiva Rao 1939:29)

The government set up an Industrial Commission and an Indian Munitions Board, and reversed its old policy in favour of active state encouragement of industry, through technical and financial assistance and the purchase of stores.

The effects were mixed. 'The almost complete lack of organized industry in light engineering meant a trickle of inferior replacements to industries subject to heavy wartime strains' (Myers 1958:16). Irrigation works deteriorated, and the railways nearly broke down. Some light engineering industries were set up, but were 'allowed (and even encouraged) to die after the crisis passed' (:18). From a combination of causes, the cotton and jute mills made fabulous windfall profits, but not much was reinvested (Bagchi 1972:79). The Tata steel works grew steadily.

Between the wars only the cotton textile industry expanded much. Growth in other industries, especially light engineering, was slow and wavering. It was not until the Second World War that a serious engineering industry was established, to supply machinery to existing industries like the cotton and jute mills, and aircraft and other requirements for the war against Japan. After Independence in 1947, tariff protection and government assistance led to the first real expansion and diversification of Indian industries since the nineteenth century, into light and heavy engineering, chemicals, cement and new steel works, and later into electronics and pharmaceuticals. Yet this expansion too, though remarkable, was held up at intervals by crises and depressions.

I shall come back later to the implications for labour of this post-war expansion. The important points about the earlier industrial growth are that the base was narrow – cotton, jute, mines and railways – not supported by indigenous engineering because almost all machinery and supplies were imported; and industrial growth was

not a gradual diversification, building on existing industries, linkages
and skills, but happened in fits and starts, determined by foreign wars,
booms and slumps. The character and social composition of the work
force depended largely on the ways in which the first industrial
workers were recruited, especially into the four main industries.

The mass of these workers, as in the first English factories, were
unskilled, and drawn mainly from the countryside: poor peasants and
landless labourers, with a high but not overwhelming proportion
from low castes. Morris' sources do not show how many of the early
migrants to Bombay came from artisan rather than exclusively
agricultural families;[7] but R. Das Gupta (1976) has examined Census
and other material on the industrial work force in eastern India, both
in the jute mills around Calcutta and in the engineering industries
which needed more skilled labour. The 1911 Census shows that '*the
ruined artisans, labourers failing to get adequate employment and subsistence in
the rural economy, agriculturists unsettled by the sort of changes taking place in
the agricultural economy, unskilled of all trades, and peasants, artisans and
labourers turned into destitutes and paupers were the most numerous* among the
working mass employed in the jute mills' (:315; Das Gupta's words
and italics). However, many employees at the Jamalpur Railway
Workshops were from castes of carpenters and other skilled artisans.
Overall there was considerable 'industrial migration', of weavers,
iron-workers, carpenters and others, distressed or displaced from
their traditional caste occupations, and 'these industrial migrants
constituted a kind of pool of skilled labour for the new factories'
(:326).

Clearly this pool of skilled workers, who could quickly learn new
techniques, made the establishment of modern industries easier; and
a minority of the traditional artisans moved straight into the ranks of
the skilled and better-paid workers. The rest, the mass of unskilled
labourers, were from very mixed social origins. Before going further
into the social composition of the work force in these early industries,
we should look at the industries' financial structure, management and
recruiting practices, and at regional differences: especially between
the two early industrial complexes centred on Bombay and Calcutta.

---

[7] Morris (1965), ch. IV 'Supply of labor'. It is interesting that, already in 1864, the Census
   Commissioner of Bombay could write: 'It is supposed that at one time caste determined the
   occupation that a Hindu was to follow. Now it is but a limited influence, and there are few
   castes of which the members will not engage in any occupation, and but few occupations in
   which the persons of any caste will not seek a livelihood' (:78).

Ownership, management and recruitment in the first industrial centres

The first investments in Indian manufacturing industries were made by British trading companies, mainly around Calcutta. They were followed soon afterwards by Indian businessmen, especially in the textile mills of western India. Morris (1965:27) suggests that most of the 'British' capital invested in the Bombay cotton mills, and probably elsewhere, came from British merchants resident in India and reinvesting their earnings: there were no large-scale transfers of resources from Britain to India, by way of investment, in the nineteenth century.

The distinctive feature of Indian industry, from these early days until very recently, was the managing agency system. The British trading companies appointed British businessmen in India as their agents, originally to conduct their import–export trade, and then to organize industrial firms which they watched over on behalf of the stockholders in Britain (Baldwin 1959:21–5). Indian businessmen soon took over the system; most operating companies came to be controlled by managing agencies, some of which built up industrial empires. In most cases a managing agency is a private limited company, dominated by one family or community.

A managing agency is not usually a holding company with a controlling interest in subsidiaries, though this is how the first agencies began. It stands in a contractual relationship to the firms it manages: an 'agency agreement' gives it the right to buy and sell for the operating company, to raise capital and manage the finances, to provide technical management and usually to appoint the managing director. The agency takes a management fee and has the first claim to a percentage of profits before any dividends are paid to shareholders.

The advantages claimed for the system are that it spread scarce managerial talent over many companies, and that managing agencies had access to capital which smaller companies could not raise for themselves. The chief drawbacks were that agencies often maximized profits, not by building up companies under their control, but by milking them of cash and by speculative transactions among the different companies, sometimes as a way to avoid taxes. Thus Morris (1965:33–8), though he does not think the system is responsible for all the evils blamed on it, shows how the agencies treated the Bombay cotton mills as 'a milch cow to be drained of profits at all costs'. For example, until 1886 managing agencies received a commission on mill output regardless of the firm's profitability. Generally 'profit maximization for the decision-making group in the enterprise, the managing agents, did not relate specifically to the efficiency of the cotton mill itself but to the wider and more complex system of commercial relationships of which it was merely a part' (:35), and this led to slack administration, corruption and divided responsibility in the mills. Department heads and their assistants were nominally responsible to the manager but were appointed by the managing agents (often as a result of nepotism), and sometimes spied on the manager for the agents.

The managing agencies did little to develop middle management or skilled supervisory staff. In factories of all kinds the recruitment, discipline, supervision and training of labour were in the hands of promoted workers, the jobbers:

> The jobber . . . is almost ubiquitous in the Indian factory system and usually combines in one person a formidable series of functions. Promoted from the ranks after full experience of the factory, he is responsible for the supervision of labour while at work. In a large factory there may be a hierarchy of jobbers, including women overseers in departments staffed by women. He has also, on many occasions, to act as assistant mechanic, and to help in keeping the machines in working order. So far as the worker is given technical teaching, the jobber is expected to provide it. He is not, however, merely responsible for the worker once he has obtained work; the worker has generally to approach him to secure a job.
>
> (Royal Commission 1931a:23, quoted in Morris 1965:23).[8]

The jobber's role as a recruiter of labour brought him a good income in *dastuurii* or bribes. Two Ahmedabad weavers told the Commission: 'At the time of our engagement we had to pay bribes to the head jobbers and the line jobbers [who also had to pay the head jobbers] . . . We have also to pay Rs 4 or 5 to them on every pay day, and in some cases we provide them with liquor' (Royal Commission 1931c:161, 163). Harilal, a Calcutta jute spinner, said: 'When there is a big surplus labour then we have to pay bribes to the *sardar* [jobber] to get employment, but when there is shortage of labour we get in

---

[8] The observation about technical training applied to ordinary mill workers: not to highly skilled artisans and mechanics, about whom Morris writes: 'I have found no complaints in the literature of shortages, instability, inefficiency, or truculence relating to these skilled workers. There is need for a thorough investigation of the methods by which workers were trained for highly skilled tasks. I suspect that the role of the railway workshops will prove very important' (1965:130–1).

somehow or other. I came in when labour was short' (Royal Commission 1931e:78).

The jobber built up a following of workers he could bring with him *en bloc* if he took employment at another mill. He could range more widely, in the Bombay slums or the villages around, to break strikes.[9] No doubt he could offer the workers who were his clients some security in the labour market.

> The sirdar [jobber] stands, in his crude way, both for the interests of the employer and for those of the labourer. It is his part to see that an adequate amount of work is done and to minimize as far as possible the fluctuations in the supply of labour. From the worker's point of view, he is necessary, not only as a protector of his rights against vague, unknown powers, but also as a security against arbitrary dismissal. In many cases he is oppressive, but he is so much an institution of the country that the labourer scarcely understands how work could be carried on without him.   (Kelman 1923:105)

The jobber lent 'his' workers money at interest, and took a commission from local shops where he made them buy their provisions: thus the jobbers managed to wreck a government scheme to provide cheap food through mill workers' co-operatives in the First World War (Morris 1965:144–5). Morris describes these profitable roles, inside and outside the mill, in his account of the jobber's rise and gradual fall, from the 1930s onwards, under the pressures of the new technology, unions, the state and the Millowners' Association.

In a recent article, Morris suggests that dastuurii represented the difference between the muster roll wage rate and the equilibrium price for millhands:

> Employers favoured the system because it was clearly the cheapest way to get the labour supply they needed with the flexibility they preferred. All the system cost them was the fluctuating amount the jobbers extracted from the workers under them. In return, the jobbers bore the responsibility for organising the job market and suffered the variation in income.
>   (Morris 1979:1685)

The alternative of permanent personnel officers would have cost more:

> The end of the traditional system of labour recruitment and administration by jobbers in the Bombay cotton mill industry was not proof that the system had

---

[9] 'In times of strikes these men [jobbers] are seen running about from locality to locality in the city to find out labour to break the strikes; and on some occasions some of them or their agents are reported to have gone, or sent false telegrams, to the villages asking men to come back or to get new recruits' The Bombay Textile Labour Union's evidence (Royal Commission 1931b:296).

been irrational before. It was merely evidence of the fact that costs internal to
the industry had changed and that under the impact of ruthless competition,
adjustment had to be made to that overriding fact.   (:1686)

In the early days, British employers and technicians saw no
alternative to the jobber system: like the civil servants (see Frykenberg 1965) they had to delegate sweeping powers to Indian subordinates who were hard to control. The British could not speak the
workers' language, and the social distance made close contact
impossible. When middle-class Indians took over the administrative
posts in cotton and jute mills, the social barriers remained: though
Morris points out that the system of powerful jobbers never developed
at Jamshedpur or on the railways, where there were both social and
language barriers between staff and workers. Morris thinks the
jobbers were intended from the beginning to play the role of a 'middle
management cadre'. More expensive technically trained staff would
not have been justified by the industry's technology and
organization.

The employers finally turned against the system when they realized
it was grossly inefficient and benefited no one but the jobbers
themselves.

> The jobbers' category is the highest to which an Indian industrial worker can
> rise. All classes and categories of work in an industrial establishment above the
> jobber's post are now closed to the ranks of Indian workmen. This
> circumstance has contributed in no small measure to engender in the jobber,
> who has no prospects of rising higher, the temptation to abuse his present
> status.   (Mukerjee 1951:52. This book refers mainly to an earlier period.)

These abuses were a cost to employers as well as workers. Wages
had to cover not only workers' subsistence, but also the jobbers' illicit
earnings. Above all, the work itself suffered from the constant
turnover of labour, selected on grounds of ability to bribe rather than
efficiency or experience, haphazardly supervised, sometimes working
long hours in appalling conditions, or wasting time hanging around
the factory 'compound' while others tended the machines. Employers complained constantly of a shortage of suitable labour, and of
an 'undisciplined' work force who were peasants at heart.[10] Morris
shows that these complaints were nonsense: workers responded

[10] Burnett-Hurst (1925:61) echoes these complaints: 'What really accounts for a considerable
      amount of loafing is that the mill worker is essentially an agriculturist. His heart is in the
      country and not in his work, and so long as he makes a certain wage he is indifferent to what
      else happens.'

rationally to insecurity and bad working conditions, and there was no difficulty in building up a stable trained efficient work force when it was in the employers' interest to have one, as at Jamshedpur from the beginning and in the Bombay cotton mills after the 1920s (Morris 1965:202).

In the early days the jobbers had to go out and recruit labour, as distinct from merely taking on those who applied for work. When the first cotton and jute mills were set up, the urban population of Calcutta, Bombay and Ahmedabad could only supply part of the labour that was needed. The first jobbers (also known as mukadams or sirdars) were often men the employers trusted and who had contacts in the villages, where they went in search of men who could be persuaded by an advance of pay to sign a legally binding contract of employment (Broughton 1924:111).[11] The jobbers built up their own network of agents. In some cases barbers were used to recruit labour: an extension of their traditional role as matchmakers, since they had a wide range of acquaintances in different castes as well as their own caste network extending into distant villages (Ornati 1955:37). It was necessary to offer greater inducements to get men to move to plantations in remote areas, or to very unpleasant work like coal mining: thus the Bengal and Bihar colliery owners 'had to use the *zamīndārī* method of recruitment by which the Santhal tribesmen were attracted by offers of plots of land', until the owners found a stable labour supply from the United Provinces (Gupta 1974:422). Jobbers or mukadams continued to supply seasonal migrant labour, or workers for industries like salt pans – evaporation beds which are often far away from towns and villages (Streefkerk 1978:244).

But the factories were soon turning away applicants at the gates: it was only in emergencies like strikes or plagues that they had to send out for labour. Thus the Bombay Textile Union claimed in its evidence to the 1929 Royal Commission, 'Scarcity of labour there is none; if anything, there is superfluity of it', and the jobbers no longer did whatever good they might once have done (Royal Commission 1931b:296). Mrs Wagh of the Bombay Labour Office told the Commission that the mills still recruited through jobbers and mukadams, but since there was always a great rush of hands at the gate and the managers did not want the machines to stand idle, there

[11] Broughton notes that the Workmen's Breach of Contract Act, which made workers criminally liable if they broke the contract, was soon to be repealed.

was less chance than before for jobbers to extort money; or at any rate the amounts were lower (:192).

By this time a new division had appeared within the labour force, between those on the payroll of registered factories – even as temporary or substitute workers – and other industrial workers employed on less favourable terms in small unregistered factories, or by labour contractors to the large factories. This foreshadowed the split between the organized and unorganized sectors, which became much sharper after Independence when stronger unions and new legislation gave organized sector workers some job security.

Where jobbers still exist, their old power and status have gone. Thus in the Coimbatore textile mills:

> Till the mid-forties a worker had to be in the good books of the jobber to move up or even to keep his job . . . Workers now seldom express fear of the jobber. A unionist pointed out: 'The jobber is no different from us except that he has an easier job and gets a few rupees more. He is even a member of our union. He can't send me out on the ground that I don't please him. The mill will grind to a halt if he tries to be difficult.' (E.A. Ramaswamy 1977:42–3)

The first Factory Act of 1881 was intended mainly to restrict child labour. It applied only to factories using power and employing over 100 workers, and in any case it remained largely a dead letter. It was amended in 1891 under pressure from Indian and British humanitarians, and from Lancashire textile interests concerned about unfair competition.

> In November 1888, the Manchester Chamber of Commerce passed a resolution that in view of the excessive hours of work in the cotton mills of British India, the provisions of the British Factory Act, in so far as they related to the employment of women and young persons and children, should be extended to include the textile factories in India. On that occasion even the European Chairman of the Madras Chamber of Commerce – a British organization – was moved to write to the Government of India expressing his Chamber's disapproval of the interference of Manchester and its claims to have Indian labour conditions regulated by British standards. The proposal to extend British factory regulation to India, he caustically observed, was not prompted by disinterested concern for Indian operatives. Indeed, the Madras Chamber of Commerce went so far as to attribute Manchester's action to jealousy, to the dictates of self-interest and to the discovery that competition in India was becoming too severe for Lancashire. (Shiva Rao 1939:21–2)

Of course Indian businessmen reacted strongly against this Lancastrian interference: this was one of the main reasons for the setting up of the Bombay Millowners' Association in 1875 (Morris 1965:38).

The new Act provided for further restrictions on hours and conditions of work for women and children in powered factories employing at least fifty workers, and an Inspectorate to enforce the law. The Indian Factories Act of 1911, which extended the definition of a 'factory', was the first to limit working hours for adult males to twelve a day in textile factories, reduced to ten in the 1922 Act, which also applied to non-textile labour. The Workmen's Compensation Act of 1923 covered accidents and industrial diseases. To escape these restrictions some industries moved to the princely states, most of which had no Factory Acts (Vakil 1931:139).

These laws – where they were enforced – tied employers' hands with respect to working hours and conditions, weekly holidays and rest breaks, safety, sanitation, and the age at which children could be employed; but they gave workers no security against arbitrary dismissal, beyond the security that came from the employers' interest in having a stable contented work force, from the jobbers' reciprocal obligation to their clients, and from the small but growing power of the unions. Thus Broughton (1924:113) wrote: 'It is true that men sometimes go on strike if one of their number has been unfairly dismissed, but, owing to the unorganized state of labour, it is not difficult for a manager to engage substitutes for those who strike.' Yet if the strikes had never succeeded it is unlikely that they would have continued to happen, and some strikes in this period did lead to better wages or conditions.

In 1931 the Royal Commission on Labour in India drew attention to the difference between conditions in large perennial factories using power – mainly cotton and jute mills – and other kinds of factory. In predominantly seasonal factories processing cotton, tea or jute, most workers were 'essentially agriculturists' living in villages. Here 'The worker is generally quite unorganized and wages tend to be low' (Royal Commission 1931a:79). The Factory Act applied to these seasonal factories, but there was more 'latitude' in its enforcement. Then there were factories not using power, which sometimes employed up to 800 workers, in a wide range of industries: mica, wool cleaning ('a foul process'), shellac manufacture, making bidis or country cigarettes, carpet weaving, tanning etc. The 'main defects' of these factories were 'the unsuitability or the dilapidated nature of the type of building used, the absence of adequate sanitation, poor lighting, defective ventilation, overcrowding, long hours and – above all – a preponderance in certain cases [especially bidis and carpets] of the labour of under-age children' (:94; cf. Shiva Rao 1939:228ff, on the appalling conditions in these large factories, which effectively escaped the Factory Act because they were seasonal or without power).

The other establishments which escaped the Act were small powered factories with less than twenty workers. These workers were not protected by laws on safety, workmen's compensation or child labour; though the Commission thought it unlikely that child labour was widely abused here, as the work was mostly unsuitable for children. In these small factories 'the hours of work, though frequently covering a big spreadover, are normally not excessive as discipline is much laxer than in the large factories and the atmosphere is more that of the domestic workshop than of the factory proper' (Royal Commission 1931a:92. This idyllic view of the patriarchal small workshops – contrasted with the harsh anonymous discipline of the large factory – has remained part of the ideology of 'small industries'). These workshops included 'the many small machine shops to be found in the back streets of all modern towns with the advent of mechanical transport and the extended use of electricity and machine tools' (:92): a type which has expanded greatly since then. Altogether the Bombay Director of Industries thought that not more than one-eighth of those engaged in 'industry' were employed in factories covered by the Factories Act (Royal Commission 1931b:207), and others gave similar estimates.

There is not much evidence about the history of these small workshops; but it is clear that the owners normally supervised the work themselves and recruited labour as they do now, through their own workers who recommended friends and relations:

> The usual practice in Sholapur for the existing small factories is to ask their employees to induce their friends to join the factory. It is almost a universal practice for the small factory owners to give an inducement in the form of a loan to new employees. When a new factory is being established the owner gets in touch with a local mukadam and gets through him the first batch of employees . . . Wages are paid directly to the workers by the owner himself. The men have direct contact with the master and the evil of jobbers extorting money from them as it obtains in the mills does not exist in connection with these small factories.   (:208–9)

By this time contract labour – workers employed and paid by a labour contractor, not directly by the factory management – had emerged as a separate type. Thus the Chief Inspector of Factories, Bombay, told the Commission: 'Where the labour supply is adequate, it is engaged direct and weekly payments are made by the management . . . Where labour is scarce a contractor is often employed' (:185). The contractor paid the workers, or sometimes the management paid them and debited the contractor's account. 'In other instances the contractor simply contracts to supply labour which is paid by the factory management' (ibid.).

It seems that outside contractors were taking over the jobber's role of recruiting extra labour when it was needed, and that these contract workers had a different status – less secure and worse paid – from directly employed workers, even when they stood side by side doing the same work: a situation which has recurred in recent years. In the absence of detailed evidence, it is likely that the reasons were the gradual limiting of the jobbers' powers, growing union militancy over pay and security, and the employers' wish to limit to one part of the work force any concessions they were forced to make. By the Second World War the distinction was firmly established:

> In some of the best organized industries in the country, such as the cotton and jute factories, engineering and metal works, contractors recruit and engage workers to an extent unknown in any other country, although the management can easily secure labour at the factory gates in the industrial centres. Apart from temporary construction work or erection of plant and machinery, where contract labour may be suitably and economically employed, many normal industrial operations are now left to contractors who work within the factory premises virtually as subordinate employers . . . Spare labour employed in place of absentees is also sometimes supplied by the contractor or jobber, the two kinds of labour working at different wage rates before the same machinery. (Mukerjee 1951:35)

> In all engineering and metal works in India contractors and petty jobbers play the role of intermediate employers, so that contract labour works side by side with the labour under the direct employ of the management, and without the privileges of the latter. (:51)

Labour supplied by the jobber, like contract labour, had now become a separate category without 'privileges': while in earlier days all except highly skilled labour had been hired and fired by jobbers. Moreover the status of a 'regular' worker – even without legal safeguards against dismissal – had become clearly distinct from that of all the other categories of contract, temporary or badli (substitute) workers.

> In a number of industrial establishments it used to be the practice until a few years ago to keep a certain number of workers on a waiting list, and offer them a small daily allowance even if there was no work for the day. But this

practice . . . has practically disappeared. Indeed, certain mills are now not only not paying any waiting allowances to the *badlis*, but enter into an agreement with them that no wages will be paid while they are learning work. There is such keen competition to secure even temporary work, that the workers (the vast majority of whom are illiterate) do not hesitate to sign any agreement that is put before them, in the hope that at least after serving their apprenticeship for a few months, they will be entertained as regular workers with a fixed wage. (Shiva Rao 1939:90)

The 1931 Royal Commission said unskilled factory labourers

fall roughly into two classes. There are a number of labourers regularly employed on manual work in factories and other industrial establishments . . . The other class consists of the large volume of unskilled labour engaged in other miscellaneous occupations on daily rates finding employment in industry either casually or for limited spells.
(Royal Commission 1931a:203).

Both in large and small factories, which villages or castes or language groups were first recruited into particular industries was largely a matter of chance; but once the pattern was established it was often perpetuated, as workers' friends and relatives followed them to town and got their introduction to jobbers or, when the jobbers ceased to hire labour, direct to factory managers.

Migration has, in fact, been dependent upon opportunity. It is noteworthy, for example, that where a connection was established between a factory and a particular village or group of villages, recruits would continue to come from these, while adjacent areas yielded none. Some of the minor currents in the streams of migration owe their force to little more than accident.
(Royal Commission 1931a:15)

This is why it is so hard to generalize about the social or caste origins of the early work force. There were one-caste or language pockets: thus Bombay foundry workers have long been Hindi-speakers from UP (United Provinces, renamed Uttar Pradesh at Independence); large numbers from the same area and Bihar went in the opposite direction to work in the Calcutta jute mills. The Bombay cotton workers were from many areas, especially the Konkan, and a wide range of castes (Morris 1965:39–83). The work was sought after and there were few caste or other barriers which prevented workers from applying or employers from hiring them: except that Untouchables, whose share in the work force gradually increased, were excluded from the weaving sheds – ostensibly because they might defile other workers when they had to suck yarn into the shuttles, though Morris suggests a stronger motive may have been 'to preserve the monopoly of particularly well-paying jobs for all Muslims and clean-caste Hindus against all untouchables', as Untouchables moved into the lower-paid jobs which higher castes were leaving (:201). In any case: 'The labor force did not, as Weber suggested, come mainly from the "declassed and pariah castes" of the countryside' (ibid.); and this was true not only in Bombay but in other industrial cities.[12]

Differences between regions and between cities: early studies of employment, migration and living conditions

I have drawn heavily on Morris' book (1965), which is mainly about the Bombay cotton mill workers but with comparative material on the Jamshedpur steel works and many valuable comments on the growth of an industrial work force in India generally. Bombay is the best-studied Indian city, and the one with the longest history of relatively uninterrupted industrial and commercial growth. Mills, docks, railways, shops and offices were the foundations on which new kinds of work were built up: engineering and metal working, chemicals and printing; and, especially after the Second World War, consumer goods, man-made fibres, petrochemicals, pharmaceuticals, electronics and the Indian film industry of which Bombay is the capital. But the few early studies of living and working conditions, and of labour migration and recruitment, were mainly about mill workers.

Thus Broughton (1924:180) writes 'Probably in no industrial city in the world are conditions as bad as in Bombay.' In Bombay Presidency as a whole, the textile and connected industries employed 67 per cent of the men and 85 per cent of the women working in industrial establishments. Until 1922 men's working hours in non-textile factories were unlimited, and 'it was largely in the smaller factories that abuses took place' (:123) but the appalling conditions all industrial workers lived in, and the insecurity of their employment, ruined their health and broke up families.

> This fear of unemployment is an ever-present anxiety in the minds of workers. Wage-earners have not yet obtained the right of continuous employment, but are liable to be dismissed at short notice. Employers are therefore not obliged to look ahead and to spread out the work. They can take on men and women

[12] For a review of the slender evidence on the composition of the early industrial work force, and some tentative conclusions (mainly that caste made little difference to recruitment) see Morris 1960b. In the discussion of the subject, there has been 'a systematic confusion of caste with village, region, language, occupation and religion' (:127–8).

and dismiss them at will. In most cases savings from the wages earned during the period of employment are quite insufficient to tide over periods of enforced idleness. A man loses his physique, his clothes get shabby and he finds it even harder than before to get engaged. (:103)

A notable peculiarity that strikes one in large industrial centres in India, such as Bombay and Calcutta, is the difficulty that confronts a man who wishes to continue the family life to which he has been accustomed. So great are these initial difficulties that many a man has to decide from the start to leave his family behind him. (:107)

Burnett-Hurst (*Labour and housing in Bombay*, 1925) described the filthy slums where mill and dock workers lived, and the rural areas they came from. Kelman (*Labour in India*, 1923) wrote about the mill workers' chawls or tenements, especially the conditions in which their wives and children lived (:142ff), and about women working in the mills. There is a great deal of information in the *Report of the Royal Commission on Labour in India* (Royal Commission 1931a) and the evidence given by employers, officials, and industrial workers themselves (Royal Commission 1931b and 1931c, for Bombay Presidency). From these sources one can piece together a picture of the interdependent relations between the dominant textile industry and a few other large factories, offering relatively secure and well-paid employment; a growing number of back-street workshops; a large service sector; and a centre of national and foreign trade, mainly in the hands of Indian businessmen. Thus the Bombay Council of Social Workers told the Commission that one reason why people continued to live in the most crowded areas was

the uncertainty of securing satisfactory work in the less congested area of the city. A job secure is worth two jobs in prospect . . . In every crowded locality there are hosts of small shopkeepers and small factories. The owners of these hesitate to give up a more or less assured income for the unknown.
(Royal Commission 1931b:370)

A more recent study of Parel, one of these old mill areas (Patel 1963, *Rural labour in industrial Bombay*), describes the transformation of a floating migrant population into permanent residents of Bombay, who married in their original villages but brought their families to live in Bombay whenever they could afford it, educated their sons for a new labour market in which mill workers needed some education, and earned as much as lower-grade clerks. This older working class of cotton mill employees – the result of continuous migration mainly from other parts of Maharashtra – shaded into the more cosmopolitan literate class of workers in the new engineering and chemical factories, or in the industrial estates which spread across the hills as Bombay expanded northwards along its narrow peninsula.

Bombay's workers, like its businessmen, differed in important ways from those elsewhere, particularly in the other main industrial region centred on Calcutta. The city of Calcutta, still the largest in India, was the imperial capital of India until 1912, the headquarters of the chief British trading companies, and the centre of international trade for a vast hinterland including the tea and jute plantations and coal mines of eastern India. It was also the city home of the landed Bengali upper classes, and a large middle class of professionals, officials and clerks working under the British, with a flourishing intellectual and artistic life.

The best discussion of the differences between the two regions is in Bagchi's *Private investment in India 1900–1939* (1972). Before 1914:

> cotton and jute were the most important manufacturing (as opposed to mining or plantation) industries. While the cotton industry was concentrated mainly in the Bombay Presidency, that is, in western India, all the jute mills worth mentioning were situated in or near Calcutta in eastern India . . . While the cotton industry was controlled mainly by the Indians, the jute industry was almost the exclusive province of European (mainly British) businessmen. India held a monopoly of raw jute production, whereas she was only one of the major producers of raw cotton.   (:5–6)

> Western India, and in particular Bombay and Ahmedabad, differed from other centres of trade and industry in that they had a much larger proportion of Indians controlling trade and industry.   (:174)

These western Indian businessmen came from the Bania (merchant) castes or were Parsis; and although British capital was also important in western India, there was 'a greater degree of collaboration between Indian and European businessmen' (:182) than in Calcutta, where 'in most fields, the European businessmen were well organized to maintain something approaching collective monopoly' (:171). Eastern India entrepreneurs remained weak until after the First World War, partly perhaps because of '"values" or caste restrictions' but mainly because of:

> (a) the thorough orientation of eastern India to the raw-material-supplying function associated with a colony and (b) the persistent advantages enjoyed by the Europeans not only because of their early start and acquaintance with external markets but also because of the racial alignment of government patronage and the financial and other services supporting and reinforcing European control over trade and industry.[13]   (:205)

---

[13] 'European' still has this racial connotation in India: it means 'white' or (as Fielding says to the disgust of his fellow club members in E.M. Forster's *A passage to India*) 'pinko-grey'.

The first jute mill was set up in 1854, the year when the railway first connected Calcutta with the inland coal fields. By 1877 there were 4000 looms in the jute mills; and between 1900 and 1920 the number of looms increased rapidly, from 15 000 to 40 000 (Myers 1958:14–5). At first the mills drew their work force from landless Bengali labourers in the surrounding countryside: the 1890 Factory Commission found that most of the workers were Bengalis, and almost all were landless (Gupta 1974:416). But this regional labour supply seems to have been exhausted by the end of the century. In the period when the jute industry was growing most rapidly, between 1891 and 1911, there was a marked shift towards the recruitment of migrant workers from distant areas and speaking other languages: especially Hindi- or Urdu-speakers from Bihar and the United Provinces (Uttar Pradesh), also Oriyas and south Indians (Das Gupta 1976). In this Calcutta differed from other industrial centres like Bombay, Ahmedabad and Kanpur, where the bulk of the work force came from the surrounding regions. By 1931 less than a quarter of Calcutta jute workers were Bengalis (Royal Commission 1931a:8). Non-Bengalis were in a smaller majority in the city's metal-based industries and railway workshops, though most skilled workers were Bengalis (Das Gupta 1976:308).

Unlike the original jute labour force, the new immigrants were very mixed in their social and caste origins. Commenting on the 1911 Census Report, Das Gupta writes: 'Perhaps it would not be wrong to argue that migration to jute mill centres – be it from nearby places in Bengal or from distant eastern U.P. or western Bihar or Orissa – represented a sample of the rural population of the emigrating areas (:314) except that the proportions of Untouchables, Muslims and men from a 'craft background' were higher.

Calcutta was also where the India engineering and chemical industries began. The first big engineering firms (Jessop's, Burn's etc.), controlled by Europeans, supplied structural steel work to cotton and jute mills, to public works departments and later to railways. But after 1914 a more diverse light engineering industry, organized in much smaller units, grew up mainly in Howrah, Calcutta's twin city across the Hooghly river. In particular, small businessmen of the Mahisya caste – traditionally cultivators and quite low in the caste hierarchy – set up workshops and brought in relatives or caste men, whom they employed for some years and then helped to start their own firms (Owens and Nandy 1975, 1977; Owens 1973; Reserve Bank 1964:89, 119).

Though there are historical studies of the formation of Calcutta's work force (Das Gupta 1976; Gupta 1974), I know of no early studies of living and working conditions in the city, except for some of the evidence given to the Royal Commission on Labour in India (Royal Commission 1931d, 1931e, 1931f) and Kelman, *Labour in India* (1923), which is specially but not only about women. Kelman also wrote about long-distance migration to Calcutta (:97ff), conditions in the bastis or colonies of huts which workers built for themselves (:153ff), and the 'lines' or housing that some employers provided for their workers (:155ff; see pp. 163–4 on the reasons why many workers disliked living in 'lines', where employers had too much power over them).

Yet Calcutta's history – more than that of any other major city in India – is reflected in the divisions of its present population; and specially in the distribution of ethnic groups in different occupations and neighbourhoods, like geological strata recording distinct stages in the city's growth and a series of devastating shocks to its economy. 'Since the 1940s the waves of immigration which have episodically overwhelmed Calcutta have consisted not so much of migrants seeking work as of refugees fleeing from disaster' (Lubell 1974:36). In the great Bengal famine of the Second World War, country people poured into the city seeking food, often to starve in the streets (Satyajit Ray's film *Distant thunder* is about the rural famine which drove them to Calcutta). Partition in 1947 brought a wave of Hindu refugees from East Pakistan (now Bangladesh). The new border cut off Calcutta's jute mills from the best jute-growing areas, and jute exports faced competition from the more modern East Pakistani mills: employment in the jute industry fell by half in the twenty-five years after the war. Distress and unemployment in the city's traditional industries fuelled the political violence of the 1960s and 1970s, as naxalite left-wing terrorists fought against their political and union rivals and an increasingly ruthless army and police. Investors took their money elsewhere. The 1971 rebellion in East Pakistan brought another influx of refugees, not all of whom returned to the new Bangladesh.

Besides this succession of disasters, Calcutta faced a long-term economic decline: 'Metropolitan Calcutta suffers from a disadvantage faced by many industrial pioneers: an industry oriented towards demands which are often not the most up-to-date and based on raw materials which are becoming obsolete' (:82). Although value added (but not employment) in engineering grew quite fast between 1959 and 1965, the industry was too dependent on railways and on heavy engineering, with the small workshops almost entirely dependent on large factories. The factories' first reaction to any recession was to stop putting out orders for components to the smaller firms, in order to keep their own unionized work force if possible. Calcutta has India's biggest car factory, but protection made it possible to continue for years turning out a single obsolete expensive model for a limited home market. Since 1965 one firm after another has run into trouble, and some of the biggest have been saved from bankruptcy only by nationalization and mergers imposed by the central government (the state government has its own 'Closed and Sick Industries Department'). More diversified and modern engineering industries grew up in Bombay and in newer industrial centres like Bangalore and Poona.

In Calcutta the chemical and pharmaceutical industry was based on traditional raw materials – coal and alcohol; in Bombay, on petrochemicals, with growing local sources of supply. In foreign markets, jute gave way to man-made fibres. The textile industry contracted everywhere in India, but in Calcutta there was little alternative employment for the displaced mill workers.

For a long time Calcutta people have had few chances to move between jobs. Those who had work clung to it. Sons took their fathers' jobs if they were lucky. Those who lost their jobs, or arrived in the city without work, fitted into whatever miserable niche in the city's economy they could find, and stayed there (see Mukherjee 1975 on the pavement-dwellers who live by begging, casual labour, ragpicking and prostitution). There was no labour market, but a number of self-contained compartments in the work force, and little movement within some of these compartments. This is perhaps an exaggeration, but is broadly true.

Since people live near their work and seldom change it, each period of growth or stagnation between disasters has left its evidences in Calcutta's human geography. Around the jute and textile mills, the population is mostly Hindi or Urdu speaking (more or less the same language with different scripts: 'Hindustani' can mean either), poorly educated and poorly housed. These are the descendants of the first Hindu or Muslim immigrants from Bihar and Uttar Pradesh. Many still keep to the old custom of leaving their wives and children in their villages, sending remittances, and visiting their home perhaps every two years. The Bengali minority in the mills includes some refugees from East Pakistan who were lucky enough to get jobs.

Bhattacharya and Chatterjee (1973) found that 75 per cent of a sample of jute workers were Hindi- or Urdu-speakers, 78 per cent had their own house in a rural area and 86 per cent were born there, few had ever done anything but mill or agricultural work, half were illiterate, and half the workers' households in Calcutta had no female members.

The work force in the big engineering factories, by contrast, is mainly Bengali, Hindu, and educated. These are often people of middle-class origin, sometimes landowners who fled from East Pakistan after Partition. They live with their families if they can, if necessary commuting long distances to work. Twenty years ago they would have sought clerical work and regarded a factory job as second best: but not now, since a skilled factory worker's pay, status and prospects are better than a clerk's (Béteille 1970b). Bhattacharya and Chatterjee (1974) found that two-thirds of a sample of engineering workers were Bengali, only 21 per cent were illiterate, and 69 per cent of married workers lived with their wives (cf. 39 per cent of married jute mill workers). In areas where there are both mills and engineering factories (like Matia Buruz, near the Garden Reach Shipbuilders and Engineers) the population is mixed.

Small engineering workshops and foundries are concentrated in Howrah across the river, linked to Calcutta by a bridge. In these workshops, the owners and most skilled workers are Bengalis, like most other engineering factory workers. But factory employment is shrinking, and the few factory jobs that become available are quickly filled by the present workers' relatives. Although many workers in the small engineering workshops are both skilled and experienced, it seems they have little chance of ever finding well-paid steady factory jobs.

In addition to these three self-contained groups of industrial workers – jute and textile mill workers, engineering factory workers, and employees of small engineering workshops – there are of course a large number of groups, often equally self-contained and each showing a strong concentration of one ethnic group, filling niches in Calcutta's industrial and commercial economy. N.K. Bose (1965, 1968) conducted a major study of ethnic clustering in the city, which he called 'a premature metropolis' because it had appeared in a traditional agricultural economy in advance of a real industrial revolution. As a result, ethnic groups clustered together for preference, each speaking its own language, eating its own food and finding jobs exclusively in the trades where it was already established; and this was a carry-over of attitudes from the traditional village, where each caste was associated with an occupation, clung to its own cultural practices, and tended to live in its own quarter. Biswas *et al.* (1976) made a map of these ethnic clusters in Calcutta, based on the 1961 Census, and argued that Bose had exaggerated the part played by caste preferences and prejudices in determining people's residence or occupation: the present pattern is a direct result of limited opportunities and nothing else; and 'more than any ethnic bias, occupational considerations direct a person to choose a residence' (:165).

Industries in Calcutta's hinterland show a similar pattern of ethnic specialization. Thus workers in the Bengal collieries are Hindi-speakers or 'tribals'. In the tea gardens of Bengal and Assam, almost all are 'tribal'.

Calcutta's problems are special, the result of long stagnation punctuated by disasters. This history is reflected in a fragmented work force and labour market, and the fragments are scattered across the city like pieces of a jigsaw. A better pointer to the future is in Bombay, with its more dynamic economy and mobile mixed work force; or rather, in the interdependence of Bombay's industrial economy with those of smaller towns.

The other important industrial cities of India fall roughly into two types. First, the older industrial cities still dominated by nineteenth-century industries, which used to employ large number of un-educated, mainly unskilled workers from rural backgrounds: especially the textile towns of Kanpur, Ahmedabad and Coimbatore. Twentieth-century legislation and unions gave at least some workers the status of permanent employees, more secure than the badli or casual workers waiting for permanent jobs. The 'unorganized sector' which served the large factories was small and undeveloped. In these cities the more modern engineering and other post-war industries have drawn on labour from other social origins; and in these newer industries, firms which are technically and economically inter-dependent are divided into organized sector firms, where workers have some security if they are 'permanent', and small unorganized sector firms where they have none.

The second type are cities which may have some nineteenth-century factories, but were mainly administrative, trading and military centres until the post-war growth of engineering industries, in many cases as a result of government initiative. These include the capital Delhi, whose main industry is government, but which is also the centre of a fast-growing industrial region extending into two neighbouring states; Madras in the south; and especially a number of cities in the middle range – with populations of about 1–2 millions – old and attractive towns which are now mainly industrial, and which grew most rapidly in the 1950s and 1960s. In places like Bangalore, Poona and Hyderabad, the image of factory work is not of hard labour in dark satanic mills, but of educated workers with new skills in modern factories, taken largely from the lower middle class of these old towns and the peasantry of the surrounding villages. A vast number of small firms – often in the 'unorganized sector' – has grown up in back streets and industrial estates to serve these factories, and here conditions are much worse. But technology has its glamour and prestige. In these cities the labour movement is dominated, not by lawyers and middle-class philanthropists, but by articulate workers who hire and fire the professional leadership they want.

There are few comprehensive early studies of labour in the older industrial centres, a limited amount of material in official reports and a few books. Kanpur in Uttar Pradesh (population 1 275 242 in 1971) became prominent in the late nineteenth century as a centre for cotton and wool textiles and leather goods, being an important railway junction surrounded by fertile cotton lands and having an early concentration of Camaars (Chamars), untouchables who traditionally worked with leather (Niehoff 1959:18). These low-caste workers, and Muslims, are found specially in the older textile mills. V.B. Singh sees this as a result of a deliberate policy of the British employers and government:

> During the 1920's and 1930's, when the British Government started pampering and encouraging communal interests against the militant national and trade union movements, the Kanpur British employers contributed their share by employing a disproportionately larger percentage of 'lower castes' and Muslim workers. The two Indian-owned mills, coming on the scene later, have 'counteracted' this 'imbalance'. (Singh 1969:108)

But the middle and higher castes also moved progressively into the cotton mills in other places, like Bombay, where from the beginning most mills were owned by Indians.

An early study of Kanpur by Margaret Read (1927) describes the mill workers' miserable living conditions, oppressive foremen, how the restrictions on child labour were evaded, etc. The theme of this

well-meaning superficial book is that the mill worker is uprooted and
lost among strangers in the town:

> Add to this the monotonous regular work, the terrifying noise of machinery all
> day, the none too kindly supervision of the foremen or overseers – all these
> causes plant in the heart of the factory worker deeper than ever the conviction
> that he is not a mill-hand and that he is a village man.   (:36)

> A new kind of herd spirit possesses them in the factories, far less balanced and
> reasonable than their old village community spirit, and it is ripe for the
> stirrings of agitators.
>
>   (:74)

W.H. Wiser (1922) wrote on conditions in the city: especially the
congested housing in the narrow lanes, and the lack of privacy for
workers who brought their families to Kanpur. Niehoff (1959:47–53),
in a more recent study of Kanpur factory workers, shows that
conditions have not changed much. Kanpur now has a variety of
newer industry – an aircraft factory, the very capital-intensive Indian
Explosives, firms supplying small arms and parachutes to the armed
forces, and many small engineering units – but the town is still
dominated by the cotton textile industry, which has stagnated since
1960.

In the report of a seminar on Kanpur's industrial prospects (P.B.
Desai *et al.* 1969), J.N. Sinha writes, 'Of the three textile centres
(Kanpur, Bombay and Ahmedabad), Bombay alone shows a diversified and broad-based industrial pattern with sizeable employment in
new and basic industries. Employment in the chemicals, metal-
lurgical and engineering groups has shown a rising trend in recent
years in Kanpur and holds greater promise in the long run but still
remains only marginally important' (Sinha 1969:120). Yet in
Ahmedabad, where 75 per cent of organized sector workers are
employed in textile mills, the engineering and metal working firms –
largely in the unorganized sector – have grown quite fast, in spite of a
shortage of skilled labour (Papola and Subrahmanian 1975).

Ahmedabad (1971 population: 1 741 522) is an older, more
attractive town in Gujarat north of Bombay, with a long tradition of
trade, finance, weaving, and crafts. These were regulated by guilds
(mahajan), with members from one or several castes (Gillion
1968:23) and based in the mainly one-caste walled streets (pol) for
which Ahmedabad is still famous. Each street had its temple, its
council and a gate which was locked at night (see Doshi 1968, 1974,
on these streets as they are now). There is a clear continuity between

the traditional guild institutions and the indigenous industrialism of the nineteenth century:

> there was already a well developed market based on contract, indigenous systems of banking and insurance, a high level of commercial morality, and machinery for the settlement of disputes through the mahajans and seths [hereditary guild masters] . . . A dominant ethic of hard work, frugality and money-making [which] suited the rigors of modernization and met the need for capital. (Gillion 1968:76–7)

> It is true that there was little interest in science or technology and this would certainly have prevented an autonomous industrial revolution, but this was not required in the early Ahmedabad textile industry which could draw on England's experience and expertise [by employing weaving masters from Lancashire].
>
> (:78)

The old family or one-caste firms became managing agencies:

> The old-style [mill] agent lived frugally, walked to work, stayed there fifteen hours a day, employed a relative or two to help him with the paperwork, and knew every detail of the business, at least on the financial side.
>
> (:94–5)

The workers too were more rooted in the traditional city than elsewhere. Though many were immigrants, they were regarded as more settled than Bombay mill workers, and the city's sex ratio was nearer equality (:101). Union organization in Ahmedabad took a form which can be traced to the older craft guilds. Thus the 1929 Royal Commission wrote:

> In Ahmedabad the [textile] workers, excluding the Musalman weavers, are organised in a group of craft unions which, participating in a common central federation, have a strength and cohesion probably greater than those of any other labour unions. This may have some connection with the survival, until a comparatively late date, of a strong guild tradition in Ahmedabad. This lateral method of organisation is comparatively rare in India, where the tendency has been to organise vertically, i.e. by industrial establishments. Even where more than one union is formed in the same industry and the same centre, the division is generally by factories and not by occupations.
>
> (Royal Commission 1931a:320)

Gillion (1968:101ff) describes nineteenth-century working and living conditions, and the close personal relations between workers and jobbers, and Kelman (1923:147–50) writes about conditions in the slums. Nineteenth-century sanitary reformers struggled to improve these conditions, setting the pattern for a tradition of middle-class philanthropy.

In 1918 Gandhi founded the Ahmedabad Textile Labour Association (TLA) or Majur Mahajan (workers' guild), a centralized federation of craft unions under firm middle-class leadership (Revri 1972:75–8). Most of the workers were unskilled, uneducated, and often of 'tribal' origin though 'the exclusion of the Muslims in general, who were the traditional weavers of Ahmedabad, from the Labour Association, would require some explanation' (:78).

In the same year Anasuyabehn Sarabhai – the sister of the Millowners Association chairman – led the union in a city-wide strike for higher wages, which was settled by Gandhi's mediation. The TLA has continued as the strongest union in Ahmedabad, well known for its gandhian ideology, committed to settling disputes by arbitration and avoiding strikes wherever possible, and backing social work projects like a hostel for homeless girls and a bank to help self-employed women.

A recent study of Ahmedabad (Papola and Subrahmanian 1975, *Wage structure and labour mobility in a local labour market*) says something about relations between the dominant textile industry and the new smaller engineering firms, which get labour from different sources; but nothing about firms which are smaller still and fall on the wrong side of the organized–unorganized divide, and this is a serious gap in an important study of a fragmented labour market (or 'markets within market').[14]

Both Kanpur and Ahmedabad are nineteenth-century textile towns, where the first mills drew on local skills and attracted unskilled immigrant labourers; but the contrast between the two towns is in some ways like that between Calcutta and Bombay. Kanpur's industry was run by outsiders, largely by British firms with expatriate managers. Ahmedabad was the home of vigorous Indian capitalists, sharing a language and a regional culture with their workers, and these capitalists reinvested in new or smaller industries, whether in Ahmedabad, Bombay or elsewhere.

Coimbatore in Tamil Nadu, south India (1971 population: 736 203), like Ahmedabad, is a nineteenth-century textile town which was built up mainly by local capital and now has a considerable engineering industry, mostly small-scale. The town is not too big, and two-thirds of the mill workers commute from the surrounding half-urban villages. There is some good historical

---

[14] See Heather Joshi's review of the book (*Economic and Political Weekly*, 2 April 1977, pp. 575–6).

material on these mill workers in E.A. Ramaswamy *The worker and his union* (1977), which is almost the only study of an Indian union as ordinary workers see it, and a masterpiece of industrial anthropology. In Coimbatore, also, Enid Perlin (1979) has done pioneer work in using mill workers as historical sources, to 'convey the human experience of industrial life'. In a short paper, she has put together a picture of working and living conditions since 1920, from interviews with older workers in six mills, and from mill records and other documents: a picture of long hours worked in appalling physical conditions, which workers tolerated only because the job was relatively secure; of widespread illegal child labour, brutal punishments and accidents. Workers specially resented the tyranny of the clock, an unnatural rhythm of life, and 'the lack of *dignity* in mill work, as compared with land-owning or leasing, or small-scale trading or shopkeeping'.

> The sum of ambivalent attitudes towards mill work can be typified by the remark of one man that his father had encouraged his children to seek mill work '. . . because the mills never perish'. Conversely, the word most frequently used by workers, in many contexts, was – Kashtam (trouble) . . . In spite of the vast improvements in conditions and welfare since Independence, mill employment for Indian workers still means subjection to machine speeds which confuse the eye and mind – to cotton dust and humid heat (especially in the spinning department) which still produces or exacerbates lung disease – to a noise level in the weaving shed which defies description . . . and to an alien time regime which diminishes human dignity.   (:457)

No one who has been inside an Indian textile mill could challenge this. Yet Enid Perlin does not make enough allowance for the real improvements the unions have obtained, not only in pay and conditions, but in giving workers a feeling of dignity and independence. Thus Ramaswamy says the oldest members show the least concern with the union's purely economic functions:

> One of them observed, 'There is a limit to what we can ask from the millowner. I get four times as much as my neighbour who toils in a field all day, and yet my job is easier and not very much more skilled than his. Unless conditions improve all around it is difficult [for the union] to get us to ask for more.'
> (E.A. Ramaswamy 1977:182–3)

Madras, the biggest south Indian city, also had large textile mills. I know of no early studies of the work force, except for some references to B.P. Wadia's Madras Labour Union of 1918, generally regarded as India's first real trade union (Revri 1972:71–5; Hafner 1978), and a description of the city's industrial and non-industrial workers in

Ranson (1938), *A City in transition: studies in the social life of Madras*.
Parthasarathy (1958) writes about the importance that caste had,
especially in recruitment, at a textile mill in another southern city,
Mysore.

There is one striking difference between cities in the south and the
rest of India. Since the first wave of industrial migration in the
nineteenth century, the sexes have been more evenly balanced in
southern cities, though the gap between north and south has
narrowed in recent years. Every census since the first in 1871 has
shown a large excess of males in northern cities: in 1951 the sex ratio in
Bombay was only 596 (females/1000 males), though by 1971 it had
risen to 717 (cf. 701 in Calcutta, 664 in the Bihar mining town of
Dhanbad). Every census has shown that over 70 per cent of Bombay's
population were born outside the city (Devanandan and Thomas
1958:13). Many were unmarried migrants or men who left their
families in the villages, sent money home, and returned only for
festivals or occasional visits. But successive censuses have shown sex
ratios for the chief southern cities in the region of 850–950, that is,
only a small excess of males: in 1931 the sex ratio for home-born
residents of Madras City was 962, and for out-born residents 781: cf.
729 and 505 in Bombay (Davis 1951:135). The typical south Indian
migrant brought his family to live with him, in cheap rented
accommodation in one of the suburban villages which became centres
of urban growth; or he sent for them as soon as he had a job and
somewhere to live. Ranson wrote of Adi Dravida or Tamil Harijan
migrants, who had mostly been landless labourers in the villages:

> Adi-Dravida migration to Madras city is frequently family migration, as
> opposed to the industrial migration in other centres, which is largely confined
> to men. The Madras Adi-Dravida tends to establish himself in the city in mud
> and thatch huts and to retain his own form of community life, within the larger
> city community. The transition of a family from village life to an Adi-Dravida
> hutting ground in Madras is much less violent and confusing that the removal
> of an individual labourer from his village to a 'bustie' or 'chawl' in Calcutta or
> Bombay. It is perhaps a permissible conjecture that, because of the fact that in
> South India the gulf fixed between the urban and rural populations is less
> deep, the influence of a city like Madras upon the rural areas which surround it
> is more effective, because less violently contrasted, than that of other large
> Indian cities.   (Ranson 1938:3–4)

This habit of family migration, among people of all castes, has given
southern cities a different look and feel – really urban, settled
neighbourhoods of working-class people, with a vigorous community

and religious life centred on the temples and festivals of old suburban villages, and a high level of interest in local politics (Holmström 1969, 1971, 1972). These mixed neighbourhoods support an economy of services, secondary occupations, and small businesses, and encourage movement of labour as workers learn skills and make contacts.

It is not clear why there has been this regional difference in urban sex ratios. It may have something to do with the high proportion of landless people in the south, southern family structure, or the greater traditional independence of southern women.[15] But it is now clear that northern workers too are less willing to endure separation from their families, and regard it as temporary not normal.

According to the 1971 Census Commissioner, 'The cities of the south . . . generally show a stabler state of society as reflected by the fairly balanced sex ratio . . . Or does it reflect a relative state of backwardness, stagnation and poor industrialisation?' But these same cities have a long record of successful industrialization, and now provide some of the best examples of diversified modern industry.

There is not much else to read on conditions in industrial towns before the Second World War – particularly on how the work force came to be divided into those with and without steady 'organized sector' jobs – except for brief comments in books about India's industrialization, and histories of the union movement.

Most studies of early industrialization are about the work force in big factories, how it was recruited and disciplined, and specially how rural migrants adapted to industrial life (several writers continued to flog the horse of 'labour commitment' long after Morris had killed it: see Munshi 1977 for a post mortem). There are comments on the system of badli or substitute workers, on contract labour, and on the networks of jobbers, relatives and friends who could give workers some security and continuity in employment: very little on labour in small workshops, or relations between large firms and small ones which supplied and served them.

The chief general studies of industrialization have already been mentioned. Bagchi's *Private investment in India 1900–1935* (1972) is

---

[15] The 1961 Census Commissioner commented that these regional variations in urban sex ratios 'are not entirely explained by male selective migration. While very few towns (not certainly cities) in the North have their sex ratios anywhere near par, there are few towns or even cities in the South . . . where the sex ratio even drops below 900 females per 1,000 males. This is a matter of great sociological interest to urban planning in India' (A. Mishra, quoted in Natarajan 1971:104).

indispensable on the financing and growth of the main industries, on
relations between Indian business and the British, and on the contrast
between eastern and western India or Calcutta and Bombay. Myers,
Labor problems in the industrialization of India (1958), gives a useful
summary of the history of Indian industry and its economic and legal
background. He attacks the myth that industrial workers are lost and
insecure when thrown into an impersonal city life, and argues that
industrial workers are 'an élite group' in Indian society. Ornati, *Jobs
and workers in India* (1955), has interesting historical information on
the recruitment of the first work force. Broughton, *Labour in Indian
industries* (1924) and Kelman, *Labour in India* (1923) are sympathetic
early studies of working and living conditions, mainly among mill
workers. The 1929 Royal Commission on Labour in India produced
not only a full report (Royal Commission 1931a) but a mass of
evidence collected from employers, officials, unionists and ordinary
workers all over India (Royal Commission 1931b–e, and other
volumes). Gadgil, *The industrial evolution of India in recent times,
1860–1939* (1971) is the updated fifth edition of a book which first
appeared in 1924, and relates the growth of powered industry to
developments in agriculture and the older craft industries. Mukerjee,
The Indian working class (1951) is a good general history: also, Shiva
Rao, *The industrial worker in India* (1939) which describes the
background and working of early factory legislation, and the
appalling conditions of unprotected labour.

There is a large literature on the history of Indian trade unions, but
most of it is concerned with central organization, politics, splits in the
leadership etc., rather than branch activities or the union's meaning
and practical importance for ordinary members. Revri, *The Indian
trade union movement* (1972) is the best general history, and emphasizes
the beginnings of Indian trade union organization in an older
tradition of spontaneous strike action organized by temporary
informal committees, with which the new middle-class union
'leaders' had a tenuous relationship (see Royal Commission
1931a:316ff). Johri, *Unionism in a developing economy* (1967), which
covers the period 1950–65, is mainly about the leadership, and has a
useful bibliography. The *Report of the National Commission on Labour*
(National Commission 1969) has chapters on the growth of workers'
and employers' organizations. E.A. Ramaswamy, *The worker and his
union* (1977) gives a full history of the Coimbatore District Textile

Workers Union and workers' involvement in it, as well as a study of the union now. Uma Ramaswamy, 'Tradition and change among industrial workers' (1979) is about the changing significance of caste for these workers, and the extraordinary importance of union loyalties and leaders in Coimbatore (at one time intermarriage between families belonging to different unions was unthinkable; and even now a union leader should attend every wedding and bless the couple). Another good local study is Sheth, 'Workers, leaders and politics' (1968b) on the history of rival mill unions at a city in Gujarat.

Labour in the new industries: historical and field studies

In this book I am less concerned with these older industries than with new or expanding ones, like engineering, plastics, chemicals and electronics; and in particular, with relations between 'organized' and 'unorganized sector' labour.

The few anthropological or sociological studies of labour in the new industries and new industrial towns are mainly about the 'organized sector'. I think there are two reasons. First, it is easier to study a factory than a roughly bounded group of people employed for differing periods in a wide variety of small firms, and anthropologists trained in the structural–functionalist tradition tended to look for relatively closed units like the villages or tribes or island communities of 'classical' anthropology (see p. 3 above). The other reason is that, until recently, for most writers the factory sector giving regular employment *was* the modern industrial sector. Its dependence on small firms for components and services was a passing phase, or a way this dynamic sector could help smaller firms and the economy as a whole to grow quickly into something recognizable as a modern industrial economy. The use of 'temporary', contract and sweated labour was part of the growing pains of an industrial society, and the 'commitment' theory provided some justification for it. Workers in countries like India were not 'committed' to the norms of industrial life – regular timekeeping, the legitimate authority of a management hierarchy, a career of orderly progress up the ladder of skill and responsibility and so on. Therefore they were worth less to employers than workers in the west or Japan – who of course *were* committed, almost by definition.

> Commitment involves both performance and acceptance of the behaviors appropriate to an industrial way of life . . . The fully committed worker . . . has internalized the norms of the new productive organization and social system. (Moore and Feldman 1960:1)

> Acceptance refers to the phenomenon of internalization or moral conformity. (:9)

However: 'An antimanagement ideology is part of the tradition and culture of industrial labor and . . . commitment includes the acceptance of such an ideology' (:4).[16]

The two best factory studies (Lambert 1963 and Sheth 1968a) are both of workers in western India, living in the middle-sized old towns which had attracted so many new industries. Lambert's *Workers, factories and social change in India* (1963) is about five factories in Poona, and relates the workers' attitudes to a 'production process typology' of factories. In 'type A factories', which do simple processing of raw materials (a paper factory, a chocolate and biscuit factory, and a rubber factory), gangs of unskilled men tend each machine, carry away and pack the product, etc. In type B (represented by a cotton textile mill) most workers are semi-skilled; 'each worker tends one or more machines, performing operations which are almost entirely repetitive' (:12); and there are also more skilled specialists, like repairmen and machine setters. In type C (here, a factory making oil engines), 'except for the supplementary service operations, each worker not only feeds but individually directs a machine' (:13); 'men use machines as tools and use their skills to direct them' (:113). Lambert compares the social composition of the work force in the five factories, and in the non-factory population of Poona.

His main conclusions are that factory employment is not bringing about the transformation of attitudes and social relations implied in theories of 'modernization' – the move from *Gemeinschaft* to *Gesellschaft* etc. – because workers are rooted in their traditional culture which is consistent with industrialization. In particular, workers regard a factory job as property rather than a challenge or a career: 'Most of the workers were interested in acquiring "permanent" property rights in a job and . . . this carries with it a notion of minimal quality of performance but not an internalized drive for continuously enhanced productivity . . . A factory job is a form of property to the worker and . . . he will seek to retain, but not improve

---

[16] The same book contains Morris's article demolishing the whole commitment theory (Morris 1960a).

it' (:179). Indian workers are not just committed to their jobs, but 'overcommitted'. These attitudes to work are carried over from the traditional village jajmaani system, where the right to serve a patron is the specialist's privilege and property.

This is an excellent pioneering study, but are workers' attitudes to the job really so different from those of industrial workers elsewhere? Or if they are, could this not be explained as a rational response to greater insecurity outside the 'organized sector', rather than a carry-over of traditional attitudes? Moreover the conclusions about workers' attitudes – as well as more objective measurable facts about them – are based almost entirely on the statistical analysis of answers to set questionnaires, without the open-ended interviews and participant observation of workers' lives which should complement this method and show the relevance of the questions.

Sheth's *Social framework of an Indian factory* (1968a) is about workers and managers in the 'Oriental' factory, making pumps, electric motors and switchgear at an unidentified town in Gujarat. This was the first sustained attempt to use anthropological methods of participant observation, as well as formal interviews and questionnaires, in an Indian factory. The book's many virtues and few faults can be traced to the structural–functional tradition of anthropology: the concern with formal and informal structures of organization, and how values and norms give these structures the moral cohesion they need in order to endure, to function and to adapt. Also the attempt to find a social unit which can be provisionally isolated for study, a unit where loose ends can be tied up and external relations allowed for, and the social system can be studied in miniature. At every point, workers' opinions and values are related systematically to their parts in a bureaucratic organization with specific goals, and the parallel organization of the union in relations of regulated conflict with the management. Sheth says little about the rest of the workers' lives – about social relations not directly linked to factory roles, about leisure, conversation, festivals and religious activities, life in industrial neighbourhoods – all the things which for many people are more significant than the time they spend at work. The general picture is of rather conservative status-conscious workers, who take for granted particularistic norms of obligation to caste and kin as the right criteria for recruitment and promotion, and are often bound to the management by ties of personal obligation which may be rationalized as religious duty to natural superiors. Sheth refers briefly (:56–7) to 'temporary' or contract workers in the factory, who had no security and much worse conditions of employment.

Sheth considers the ways in which the difference between pre-industrial and industrial society, or the conditions for industrialization, have been conceived of: Weber's contrast between traditionalistic and rationalistic bureaucratic values, Parsons' particularism and universalism, ascribed and achieved status etc.; and the 'logic of industrialism' which is supposed to break down (or to require as a precondition) the breakdown of traditional roles, particularistic relations, joint families and so on. But he finds this too simple and deterministic. There is no necessary contradiction between 'traditional' values and industrialism: in this factory both sets of norms coexist without strain. 'Some forms of particularism may be functional to industrial organization' (:200), and we cannot yet say which social structures are compatible with modern technology, or whether all industrial societies are converging towards a single type. The last chapter gives a useful critical survey of the literature, both on India and on industrialization generally.

Kapadia and Pillai, *Industrialization and rural society* (1972) combines questionnaire methods with extended fieldwork. It is not about a city but about another kind of industrial environment which is becoming common: three factories owned by the same firm, in an isolated township where some of the workers live; and the impact of these factories on surrounding villages in an area where there is little other work except agriculture. Vaid, *The new worker* (1968), a study of workers in new factories at Kota in Rajasthan, and B.R. Sharma, *The Indian industrial worker* (1974), about a Bombay car factory, are both questionnaire-based social-psychological studies of 'commitment', alienation, adjustment to factory organization etc. Holmström, *South Indian factory workers* (1976) is about the careers and thinking of workers in four engineering factories in Bangalore. Baldwin, *Industrial growth in south India* (1959) gives an excellent history of the industrialization of Mysore State (now Karnataka), especially the capital Bangalore, and the formation of a skilled engineering work force during and after the Second World War; with case studies of public and private sector factories and of entrepreneurs. Bhagwati and Desai, *India: planning for industrialization* (1970), is an economists' study of problems and prospects.

Three useful collections of readings on Indian cities and industrial labour are Rao (ed.), *Urban sociology in India* (1974); Turner (ed.),

India's urban future (1962); and Fox (ed.), *Urban India: society, space and image* (1970). Ashish Bose, *Urbanization in India: an inventory of source materials* (1970) gives a critical overview of research in demography, economics, and sociology. E.A. and Uma Ramaswamy, *Industry and labour* (1981) is an introductory guide for students.

There are summary references to current work, and bibliographies, in *A survey of research in sociology and social anthropology*, vol. 1 (Indian Council of Social Science Research 1974) and in the *Second digest of Indian labour research (1962–1967)* and *Third digest of Indian labour research (1968–1972)* (Labour Bureau 1974, 1978).

An indispensable source is the *Report of the National Commission on Labour* (National Commission 1969), which brings together a large amount of historical and statistical information on 'industrial' and other labour, with a good critical discussion of issues like the relation between the 'organized' and 'unorganized sectors'; political obstacles to labour migration between Indian states; choice of technologies and their social consequences; and the future.

3

The rise of 'small-scale industries'

Before Independence in 1947 there was no 'small-scale sector' and therefore no 'organized sector'. There were many small firms, mainly in engineering, which served and supplied the cotton and jute mills and other big factories, but no clear line between workshops and factories. Big firms were bound by the Factory Acts in matters like health and safety, and were more likely to have unions, but their workers were often no better paid and no more secure than those in small workshops. Labour earned its market price, which was low, and could be laid off at any time.

The idea of small industries as a distinct 'sector' emerged after Independence, to mean firms which escaped a whole range of laws about dismissals, social security, taxes, union recognition and labour disputes; offering a new kind of employment, worse paid and less secure but easier to get; and with its own needs and problems, to be remedied by special policies, government agencies and assistance.

Even now, when the two sectors are thought of as separate compartments in the economy, there is no one clear dividing line, but several lines based on at least three criteria. First, whether a firm comes under the Factory Act and is therefore in the 'organized sector' depends on the number employed (ten, if the factory uses power, with similar limits for purposes like Provident Fund and Employees' State Insurance). Secondly, it is a 'small(-scale) industry', entitled to special help and privileges, if its investment is below a certain amount: but a very small firm may prefer to remain unregistered and invisible, especially to tax inspectors. Thirdly, an individual worker's position, even in an organized sector firm, depends on whether he is permanently employed, or is a 'temporary', casual or contract worker not protected by the same laws. All these limits are theoretical, since the laws can be evaded up to a point. But on either side of the grey area there appear to be two very differently placed kinds of firm, and two kinds of worker. 'Organized' and 'unorganized sector' will serve as shorthand. 'Unorganized sector' firms have both kinds of workers.

This is the result of the growth of new industries and technologies since the Second World War, and of political changes which largely determined the way these new industries were organized.

Since the Second World War and Independence

On the eve of the Second World War the industrial economy was still dominated by the four main nineteenth-century industries – jute, cotton textiles, railways and coal – with the notable addition of Tata steel. The engineering, chemical and other industries which had grown at a modest rate between the wars, helped by the gradual introduction of tariffs, were not only tied to these traditional industries for markets, but were largely controlled by the same managing agencies.

The Second World War, like the first, cut off imports from the west. This time the government's defence needs were far greater, since the war with Japan was being fought on India's doorstep, and Indian industry had developed to the point where it was better able to meet the demand. Yet:

> As with the first world war, the increased demand could not *pro rata* be translated into investment and capacity: again, transportation bottlenecks on imports of capital goods were to be important in preventing fuller exploitation of this 'opportunity'. (Bhagwati and Desai 1970:35)

Though industrial employment rose by 103 per cent during the war, production went up only 20 per cent.

> The incremental production . . . occurred principally through fuller utilization of idle capacity, through additional shifts, and through more efficient utilization of capacity in other ways. New plants were also added in the numerous newer industries: ferro-alloys such as ferro-silicon and ferro-manganese; non-ferrous metals such as copper, copper sheets, wires, and cables; mechanical industries such as diesel engines, pumps, sewing machines, machine tools, and cutting tools; some items of textile, tea and oil pressing machinery; and chemicals, which grew from minute proportions to include caustic soda, chlorine, superphosphates, photographic chemicals and bichromates.
> Among the older industries to expand . . . the most prominent were cement, paper, cotton textiles, iron and steel, and sugar. (:35–6)

The war also saw the setting up of the Hindustan Aircraft factory in Bangalore (now Hindustan Aeronautics, with factories throughout the country) by a Bombay businessman who had tried unsuccessfully to get backing for a car factory before the war. In 1942 it was nationalized, and with 16 000 employees it was perhaps the largest industrial establishment in India (see Baldwin 1959:135–45 for a study of its history and work force).

By the end of the war the industrial base was much broader. The country had new workers with new skills, and entrepreneurs with confidence and experience. Many new firms survived the falling off of wartime demand and the chaos of partition which accompanied Independence in 1947. Yet in 1946, when the first Census of Manufacturing Industries was taken, cotton and jute still dominated Indian industry. Cotton textiles accounted for 46 per cent of value added and 44 per cent of industrial employment; jute, for 17 per cent of value added and 22 per cent of employment (the Census did not cover mining, railways or firms with less than twenty workers). In contrast, general and electrical engineering provided 5 per cent of value added and 7 per cent of employment; chemicals including pharmaceuticals, only 3 and 2 per cent. The whole 'industrial' work force was very small indeed: 1 514 382 in a population of well over 300 million.

After Independence several things caused a shift to new industries and technologies: allocations of resources and licences under the Five-Year Plans; direct public investment; import substitution policies and markets for new Indian exports; newly available skills and technologies, and entrepreneurs to take advantage of them. Cotton textiles lost their share of the market, mills closed down or were kept alive with public money, rationalization reduced employment. While cotton declined relatively, jute declined absolutely, since the industry depended heavily on export markets where there was stiff competition from East Pakistani mills and from synthetic fibres.

As cotton and jute went down, engineering and chemicals came up, stimulated by government action, the market, or both. The new or expanding industries included machine tools and other machinery, agricultural equipment, fertilizers, electrical equipment, aluminium, petroleum products, rubber, paper and transport equipment including bicycles, scooters, cars, lorries and tractors; from the 1960s onwards, consumer goods for the home market and for export – plastics, synthetic fabrics, pharmaceuticals, detergents, radios and domestic appliances; and most recently, the fast-growing electronic industry.

The new division of the work force – organized sector on one side, unorganized sector and 'temporary' workers on the other – came about partly because of the nature of the new industries, requiring skilled educated workers who were sometimes harder to find, expected more, were more articulate and able to organize themselves; partly because of political developments – labour legislation enacted under the influence of fabian welfare ideology, the unions' political links, perhaps the very fragmentation of unions into competing federations. Similarly the growth of new industries was partly a direct response to markets and available technologies, very largely the effect of government policies: yet these pulled in more than one direction.

The big firms, publicly or privately owned, set the pace, stimulating smaller firms and sometimes depending on them for parts and services. This was, on the whole, what the planners expected. The main aim of government policy, under Nehru and his allies on the Planning Commission, was clear: first lay a foundation of basic and heavy industries, necessarily organized in large units, on which a more diverse industrial economy could be built. This was to be done through planning, rapid import substitution especially in consumer goods, restrictions on foreign firms, licensing and controls on private industry and public investment, especially in basic industries where the returns were long-term and uncertain.

This policy was criticized, in India and abroad, as one of mindless imitation, import of inappropriate technology, the worship of gigantism and modernity, and neglect of agriculture and village industries. In particular, the new steel mills built with foreign aid were held up as bad examples, mere status symbols irrelevant to the needs of the masses. Yet the policy was intelligently and flexibly applied. It is not clear that higher government expenditure on agriculture could have been used productively at that time. Rural community development was held back by administrative problems and inexperience as much as by shortage of funds – after all, Indians were the pioneers in this field. The encouragement of small industries to complement large modern ones was an essential part of the Plan strategy from the beginning. The planners were influenced by strong pulls in other directions: on the one hand, towards an open laissez-faire economy free of bureaucratic controls; and on the other, towards the gandhian ideal of village industries using traditional methods.

Small firms and the government

The modern small firms, like the large ones, grew as a direct response to new opportunities, markets, available technologies and skills. They would probably have come up in any case, given a private enterprise system. The efforts to 'stimulate entrepreneurship' were not always necessary, because there were enough entrepreneurs with access to capital. But the place these small firms came to have in the economy was also a response to special political developments: government encouragement springing from an ideology of 'small-scale industries', as well as the indirect effect of labour legislation and unions on the larger firms.

Dhar and Lydall write 'In no country . . . has the doctrine of small industry received such strong support as in India. There are a number of reasons for this. The most important is the legacy of Gandhian teaching' (1961:xv). Yet the results have been very different from what Gandhi intended. To revive crafts and cottage industries through subsidies was one thing: to revive the economically self-sufficient village community – assuming it had ever existed – was another, and was never seriously attempted. If it had been, this would have made it impossible – instead of just very difficult – to achieve other objectives dear to the hearts of the planners and modernizing intellectuals like Nehru: socialism, equality and especially an end to the oppression of Untouchables and women.

Gandhi saw no contradiction. He believed in equality too, though he thought it could be reconciled with a revival of the original hereditary division of labour without exploitation or competition – something that had degenerated into 'caste'. Nehru and the planners, for all their differences with Gandhi, were influenced by his thinking and acted as if the problem could be overcome by democratic village self-government, education and the like. The Village and Small-Scale Industries Committee, or Karve Committee, declared that 'the principle of self-employment is at least as important to a successful democracy as that of self-government' (quoted in Dhar and Lydall 1961:10); and self-employment (in practice, a high ratio of employers to employed) was seen as a good thing in any kind of industry. Pocock writes in criticism of the Draft Fourth Plan:

the Draft Plan seeks to answer the question of decentralizing industry *both* through 'small industries, especially for the production of a variety of ancillary parts and components required by large industries' *and* by the development 'of some of the traditional village industries which have been languishing' (p. 240). This demonstrates a failure to distinguish between the social functions of these two kinds of small-scale industry. The first, whether it is established in a village or a town, encourages workers to move away from the village ethos, which is the ethos of caste, and creates contractual relationships between employer and employee in a labour situation to which caste is much less relevant. To this extent it gives the labourer, of whatever caste, a moral and economic independence from traditional relationships and pressures. The 'traditional village industries' on the other hand are without exception linked to caste and thus to the caste hierarchy. To revive those that are languishing is, whatever the economic benefit to the individuals concerned, to reinforce caste values and thus to encourage the practice of untouchability.

(Pocock 1968:273)

There are other possibilities. If all 'traditional village industries' are caste-bound, it does not follow that the only caste-free small industries are ancillaries to large ones. Small firms can use any level of technology to supply consumer goods and services. Pocock says small-scale industry 'is socially valuable to the extent that it creates a landless villager free from independence on a status-tied occupation' (p. 277), and he suggests ways in which the planners might encourage such industries in rural areas.

In chapter 1 I discussed the various social and economic arguments put forward for helping small industries. The policies actually followed have to be understood in relation to Gandhi's ideas and the reactions they stimulated. The hard-line gandhians were powerful in the ruling Congress Party; and for reasons rooted in the history of the Independence movement, they often found themselves – like Gandhi in his lifetime – in a bizarre alliance with right-wing millowners and industrialists, who claimed to regard themselves as trustees or stewards of their wealth on behalf of the masses.

The gandhians fought a rearguard action to revive khadi or homespun cloth, handlooms and village crafts. 'Spheres of production' were reserved for small-scale, especially cottage industries, and production by large firms was restricted or taxed. Through the Khadi and Village Industries Board and similar bodies, the government subsidized cottage industries directly: with limited success except, in the 1970s, in the export market for 'ethnic' clothes sold at high prices in the west. The subsidies went largely to middlemen (including some 'co-operatives') not craftsmen. Little new employment was created, and it was clear that the movement was unlikely ever to provide the masses with cheap alternatives to mill and factory-made goods.[1]

Gandhi himself made concessions. He would accept the sewing-machine and the bicycle and a few other machines he thought compatible with human dignity and a small scale of economic organization. 'Gandhian economics' is still very much alive, indeed fashionable in India and the west, but the ideal of the self-sufficient village community has been tacitly abandoned or compromised. The main practical effect of 'gandhian economics' has been to strengthen the growing official emphasis on the virtues of small-scale industries as a means to create employment, to tap unused resources and to disperse industry: even when these small firms use modern machinery to supply or compete with the big factories.

The principle was set out in the First and Second Five-Year Plans, the Industrial Policy Resolution of 1948 and the Karve Committee's report. Concerted action by the central government to encourage modern small industries began in the 1950s. A group of Ford Foundation specialists, invited by the Indian government, stressed the potential of small industries as a way to regenerate the whole Indian economy and suggested specific measures (Ford Foundation 1954). The Industrial Policy Resolution of 1956 took up these ideas, and from the late 1950s onwards a number of overlapping organizations and programmes were set up or strengthened, aimed at various targets: the Small Scale Industrial Development Corporation (SSIDO); the National Small Industries Corporation (NSIC); the Small Industries Service Institutes which give advice, technical training, and some workshop services with specialized machines in towns; the industrial estates programme, under which sheds are made available at subsidized rents; programmes to help unemployed engineers and other graduates; special officers in the nationalized banks to deal with small businessmen's problems; the Small Industries Extension Training Institute (SIET Institute) in Hyderabad; and legislation enabling state government to set up their own independent development corporations for small industries. The list of products reserved for the small-scale sector was constantly added to; production of others in large factories was restricted by licences

---

[1] Gandhi's two great ideals were prohibition and reviving village industries. In the 'dry' states, and especially round Bombay city, prohibition may have brought into being the one viable village industry: distilling.

and quotas. Banks and government agencies gave cheap loans, amounting to subsidies, to entrepreneurs in certain categories. Small firms were given quotas of scarce or imported materials and exemption from some taxes (though others, like the excise levied until recently on each firm's turnover rather than value added, worked against them). The government's own public sector units were told to order from small firms, and to encourage the setting up of ancillaries which could supply the 'parent' units on long contracts and sell their surplus production on the market. State governments developed similar policies.[2]

Small industries have not yet justified the high hopes placed in them by producing cheap wage goods, exports, social stability and above all providing employment. Partly this is the result of a misdirection of effort, caused by the confusion of modern small industries (which are often viable) with revived village industries (which on the whole are not). But with that exception, this does not mean the expenditure of money and administrative talent on the small industries programme has all been wasted. The whole 'industrial' economy is very small in relation to India's population and needs, and the small-scale 'sector' is now an essential and large part of it. The growth of large firms – public or private – is a necessary condition for the successful growth of small ones, and it would have been more economical to recognize this instead of chasing the mirage of a massive expansion in employment led by the small-scale sector. Large firms also depend, increasingly, on small ones. Indeed the idea of two 'sectors' makes it harder to see the very diverse kinds of linkages which exist or could be fostered in different industries.

Small-scale enterprise

It is useful to distinguish between different kinds of small manufacturing units, which overlap in practice and may not all come under the official definition of 'small-scale ·industries'. Some (like car-component makers) use modern technology to supply larger factories, to serve them (sharpening tools etc.) or to compete with them by making finished goods for the market (plastics, electrical goods). Some use simple technology to serve modern factories (wooden

[2] Subrahmanian and Kashyap (1975) give a useful account of the debates about small industries, the policies designed to help them, and the disappointing results over the last twenty years, with a full bibliography; and see C.T. Kurien (1978) on recent developments.

cabinets for radios, packing crates; but carpenters often work independently). Some use new technology to make traditional products (leather, powerlooms, food). Then there are the real cottage industries, making traditional products in the old way (mostly handlooms; also, for example, shoes, and bidis or country cigarettes, which can also be made by hand in big factories with no machines at all – see Lynch 1969:32–65 on the Agra shoe industry).

Here I am concerned with small urban firms that depend on larger factories or compete with them. The most important are light engineering firms, because they are the most numerous and because all other industries (plastics, textiles etc.) need their services. The rest include firms in the chemical, pharmaceutical, plastic, electronic, rubber and printing industries.

Most of these small firms are run not by paid managers but by their owners. However the 'owner' who manages the day-to-day work puts his own capital at risk but may not have much capital. The rest comes from a rich partner, relatives, a big company, or a bank or government agency loan. The visible employer, the manager, the boss is a classical entrepreneur, bringing capital and labour together.

There is a mass of literature on entrepreneurship in developing countries and especially in India (e.g. Gerschenkron 1966; Leibenstein 1957; McClelland 1963, 1966; Baldwin 1959), much of it written on the assumption that economic or at least industrial growth depends on a supply of well-motivated entrepreneurs, the leaven which will cause any mix of human and material resources to rise.

Entrepreneurship is a special skill, which can be taught, and a psychological disposition – the will to achieve great things for oneself and the community – which can be instilled by propaganda or conditioning. Some cultures already emphasize achievement in their values and child-rearing practices: that is why they prosper. The presence of 'achievement-oriented' people (McClelland's phrase) is not only a necessary condition of growth, but for some writers a sufficient one. They will rise above every obstacle which governments and traditional conservatism can put in their way, though it is better if governments remove these obstacles and stimulate entrepreneurship or achievement-orientation, which becomes a moral quality: individuals who have it are to be admired, countries which discourage it are to blame for their own backwardness. God helps those who help themselves, and rich aid-giving countries should follow His example.

Perhaps I have strayed into parody, but it is clear that the roots of this attitude are in the moralizing western tradition of self-help, character building and sturdy private enterprise. No development without entrepreneurship; no entrepreneurship without the protestant work ethic or some functional equivalent (a view that is illegitimately fathered on Max Weber). This ideology has spread from foreign and Indian academics to officials concerned with schemes to help small industries, and the vocal new class of educated small-scale entrepreneurs with their own organizations and contacts in high places; and it fits well with the more homespun philosophy of an older generation of businessmen, especially those reared (like Gandhi) in the puritanical sectarian tradition of the merchant castes.

Clearly there is something in the idea. Someone – in private firms, public agencies or the work force – must be imbued with a special kind of energy and imagination if new opportunities are to be grasped and work organized. Some social systems or traditions encourage this spirit more than others: and though this view of entrepreneurship is usually an apology for capitalism, McClelland (1966:38) finds some of the best examples of the spirit of achievement in the Soviet Union and in communist China. Where the political and economic institutions are the same, as in a single country, differences in the emphasis placed on individual achievement may explain why people of some communities or regions take opportunities before others can see or take them. I doubt that they explain the development of the whole country.

I begin my account of small firms with the entrepreneurs – their background, sources of capital, links with the large-scale sector, careers and attitudes. This is not because I think of entrepreneurship as the main determining factor in industrialization: if the political and economic structure provides opportunities for entrepreneurs they will probably appear anywhere. Anyway, there is no shortage of them in India. A tradition of ruthless entrepreneurship has always been strong, though not equally spread throughout all communities and regions.

Pre-war entrepreneurs and their caste links

The older (pre-war) entrepreneurs could usually be identified as members of particular castes or religious communities, who went into business at the same time and helped each other. They generally

started in a small way and reinvested their profits. In some cases
artisan castes adapted their traditional crafts to new products: some
handloom weavers brought powerlooms; the Karkhanedars or
Muslim armourers of Delhi became blacksmiths under the British,
and later went into light engineering products like ball bearings and
motor parts while remaining a tightly knit community in the old city
(Rizvi 1976:28–31).

More often, I think, when members of the same caste went into
small-scale manufacturing, there was little direct connexion between
their traditional and new occupations. I have described the way in
which early recruitment gave people from certain communities or
areas a partial monopoly of some factory jobs, which no one else
wanted until it was too late to get in. Similarly among small-sector
employers, only local accidents and opportunities, and perhaps some
peculiarities of custom and belief, can explain why castes – sometimes
low castes – came to dominate branches of small industry in a city or
region: for example, the Mahisyas who control most small-scale
engineering in Howrah near Calcutta (Owens 1973; Owens and
Nandy 1975, 1977; Reserve Bank 1964:89, 119; p. 58 above).

In a comparative study of three Punjabi castes since the nineteenth
century, Satish Saberwal writes:

> *Who* can successfully take advantage of the new opportunities will depend on
> *marginal advantages*: this applies to corporate groups . . . as well as to
> individuals; and such elements as particular skills (say, literacy), the
> achievement motivation acquired in the family context, and fortuitous
> connexions with unusually resourceful individuals or networks are relevant.
> (Saberwal 1976:42)

Saberwal tries to explain why the Sikh Ramgarhias – originally
carpenters – have been very successful small-scale entrepreneurs,
especially in engineering; the untouchable Ad Dharmis have been
only moderately successful in this line; and the untouchable Balmikis
hardly at all. Though the Ramgarhias' skill with wood and metal
helped them, Saberwal thinks their main advantages were psychological or ideological – an openness to change and an emphasis on
individual achievement – and especially the wide network of contacts
they could exploit. The Ad Dharmis – traditionally cobblers and
weavers – had manual dexterity, numbers and political connexions
on their side. The Balmikis or scavengers were discouraged and
discriminated against; the education and jobs reserved for Untouchables went to the more confident Ad Dharmis, and the Balmikis
fell back on their traditional occupation:

The mobility experiences in Modelpur [a pseudonym] have been influenced not so much by the caste *rank* as by its hereditary occupation, and the new opportunities coming its way, which gave it a particular mix of resources and handicaps in a changing economic and political setting. In Modelpur's circumstances, the capacity of the three caste groups to build on those resources did rise with caste rank, but . . . such an association, plausible in Modelpur, may have been fortuitous, without general validity.   (:220)

Lynch (1969) has studied another caste whose members tried and generally failed to use their traditional skills in small firms supplying new markets. The Jatavs of Agra are cobblers, like the Ad Dharmis, and there is a flourishing export market for the shoes they make at home or in factories. They have political influence, many are educated and in government jobs and for some time they have actively demanded integration into national life and recognition of their improved status. Yet their 'big men' have been displaced, both as factors marketing shoes and as factory owners, by Punjabis who have more business experience, more capital, and better contacts with retailers and foreign markets; and who can, if necessary, 'freeze out a lower caste competitor by making salient the Jatavs' Un-touchable status within the market networks' (:39).

The new industrialists: financiers or technicians?

Those studies are of men who used – or failed to use – their caste contacts and traditional skills to build up small firms: not whole castes, but many from the same caste. They competed with each other, but their success depended largely on caste links.

Entrepreneurs in the new small industries are not of this kind. Their caste or religion is a relevant fact about their background and personal history – some castes have a business tradition, some value manual skill or abstract thought – but their success depends more on contacts with all kinds of people, besides close relatives. To see their careers in terms of the rise and fall of castes is an anachronism.

There is however an important division among the new en-trepreneurs, which sometimes has to do with their caste background: between *financiers* and *technicians*.

The old-style craftsman entrepreneur was a technician of sorts, who learned new skills by trial and error and improvisation. He built up the business gradually by reinvesting profits. The new en-trepreneur needs more capital and needs it quickly to start produc-tion. He must have it in the family, take a partner or borrow. Thus a new firm often represents an uneasy compromise between capital and technical skill.

A firm's character depends crucially on which kind of person has the upper hand. If a financier runs the firm he may learn a good deal about the technology, or very often he sends his son to study engineering, but he thinks of the firm as a family investment, to be kept going for as long as it is more profitable than alternative investments. A technician may have access to family money, and he may take to the commercial side of the business, but his attitude to the firm is different: the product matters more to him, because his main assets are his knowledge of how to make it and his ideas about how to improve it or to use the experience to develop new products.

Not everyone fits neatly into either type, but entrepreneurs themselves often make a similar distinction, between engineers who need capital to make their ideas pay, and capitalists who need engineers to make their money grow. Relations between the two are not always easy. Financiers say engineers or ex-workers do not know how to run a business and should stick to the technical tasks they understand – a view expressed in an article from the Small Industries Extension Training Institute:

> A study of sick units will reveal that a majority of them were set up by engineers and techno-entrepreneurs. Such entrepreneurs are better-suited for production than other aspects of management. Obviously they concentrate more on producing goods and thus pile up inventory and run out of money.
>
> (SIET Institute 1976:D2)[3]

Technicians think financiers exploit them and the consumers, and selfishly prevent real industrial development: thus industrial leaders in Faridabad argue that they themselves are not just interested in making money but in contributing something worthwhile to the country, but 'in this they are thwarted, they say, thanks to the "*bania*-minded capitalists" who control the economy' (Panini 1977:112; banias are merchant castes).

R.K. Ray makes a similar distinction in a study of pre-war businessmen operating on a much larger scale, and their relations with the British:

---

[3] Cf. Lakdawala and Sandesara 1960:257, *Small industry in a big city: a study of Bombay*: 'In most cases, this [entrepreneurial] ability is associated with technical talent. But the latter without a more powerful ability of the former type has retrograded many a master into workers [*sic*]; and this, we understand, has happened for more than once in the history of the same persons.'

it will not do to present the divisions within the Indian capitalist class in terms of a simple dichotomy between comprador and national bourgeoisie. In basic economic terms, the most readily recognizable distinction was between the traders, merchants, speculators, brokers and marketeers of different sorts on the one hand and the industrialists on the other.　　　(Ray 1979:309–10)

The line was blurred because industrialists like Tata and Birla also engaged in import–export trade, while the big merchants were made directors of industrial companies: 'Nevertheless the distinction between "marketeers" and "industrialists", recently advanced by A.D.D. Gordon [1978], is a useful one' (ibid.).

Financiers and technicians differ in their background, attitudes, motivation, and style of management. Financiers often come from the old trading castes: the Banias and Marwaris of western India, the Cett'iaar (Chettiar) in the south, some Muslims etc. K.L. Sharma and Harnek Singh (1976:vi), comparing the growth of entrepreneurship in Punjab and Uttar Pradesh, found that although artisans and others without a business background were moving into small-scale industry, most entrepreneurs in both states came from business castes or families. They got their initial capital from their families, and borrowed from government agencies only when their firms had already been set up. In their book on small industries, Dhar and Lydall write:

> Many of the entrepreneurs now trying to find a foothold in industry are ex-merchants, especially importers whose supply of goods has been cut off by the import restrictions. There are also other men of capital (including ex-landlords) who, for one reason or another, are shifting their interests into industry.　　　　　　　　　　　(Dhar and Lydall 1961:80).

Even when the 'owner' has only one small firm to manage, it may be part of a family business empire which includes trading ventures, big and small manufacturing units and even a managing agency; and the family capital is frequently switched from firm to firm. 'Family' in this context can mean a traditional joint family of married brothers living together under their father's authority – some of the sons are given a technical education to manage that side of the business – or a more distant family connexion, often through marriage. An ancillary unit is said to supply the 'parent' firm, and this kinship idiom may be more than a metaphor.

Technicians (apart from the old-style craftsmen) include graduate engineers and chemists. These 'technocrats' (in the jargon of agencies set up to help small-scale industries) are generally from professional or landowning families, with a high proportion of Brahmans.

> The [industrial] estates are not recruiting entrepreneurs from amongst low-
> status social groups. They are providing an arena for the growth of a new
> entrepreneurial class, owning typically relatively large and sophisticated
> units, and drawn from landed interests and professional groups, which is also
> developing outside the estates.   (Mars 1973:22)

Anil Awachat tells me that the pioneers in setting up small industries
in Poona and other Maharashtrian towns were Brahman village
landlords, driven to town by the Land to the Tiller Act and other laws
aimed specially at breaking Brahman power. The same thing
happened in Tamil Nadu (formerly Madras State).

Most 'technocrats' have spent years working in large factories as
managers, or even ordinary workers, before setting up their own
firms. They shade into the much larger group of skilled workers, who
left factories or workshops to set up their own firms or to expand small
businesses in which they were already working part time (see
Holmström 1976: 108–9 on these embryo industrialists).

These ex-factory workers come from all kinds of backgrounds, with
widely differing levels of skill and education, and very varied past
careers. In Faridabad – where almost all industrial entrepreneurs
seem to have factory experience – Panini (1977:95) classifies them as
former craftsmen (i.e. factory craftsmen not traditional ones),
supervisors and executives. Their assets include not only their skill
and savings, but especially the vital contacts with factory officers who
can pass on orders for components, or mention their names to others.
They also know where to get materials and second-hand machinery
cheaply. Lakshman (1966:338–9) describes the way Bangalore
entrepreneurs used to fabricate tools and equipment from worn-out
machine parts, so that their products lacked precision and quality,
and had to be finished in better-equipped workshops; but Panini tells
me it is now much easier to set up a small workshop in Faridabad – a
new industrial town – than in Bangalore, where entrepreneurs have
been trained in strict quality control by the factories and will not use
the old lathes and machinery which Faridabad entrepreneurs can get
cheaply.

Studies of entrepreneurship tend to over-generalize from experience of one or other of these types. In areas like Gujarat, where
there is a long tradition of merchant capitalism, and to a large extent
in Bombay, small industries are owned and managed directly by
merchants. As an engineer with a small firm in Bangalore told me, in
Bangalore and Poona many entrepreneurs have an engineering

background, but in Bombay they are people with a financial background who see an investment opportunity in engineering and employ engineers. In places like Bangalore, the engineers or ex-workers who run the firms depend uneasily for capital on financiers or official sources or both. In Calcutta and elsewhere a common complaint – which may or may not be well founded – is that much of the economy is dominated by capitalists from other parts of India, whose instinct is not to build up stable local firms, but to take the money and run. If they do the same thing on their home ground, at least they are more likely to reinvest locally.

Thus one image of the small-scale entrepreneur is of a grasping capitalist, the nearest thing to economic man walking on two legs, whose acquisitive nature is poorly hidden by a veneer of religiosity and paternalistic care for his workers.

Yashodhara Dalmia, a journalist, spoke to one of them, who makes tubelight chokes on a Bombay industrial estate.

> The business is profitable because there is little competition and he knows where to buy raw materials more cheaply than the big firms can; but: 'They [the dealers] are not really aware of the profit margins and in front of them we also pretend that we get little profit.'
> His workers earn much less than the legal minimum: 'There is so much unemployment and labour is freely available. When you can get a person at a lower rate why not? . . . You must be thinking that if I pay them more they will be more sincere? Well, the fact is that the really hard-working person, we do increase his scale. We try to keep him happy so that he may not go over to someone else'. Only eight or nine of his 100 workers are 'sincere': the others 'don't have the feeling that the boss is a nice person and they should be loyal to him'. 'In this business you don't know whether the workers will let you open the factory tomorrow. My mind is always busy pre-planning all the moves I might have to take in case something happens. But now I plan to start something on the side, like a shop.' 'Any day, my profits can decrease . . . Of course, I can start manufacturing some other item where there is less competition. But you have to be constantly alert about what will fetch the most profit with minimum investment.'
> (Based on Dalmia, 'The rules of the game', *Times of India*, 21 August 1977)

Hein Streefkerk (1978, 1979) describes these financier–industrialists in an almost 'pure' form, in the Gujarat town of Bulsar. The rapid growth of Bulsar's small industries in the 1960s was mainly the result of rising land prices and labour unrest in Bombay. This caused Gujarati businessmen to find a safe home for their investments not too far away – Bulsar is on a main line to Bombay – where they could continue to buy materials and sell their products in the city, and in many cases to look after their remaining offices and assets there; 'Only labour is provided locally. It is cheaper than in Bombay' (1979:103). Bulsar also attracted them because it was an administrative centre, where they had access to officials through friends and relatives.

> Industrial development in Bulsar is furthermore characterized by 'switching' activities (Baks [in an unpublished paper] uses the word 'vacillating', i.e. 'a change to divergent types of small scale industries during the entrepreneur's career'). From Baks' research among the Jain Banias it appeared that during the last 20 years 16 of them were involved in at least 33 industrial activities. My study of small-scale industrialists in Bulsar shows that this is equally true outside the Jain community . . . Wavering industrial activities, often combined with non-productive enterprises, are indicative of a predominantly commercial entrepreneurship aimed at easy profits and short term results.
>
> (Streefkerk 1979:104)

Streefkerk gives case studies, for instance of the several men who have gone into the capital-intensive plastics industry:

> The production process requires general insight into the working of the machines but no specific technical skill; as one Bania put it, 'we are not industrialists; we simply buy the machine and try to sell the plastic buckets'. At the start the maintenance work on the plastic injectors is done by technicians from the firm that delivered the machine and later on by a worker trained on the spot or recruited from an urban centre.
>
> The success of such an enterprise is determined only partially by the quality of the product. Since all the machines are almost the same the quality of the products cannot differ to any great extent. The important point therefore is to capture a market at an early stage and to have a regular supply of raw materials. This is mainly a matter of knowing the 'right' people, viz. the middlemen. The Artisan [by caste] was proud to point out that the other shareholders were important businessmen who had good contacts with the administration, trade and industry. (:106)

> A major determinant of profitable enterprising . . . is the range of the particularistic potential of an enterprising family. (:119)

In an earlier study of Bombay small industry, Lakdawala and Sandesara (1960:197) found that: 'For as many as one-third of the total units, industrial activity did not constitute the sole source of income, but a primary or secondary source with the non-industrial activity, generally trading, as the main or the supporting cast.'

Switching capital between firms is also an insurance against unions and against enforcement of the labour laws. If workers in a small firm join a union or demand the legal minimum wage, or if the union takes a case of unfair dismissal to court, it is easy to close the firm, transfer the machinery and stock to another firm owned by the same man or family, and offer jobs to 'loyal' workers. This happens constantly in Bombay; the assets may be taken out of the city and then back again. Long before the slow legal processes can catch up with the employer, the firm has ceased to exist. It may even reopen under another name, a few months later, in the same building.

Streefkerk suggests that this 'commercialism' – 'the inclination of different entrepreneurs, whether successively or simultaneously, all to involve themselves in too wide a range of disparate commercial and industrial activities' (1978:304) – is typical of successful small-scale industrialists all over India. It is not adequately explained by the traditional occupational background of the trading communities, or by psychological factors:

> Commercialism is . . . inherent in the Indian social and economic structure. In the first place it is command over access to government and business circles which determines who go in for industrial production. Such access not only makes investment in light industry possible, and even more, attractive, but it also provides the favoured entrepreneurs with other lucrative opportunities for profit-making. They can thus spread their risks, help members of their family, and others, to enjoy the same facilities, and switch from one line of business to another when profits begin to decline.
>
> But the most important explanation must be looked for in an economic structure which encourages, rather than discourages, the switching and spreading of investment.   (Streefkerk 1978:305)

Industrial expansion is limited by the narrow export market, and especially by the insignificant purchasing power of many rural people. The best opportunities are pre-empted by big firms which have foreign and government contacts and steady access to resources: especially since Indian industry, large and small, is becoming dependent on imported petro-chemicals with the shift from natural to synthetic products (plastics, chemicals, textiles):

> A regular supply of raw materials at reasonable prices cannot be relied upon, nor can the market be extended indefinitely, and what starts off as a lucrative line of business is soon stretched too far. In such a situation it is no more than reasonable entrepreneurial behaviour to place bets on a number of different horses. The commercialism that characterizes much of light industry is thus an inevitable facet of Indian socio-economic structure.   (:305)

But this does not account for the success – and in places like Bangalore, the leading position – of the other kind of entrepreneurs, the technicians.[4] It is certainly rational, in the Indian situation, to

---

[4] Things seem to be similar in Coimbatore: see John Harriss' account (1981; 1982:950–1) of the different types of small-scale entrepreneurs there, few of whom behave like Streefkerk's 'commercialists'.

switch capital between industrial and trading ventures, and to exploit
a wide range of one's own and one's family's contacts, but this
strategy is open only to those who have enough capital, contacts and
business experience – an experience which begins from childhood in
these families. Technicians, on the whole, have different contacts, less
capital and no commercial experience. The only way they can
succeed is by taking the alternative path, concentrating on the
product and technology.

If technicians need capital, financiers need technicians: even
Streefkerk's maker of plastic buckets needed someone to maintain the
machine. The easiest way is to employ a technician: but he may want
a high salary, he may have ambitions for a firm of his own, and he
may also have contacts with other technical men and with factory
officers, which would make a useful complement to the financier's
business contacts. All these things may point to some kind of
partnership.

'Mr Chawla' runs a Bombay toolroom making replacement parts for
factories and doing other job work, with 'nine to fifteen' regular skilled
workers and eight or ten casuals (not committing himself to any number
above ten permanent workers, the threshold for Factory Act registration).
He began as a rice merchant in Burma, until Indian businessmen were
forced out. Then he went into partnership with a friend who wanted to make
refrigerator compressors, which were not made in India at that time.
Chawla had bought the materials and tools when his friend died. Since
Chawla knew nothing of engineering – 'I'm just a commercial man totally' –
he employed a foreman and took jobbing work instead. He tried to market
his own finished products: he made some clutch plates just before the Indian
car industry slumped: boxes of unsold clutch plates are piled on a shelf in his
office. Now he is making an ingenious patent lock, designed by an engineer
friend, for which he has orders from America. Even if Chawla is no engineer,
he is fascinated by gadgets and delights in showing them off.

His machinery is hired, or on hire purchase, from an agency of the state
government. Workers come and go: some have left to set up their own firms
with perhaps three or five workers, and he passes surplus job work on to them
since their labour costs are even lower than his.

'Kris'nasvaami', Managing Partner of 'Shriidhar Tools', advertises his
Bangalore firm as 'Manufacturers of special forming tools; all kinds of
general machinery spare parts and re-sharpening in any type of cutting tools
etc.', but his work consists almost entirely of sharpening cutting tools for
firms of all sizes. He had 18 years' experience as a skilled grinder in three
factories. Six years ago he went into partnership with a textile financier, who
was not a technician but just provided the money, apparently leaving the

management to Kris'nasvaami. They also borrowed from the Karnataka State Finance Corporation, on the security of the three expensive milling machines. He employs a supervisor, two skilled men he trained himself, and four 'trainees'.

Though two or three other local firms have the machines for this specialized work, he says they lack his experience; so that all kinds of firms – even big factories – bring their cutting tools to his small workshop and collect them afterwards;[5] he puts out some jobs to other small firms, and he has started manufacturing his own tools.

He is a self-made man who takes great pride in knowing the job, and explains the details with enthusiasm; approachable and open, and in character like many Bangalore factory workers. Like them he emphasizes the value of practical experience over paper qualifications, and complains that banks and government agencies discriminate against applicants for loans who are 'unqualified', without degrees: something that rankles, since he mentioned it several times. He talks of the firm and its future as if it were his own, hardly mentioning his partner the financier.

Two kinds of partnership: Chawla the businessman manages the firm and borrows ideas from his engineer friends; Kris'nasvaami the skilled worker takes a rich sleeping partner because, lacking paper qualifications, he cannot raise enough capital otherwise.

A financier would usually prefer to keep control of the firm and to employ a technician to manage it: but then – and this is a fear constantly voiced by men with money but little technical knowledge – the technician will go elsewhere taking trade secrets with him. It is safer to pass these precious secrets only to close relatives.

Five Gujarati brothers manage an electronic factory in Bombay, with about forty workers. The eldest brother, the 'President', studied science but 'didn't appear' for the examination; however, he worked in a factory abroad for two years and learned enough to start the business. They keep ahead of the competition by improvising copies of the latest foreign models. The youngest brother has enough technical knowledge to look after 'research' (i.e. copying?) and production, so things are under the owners' control.

---

[5] He gave me a pink handbill, decorated with printer's blocks of a holy lamp, a rose, and a hand holding a lotus, and beginning:

> Entrepreneur dear
> Why do you fear?
> When 'SHRIIDHAR TOOLS' is here . . .
>
> Production Bottleneck?
> is the result when you over look
> Resharpening of the Tool
> which is but natural!

The owner of another small electronic firm lamented that he could not expand, because he had no son or other close relative he could trust with the firm's secrets.

Not that this emphasis on secrecy is confined to the financiers: when I asked a graduate chemist whether the workers in his pharmaceutical factory understood anything of the technical processes involved (for in my experience Indian workers are often very interested in the technology they work with), he said they knew nothing and were not encouraged to delve, since they might take his secrets to a competitor.

'Deshpande', an engineer, employs about seventy people making electronic components in Bombay. After working in Britain, he borrowed money without security under the State Bank of India technician's scheme to start a factory. Entirely by himself, he developed a method of making a product which other firms can only make with foreign collaboration and imported material. It is chemically the same as the foreign one – 'If you like I've pinched their patent', but indianized it, overcoming the problems of using Indian material.

To develop his technology and instruments, he went to all kinds of ink, paint and plastic technologists, who helped because they knew he would not compete with them. He can pass technology on freely to his nephew, also an engineer. He does not like employing highly qualified people, as they will blackmail him by threatening to start their own firms: in fact one or two have done so, using his ideas, but they failed. Yet if they had asked, he would willingly have given them the information they wanted – in general he has never kept secrets, and he deplores the 'Indian tendency' to keep everything to oneself (why then is his nephew to be specially trusted?).

Firms everywhere have their secrets. It is perhaps more rational to guard them in India, where patents give so little protection that some inventors never bother to take them out. If you cannot get a machine, or your old imported model wears out, copy it: I have seen managers and technicians standing round a fabricated copy of an old British machine for putting bristles into plastic toothbrushes, comparing every detail of its performance with the original which stood beside it.[6] The same thing can apply to the product: a Bangalore diemaker said firms send him imported plastic components for which he tries to design a mould – he was copying a foreign machine tool handle for use on buses, but had not yet matched the original finish and quality. But financier–industrialists seem to regard technical knowledge as *property*

[6] This is not a parody, though it may look like one to devotees of Peter Sellers.

and to be suspicious of outsiders who might take it from them, while technicians lay more stress on the process of learning it, on practical experience which becomes part of a man's personality and makes him more valuable: not just economically, but in an almost moral sense.

The picture of the small-scale entrepreneur as a grasping capitalist – economic man incarnate – is grounded partly in fact, partly in polemics from the left and other quarters, partly in popular prejudice against the merchant castes: especially Marwaris, whose very name has become a byword for usury and crookedness. I do not suggest that these stereotypes are fair or true, only that popular opinion associates whole communities with a business style which is very widespread, and perhaps a rational response to a social and economic situation. There are two sharply different styles of business, and various compromises between them, and people from some communities may be predisposed by their upbringing and situation to one style or the other.

People's motives are complex, and change in the course of a lifetime. The merchant's son sent to study engineering may not share his father's values when he takes over the firm. But even then the style of business and management, relations with workers and attitudes to work, can continue with little change but different rationalizations.

Contrast this type of financier–industrialist with the energetic technician translating his knowledge and ideas into production and profit. Again one can find him in an almost 'pure' form:

'Divaakar' owns a chemical firm with fifteen employees on a Bombay industrial estate: not one of the private 'estates' which are really industrial slums, but a well-laid-out industrial area provided by the state government. His main product is a compound which he sells to the main pharmaceutical companies.

His story (told in the press cutting he showed me) is of a classic rise from humble origins. The son of a village policeman, and apparently a Harijan, he went from his village school to high school on an 'open merit' scholarship, studied chemistry in Bombay, became a lecturer and did post-doctoral work in America.

After his return he set up this company with help from the Maharashtra State Financial Corporation through its Technicians' Assistance Scheme to make, for the first time in India, the compound by a process he had developed in his university research. He struggled to compete with government imports of the compound, which was much cheaper abroad; but since it is now made in India the government banned imports and controlled the price. Now he has three-quarters of the market and one competitor.

Imports of one essential input are 'canalized' by the government, so he goes to Delhi from time to time to make sure of supplies.

His process is different from the one used abroad, using cheap indigenous machines in a laboratory which looks like a kitchen (pointing at one vessel in which a reaction was taking place, he said 'that cost Rs 5000'). Four of his fifteen employees are experienced chemists: the firm is 'neither capital-intensive nor labour-intensive but talent-intensive'. The other workers, apart from two electricians, just mix the materials, watch meters etc.: they need no experience, and he can train any 'smart' young man in a week. They have no chance of promotion but he claims to pay them better than in most small firms, and since 'the psychology of the workers' is such that they would rather demand and get Rs 10 than take Rs 15 which he would give freely, it would be best to have someone to negotiate with – 'I'm thinking of forming a union myself for them'.

He is not dependent on any big customer. Since he has space, he plans to diversify the product and to export.

'Naaraayan'a', in partnership with his brother, runs a silk screen printing business with twelve permanent workers, on a Bangalore street which contains an astonishing variety of small engineering and other firms working not only for the big factories but for each other.

His father, a retired railway official, lost all his money. Naaraayan'a had to leave school at seventeen and work as a building labourer, then as a small building contractor. At school he had been interested in photography, and he became an approved photographer for the Public Works Department. Since he could not get his own studio, he turned to civil engineering contracting, which paid well but involved too much corruption. (I came to know him quite well, and I believe his hatred of corruption was sincere.) He bought his brother a radio repair shop, which failed; and he put his money into a partner's firm making decorative light fittings, which also failed.

There was then no silk screen printing firm in Bangalore, so he borrowed library books and experimented at home. He developed his own emulsion by trial and error, before setting up the firm with his own money, nine years before I met him.

The best equipment and materials are unobtainable in India or too expensive, and foreign automatic machinery (even if he could afford it) is designed to print much larger quantities than his customers need. There are now many silk screen printers in Bangalore, but he has kept ahead by improvising cheap labour-intensive solutions to technical problems. Since he cannot afford a vacuum printing frame, he piles books and sandbags on the frame to get close contact; but an air-conditioned dust-free room, for high precision work, is beyond his means. He cannot get rub-down lettering, so he uses a small press.

He takes all kinds of work: wedding invitations, stickers, visiting cards, printing on plastic; but he wants to concentrate on printing anodized aluminium plates for electronic and electrical firms, and printed circuit boards etched on copper-plated plastic (two firms which are his customers are literally next door). He has acquired equipment to do the anodizing himself.

He employs a full-time cameraman, and a draftsman and printer with full-time jobs elsewhere. Everyone, including him, will turn a hand to any job, except that the women do no heavy work like drilling and punching. He taught the stenotypist photography; and everyone learns to print. He was working on a process for printing greeting cards, not with the usual dyes, but with sandalwood paste: he had managed to get the colour on to the paper, but not the pleasant smell.

This is the kind of person who figures in much of the writing on entrepreneurship as the catalyst of economic development: the man who identifies new markets, backs ideas at his own risk, finds capital and labour to organize production and overcomes obstacles by improvising and innovating. Government plans and programmes are designed to help such people where they exist or to stimulate these qualities ('the objective of the rural industrialization programme should be to make the rural artisan a better artisan today, a skilled worker tomorrow, and an entrepreneur the day after'[7]).

Financiers and technicians differ in their management styles and often their social origins; perhaps less in their motives. Of course it is difficult to generalize about motives, but they are often quite plain from what people do and the reasons they give.

Everyone wants money. The main reason why people start their own firms is because they believe they will make more money than they could otherwise. This may seem obvious, except that for some people who do believe this some other motive appears to be stronger, and a few may sincerely think they must sacrifice the chance of a relatively high steady income to be their own masters.

Factory workers and managers spend years exploring possibilities before deciding to take the plunge and go for maximum income; unlike a young tool and die maker in Bangalore.

His employers sent him for nine months' training in Switzerland. On his return he moved to another factory, where he and a friend at once started planning their own workshop. They made up their minds (he said) when they both asked for a rise in salary, were refused, and resigned the same day. They had only Rs 12 000 to invest in machinery and a shed, and contacts in

[7] P.C. Alexander, *Entrepreneurs in India*, quoted in K.A. and U. Chopra (1974b).

several big factories who were sending them orders. When I met him they were waiting for a bank loan of Rs 110 000 to buy machines.

Again it may seem obvious why everyone wants money: to buy goods and security, for dowries, status symbols and conspicuous consumption. Another reason is: to give it away. Especially in the old merchant castes, there is a tradition of religious giving, sometimes on a lavish scale, to sectarian gurus as well as established temples, and 'status' is an inadequate explanation for this. Old and successful entrepreneurs tend to withdraw gradually from business and to devote themselves to philanthropy:

> Many have donated large sums of money to build hospitals, schools and colleges and take active interest in managing these institutions. They stress that they do not obtain any personal benefits from their influential contacts although no one creates any obstacle in their way.   (Panini 1977:113)

But membership in social service organizations like the Lions Club is also an important source of status and useful contacts (:111). A commoner and more informal kind of philanthropy is patronage: helping out one's own employees or others in need, with gifts or loans which are really gifts, using contacts to find people jobs or to help them in their dealings with government offices, and so on.

Especially for technicians, money has a special value if one started with very little and made it by one's own efforts: though hardly to the same extent as Weber's calvinist businessmen who saw profit, not as an end in itself, but as a sign of God's grace shown to the chosen souls who laboured successfully in their calling. In India today a special prestige attaches not just to wealth, but to being a self-made man. Thus one of the four partners in a Bombay engineering firm, who had all been supervisors in the same factory, said proudly that none of them had any family money: all their investment had come from their earnings, and from bank loans granted on their records.

> Thus we notice the craftsman spirit even in their external style. It is also evident in the robust philosophy of self-reliance and independence they express. Their ideal is to succeed through one's own hard work rather than through gaining 'approach' to important people.   (:102)

Another strong motive – in some cases perhaps stronger than money – is *independence:* to be free, to be one's own master and other people's master as well.

The managing partner of a small Bangalore firm making power tools never considered working in a factory, since his family were business people and for generations none of them had taken employment. He studied engineering, and set up his own firm at once.

The owner of a new Bangalore firm with seven workers, making electronic instruments (the man who remarked on the different background of Bombay and Bangalore entrepreneurs, p. 90 above) was a factory manager in Kerala. He saw so many uneducated men setting up their own firms and doing well that he decided to take the risk himself. Now he has more freedom and the satisfaction of giving employment. His father had done the same thing.

I asked a Sikh taxi driver in Delhi whether he owned his taxi: he said yes, Sikhs will always try to be their own masters, unlike people from U.P. who are content to work for a taxi owner or a company.

In *South Indian factory workers* I described some of the factory workers who were actively planning to leave and set up on their own (Holmström 1976:108–10), and the much larger number of 'risk-minimizers with a wistful eye on the job market' who dream either of a better job or of having their own business, but can never bring themselves to give up a secure job (:110–14).

Ex-factory employees want to gain independence, sometimes even at the cost of security or income; business people do not want to lose it. The technicians sometimes stress, not only freedom from other people's direction, but the moral independence of a small-scale industrialist who makes things, as against the corruption and compromises which are inevitable in other kinds of business. This is why 'Naarayaan'a' (p. 98 above) gave up civil engineering work. In Faridabad:

> Conversations often refer with admiration to one or another ordinary worker who rose to own a large factory; and considerable status attaches to being an independent entrepreneur. Being an entrepreneur implies that one is *not* working for others; and being an industrial entrepreneur implies that one is not 'cheating' or 'lying' as is believed to be necessary for a contractor or a shopkeeper. An industrial entrepreneur is believed to earn a living through hard work. (Panini 1977:98–9)

Of course any kind of business involves shady dealings, especially with government officials who give quotas and licences. Yet in spite of the general cynicism about businessmen and officials, not all are willing to give or take bribes. As an informant from a large firm in Howrah said:

> The successful factory owner in Howrah is not a qualified engineer. He is aware of how to get jobs done and has a knack for getting the best out of a contract. This requires a certain intuition about when to give a kickback. The inexperienced man will try to convince the man on the wrong grounds, such as the quality of his product, when this is not required. Some government officers won't budge an inch on quality; others want a kickback. You must judge which man you are dealing with. If you offer the wrong man a bribe you may be thrown out. (Owens and Nandy 1977:42–3)

Hypocrisy is the homage which vice pays to virtue, but it may be a sincere homage:

> bribery has been institutionalized to such an extent that there are agents who regularly visit the executives, especially those who are shy of paying bribes, and offer to solve their problems for payment of a commission. (:111)

The fixer takes the client's sin upon himself. It is a common opinion among these people – unlike other businessmen – that corruption is wrong, and both the sinner and the country would be better off without it. Tax evasion is different: no one sees anything wrong with that; and only unions and workers object to the widespread evasion of labour laws.

The technician entrepreneurs' pride in the work, their delight in new technology and their stress on technical perfection are said to blind them to cost (see p. 88 above), though I doubt whether this is generally true (again, see Panini 1977:105). Technicians who have been factory workers, and some graduate engineers, are proud that they can work with their hands and do any job in the workshop. The engineer owner of a Bangalore firm with fifteen workers, making pressed components to high standards of precision, said he has 'no overheads', being supervisor, proprietor and a worker. A Bombay tool and die maker said all his ten workers were trained on his full range of machines; he himself could operate any of them, and he proudly held up his hands covered in oil.

This pride in being a worker and turning one's hand to anything, the show of camaraderie and toughness, can also be a front put on to impress employees and outsiders (like me): the image of a hard-headed fellow worker, friendly but not easily fooled, rather than a desk-bound paternalistic businessman (the type who says 'My door is always open: my workers feel they can always bring their problems to me'). Technicians tend to emphasize that they are workers too, but there is probably not much difference between them and the financier–industrialists in their approach to labour relations. In small firms the margins are too small, and the employers' ability to drive a hard bargain with workers is why they stay in business.

The small-scale industrialists' public image is contradictory. On the one hand, toughness and self-reliance: men who want only to stand on their own feet. The engineer 'Deshpande' (p. 96 above) said the reservation of certain products for small firms was a mistake, and had brought about a new kind of caste distinction between big and small firms. Other employers made a similar point; some prefer to have as little as possible to do with official agencies. On the other hand they complain constantly of discrimination against small industries by the government and big firms, of unfair burdens and legislation, of special problems requiring special help, and what a hard time they have (like British businessmen who extol the virtues of sturdy private enterprise and demand state aid in the same breath).

Indians are pioneers, exporting 'the philosophy of small-sector industries', yet small industries are exploited by labour and the banks, and face a wall of official obstruction and delay. The entrepreneur is at the mercy of everyone, especially government officials; 'he has only bosses', though he is supposed to be a capitalist, and on his limited capital he must dress well, have a telephone etc. It takes guts to tackle 'the sixteen agencies that pounce on small-scale industries', like the Employees' State Insurance and Provident Fund men, who take all the time he should spend on the business. Small industries are not yet ready to face the rigour of the labour laws. Over the last few years, simply to survive was an achievement. Young men should be warned of all these dangers before they take the plunge. (All these comments were made at a one-day conference of 'successful' entrepreneurs called by the Indian Institute of Management, Bangalore, to discuss a three-month course in entrepreneur develop-ment for selected candidates, who would get a 100 per cent loan to start businesses.) Another well-founded complaint is that the small industries' customers pay them months or years late – public sector factories being by far the worst offenders. Small industries have the greatest difficulty in getting materials either through official channels (on quotas or licences) or otherwise.

In some cases this is a front (like 'I am a worker too'): special pleading for protection and advantages by hard-nosed businessmen who can look after themselves. As a Bombay trade unionist told me, there are conflicting 'pulls' on any manager; if he shows a good profit he cannot avoid tax or his workers' demands: they will expect more, and the law says wages should depend on the company's capacity to pay. But if the company is not seen to be doing well, he will lose the confidence of partners and shareholders, and find it hard to get bank credit. So public statements of the company's financial position represent a compromise between these pulls and (in answer to my suggestion) the truth.

But these pictures of entrepreneurs – whether financiers or technicians – are built up from studies of those who stay in business. There is a high rate of failure, especially in the early years, and the problems of survival are daunting even if entrepreneurs exaggerate them. Firms controlled by financiers very often close down because the owner or chief investor sees a more profitable use for his money, and may have already milked the firm of its assets: he survives, though the firm does not and the workers must survive as best they can. But the technician–entrepreneur typically has all his eggs in this one basket, and if the firm fails he fails with it. Small marginal firms can only make up for lack of capital if they have sponsors and contacts.

In Bombay's Dharavi, known as 'the biggest slum in Asia', men make small components like springs at home, with primitive equipment. A Tamil employed as a dockyard welder told me that some try to set up regular workshops on roads some distance away – not in Dharavi, for 'who would buy things from a place like this?'. They borrow the capital from well-employed men like this welder, at 10 per cent a month.

In Faridabad 'infant mortality' is high among the craftsmen–entrepreneurs, who take labour jobs at low rates in the hope of building up goodwill, and often lose heavily: 'Crucial for survival is the nature of the tie between a craftsmen and his sponsor' (Panini 1977:99). The more sophisticated firms, born with the official agencies' blessing, may last a little longer: Mazumdar and Nag (1977:26) found that 'if births are induced by sudden promotional measures and possibly not followed up consistently, the units die a natural death within two to three years', mainly because of the lack of finance, then shortage of materials, 'management problem', and poor demand.

Technicians' firms, financiers' firms and compromises

As an anthropologist, I begin by observing and questioning people, before trying to fit them into the big economic and social structures which largely condition their deeds and words. That is why I have dealt with entrepreneurs first, before coming to the financial and technical relations between firms.

Real small-scale entrepreneurs range between two extreme types – the financier and the technician – in their background, motives and management styles. Real firms, successful or not, represent various compromises between finance and technical skill. They range from firms dominated by technicians to those where financiers clearly have the upper hand:

1. The technician may be the real entrepreneur. While a financier–industrialist wants a technician he can trust to run his business (though he can really trust no one outside the family), a technician wants access to capital without control or interference. He would rather borrow from a bank or government agency than from a private businessman (an ex-worker running a Bangalore machine shop, who thinks of marketing his own product, said 'Without bank there is no finance at all'). He may also have savings from employment (like the four factory supervisors who pooled their savings and went into partnership, p. 100 above) or family money.

A participant at the conference on training entrepreneurs (p. 103 above) said a young entrepreneur should be unmarried, with no family cares to bring him home from work in the evening; but he needs a 'godfather' or family friend to advance extra funds for contingencies, or when the bank loan runs out.

An entrepreneur not only needs working capital, but access to markets, contacts, efficient cost accounting etc. Technicians are not always aware of their own shortcomings in this area (thus ex-factory workers in Faridabad despise paper work, put off applying for licences and cannot exercise proper financial or administrative control: Panini 1977:100); or if they are, they may not be able to afford the right people or know how to delegate power to them. Financiers may not like delegating to technicians or anyone else, but they know the importance of accountancy, administration and marketing, and can find the right men if they must: 'Mr Chawla' (p. 94 above) already hires an accountant, and if his expansion plans succeed he will need someone to look after labour problems, Employees' State Insurance etc.

Technicians are said to be inflexible, pursuing an idea instead of maximizing profit by rational allocation of resources (p. 88 above), but this is largely a caricature. Technicians are committed to a product and a technology not just by temperament and conditioning, but because it makes economic sense for them. It is rational to put all your eggs in one basket if that is the only basket you have. If the failure rate is high, the successes benefit the national economy by raising production and employment, and by technical innovation. Technicians sometimes fail. Financiers deliberately close firms down: the consequent reallocation of resources may benefit them but not the nation, and is disastrous for their workers.

2. The technician owns the firm but depends for capital on a financier or a big company. This usually happens when the small firm is an ancillary supplying a big firm, which advances the capital and is the main or only customer. I deal with ancillaries later, when I come to the relations of dependence between firms rather than entrepreneurs.

3. Technicians and financiers – usually one of each – may be partners. This is not so common. If both are normally present in the workshop, they may split the work – one looks after production, the other after accounts, marketing, and contacts. Or the financier is a sleeping partner – from the technician's point of view, as fast asleep as possible. An example is 'Kris′nasvaami's' engineering partnership with a textile financier (pp. 94–5 above).

4. The manager is a qualified technician from a business family with diverse interests. Such people (women as well as men) are increasingly common, especially in Bombay. They blur the neat distinction between financiers and entrepreneurs, but their business style is sometimes recognizably closer to the financier end of the spectrum.

'Iqbaal' manages a Bombay die casting factory with forty workers, started by his father; and his own electronic instrument firm nearby, with twelve workers but growing, which takes components from the die casting factory. Both firms are partnerships, I think within the family.

Iqbaal studied electronic engineering abroad. His instruments are adapted from foreign models, without licence, as he cannot afford his own research and development. His success depends on selling products which are also available from other sources to big factories. He trains his own engineers, who then leave to work for public authorities.

The die casting workers switched to a militant union, whose leader insisted Iqbaal should go to the union office to negotiate. Iqbaal refused, closed the factory for six months, and reopened with a few 'skeleton' workers. They are not 'loyal' but 'they know their fate very well', and know they will get nothing from the union. Any worker with a grievance can come straight into his office, without knocking.

Though Iqbaal is a trained engineer, his business style, and his ruthless approach to labour relations behind a façade of paternalism, are characteristic of financier industrialists. The technically advanced unit he has developed himself is closely integrated with the family's other interests.

5. A financier runs the firm, attending personally to costs, marketing, labour relations, and so forth, and employing technically skilled people to do only those things he cannot do himself: like Streefkerk's plastic bucket maker (p. 92 above) or 'Mr Chawla' with his Bombay toolroom (p. 94). Very often the individual firm is not a stable profit-maximizing unit, but part of a family business empire. This would be the end of the spectrum, if it were not for

6. Phantom or bogus firms, which exist in large numbers to obtain licences, cheap loans available to small industries, or quotas of scarce or imported materials. These are sold on the black market or passed on to other units belonging to the family, who could not legitimately get any more licences or loans or quotas for themselves. The *Hindustan Times* reported that 'the recent census of small-scale industries revealed that some 40 per cent of registered small-scale units were either dead, bogus, or untraceable' (27 April 1977). 'A majority of small-scale units in U.P. [India's most populous state] . . . were found to exist only on paper when a survey, perhaps the last, was conducted during the emergency' (Girilal Jain, *Times of India*, 3 May 1977), though the Commissioner for Small-Scale Industries claimed that liberal imports and easy availability were putting an end to bogus units (*Times of India*, 12 May 1977).

Most phantom entrepreneurs probably employ no technical staff, because they produce nothing. In some places, however, it seems necessary to allay official suspicion by putting on a show of production. Thus a 1968 study showed that 'phantom entrepreneurs' in Rajasthan took sheds on industrial estates to get government quotas of imported and other materials: 'The sheds were "occupied" in name, the real business being conducted through quick, under-the-counter disposal of import quotas' (K.A. and U. Chopra 1974a).

Other entrepreneurs got machinery and equipment through the National Small Industries Commission and financial assistance from the state Department of Industries, sold part of the imported material on the black market, and used the rest in manufacturing to stay out of suspicion.

The great chain of dependence

> The employers in the small factories are the sons of rich peasants and merchants, the sons of bureaucrats, the very basis of the ruling party; 'small business' is the urban equivalent, in both economic and political terms, of the 'green revolution'.
>
> ('Engineering workers: struggle for minimum wages', *Economic and Political Weekly*, 12 April 1975, p. 612)

This may be true (and it may not make much difference which was the ruling party at the time). Small industries and the 'green revolution' create lucrative opportunities mainly for the rich and those in the middle ranks of society. In an unequal society this is to be expected, and the exceptions (like successful Untouchables) stand out. One can see this either as a necessary stage in industrial development, or a sterile diversion of resources from wage goods and social services for the masses to upper-class consumption. The question is not whether the position of the rich is strengthened, but which rich, and with what effects.

In general, an industrial entrepreneur's success depends on personal contacts with suppliers of capital and materials, and with larger factories which buy his products or middlemen who market them, rather than on technical ability. This is clear from the work of Panini, Streefkerk, Breman and others, and borne out in my fieldwork. But one should not exaggerate (as I think Streefkerk does, not because he misrepresents the situation in Gujarat but because he implies it is typical throughout India and of all kinds of entrepreneurs). Market forces may not operate freely but they are not abolished. Technical innovation and productivity can give a critical advantage even to a man whose contacts are not so good. The industrialists' admiration for the self-made man who came up from nothing goes with the belief that anyone can make it if he has it in him, there is always room at the top: this is an ideology justifying the distribution of wealth, and is usually but not always false.

Since personal contacts and affinities count for so much, it is useful to examine the background, motives and business style of the kinds of people who start and manage small firms. So far my focus has been on individual firms. In the next chapter I say more about the financial and technical links between strong and weak firms, and the chains of relationships – mainly dependence, but sometimes genuine complementarity – reaching down from the big corporations (including public sector companies) which dominate the economy, through firms of different sizes and the ancillaries which supply them, to the smallest most insecure marginal producers.

4
Factories and workshops

My subject is the different kinds of industrial workers, and whether some are privileged at the others' expense. But workers are links in a longer chain of relations of dependence and interdependence, extending to the owners of capital, large- and small-scale entrepreneurs and, at the other end, all who depend on industrial workers for markets, remittances or help.

The last chapter was mainly about small firms and those on the margin of the 'organized sector': how they have grown, and the kinds of people who set them up and manage them. Here I move away from the study of individual firms to the economic and technical links between the strong and the weak, whether these people are entrepreneurs, 'workers' or employees, or those outside the system of formal employment relations because they are self-employed, 'unemployed' or family dependants.

Dependence, interdependence, independence?

Consider three kinds of dependence:

'Raajan', a young engineer, worked in a Bangalore electronic factory, when the firm's foreign collaborators suggested he should start his own ancillary supplying components to their factory in India. They put up 75 per cent of the capital and gave him a five-year contract to work exclusively for them. He now employs about twenty workers, mostly girls. Although he gives out work to other firms, none depends on him exclusively, as he does on the foreign firm.

The contract ends next year. Raajan is very worried that it may not be renewed, or not for the same output, and he does not know where to find another contract. He may have to sack workers: when he employed them he warned them about the contract, and told them only about half could eventually be made permanent.

They ['craftsmen entrepreneurs' in Faridabad] assiduously cultivate the bigger entrepreneurs who give labour jobs. The relationship between these entrepreneurs and the craftsmen has the patron–client flavour. The patron not only recommends the craftsmen to his friends but occasionally helps him [*sic*] too. He may lend his client some small machine or a component which he is not using. He may also give him technical advice and help him with officials. The relationship may become close enough for the patron to stand surety for his client in getting bank loans and the like.

A good client is loyal, striving not only to do his patron's labour jobs efficiently but also to help him get reliable workers. If the patron is under pressure to keep a deadline, the client may offer to work himself or supervise work. Or, if the patron needs a job done from outside, the client may get it done through his friends. (Panini 1977:101–2)

Influence is also of crucial importance in trying to change one's position from a temporary to a permanent basis [in the Gujarat 'formal sector']. For that you need help of mamas and kakas [literally, maternal and paternal uncles] from higher circles, I was repeatedly told. This means that you work in the boss's house in your spare time, run errands for him, occasionally take him some liquor, a chicken, some mutton or some other treat – in other words you make your services available and behave as a chamcha (literally, 'spoon'), that is you bow and scrape. (Breman 1979:133)

In the first case, an ancillary entrepreneur depends totally on a formal contract with the 'parent' firm: renewal of the contract, and continued employment for the workers, probably depend on quality and market forces more than personal contacts. In the second, there is a diffuse patron–client relation between small and large entrepreneurs; a worker's security also depends largely on building up such a relation with his employer, who may even set him up in business. In the third case, organized sector managers can extract services and presents from subordinates in a calculating way by dangling the prospect of security before them.

Relations between firms are part of this chain of dependence; so are relations between employers and workers. Similarly, employment relationships range from sheer naked domination, through patron–client relations where domination is tempered by emotion and ideas of loyalty, to relations where even the inferior party has some options, some bargaining power, and is prepared to stand on his rights.

Perhaps dependence is in the eye of the beholder. I may be imposing a western view of society as transactions between individuals, or left-wing ideas about exploitation I share with many Indian intellectuals, on a reality which the people see differently, as a

hierarchical system of protection and obligation, patronage and
loyalty as moral duties. Even in purely economic terms, dependence
may be a one-sided view of these relations, especially between big and
small firms.

Typically, small firms depend on large ones for markets. Small
firms sell components or services to large firms, either on long
contracts (as 'ancillaries') or wherever and whenever they can in
competitive markets, under all sorts of arrangements which give the
small supplier varying amounts of security and profit. The price of a
secure market may be loss of freedom: the freedom to diversify and to
explore more profitable options, or the independence which is the
second most important motive (after money) for setting up one's own
business. Thus the owner of a Bangalore workshop supplying tools to
the big factories' ancillaries said he would not like his own firm to
become an ancillary, though he would be better off financially – 'I
would not like to be married to a particular group' (this may be sour
grapes but I think not). 'Deshpande' (p. 96 above) tried from the
start to sell his electronic components as widely as possible and to
avoid becoming dependent on a single big firm, 'otherwise they crush
you and kill you'. On the other hand, entrepreneurs scramble for the
favoured position of ancillary: 'Raajan' (p. 110) is frightened of
losing it, and will diversify only as a last resort.

The division of labour between linked firms may correspond to
technical requirements – successive stages of manufacture or assembly which can conveniently be done in different places, economies
of scale, special machines or skills needed to make products which the
biggest firm can sell. Or a small firm may do exactly the same work as
the large one does or can do, but with labour which is cheaper or more
flexible: workers can be taken on or laid off, they will turn their hand
to any kind of work without formal training, or come in at odd times
for a few hours work. The Bombay chemical, rubber and plastic
industries rely largely on such part-time labour, paid at piecework
rates.

Sometimes almost all the work has already been done in small
workshops which make the components. Only the final assembly is
carried out in the factory which markets the product. In some cases
(soap, cosmetics, toothbrushes, cloth) the factory's only contribution
is to stick its own well-known label on the finished products it buys
cheaply from many small units.

Four brothers run a small but growing workshop making textile machinery, which I visited in Ludhiana. Their design is adapted from that of the firm where they and most of their seven employees used to work: anyone can copy a machine, but their trade mark is their 'patent'. They not only buy needles from Bombay and forgings from local firms, but fully assembled machines to supplement their own production. These are sold all over India by their representative, whom I first met on a train from Bombay to Delhi.

A Bombay engineering firm with sixteen workers makes a wide variety of machine parts, which are sold to many large firms but mostly to one 'American-based' company which resells them under its own trade mark, as a guarantee of quality. This Bombay firm puts out turning jobs to other small companies, but only when extra production is needed.

These arrangements allow the bigger or better-known firm to supplement its own production when necessary, or to reduce sales when demand falls without laying off its own skilled workers. Some of the risk is passed on.

In these cases the big firm is also a manufacturer, insuring itself against fluctuations in demand. But often the marketing firm is simply a commercial agency for small firms, which have not the contacts or resources to sell under their own name. This happens with handicrafts like made-up garments or sandals, especially in export markets (where the middlemen may be foreigners, or Indians settled abroad who visit India from time to time). Small factories too need outlets and salesmen, both for consumer goods and for intermediate goods sold to other factories: here the links between manufacturing and trading firms owned by the same family are important. Manufacturing firms which build up a foreign sales network become agents for quite different products from other companies: especially since a firm which exports goods of a certain value for some time gets the status of an 'eligible export house', entitled to tax rebates and other privileges like easy imports of its own requirements.

A.N. Bose found that in Calcutta the big firms systematically market the small units' products, not just to cope with fluctuations in demand for their own products but to take advantage of lower capital costs and wages:

> The existence of the large houses controlling the market ensures effectively that the informal sector producers hand over their produce to the organised sector for marketing the goods, they themselves have produced, under well-known, often internationally famous, brand names, at a far higher price. This 'cost' of

marketing often exceeds by far the total cost of production. This is the typical case of that part of the informal sector, which is modern, and produces – despite low capital intensity, low wages, unsophisticated factory shed, etc. – really skilled, sophisticated products which also often includes embossing the labels or trade marks of the other larger factory under whose name the product will ultimately be sold in the market. This also applies to those who produce significant parts or components which are then assembled by the larger producer or some other sub-contractor engaged by the larger 'producer'.

(A.N. Bose 1978:98)

Thus a small engineering unit sells pipeline control valves for Rs 2200 to the 'producer', who markets them for Rs 5000. Another firm's light fixtures, sold for Rs 32, are marketed at Rs 90; yet the same firm pays over Rs 5000 a ton for cold rolled steel, which the big firms buy at the controlled price of less than Rs 2000. Moreover the small firms in Howrah put out much of the work to still smaller ones: 'Even an order for a simple product, such as pipe fittings, is often jobbed out as many as six times before it is completed' (Owens and Nandy 1977:44).

The main link between large and small firms may be *ownership*, whether or not the small firm also supplies the large one with components or finished goods for the market. Many small firms are owned outright by manufacturing or trading companies, including some of the big industrial houses which dominate the economy; or they are controlled by companies which advanced the capital. The owner or chief investor profits not only from cheap unregulated labour, but from privileges reserved for small industries:

> Advertiser interested in T.V. manufacturing plant, with a view to outright purchase. The plant should be licensed in the small industries sector. Interested parties please reply sharp to box . . .
>
> (*Times of India*, Bombay, 15 May 1977)

This kind of thing is common, especially in electronics where there are tight restrictions on larger units' output. Small firms are often set up to provide for junior family members, or for clients:

> If . . . there was growth in small units, these were broadly of three types. First, there were small-scale units set up by members of family/friends/relatives of entrepreneurs and of professional managers of the large units. These units, in many cases, were 'ancillaries' of large units. Linkages in these cases were more strong in terms of ownership than of processes of production. The policy of 'small is virtuous' boosted the growth of such small-scale units. Additional advantage of small sector of this type was that it facilitated availment of priority allocation of inputs and enabled manipulation through transfer pricing and so on. Many of these units existed only on registers. In any case, 'diffusion' of ownership in these cases was illusory.

The second type of small units were set up on small-scale primarily because of financial constraints; these did not necessarily represent the use of labour-intensive instead of capital-intensive techniques of production. For instance, the use of one multi-purpose machine tool or five powerlooms makes a unit small compared to another using five of such tools or fifty powerlooms. But, compared to a single-purpose machine tool and handloom, the respective techniques were definitely less labour-intensive.

The third type of small units [like handlooms] were small in both these senses, namely they required small capital investment and were labour-intensive. *(Econ. and Pol. Weekly*, 30 July 1977)

Raymond Owens, writing about Howrah, says the relation between small firms and bigger ones which give them orders, loans and materials tends to become outright ownership or partnership:

> As orders pass from factory to factory, so do loans, often in the form of raw materials advances to manufacturers. The more financing a man receives with an order, the lower his profit margin is likely to be, depending also upon his skill in bargaining with the order-supplier and those persons to whom he may job out part or all of the order . . . Men with skill in commercial bargaining may profitably act as order-supplier links in the huge network of relations through which orders are received and manufactured, without even owning a factory. The strong tendency over time is for order-suppliers to become factory owners (prompted by a new law which makes it illegal to order-supply without owning a factory). More passively, a person might simply act as a financial partner of a factory owner and/or order-supplier. (Owens 1973:135)

So far I have painted a picture of almost universal one-way dependence, of small firms on large ones which get all the advantages. Is this perhaps a biased view of the typical relations between large and small firms, or true in some cases only? Another possibility is complementary interdependence, a division of labour between specialized units which benefits both sides and the national economy, involving rational allocation of resources, the best use of locational advantages and of management and entrepreneurial talent, higher employment and the most appropriate levels of labour- and capital-intensity. 'The relationship between large and small enterprises is not always competitive; often small and large enterprises support each other through mutual buying and selling and also through the process of sub-contracting' (Subrahmaniam and Kashyap 1975:95), though the government has had only sporadic success in developing ancillaries.

> The Executive Secretary of the Small-Scale Industries Association in one state depicted the ancillary and subcontracting firms, which make up most of his membership, as a nursery of talent and opportunity, giving technical training

to men who otherwise would not get it (but who are ungrateful enough to leave for higher wages). A small employer cannot afford high wages, but makes up for it by treating workers 'as his own', lending money, taking workers to the doctor in his own car and paying the medical bills – with this close understanding, there is no question of labour disputes. He trains up children from the age of ten if they cannot get to school, 'which itself is a social service' (Subrahmaniam and Kashyap 1975; cf. Marsden, Schumacher *et al.* on the closer human relations in small firms: p. 20 above).

This or something like it (without the justification of child labour) is the theory behind official programmes of help to small industries, especially the encouragement of ancillaries and subcontracting; and there is something in it. The model is Japanese, not the gandhian ideal of self-sufficient village industries. Industrial development must go forward on two legs. Large firms need the specialized flexible services of a thriving small-scale sector. Small firms need the markets and the stimulus to higher quality which only big firms can give. Each kind is said to have its own advantages for labour.

Few people expect market forces alone to replace dependence with interdependence. Government action to do it starts in the government's own public sector factories, which are supposed to buy components wherever possible from small firms, and to help their own employees or others to set up ancillaries to supply the 'parent' firm. Thus A.P. Sharma, Union Minister of State for Industry in 1976, announcing a programme to stimulate sub-contracting and ancillaries, said the growth of ancillaries had been disappointing. Public sector industries with a turnover of Rs 100 000 million a year bought products worth only Rs 360 million from ancillaries: they should encourage employees with entrepreneurial talent to set up ancillary units, and should buy up to half the ancillaries' production (*The Statesman*, 22 Oct. 1976). The most successful example so far is Hindustan Machine Tools in Bangalore, which has an industrial estate for ancillaries set up mainly by its ex-employees to supply the factory itself and other customers. The new Government Electric Factory, also in Bangalore, announced that it was to have an 'ancillary campus' for 100 units with 4000 workers, with a 'raw material bank' to supply critical imported or Indian materials. The 'mother company' would buy at least one shift's production, and: 'The ancillary units, open to small entrepreneurs and technocrats, will be free to diversify production in their second and third shifts and sell the output to other industries' (*Times of India*, 16 Aug. 1977).

It is harder to persuade the private sector to help ancillaries. Restrictions on the factories' licensed capacity are intended to make them buy from small firms (where these firms cannot market their own finished products) but the restrictions can be evaded: one way is to buy up the small firms themselves and not just their products. 'Subcontracting exchanges' exist to put customers in touch with suppliers. The Small Industries Service Institutes, which provide technical advice, training, and some services in their own workshops, reach the recognized ancillaries run by educated men rather than marginal back street workshops. Under various schemes, ancillary units can get loans on preferential terms: again, this accentuates the division between firms which have 'ancillary status' and subcontractors without it. In some ways this is like the distinction between 'permanent' workers entitled to keep their jobs, and 'temporaries' trying to get into the citadel. At a National Workshop on Ancillaries Development in Bangalore, entrepreneurs and officials suggested it was desirable for large firms to 'adopt' small ones as ancillaries – the relationship is regularly compared to that of parents and children – but they hesitated to do so and those who ought to have 'ancillary status' were deprived of it. In some states, only units on industrial estates are recognized as ancillaries. Ancillaries must be carefully selected: entrepreneurs already chosen think they have a right to protection against competition from unrecognized subcontractors.

Even if official programmes to encourage ancillaries and subcontracting have had limited success (and may have the side effect of creating two tiers of small industries), this does not rule out the possibility that the present pattern of relations between large and small firms in industries like engineering is more economically rational, and less exploitative of entrepreneurs or workers or both, than strong dependency theory suggests; alternatively, that the pattern is irrational and exploitative only because market forces, which could bring about a healthy complementary development of firms of different sizes, are inhibited by licensing, subsidies and, above all, indiscriminate import substitution.

Another possibility is that there really are two sectors; small industries are or could be relatively self-sufficient, supplying their own markets; and links with large firms are not so important. Dualism is commonly thought to be a bad thing, but this is what Gandhi wanted when he proposed to his industrialist friends that mills and factories should produce for the cities only, while the rural market should be reserved for handicrafts. A relatively self-sufficient small-scale sector need not consist only of handicrafts: it can use modern machinery, perhaps bought secondhand, and the large firms' by-products or waste as one possible source of raw materials.

Cheap bangles are made almost entirely in small factories for a vast mass market served by small shops and wandering bangle sellers who visit the remotest villages. Cheap metal bangles are quite popular; but glass bangles are in many attractive colours and are traditionally broken and replaced when the bangle seller comes. Bangle making was important for the early growth of the Indian glass industry, but now glass has been partly replaced by plastic. The plastic bangle industry is found mainly in Bombay (the seat of the All India Plastic Bangles Manufacturers Association), Bangalore and Madras.

A former union official employs fifteen to twenty men in a Bangalore suburb, to finish bangles by hand. He gets the moulds from a diemaker who employs two or three men, and the moulding is done at another 'branch' in a nearby town. There is only enough work to keep the factory open for ten months each year.

In Bombay, the film capital of India, old film is scraped clear and rolled tightly round a core to make bangles with coloured patterns. Even the waste from this process is used to make decorations. Bangles from these tiny workshops are sold as far afield as East Africa.

Not only bangles, but the making of toothbrushes and other small plastic goods is almost a cottage industry in and around Bombay, carried on in small rooms by men with one or two moulding machines. But these products seem to be marketed more often through the big firms.

If the small-scale sector is more or less self-sufficient and serves its own markets, the main form of interdependence will be links between small firms: like the plastic workshops and the diemakers who supply moulds. Small firms cluster together partly because each needs innumerable small jobs done by neighbours with spare capacity or time or special machines, often at short notice, within easy walking distance so that the entrepreneur can keep an eye on the work and the materials can be transported in a handcart. In Bombay,

> the machine shops are not only, as a rule, dependent upon casters, blacksmiths and welders who run specialised plants, but also they are often dependent between themselves for a few of their needs connected with drilling, planing, polishing etc. (Lakdawala 1960:248)

Small engineering industries are concentrated in parts of Howrah (near Calcutta) because there is a steady flow of customers who know that multifarious odd jobs can be done somewhere, and because of the facility to start [a workshop] with only a few machines, because other machine jobs could easily be arranged with neighbouring firms. The interdependence between the different units was a remarkable feature of Howrah engineering units. It was this characteristic which induced a skilled craftsman with some little capital to start a shop with the hope, seldom fulfilled, that some day his enterprise might become big.

(A.N. Bose 1978:36, commenting on the Reserve Bank of India (1964) survey)

Yet both Lakdawala and A.N. Bose show that these dense neighbourhood networks of small firms produced finished goods for their own markets, as well as intermediate goods for the big factories they continued to depend on for orders:

The low price of informal sector products matched well, on the one hand, with the demand for mainly cheap, low quality industrial goods from the poorer majority of consumers. It also added to the profits of the large, organised units who could use the cheap labour to produce at low cost more sophisticated goods (as also the cheap products) for sale under their own well known brand names at relatively high prices. Thus, by keeping the poor satisfied with cheap consumption goods, and guaranteeing at the same time an excessive profit for big houses controlling the market, the small units today play an essential role in making the present economic structure function.   (A.N. Bose 1978:64)

To the extent that the small-scale sector is really separate, the large-scale sector may also be relatively self-sufficient, as firms concentrate as many processes as possible within their own factories, or give orders only to other large or medium-sized firms, not to smaller ones. There is some evidence that individual firms, or each sector, tend to self-sufficiency: thus Berna found that even the smallest metal working units in south India had their own foundries, even when these were used for only three months in the year (cited in Subrahmaniam and Kashyap 1975:95). The *Statesman* newspaper, commenting on the slow growth of ancillaries, said that the bigger units had tried to be self-sufficient even where this apparent self-sufficiency was 'self-defeating' (22 Oct. 1976).

One reason why big firms may prefer not to save money by putting out work to subcontractors is the uneven quality of the small industries' products, and the difficulty of maintaining the kind of quality control the big firms' reputation depends on. An ancillary can be watched more closely, but requires some long-term commitment by the bigger firm. Products from a little-known small firm are assumed to be second-rate until they are proved otherwise:

The other day, the writer bought a 40 watt GLS bulb. After a day it fused. When I complained to the dealer, he smiled and said: 'Oh it is quite likely. The bulb you bought was manufactured by a small-scale unit.'

(K.K.G. Nambiar, 'Should small-scale units be propped up?', 1977)

The managing director of a component factory with 150 workers, supplying the two big vehicle factories in Bombay and one in Poona, places no regular orders with small units (though they could supply for Rs 1.75 a part that the firm buys from a medium-sized unit for Rs 2) and sends them components for further processing only when it is urgent and there is no alternative: it is better to ask the firm's own workers to come in after hours and finish the job as a group contract, with one of their number as contractor. The same managing director said a pharmaceutical company could send its compound to a small unit for pressing into pills and packaging, but no good firm would do this because it must guard its reputation for cleanliness. Another car component factory in Bombay, with 200 workers, does most of its own toolmaking and puts out the rest to other organized sector firms: never to small toolrooms, which work to an example rather than a design and may use the wrong steel, so that the tool will not last. The secretary of a trade association said the quality of the small firms' products is uneven, because their workers keep leaving like cooks in a restaurant.

A partner in a much smaller firm with eighteen workers has only two customers, including a big vehicle factory where he worked as an engineer: large firms would not discuss orders with a smaller manufacturer unless they knew him, and even then they sent him a detailed questionnaire. He puts out work to firms with specialized machines, but almost always to bigger firms as a precaution – in the vehicle industry quality is more important than price unless you supply 'the market', that is replacement parts only: garages fit these dubious parts and pass them off as genuine parts from the manufacturer.

In a case like this, the firm at the top of the chain – the vehicle assembly factory – can afford to deal directly with selected small suppliers, because its reputation is solid: a medium-sized firm lower down the chain would risk its own reputation and its vital link with the assembly plant.

So there is some tendency, especially in industries like motor vehicles with a very expensive product, for large- and small-scale industries to form themselves into two closed sectors: but there are very strong countervailing advantages for a large firm in using the specialized services and cheap labour available in smaller units, and these smaller units also supply their own markets with a wide range of goods – consumer goods for the poor, as well as for the middle classes.

A chain of dependence, tempered by complex technical and financial interdependence at every level, would be a better image of the relations between *firms* than that of two sectors. But it is a mistake to assume that firms of the same size (or rather, their owners) all occupy the same place in the chain: some have much more bargaining power than others. For example:

> The implications of the sub-contracting and product linkages between workshops and factories in Coimbatore are not homogeneous, and there is a good deal of variation in the extent of subordination and exploitation which is involved, depending, of course, upon the bargaining power of different workshops. Some workshops have bargaining power by virtue of providing specialised services, and others by virtue of having secure access to finance.
> (Harriss 1982:998)

Workers in a strong firm may be in a weak position, depending on their terms of employment and degree of union organization. If there is a chain of dependence, the workers' place in it may have little relation to the places occupied by their employers.

The examples of linkages between firms which follow, drawn mainly from my field experience, do not suggest a dual economy, but a complex network of interdependence both between firms of similar size, and between large and small firms, in which the bigger firm is not always in the stronger position.

Linkages

This is not a systematic account of linkages between firms or industries, but some examples to show how the industrial economy creates job opportunities, secure or insecure, well or badly paid. I start with 'industries' like chemicals or electronics, defined by their products. Whatever other linkages there may be across 'industry' boundaries, one linkage is always with the engineering and toolroom trades. Engineering is the foundation, or at least one pillar, on which all the industries are built. Every firm must employ people with these skills or have access to a toolroom to maintain the machinery, if for nothing else.

First the *automobile* or motor vehicle industry, which is all engineering and where linkages are strong and complex. For practical purposes there were only two Indian car manufacturers in 1976–7: Premier in Bombay (making a version of the Fiat) and Birla's

firm Hind Motors (making Ambassadors) in Calcutta.[1] Output was
very low because the market, though captive, was small: few Indians
could afford cars, and those who could would have bought up-to-date
foreign models if imports had been allowed. It is hard to see how
India, with its engineering industry and skilled labour, should not
have a successful car industry supplying world markets: the Indian
car industry is a standing example of the dangers of indiscriminate
import substitution and oligopoly.

In contrast to cars, Indian trucks, buses and scooters are not only
more in demand and better suited to the country's needs, but better
made, and exportable. Indian components for cars and other vehicles
are good, and widely exported. However in 1976–7 demand for
vehicles of all kinds had not recovered from the recession that
followed the rise in oil prices. Major factories shared the work among
their permanent workers: Hind Motors, for example, stopped
ordering parts from workshops in Howrah.

To start with the assembly plants: a Bombay factory with 4400
well-paid workers makes Jeeps and small trucks. It buys leaf springs,
steering wheels, spark plugs, dashboard instruments etc. from well-
known independent factories, and other parts from ancillaries
(castings from Madras, though the firm has its own foundry). A few
parts, like a bush, come from local firms employing perhaps six men.

A Faridabad firm with 5600 workers (less well paid, no recognized
union) in six factories makes tractors, motor cycles and machinery.
Sixty per cent of vehicle components (tractor parts, sheet metal,
machining, plastic and rubber components, castings and forgings)
come from ancillaries, including 270 in Faridabad, mostly set up by
ex-employees with the company's help and sometimes a loan: these
generally employ 20–30 workers (a few have up to 200). Both the
company and ancillaries give job work (finishing etc.) to very small
firms. Some 800 local firms depend on the company.

A Bombay firm employing 190 workers makes electrical components (like voltage regulators): 15 per cent for vehicle manufacturers, 60 per cent for replacements, 25 per cent for export. As the
market is stagnant, the firm is diversifying into staplers and stationery
goods. The work is simple except in the toolroom: 10 per cent of the

---

[1] Elsewhere I have concealed the names of firms and people, to protect confidentiality. All I
know about these two firms is public knowledge: but I cannot hide the identities of some big
firms I visited, and I have had to leave out anything which was or might have been told to me
in confidence. Some unions are also easy to identify. In some cases I describe firms as making
'components' etc. because to name the product could identify the firm.

toolmaking is done outside, always in the organized sector for quality. Otherwise the firm sends out little work: some employees moonlight in their own workshops, and at least one takes electrical coils home for his large family to wind.

I mentioned a middle-sized component firm with stronger linkages in both directions (p. 120 above). Another Bombay firm with 100 workers turns out a wide variety of parts, mainly die castings in metal or plastic for three vehicle factories, and such things as television camera casings. It uses its own toolroom to make moulds and dies for other firms, and produces intermediate goods like sheet metal and plastics. Much of the work is hand assembly of components – individual orders are not big enough to justify an assembly line. Parts and materials are bought in from some twenty firms: metals from two very big companies; rubber parts from a 'sister' (family owned?) factory with eighty workers; small turned parts and pressings from firms with under ten workers, also plastic parts too small for the company's own machines; high quality brass parts from Jamnagar in Gujarat, where they cost half the Bombay price.

The owner buys some plastic parts from a relative in an older part of Bombay, whom I found in a tiny office attached to some other workshop. At first he said he had no plastic factory, then called a worker to guide me through a maze of tiny workshops to a shed with four moulding machines – operated, the worker told me, by from four to seven people in shifts. At the time, he was filling the machine with powder, watching the clock for two minutes, and pressing out car radio knobs one at a time, helped only by a woman who finished each piece by hand.

In the same area, another relative has a narrow shed packed with German and Indian automatic machinery and some hand-operated machines. His eight workers make 'precision components' of brass, steel and aluminium for many engineering firms, including I think the die-casting factory. A single order takes more than a fortnight to finish. He gives jobs like slotting and threading bolts to units round about, with two or three workers – this is the only way to make a profit – and his own workers will employ one or two men on small machines in houses or gateways.

Other firms belong to branches of this family, probably including the rubber factory and some trading concerns. Economic linkages between firms are inseparable from kinship ties within or between property-owning joint families.

I have traced some linkages down from vehicle assembly plants to small engineering and component firms. These do not serve urban markets alone. Cars may be a luxury, but not tractors. The same kinds of firms and skills supply agricultural equipment like pumpsets, which even small farmers now depend on.

In the *plastic* industry linkages are much simpler, because most products are finished consumer goods which a small unit can make with semi-skilled labour. The firm needs a constant supply of raw material (powder or granules) which can usually be had from several suppliers, though there are shortages which hold up work. The machines need servicing. The two critical linkages are with diemakers – skilled engineering workers – and the market.

As Streefkerk says, a small plastic firm's success 'is determined only partially by the quality of the product' (1979:106; see p. 92 above): the important thing is to know middlemen who can get the product on to the retail market, and this favours far-flung families with manufacturing and trading interests. Yet quality does make a difference, especially if the firm want to tap both the market for finished consumer goods, and for inputs to other industries like electronics, cars or pharmaceuticals.

Streefkerk continues: 'Since all the machines are almost the same the quality of the products cannot differ to any great extent' (ibid.), but this is not always true. The quality depends largely on the moulds or dies, which are expensive, and a good diemaker can give an entrepreneur the edge in a competitive market.

A small plastic firm will not have full-time work for a diemaker. The work is usually done by specialized firms which may also supply dies and tools to engineering firms making pressed components; freelance diemakers working at home; engineering firms or bigger plastic firms with idle toolroom capacity (a small unit may order from a bigger one); or quite often an engineering firm closely linked to the plastic firm and next door to it. Sometimes the two main linkages are combined, when a firm ordering plastic components lends its own moulds to be sure of the quality.

A Bombay tool and die maker employing ten workers, a proud self-made man with no formal qualifications (see p. 102), has a bank loan for his machinery and rents his shed, I think from the plastic firm which occupies the rest of the building and which buys all its moulds from him. He also supplies other factories.

The plastic factory (divided into two 'small-scale industries' on paper but operated as a unit) has eighty workers, making water meter boxes, buckets, beakers etc., for sale through an exclusive agent.

The factory owner is a typical financier–industrialist; the tool and die maker, a technician – another example of the complementary relationship between these two types of entrepreneurs.

Two brothers jointly own a Bombay engineering firm with eighty workers and a plastic firm with forty, in the same building. Their main product is electric torches – about 10 per cent for export (though they can no longer sell in the Gulf, where people can afford 'quality products' instead of cheap ones), and they do engineering jobs for other firms. Twenty-five per cent of the torch parts (rivets etc.) are bought from smaller firms.

Independent tool and die makers also supply small engineering firms which make pressings or need machine parts and tools.

A young Bangalore man, trained by a foreign company, not only makes dies and tools in a tiny home workshop but acts as agent for the big factories' purchasing officers, putting them in touch with small workshops. The orders (which he showed me) come through him; he makes the dies and lends them to the workshops, then takes them back for future use. He claims to do this for seven workshops (including one owned by his brother) employing sixty people altogether: I first met him in one of these, and again coming out of a plastic sandal factory.

Anyone can start a plastic factory if he has contacts to sell the product and money for the machines, which are easy to operate; but he may need a good diemaker – a man with a small firm or even working alone – more than the diemaker needs him. The tool and diemaker's skill is still in demand, and not only from the plastic industry.

The *chemical and pharmaceutical* industry is also fairly self-contained. Raw materials, especially petrochemicals, come from the biggest companies or from abroad. Some small pharmaceutical firms make ingredients for drugs, but in general each pharmaceutical factory makes up its own compounds, packages and markets them, buying packaging materials and plastics (ampoules etc.) from the small firms. The firms buy some electrical and electronic equipment; and since they may not have their own toolrooms to maintain and renew the machinery, this job is sometimes given to small workshops.

Small firms engaged in *repair and maintenance* serve both large and small firms: like 'Shriidhar Tools', the Bangalore tool-sharpening enterprise (p. 94), or this firm in Faridabad:

Two partners employ twenty-two (officially 'nine') men in their toolroom. Both were skilled factory workers, whose firm sent them to Germany for training. Eight years ago they set up their own firm to do repair and maintenance for big factories in Faridabad, Delhi and Bombay where they had contracts: mainly fabricating machine parts which would take months to order from abroad (and would cost more after customs duties, presumably). Usually they have a few weeks notice of a replacement job, but they also act as an 'ambulance', rushing to fix a broken part – managers will come to their houses at night, asking them to start at once in order to keep the machines running. They say their success depends – after their 'Satguru' or religious teacher – on their reputation for quick service. Now their spare parts for one foreign machine are exported, under a bigger company's name; and they are developing another part they plan to sell and export under their own name.

The Indian *electronic* industry is conventionally divided into consumer electronics (mainly radios), instruments (for factories and laboratories), components and hardware (technically specialized components like circuit boards); also computers, but in 1976–7 the computer industry had not yet had much impact on the smaller firms I studied. Further development of the electronic industry is reserved in principle for small industries, while the big (largely multinational) factories can continue limited production: they are mainly assembly and testing plants, buying components and sub-assemblies from firms of all sizes, producing the most sought-after consumer goods and almost the only exportable ones because of their reputation for quality. At SEEPZ (the Santacruz Electronic Export Processing Zone) firms producing for export only are allowed free imports, and bring in even foreign screws and nuts: only labour, and a small amount of Indian components, cross the high wire fence from Bombay.

The instrument sector produces limited quantities, often to order and from small units, each employing perhaps twenty workers and run by an engineer–entrepreneur developing a special line for which there may be little competition within India. Sales depend on quality and specialization, also contacts (for example, with hospital administrators). Designs are often foreign ones adapted to Indian conditions and materials, but customers' requirements pose new problems calling forth ingenuity and innovation; and there is some genuinely original design. Though the firm buys standard components, it is common to find design, fabrication, welding, assembly and other work going on in the same shed.

This is a relatively small sector but important, not only for medicine and science but for other industries, which need more and more testing and sensing instruments, temperature control equipment etc.: as one manufacturer said, even small-scale industries now buy his instruments, because light bulbs – for example – are unsaleable unless they are tested (but see the shopkeeper's low opinion of these bulbs, p. 119).

Consumer electronics means, above all, radios (in a village or working class neighbourhood it is a public service to turn one's radio up to full volume); also television, tape recorders, calculators etc. for those who can afford them. In this much bigger sector of electronics there is a longer chain: at the top, big or middle-sized firms (from 1800 workers down to perhaps 60, including some in the favoured category of 'small industries') known to consumers and in touch with the retail trade; and below them, manufacturers of sub-assemblies and often tiny components like transistors and rivets, made in every kind of unit down to the smallest workshops; by technology ranging from automatic processes in controlled conditions to hand-operated presses and monotonous hand assembly by rows of girls, and with different combinations of the steps in production under each roof. Many of these small engineering or plastic firms also or mainly supply manufacturers outside the electronic industry.

Because of the great variety of firms and technical processes, it is much harder to generalize about linkages in electronics than in plastics or cars. The nominal restriction of the larger firms' capacity certainly gives investors a motive to set up or take over 'small-scale industries' as part of a plan involving other enterprises; and although electronics is seen as an ideal industry for dispersed small-scale development (as in the plan to make Kerala India's 'electronic state'), there are great advantages for small suppliers in staying close to the assembly plants, when so much depends on personal contacts and special orders to be filled quickly.

Everyone in the industry agrees that it is becoming more competitive: customers no longer buy all that the manufacturers can make (the same with cars). This must strengthen the well-known assembly houses; their goods have a reputation for quality, and often cost no more than those marketed by small firms.

Tracing linkages industry by industry may lay too much stress on hierarchy, a chain of dependence with the top firmly in the hands of big producers and financial and trading interests, and each link supported by the one above it. A better image might be not a chain but a net hanging down – still held by a few powerful hands at the top and ragged at the very bottom, but with strong horizontal connexions between knots in the main part of the net; and these knots are the small and middle-sized firms.

Small firms produce finished goods, and have the problem of selling them. They also supply components and services to the big firms, and to each other. I mentioned the interdependence between small engineering units in Bombay and Howrah (pp. 118–19). These horizontal linkages are densest in neighbourhoods where small firms in different 'industries' cluster together. Though their owners work hard, they are constantly in and out of each other's premises, to talk business or just to keep in touch. Some have valuable connexions with big manufacturers and traders, or with small industrialists elsewhere in the city. So I saw the same faces again and again as I visited small firms in Bangalore: a scooter would pull up in the street, and an entrepreneur from some other suburb or industrial estate would appear in the doorway, holding his crash helmet on his arm in a curious knightly gesture.

'Bayann'a street' runs through a working-class suburb of Bangalore, and has its own micro-economy of small units, constantly taking in work from one another.

Several of these have already been mentioned. 'Naaraayan'a' the silk screen printer, who has installed equipment to anodize aluminium plates, is concentrating more and more on supplying the electronics and electrical goods industries (pp. 98–9).

Beside his workshop is a shed where an ex-factory worker operates an aluminium polishing machine. Naaraayan'a pays him for the work done, usually about Rs 250 a month, less Rs 100 for use of the shed, the machine and power. With outside work, Naaraayan'a reckons that this man makes a profit of Rs 400 a month after paying for materials, and may take on a helper (I was unable to check).

Two of Naaraayan'a's customers are next door, in a row of one-storey concrete sheds. He prints letters and figures on plastic for a plastic moulding firm with eight workers, owned by a toolmaker 'Diipak' and a partner, which mainly supplies the electronic and electrical industries, especially ancillaries of the public sector firm Indian Telephone Industries. Diipak has also designed and patented a plastic mechanical calendar, which is sold both through dealers on the retail market, and to companies which order calendars bearing their own name to give away as advertisements. When I first visited the workshop, they had no orders except for the calendar, and had done no moulding for three days because of a powder shortage.

Diipak, without the partner, has his own toolmaking firm with four workers in the next shed or room. He makes all the dies for the plastic firm, and supplies press tools, jigs and dies, also to ancillaries of the big factories. All his machining except milling, all cylindrical work, buffing and grinding are done by other small firms; including a workshop lower down the sloping street, where a man with one machine employs two or three boys or young men (the number varies) to buff metal or plastic.

Almost next door to that workshop, a printer with six employees (including three part-timers) prints invoices, advertisements etc. for Diipak and other local businessmen.

Diipak has two sheds in the row. The next two are occupied by closely linked firms. The bigger one belongs to two partners employing eight workers, who make transformers for factories; assemble instruments like rectifiers for sale by a friend who has a slightly bigger instrument factory down the street; and supply some turned parts to order. Sheet metal and simple transformer clamps come from outside. The other firm is a partnership between the same two men and a third, working together without employees: they assemble control panels for a crane factory, using their own transformers and other parts from big electrical firms. Naaraayan'a prints the metal panels and labels for both firms.

These partners supply rivets to a man, formerly an unemployed electronic engineer, who employs five workers making aluminium furniture in the same compound as Naaraayan'a's workshop. He hires a buffing machine, but all other work is done by hand – cutting out the plastic covering, bending the tubes in a simple machine and making holes for the rivets. He takes 'labour orders' from dealers, who supply all materials except small parts like plastic bushes for chair legs, which he buys from a firm with three workers in the next street. He complains that the dealers get all the profit; he relies on his industrialist friends to spread his name, and hopes to market his own products.

A grocer with a general store at the top of Bayann'a street also runs an optical grinding workshop with a partner, working for opticians: not very successfully, since he cannot keep skilled workers, who earn more than twice as much elsewhere.

In a neighbouring street, 'Raajan's' electronic ancillary (p. 110) – totally dependent on one multinational company – gives jobs like fabrication and painting mild steel plates to local firms. Naaraayan'a makes his printed circuits.

But in a shed behind Raajan's factory, the engineer who employs fifteen men to make precision pressings (p. 102) works for the big factories and gets his materials on the open market. The only job he sends out is electroplating, to a firm on an industrial estate. The neighbourhood suits him, not because he needs the other firms but because he can find workers who live within easy walking distance – on what he pays them, he says, they could not afford the bus.

Yet Bangalore is a relatively prosperous place. The little economy of
Bayann'a street, and innumerable areas like it in Bangalore or
Bombay or Poona, provides jobs at low but fairly regular wages, in
bearable conditions, to a large part of the city's population, including
women. This is the middle of the net, not the bottom.

The bottom is destitution, begging, crime, ragpicking; or foul work
like cleaning sewers or sorting scrap and broken glass in tiny sheds
along the railway line which bounds Dharavi slum in Bombay. These
activities are often well organized (though far outside the 'organized
sector').

Amrita Abraham (1979, 'Violence in a Bombay slum') describes
Dharavi's 'business area', where scrap merchants employ south
Indian labourers to recycle waste from the factories and mills: some of
these merchants have invested in a tower block of flats. Ragpicking 'is
the bottom end of the scrap business, but even here competition is
fierce' (:1789): an efficient mafia beats up ragpickers who try to take
their scrap elsewhere.

On a patch of open land in the same area, sewage workers and their families
put up makeshift huts of wood, matting and plastic sheets, which the
municipality clears away from time to time: then they start again. These are
mostly south Indians, more men than women, and at least one I met was a
leper. They do seasonal work not for the municipality (which pays its own
sweepers better) but for contractors, who pay Rs 7 or 8 a day: though a trade
union worker told me the municipality pays the contractors Rs 15 for each
man-day.

Sudhendu Mukherjee (1975) gives statistics and biographical sketches of
Calcutta pavement-dwellers. He describes an economy and way of family
life based on begging, ragpicking, casual labour and prostitution. Eighty-
one per cent live in families, and their conditions differ widely: 'The New
Market area is the "secluded preserve" of the most privileged among the
pavement-dwellers' (:5).

These people live off the leftovers of the industrial economy, as an
alternative to the rural poverty most have escaped from. Some of the
services they provide are valuable or necessary to the city and its
industry. Compare the slum-dwellers of Madras:

> they perform menial tasks essential in Madras. They pull the carts used in the
> transportation of goods. They work as coolies in construction projects. They
> sweep the streets and clean latrines. They collect garbage. In return for the
> advantages they seek under the patronage systems they develop, they back

those who help, with their enthusiasm, votes and other supports [*sic*]. They buy things. They attend festival celebrations . . .   (Wiebe 1978:26)

Then there is a vast floating population of migrant casual labourers, not beggars but men, women and children who work for wages when they can: they are neither urban nor rural but constantly on the move, going to town for building work or to the country for the harvest, walking or travelling without tickets on the train.

Between these lower depths and the small firms on Bayann'a street there is a whole range of ways in which settled urban families make a living of sorts, pay the rent, eat regularly and send their children to school: by working at home, working part-time, working as a 'helper' for practically no pay but learning the job and making contacts, living off relatives for long periods on the understanding that they will help them in return when their luck changes. These people attach themselves to the ragged bottom edge of the net of linkages between firms or employers, wherever and for as long as they can, and try to climb higher.

Making bidis or country cigarettes is one of the biggest home industries. Bidis were made in factories until around the time of Independence, when Factory Acts and minimum wages caused employers to change to a putting-out system. Now most work is done at home by women, also by men and of course children.

In a Poona factory worker's house, four women (neighbours, I think) sat together rolling bidis for up to ten hours at a stretch – hard work which makes the back ache. Each expected to make 1000 bidis a day and to earn Rs 5: in Bangalore the rates were similar.

There are still bidi factories, without machinery: employment is largely seasonal, and is falling. Workers have no protection or fringe benefits ('The combined cost on account of all social security contributions works out to a small sum of Re 0.01 per man-day worked . . .'! Labour Bureau 1971a:53), though there have been attempts to tighten the law. A union leader estimates that only 200 000 of India's 2 million bidi workers are covered by the Factory Act.

Anil Avachat (1978) describes the appalling conditions in some of these factories, owned by 'tobacco barons' who moved into Karnataka state to escape the relatively strict labour laws of Maharashtra.

A few trade unionists have tried to organize both the factory workers and the home workers, with little success. It is hard to see what kind of industrial action would be possible or effective.

A.N. Bose (1978:106–21) gives case studies of very poor Calcutta families who live by making garments at home, or by-products, like washers from waste leather. Some electrical and electronic components can be assembled at home, and fitted in with the housework: this can be a family's only support, or a source of extra income – one which regular employees are better able to get. I mentioned one worker in an electrical factory who takes coils home for his large family to wind (p. 123): under the bed they keep a stock of unfinished coils from this and other factories (the same man is union representative; contractor on behalf of a co-operative to which the factory management handed over the canteen; and I think – from his neighbour's comments – a moneylender).

Home workers are not always poor, exploited or dependent, though most are. Some are skilled workers who can make a fair living as independent entrepreneurs, with no expensive equipment and few or no employees: like the Bangalore tool and die maker who acts as intermediary between the big factories and engineering workshops (p. 125). Similarly carpenters are among the exceptions to the rule that anyone offered a permanent job will take it; largely because so many carpenters have gone to the Persian Gulf that they are in short supply (in Kerala, even barbers are said to be scarce for the same reason).

Thus the same person can make a living by being involved in several economic relationships, holding a different formal status in each one: full-time employee, part-timer moonlighting or doing a second job in the evenings, home worker on piecework rates, contractor or agent, small entrepreneur employing other workers. Formal status is one thing; real dependence or need is another, when the person you employ can sometimes name his price. Generally but not always, the stronger your foothold in the big organized sector firms, or the better your contacts there, the more control you will have over your own economic life and over other people.

Where the small firms are

By small firms I mean urban firms employing wage labour and supplying the markets for manufactured goods, directly or through linkages with other firms. The 'unorganized sector' includes most of them, besides petty trade and services, and activities which might be called unproductive or parasitic or criminal (see Joshi 1976a:51–7 on Bombay's unorganized sector).

Most of these firms are probably also 'small-scale industries' (i.e. below the investment limit) though some 'small-scale industries' are bogus or are parts of much larger holdings registered as small-scale industries to get concessions. As Panini shows (1977:102), many small employers never register because they want as little as possible to do with officials.

In 1974, 35 per cent of registered small-scale industries were concentrated in eighteen towns, mostly large ones.[2] Varanasi (Bernares) led with 11 173; but Bombay with 10 027 was well ahead if one adds the neighbouring town of Thana, making a total of 17 366 without counting the rest of the Bombay area. Calcutta (without Howrah) came next with 9621, then Ludhiana in Punjab with 8461. Bangalore came sixteenth with only 2611, which is absurd.

An earlier report (1968) showed that three quarters of small industries were in eight states.[3] Motor vehicle repair shops led all other branches of industry in the number of units, in employment, productive capacity and value added. The ten major branches (repair shops, chemicals, rubber, cycle manufacture, non-metallic minerals, basic chemicals, clays, motor vehicles, leather and glass) accounted for 75 per cent of small-scale units and 77 per cent of small-scale employment. 'Chemicals' (as distinct from 'basic chemicals') probably includes pharmaceuticals; but industries that have grown fast in towns like Bombay, Bangalore and Faridabad are not on the list: plastics, electronics, electrical goods, engineering components (except perhaps under 'cycle manufacture' and 'motor vehicles').

Defining and counting small-scale industries is such an uncertain business that official figures must be used with caution. They may be a rough guide to the distribution of small firms, though local factors may make for over- or under-registration. Local studies – which I have added to from my own observation – give a better picture of the small firms' environment, and help to show how far physical conditions of work within an industry vary with the size of firms. I say more about working conditions and the daily routine later, and about differences in wages.

Bombay is a long narrow peninsula, originally islands. The southern tip is the old Fort area, occupied by offices and shops and housing. To the north is the main nineteenth-century mill area: great

---

[2] Development Commissioner, Small Scale Industries, 1974, quoted in 'Small-scale industries: structure and growth trends', *Economic Times*, 25 May 1974.

[3] 'Eight states account for 76 per cent of small units', *Economic Times*, 1 July 1974, which refers to 'the ASI report for 1968'.

grim stone buildings set among chawls or tenement blocks and single-storey slums; with the fashionable Malabar Hill to the west, and to the east the docks facing the mainland across the bay, and some large old engineering works. Conditions in the mill slums appear to have changed little since Broughton and Burnett-Hurst wrote in the 1920s (pp. 55–6 above), but it is no longer true that 'Probably in no industrial city in the world are conditions as bad as in Bombay' (Broughton 1924:180): Calcutta is worse.

To the north of this mill area, where the peninsula widens gradually, the city has spread along and then between two main railway lines which run nearly parallel, as the middle classes moved into new suburbs that were soon overtaken by large and small industrial development and by slums like Dharavi: a process which continues since the 1960s among the hills at the northern end of the peninsula and on the mainland, as towns like Thana are swallowed up by ribbon development. In an attempt to turn the congested linear city into a polycentric more habitable place, the state government is building another city and port, New Bombay, to house two million on the mainland coast opposite Bombay, between the Tarapur nuclear research and power station and a petrochemical complex to be supplied by the offshore oil industry.

The old mill and dock area supported a mass of small workshops and trading firms, and people stayed in the slums because of the variety of job opportunities in these small firms (Royal Commission 1931b:370, quoted on p. 56 above). The firms are still there, though the technologies have changed. Firms cannot expand in this grossly overcrowded area. Nor can they afford to move out and break the intricate linkages between them which Lakdawala describes (p. 118 above). He gives the example of the Kumbharwada area

> where the gains of agglomeration arising out of clustering of interdependent units are most rampant and which, according to some, has a unique locational advantage of a central place in the city, with the hardware market to the south and the factory customers to its north . . . The economic advantages accruing to units located in the Kumbharwada area arise mainly due to a close clustering of interdependent units than due to any other reason. And this type of interdependence of units, though independent in all other ways, offers, in part, advantages similar to the ones enjoyed by vertically integrated plants run under a single ownership and management, and works in a way that makes the individual shifting of the units outside the area an uneconomic proposition.
> (Lakdawala and Sandesara 1960:252–3)

I described a visit to two firms in a similar nearby area: a tiny plastic workshop, and an engineering firm with automatic machinery crammed into a narrow shed (p. 123), surrounded by small engineering firms, car repair workshops, a one-room 'shoelace factory' etc.

This is a dynamic inventive local economy, linked at innumerable points to the city's industry and commerce. Contrast it with the kinds of economic activity in Dharavi, the enormous slum to the north: dealers in scrap metal, bottles and broken glass, waste paper and rags, in the 'business area' by the railway (p. 130); petty trade and services dependent on incomes earned outside the slum, with those in permanent jobs as a local aristocracy, the people one approaches for a loan or help in finding work; a man making springs and washers at home, with hand tools which cost him Rs 3000. Local producers seem to depend entirely on a few outside customers, not on linkages with each other. Anyone with wider ambitions must find premises elsewhere, for 'who would buy things from a place like this?' (p. 104; cf. Desai and Pillai 1972 on another Bombay slum, Golibar).

But the main concentration of new industries – large, middle-sized and small firms in engineering, chemicals and pharmaceuticals, plastics, electronics, rubber etc. – is further out, around the airport, among the hills to the north, and on the mainland especially in the 'Thana–Belapur belt'. Rice and vegetable fields and buffalo sheds are hemmed in by factory walls, rows of small workshops, blocks of flats with patchy concrete walls discoloured by the monsoon, old villages, colonies of working-class houses on paved lanes with underground drainage, shading into the real slums, hutments and shacks without sanitation, the homeless in makeshift shelters of sticks and plastic sheeting or in concrete pipes which lie by the road ready for use. In this area people expect to travel long distances to work, by train or bus, since both men and women in a family must take jobs wherever they can find them: in factories if they are lucky, otherwise in small workshops by the roadside or in the 'industrial estates' which have sprung up all over north Bombay: not only the government industrial estates where landscaped access roads lead to well-built factory sheds, of different sizes but all provided with drainage and services, for the more successful small firms; but also the many private 'industrial estates' which are really industrial slums, where small firms find premises they can afford.

The private 'industrial estates' are an extraordinary sight: usually three-storied concrete buildings, spread out with little order or plan across the ravaged hilly landscape among slums and fields and polluted streams, they are put up by speculators, by factory owners with extra space, or sometimes by small businessmen's co-operatives with rows of small sheds or rooms on each floor. With the constant movement of goods and people, the concrete stairs and balconies crumble, and are often blocked by piles of rubbish and packing materials which are a fire hazard; the pounding of machinery shakes the building; the common lavatories and washrooms stink; and industrial waste is sometimes (not always) thrown into the space between buildings. Usually there is a canteen where workers can buy lunch and hot drinks. 'The working conditions in these industries, mostly located in large industrial estates, are so [*sic*] appalling. Children and women working beyond twelve hours, filthy working conditions, all safety measures being ignored, not to speak of bonus and ex-gratia payments' (Kumar Ketkar, 1977). Conditions in a few private industrial estates, and in many units in the others, are much better than this picture suggests.

All this is new. When I first went to Bombay in 1959 – not as an anthropologist – the hilly country to the north was mostly unspoilt and beautiful, with only villages and commuter suburbs around the railway stations. The industrial expansion since then happened in spite of official efforts to limit congestion and to direct industrial growth away from the city.

Small entrepreneurs must be physically close to their markets and suppliers; not so much because of transport costs, but because so much depends on inside information, and close personal contacts with other small businessmen and with officers in the larger firms. Employers complain that Bombay is crowded and expensive, workers are militant and overpaid, and working premises are hard to find; yet they cannot afford to move to a small town or rural area where they would be isolated and forgotten. Some have tried and been disappointed, though it is easier for some financier–entrepreneurs to move their investments out of the city if they have relatives who can maintain a base and a listening-post there. It is even harder to set up completely new firms away from the main industrial centres in an industry like engineering or plastics: government marketing agencies cannot compensate for the lack of informal links and information about opportunities. It is the large firms, not the small, which can set up branches in small towns or even in isolated rural areas: Hindustan Lever, Tata or the Atul complex of chemical factories set down in a rural area of Gujarat.

The obvious contrast, again, is between Bombay's dynamism and the nearly stagnant economy of Calcutta, where each brief recovery was cancelled out by a new disaster – rural famine, floods of refugees, recession or civil strife.

I have described the industrial history of Calcutta and its twin city Howrah across the Hooghly river, and the peculiar ethnic geography determined by the work available to each group of migrants when they first arrived (pp. 57–62): a pattern which seems to have changed much less than in Bombay, because in Calcutta job-seekers were largely shut out from all kinds of work except perhaps the one where their own group was entrenched. The Bengali commuters still commute; other people live near the places where they work or hope to find work.

Pockets of small industry are found all over Calcutta but especially in Howrah, where the dense network of interdependent small engineering firms has been dominated from the start by the Bengali Mahisya caste, both as employers and workers (see pp. 58, 115 above; and A.N. Bose 1978, a recent book about these small units and their relations with factories). In parts of Howrah, like Liluah, Dasnagar and especially the Belilios road and the narrow lanes leading off it, small factories behind high walls or foundries sending out flames visible far away, stand among workshops in simple sheds open to the street. A passer-by – dodging bicycles, handcarts laden with iron bars or finished parts and the occasional lorry – can watch the whole work process. Men turn roughly finished machine components on lathes – evidently a big order from a factory, since so many workshops on the street are making the same thing. Carpenters' shops. A shed where men and boys work on steel chests and pipes, using an oxy-acetylene torch: a pair of thin legs emerges from a pipe, followed by a small boy pulling something through the pipe on a string, while another frightened boy still inside shouts instructions and asks for light. Men make big springs, probably for vehicles, by heating rods on an open fire in the middle of a shed, removing them with tongs and winding them round an upright bar – no one wears gloves or protective clothing. Young boys work everywhere. Near by are workers' houses, shacks for the very poor, and a few solid two-storey houses for the local middle class, or dilapidated old mansions; a few coconut trees in the open spaces, and ponds contaminated by sewage and industrial waste – women wash clothes in a pond while water oozes from piles of iron shavings on the edge – ration shops with long queues, and many smaller shops and stalls; as well as schools, banks, doctors' clinics, temples and a 'Home for dying destitutes'. Trains rush past whistling to clear people from the line. A bleak place – perhaps like English towns in the early industrial revolution – but one where most people appear to have work and food and hope, and there is some animation on the streets; then one turns a corner into a tiny patch of tranquillity and beauty left over from village days, a clump of trees, cows and a temple. After the bastis or dense slums in other parts of Calcutta and Howrah, where life is more precarious and the economic base even narrower, the Belilios road seems almost a place fit to live in. (If my account seems highly coloured, one cannot write about Calcutta without emotion.)

In middle-sized towns like Bangalore, Poona, Ludhiana or Faridabad, the small engineering and manufacturing firms lie scattered everywhere in working- or lower-middle-class suburbs, in long rows of sheds along the main roads or on government industrial estates, or in back streets where workers and often their employers live in solidly built small houses, occasionally rising to two storeys, among shops and cafés: not in the slums – where there are other kinds of economic activity but most people go outside for casual work – but in places like 'Bayann'a street' in Bangalore (pp. 128–9 above) where small employers are in close everyday contact, many have direct links with the big factories as well, and they can pass on extra work to their neighbours or get specialized jobs done quickly. The sheds may be purpose-built and rented out, or set up in private houses: as in Faridabad, where many houses built with government aid for refugees from Pakistan have been converted into workshops by their owners or rented out to entrepreneurs. In the back streets of old Poona, fine ornate old merchants' houses and temples stand among the dwellings of industrial workers or entrepreneurs who extend their little workshops into the courtyards of their houses – a neighbourhood of small engineering firms, men making steel chests with hand tools only, a sweet factory, ten men doing machine embroidery and making children's clothes in an upstairs room. In Lakshminarayanapuram, a bleak new industrial suburb of Bangalore, the workers' houses are between toolrooms, weaving sheds with power-looms or handlooms employing child labour, and bigger engineering factories divided up to avoid the Factory Act.

These are also the areas where most employees of the big factories

Table 1. *Employment (mainly in the organized sector) by industry divisions, 1974*

Industry division		Employment	%
0	Agriculture (including plantations), hunting, forestry and fishing	1 129 000	6
1	Mining and quarrying	740 000	4
2 & 3	Manufacturing	5 206 000	27
4	Electricity, gas and water	579 000	3
5	Construction	1 118 000	6
6	Wholesale and retail trade, restaurants and hotels	767 000	4
7	Transport, storage and communications	2 390 000	12
8 & 9	Services	7 350 000	38
	Total	19 280 000	100

Source: Based on Labour Bureau 1976:54

live, except the minority with subsidized houses in factory townships. Workers in the small engineering and manufacturing firms – like those who make bidis or assemble electronic components at home – are the neighbours of 'organized sector' workers, often their relatives, or dependants supplementing the household income.

How many work in each 'sector'?

In 1971 (the year of the last census before my fieldwork) India's population was about 548 million. A quarter were 'urban'; one-third (114m) were 'workers', mostly in agriculture; 6m were engaged in household industries and 11m (one-tenth of the whole work force) in 'other' industry. There were 5m factory workers (Labour Bureau 1976).

The size of the 'organized sector' is easy to estimate. By 1974, 19m people were in 'employment', including 12.5m in the public sector. All the public sector workers and the great majority of the rest were in the organized sector, and probably most had permanent jobs. There are no figures for units with less than ten workers, and 89 per cent of public sector workers are shown as working in units employing 25 or more.

The figures for private sector employment are suspect: for example, total employment rose by 18 per cent between 1967 and 1974, manufacturing employment by 17 per cent and all private sector employment by 2 per cent; yet in the same period private sector employment in mining and quarrying fell by 72 per cent, in construction by 46 per cent, and in transport etc. by 36 per cent. It is likely that real employment in these industries has not fallen and may have increased, but that employers have divided up firms, taken on contract or casual labour or otherwise moved their work force across the organized–unorganized sector boundary. They have done the same thing in manufacturing industries, but either they have not done so to the same extent or real growth has cancelled out the effect.

The figures in table 2 are low – many more work in manufacturing industries – but they give an idea of the distribution of labour among the main branches of factory industry on which smaller firms depend for markets. Engineering and metal working (including electronics and repairs) account for 33 per cent (1 884 000 workers); textiles, including jute, for 27 per cent (1 544 000, including over 1m in cotton); food, drink and tobacco for 17 per cent; chemicals, plastics, rubber and non-metallic minerals for 13 per cent.

But these proportions may not be reflected in the distribution of labour among industries in the unorganized sector, because some factory industries need or choose to buy many of their requirements from small firms while others are more self-contained; and because the process of moving labour across the organized–unorganized boundary to evade the Factory Act has gone much further in some industries (like bidis or synthetic fibres) than in others.

It is possible to make only a rough estimate of the total size of the unorganized sector manufacturing work force, which is made up both of workers in firms too small to come under the Factory Act, and workers employed in larger factories who lack legal protection because they are casual, 'temporary' or contract workers. Indian statisticians, research workers and census enumerators are experienced, ingenious and self-critical; but the intrinsic difficulty of collecting accurate figures in these conditions[4] is made worse because

---

[4] 'Even in case of sufficient description [of a small firm's registered address], there remained the problem of finding the lane, the byelane and the building, the names of which were not always indicated or were even completely erased. The unit was often located through a chain of eight to ten persons, who were all helpful, each one leading gradually nearer to the unit.' (Lakdawala and Sandesara 1960:11). I have had many such experiences: these casual meetings can often be turned to good account.

Table 2. *Estimated average daily employment in working factories, by industry, 1974*

Major group (National Industrial Classification, 1970)	Employment in selected industries	Employment in major group	%
20–21 Food products		784 000	14
grain mill products	141 000		
sugar (vacuum pan factories)	129 000		
other sugar factories including gur	66 000		
edible oils and fats	75 000		
tea processing	90 000		
cashewnuts	176 000		
22 Beverages, tobacco and tobacco products		155 000	3
preparing raw leaf tobacco for manufacture	96 000		
23 Cotton textiles		1 043 000	18
cotton ginning, cleaning and baling	153 000		
spinning, weaving etc., and finishing in mills	815 000		
weaving and finishing in powerlooms	30 000		
24 Wool, silk and synthetic fibre textiles		141 000	2
wool	38 000		
silk	30 000		
synthetic textiles	68 000		
25 Jute, hemp and mesta textiles		278 000	5
26 Textile products (including wearing apparel other than footwear)		82 000	1
27 Wood and wood products, furniture and fixtures		109 000	2
sawing and planing of wood (other than plywood)	50 000		
28 Paper and paper products and printing, publishing and allied industries		225 000	4
paper and paper products	83 000		
printing and publishing	143 000		
29 Leather and fur (except repair)		44 000	1
30 Rubber, plastic, petroleum and coal products		127 000	2
rubber and plastics	101 000		

Table 2 (*cont.*)

Major group (National Industrial Classification, 1970)	Employment in selected industries	Employment in major group	%
31 Chemicals and chemical products (except products of petroleum and oil)		308 000	5
basic industrial organic and inorganic chemicals	34 000		
fertilizers and pesticides	43 000		
drugs and medicines	63 000		
explosives, ammunition and fireworks	41 000		
32 Non-metallic mineral products		300 000	5
structural clay products	88 000		
glass and glass products	61 000		
cement, lime and plaster	40 000		
33 Basic metal and alloys industries		380 000	7
iron and steel	125 000		
foundries for casting and forging iron and steel	184 000		
ferro alloys	21 000		
aluminium	24 000		
34 Metal products and parts except machinery and transport equipment		201 000	4
fabricated metal products such as cans, shipping containers, drums, safes etc.	85 000		
structural metal products	18 000		
hand tools and general hardware	40 000		
35 Machinery, machine tools and parts, except electrical machinery		419 000	7
agricultural machinery and equipment	35 000		
prime movers, boilers, steam generating plants, diesel engines etc.	41 000		
machinery for food and textile industries	44 000		
machine tools, parts and accessories	48 000		
36 Electrical machinery, apparatus, appliances and supplies and parts		241 000	4

Table 2 *(cont.)*

Major group (National Industrial Classification, 1970)	Employment in selected industries	Employment in major group	%
electrical industrial machinery (motors, generators etc.)	70 000		
electrical apparatus, appliances and parts: lamps, bulbs, switches, fans etc.	36 000		
radio and television, recording equipment, records, tapes, telephone, telegraph and radar equipment etc.	60 000		
electronic computers, control instruments, and equipment	7 000		
other electronic components and equipment	8 000		
37 Transport equipment and parts		335 000	6
ship building and repairing	38 000		
railway equipment	120 000		
motor vehicles and parts	98 000		
motor cycles and scooters	14 000		
bicycles and cycle rickshaws	26 000		
aircraft	33 000		
38 Other manufacturing industries		62 000	1
medical, surgical and scientific equipment	16 000		
40 Electricity		67 000	1
41–42 Gas and water		15 000	0+
70–73 Land, water and air transport		7 000	0+
74 Storage and warehousing		52 000	1
90–99 Other services		23 000	0+
educational, scientific and research services	10 000		
YO Repair services		246 000	4
repairs of motor vehicles and motor cycles	142 000		
Total		5 653 000	100

Note: Here as in the source, all figures are rounded and do not add up exactly to the totals. 0+ means less than 0.5%).
Source: Based on Labour Bureau 1976:22–37.

they often have to rely on information given by employers with an obvious motive to tell less than the whole truth. Thus an unpublished survey of urban small industries, by the West Bengal government's Bureau of Applied Economics and Statistics, says the quality of the data depends on the voluntary co-operation of the proprietor or manager, 'or some responsible person such as accountants [*sic*]': and although some refused to answer, more than a quarter of those who did revealed that their firms should have been registered as factories. An unpublished Jadavpur University study of small engineering units in Howrah reported no workers under fourteen at all, which is visibly not true; yet according to the Reserve Bank (1964) study of the same units – carried out by the same university – nearly a quarter of the workers said they got their first job before that age. The 1971 Census showed that in Calcutta, 41 per cent of manufacturing employment was in informal sector or unregistered units, including 2.6 per cent in household units (A.N. Bose 1978:10–11), but both figures are almost certainly too low.

The line between organized and unorganized sector employment is hard to draw in practice.

> One has always to draw the line sharply in spite of the fact that, if it is a meaningful distinction, it is usually gradual and never sharp except in the eyes of the law. Actually, the legal distinction often complicates the situation; often the units hovering on the margin prefer to show themselves clearly on one side of the line which explains a somewhat higher concentration of the units in the employment class which falls just short of the number with which they must register their establishments as factories whilst in reality they normally employ a few more who are called 'casual' as distinct from 'regular' employees. Many of the men called casual are more regular than casual.
>
> (Reserve Bank 1964:5)

This study of Howrah took twenty workers as the limit for 'small' units.

After an employer had shown me round his engineering workshop, we sat in his office. I asked: 'How many do you employ?' He looked me in the eye, paused, and said, 'Nine', which was obviously false. Later in the conversation he said, 'When I told you I employed only nine men, that wasn't true. Actually there are twenty-two, and this firm should be registered as a factory. On Monday' – this was Friday – 'I intend to go to the office and see about it.' No doubt he found some more urgent business on Monday morning.

It is even harder to draw a line on the other side, between the 'manufacturing' unorganized sector and petty services, and to say: here the linkages stop.

If we take the broadest definition of 'manufacturing' used in the Census of India (including all manufacturing, processing, servicing and repairs), in 1971 there were 17 068 000 manufacturing workers in India. It is more realistic to take only the 10 744 000 working in 'other than household industry', including 5 083 000 (47 per cent) in factories. Assume that few household industry workers depend on linkages with the organized sector, that many of the others do, and that the differences cancel out. This is probably about right: on a narrower definition of 'manufacturing', to include only those activities which are linked to the organized sector, there are about as many manufacturing workers outside the organized sector as inside it, or a little more.

The official figures for employment in small-scale industries have similar limitations; besides, some small-scale industries are in the organized sector and others are not, because the criterion for registration as a small-scale industry is investment, not the number of workers. The most complete figures are in the *Report on census of small scale industrial units* (Development Commissioner 1977). This census, carried out in 1973–4 with 1972 as the reference year, was restricted to units registered with the Directorates of Industries, and excluded 'a large category of small scale units which come within the purview of different specialised boards, committees or agencies covering them' (:1), as well as units not registered at all: 'This was a conscious decision with a view to cover the modern small scale sector falling within the purview of Small Industries Development Organisation (SIDO) and availing assistance and facilities made available to them' (:1). Table 3 (below) gives the main figures.

The report explains the difficulties and shortcomings of the census. Thus the difference between the cumulative totals of registered units, and the number of working units, at first gave the impression that nearly half the units were bogus:

> Whereas the figures indicating the differences could not speak more than what they indicated and reflected the deficiencies and unresponsiveness of those concerned for giving a representative picture of the small scale units, later evidences brought to light the immediate requirement of a uniform regist-

Table 3. *Units registered with the Small Industries Development Organization, 1972: employment, unit size and capital intensity by industry groups*

Industry group	Employment (including self-employment)	%	Average employment per unit	Investment in fixed assets per worker, Rs
Food products	131 220	8	20	5 000
Beverages	4 577	0+	10	12 500
Hosiery and readymade garments	75 346	5	11	5 900
Wood products	94 703	6	8	5 600
Paper products, printing etc.	89 146	5	11	12 500
Leather and leather products	31 775	2	6	4 200
Rubber and plastic products	81 690	5	11	12 500
Chemicals	159 013	10	13	8 300
Glass and ceramics	202 269	12	26	3 400
Basic metal industries	109 626	7	22	10 000
Metal products	300 060	18	9	7 700
Machinery and parts	145 333	9	11	11 100
Electrical and electronic products	65 908	4	15	11 100
Transport equipment	83 492	5	14	10 000
Miscellaneous	40 025	2	5	8 300
Repairing, servicing and job work	38 995	2	11	9 100
Total	1 653 178	100	12	7 700

Source: Based on Development Commissioner, Small Scale Industries, 1977:22, 52, *Report on census of small scale industrial units*

ration procedure (which was promptly implemented . . .) and the necessity of deregistering of all units which were found to be closed or not traceable and the non responding units.   (:1)

After these corrections, 62 per cent of SIDO units were found to be working (though it was only possible to tabulate data for 54 per cent), less than 9 per cent were untraceable and 'those which misutilised imported and scarce raw material and other facilities available to small scale industries [i.e. bogus units] may be much less than even 9 per cent' (:1).

The 139 577 units covered gave employment to 1 653 178 people: an average of twelve per unit which would be over the limit for registration under the Factory Act (ten) except that it clearly includes most of the employers and managerial staff like engineers and accountants – 13 per cent of the total are 'self-employed' entrepreneur-workers – and it is unlikely that many of these units are registered factories. Only 38 per cent of those employed are regarded as unskilled. This census appears to cover mainly the modern well-established firms with good market connexions, run by educated middle-class men or skilled workers from the big factories, rather than the very marginal small units which also supply the big factories directly or indirectly. Although the units covered by this census provided only 9.7 per cent of the total 'manufacturing' employment in India, they accounted for 14.5 per cent of value added by the manufacturing sector. The engineering and metal working industries, including electronics and repairs, provide 45 per cent of the employment – an even higher proportion than in factories (33 per cent in 1974). Chemicals, plastics, rubber and non-metallic minerals (including glass and ceramics) account for 27 per cent (cf. 13 per cent in factories). Only 8 per cent of employment in these small units is in the food and drink industries (cf. 17 per cent in factories, including tobacco) and 5 per cent in textiles (cf. 27 per cent), but only 'hosiery and readymade garments' are listed in table 3 – the many small textile units do not seem to be registered with SIDO. A similar census now would show more small firms in new industries, especially electronics and plastics.

The National Sample Survey Organization's *Tables with notes on small-scale manufacturing in urban and rural areas* (1976, but referring to 1968–9) contains detailed information especially on self-employment, on household and very small industries, and on seasonal and part-time work, but no employment totals which can easily be compared with those for the organized sector. On the most comparable units, the report says:

Among the rural enterprises those belonging to industry groups of printing and publishing and food manufacturing had the highest percent of enterprises employing 6 or more workers, the figures being 9.90 and 3.49 respectively. In urban areas the first three industry groups with the highest percent of enterprises employing 6 or more workers were manufacture of paper and paper products (12.96), printing and publishing (11.79) and basic metal industries (12.56). (National Sample Survey Organization 1976:7)

Most all-India figures for unorganized sector employment are biased towards the more established registered firms, and even here there is no guarantee that over-reporting (of bogus or partly bogus firms) will cancel out under-reporting (as of child labour, or a work force which would bring a firm under the Factory Act). The excellent local studies (like the Reserve Bank's Howrah survey (1964)) do not always give the sort of information which would allow one to compare the number of workers in the two sectors. As usual the best-studied city is Bombay; and the best attempt to answer this question is in Heather and Vijay Joshi's *Surplus labour and the city* (1976a), a model of intelligent use of inadequate figures.

The Directorate of Education and Training collects data on Bombay's organized sector, defined as all the public sector and all private establishments with more than twenty-five employees, which the Joshis say is

> a good dividing line for isolating those workers who are more or less effectively safeguarded by labour legislation. Some establishments employing less than 25 are also covered by some Government legislation, but the difficulty of implementing it in these quarters is so great that they can for all practical purposes be regarded as being outside its scope. As for workers' organizations, even if they exist in the smaller establishments, they are weak and ineffective. When we think of other organized sector characteristics [like technology and products], our criterion is almost certainly too generous in classifying firms as organized . . . Another reason why our criterion probably leads us to overestimate the size of the organized sector is that in some large firms 'labour on the rolls' includes temporary, casual or contract labourers who do not share the advantages of permanent workers.   (Joshi 1976a:47)

They estimate the unorganized sector's size by subtracting these workers from the work force shown in the Census. Breaking down the Census figures by branches of economic activity, they also describe ways of getting a living which are unlikely to appear fully in the Census, like begging, bootlegging and prostitution.

In 1961 half of Bombay's enumerated work force were in the unorganized sector; but: 'Contrary to a superficial conventional view, almost as many Unorganized workers are to be found in Manufacturing . . . as in Services' (:53), and many of them are skilled. Twenty-nine per cent of manufacturing workers were in the unorganized sector. Over three-fifths of organized manufacturing employees were in textiles: in other manufacturing divisions, the organized and unorganized sectors already accounted for roughly equal numbers of workers (:50).

Between 1961 and 1971 the manufacturing unorganized sector expanded faster than the organized sector, especially in Bombay city where the textile industry stagnated, and to a lesser extent in the part of the Metropolitan Region outside the city, where new industries grew very fast in the 1960s (the Joshis take Thana District as a proxy for the rest of the region). On these figures, by 1971 the unorganized sector still had half the city's work force but 39 per cent of its manufacturing workers: over the decade the number of manufacturing workers rose by 62 per cent in the unorganized sector and only 22 per cent in the organized sector (:58–9; the table on p. 70 contains a serious misprint). In Bombay and Thana together, the unorganized sector manufacturing work force went up by 50 per cent, the organized sector by only 35 per cent, so that by 1971, 36 per cent of all manufacturing workers were in the unorganized sector. Not only are organized sector figures inflated by the number of temporary, casual and contract workers, but for various reasons (which the Joshis describe in detail, :72–8) the unorganized sector estimates are almost certainly too low. The figures for other Indian cities are probably similar: about half the non-cultivating workers in urban areas are in the organized sector, both in Bombay (49 per cent) and in the whole country (52 per cent, :61).

There are good grounds to believe these trends have continued: small firms have grown faster than large ones, and a higher proportion of factory workers are not effectively protected by the Factory Act and other legislation.

The exact figures are doubtful, but the general picture is clear. In Calcutta and Bombay, and probably elsewhere, about 40 per cent of manufacturing workers are in unorganized sector firms (including firms which should legally be registered as factories but are not). Add at least 10 per cent to this figure for casual, temporary and contract workers employed by factories but without security or any effective legal or union protection. Both these estimates are probably on the low side, because of the difficulties of counting unorganized sector labour and because of deliberate under-reporting. So, as I suggested, only about half of India's industrial workers, or probably rather less, have regular organized sector jobs. The trend is equally clear: organized sector employment is growing, but the unorganized sector is growing faster.

Do small firms exist because labour is cheap?

Some things are made and sold only by large firms or small firms. Otherwise large and small firms compete for markets, or small firms supply parts and services to large factories which market the product. How far are relations between large and small firms determined by the availability of *labour* on different terms, rather than by other constraints or advantages?

Labour in small firms is cheaper, or at any rate wages are lower; employers save on fringe benefits like Employees' State Insurance and Provident Fund; and they also save, or think they save, the costs of job security, safety precautions, union trouble, labour courts and an inflexible work force bound by precise job descriptions.[5] But factories can get some of these advantages – as well as economies of scale – by taking on extra temporary or contract labour, up to the point where the permanent workers' unions or the law prevent them. So the line between large and small firms – or organized or unorganized sectors – corresponds only roughly to the formal distinction of statuses or conditions of employment: the status of permanent factory worker being distinguished quite sharply from those of temporary, casual or contract workers, 'regular' workers in smaller firms, home workers and the self-employed. A worker's real living standards and prospects depend largely but not entirely on his formal status.

To put the problem in these terms implies there may be a choice between making a thing in a factory and putting the work out to small firms. If there is really a choice, only the bigger entrepreneurs are in a position to make it, or the government must make it for them by imposing controls (the other alternative may be not to make the thing at all, but to put the resources to some other use). Small entrepreneurs have no choice, except sometimes to change products: their survival depends on cost advantages and market contacts. Does the outcome – and the small firms' prospects – depend more on labour costs (including wages) or on other things?

The answer may differ from one industry to another. Engineering products, electronics and plastics – especially components for as- sembly elsewhere – can often be put out to small firms which do the

---

[5] In a 1961 study of 'Fringe benefits in Indian industry' (summarized in Labour Bureau 1974:47) the Employers' Federation of India claimed that fringe benefits amounted to 21 per cent of the organized sector wage bill, making India a country with high wage costs.

work just as well yet more cheaply, but not some precision work for customers with high standards of quality control. Pharmaceutical firms cannot risk their reputation. Chemical plants may put out some repairs and maintenance work, but the main process cannot be broken down into parts done in different places. Some products but not others can be made and marketed entirely by small units.

At a National Workshop on Ancillaries Development in Bangalore (29 July 1977) the opening speaker said the advantage of ancillaries was that they could produce sophisticated goods with modern technology, yet their costs were much lower because 'the working conditions are different'. Following him the Minister for Industries, George Fernandes, said pointedly that ancillaries should not mean exploitation of workers – an ancillary should be able to make things at the same cost as the parent unit, paying the same wages and giving workers the same conditions and security, even though it is not under the Factory Act; yet ancillaries were being used just to take advantage of sweated labour, and to give work to friends and relatives.

Contrast two imaginary extreme situations. In the first case – which George Fernandes seems to envisage for small firms generally – labour is employed on the same terms and conditions in large firms and small ones, whose existence depends on competitive advantages other than labour costs. Small firms tap unused resources of entrepreneurship, savings and skill, they get state aid and protected markets, they are less wasteful and more responsive to demand, they use cheaper (but safe) machinery and buildings, workers will turn their hand to anything (for the same wages as the less adaptable factory workers) and so on.

Clearly this is not so, but it is worth asking how far it might sometimes be truer than the other extreme possibility, which is that small firms are just extensions of large ones, owned outright or controlled by the same people: the small firms exist only as a way to take advantage of cheap insecure labour working in dangerous conditions, not protected by law or by unions (this is exactly the situation – except with regard to safety – where directly employed and contract workers do the same work side by side in factories). The effect would be the same if small entrepreneurs, though formally independent, depended entirely on large firms, and if cheap labour alone governed their decisions to start firms and their chances of survival.

The technician entrepreneurs (described in chapter 3) could not have set up their firms at all except on a small scale. The motive was not cheap labour but simply a chance to make money from their own skills and ideas, and to be independent. However, cheap labour helps to make this possible. Some say they would like to pay higher wages as their business expands, and they may be sincere because they aspire to the management style of the more enlightened big firms. They need capital and may have to get it from financiers, who are perhaps more likely to see opportunities for profit in cheap labour than in new ideas: like the small-scale industrialist with a commercial background who said: 'There is so much unemployment and labour is freely available. When you can get a person at a lower rate why not?' (p. 91 above). Yet even he ascribed his success mainly to the lack of competition, and to his ability to buy materials more cheaply than the big firms could.

A firm on a Bombay industrial estate employs twelve men making switchgear. The owner – a former factory worker and union official – says he has to get more productivity from his workers because, unlike other employers on the industrial estate, he pays the legal minimum wages and encourages the union. (However a union official alleged afterwards that this man has four other small firms, none of which have unions.)

In this case the evidence is inconclusive. The legal minimum wage in Bombay, though more than the pay in many small units, is about half the rate paid in bigger factories. Whatever the motives of such entrepreneurs, it is unlikely they could stay in business if they paid factory wages.

It is hard to make detailed comparisons between wages paid for similar work in large and small firms, because skill titles are deceptive and there is little reliable statistical information on the unorganized sector. In Bombay unorganized sector earnings vary around, rather than above, the legal minimum. Organized sector wages vary widely even between factories doing similar work (thus in a big Faridabad engineering factory, owned by a multinational, the minimum monthly pay before deductions was Rs 600 in 1977; in a bigger engineering factory, it was Rs 230). H. and V. Joshi use all the available figures for Bombay:

> we estimate that the earnings differential between the Organized and Unorganized sectors is unlikely to be less than 100 per cent and could easily be as high as 150 per cent. If we also make some allowance for the present value of the employers' provident Fund contributions and for the monetary value of various fringe benefits, we believe that 150 per cent provides the more likely figure.   (Joshi 1976a:100)

If costs like 'leave salary', and the cost of hiring a substitute, are added

> the private cost of hiring labour is probably about 150 per cent and possibly even as high as 200 per cent above the prevailing wages in the Unorganized sector. (:101)

The information workers gave me, and the 'Bombay labour market' study (Deshpande 1979), suggest this is about right. Generally a worker in a big modern factory earns two or three times as much as an unorganized sector worker with the same title, like a turner, and he has security and fringe benefits. Small organized sector factory wages are not much better. Some of this difference does reflect skill and experience on machines which only the big firms have; but

> the Unorganized sector is not entirely composed of extremely unskilled people. There is a very wide range of skills present and there is reason to believe that the low incomes earned are the result of lack of resources rather than of skill, effort or enterprise. (Joshi 1976a:56)

Yet in some places the wages paid in small units, especially to skilled workers, may be at least as high as in factories. One partner running a Faridabad engineering firm with twenty-two workers (p. 126 above) said his skilled men get Rs 100 a month more than they 'deserve' (meaning factory wages, since they are mostly ex-factory workers), earning up to Rs 1100. Each skilled man has a 'helper' earning Rs 150 175, but helpers tend to leave for factory jobs, 'because we are paying them less than they deserve'. The Reserve Bank (1964:120) study of Howrah shows that average earnings in small engineering units were slightly higher than in big factories. This is seen as a premium to compensate workers for the greater risk of unemployment, though it may also be a result of the higher proportion of skilled men in these small units.

Craftsmen like carpenters or tool and die makers may earn more by staying independent. A factory manager has radio cabinets made by a carpenter he knows instead of the factory carpenters, giving himself a tax-free profit and saving the firm the cost of more full-time carpenters. Assuming the carpenter also makes a good profit, it comes from savings on factory overheads and tax, and the full use of his time in a market with plenty of work for carpenters.

Small firms, as well as the self-employed, enjoy these tax savings, either by exemption or evasion. Thus the general excise duty is not collected from firms whose annual turnover is below a certain figure

(Rs 3m in 1977). The liability depended on the number employed until 1977: after that date the 1 per cent duty was doubled, but a set-off was allowed where excised goods became the inputs of other manufacturing firms, so that the duty became a value added tax without the 'cascading effect' of multiple excise (S. J. Srinivasulu 1977). This tax liability is one of the 'thresholds' which stops small firms from expanding (Panini 1977). Businessmen can simply avoid other taxes, like income tax, if their firms are either so small that the work is carried on at home and escapes official notice, or big enough to afford tax accountants, fixers or agents (:111).

Then there are the advantages reserved for small firms by law and under government programmes to help the 'small-scale sector': easy loans amounting to subsidies, sheds, advice, help with marketing, technical training, workshop services in the Small Industries Service Institutes, and items reserved wholly or partly for small-scale production (pp. 82–3 above). To enjoy these advantages a firm must be registered with agencies like the Small Industries Development Organization, but not necessarily registered under the Factory Act. Big financiers can get some of these advantages by setting up phantom or bogus firms (pp. 107–8) or buying up small firms (like the advertiser who wanted a television factory already licensed in the small industries sector; p. 114); the 'president' of a Bombay electronic factory run by five brothers (p. 95) complained that big firms allowed small ones to start production, then moved in and took them over by illegal methods. A small but growing firm risks losing these concessions if it goes over the investment limit, and this is one of the thresholds which can inhibit growth. Some entrepreneurs told me that this – rather than liability under the Factory Act – was the reason why their firms had been divided into nominally separate companies.

These concessions or privileges may be abused. One could argue that they do not go far enough to stimulate healthy self-reliant small firms; but still they have made many small firms viable, created employment and drawn on reserves of entrepreneurship and savings. This is clear from the rapid growth of some protected sectors like electronics, from the take-up of the official agencies' technical services and from entrepreneurs' own comments. They have also had the effect of preventing growth above the threshold where a firm might achieve economies of scale but would be visibly too big for the small-scale sector.

One great advantage claimed for small firms is their flexibility.

They can see market opportunities the big firms miss, and supply services the big firms are not equipped to give: like 'Shriidhar tools' which sharpens cutting tools for large and small firms all over Bangalore (pp. 94–5) or the Faridabad firm which acts as an 'ambulance', doing emergency repairs to machinery, and fabricating parts at any time of the day or night (p. 126). The workers themselves are said to be more adaptable in small units: they are not bound by precise job descriptions and will turn their hand to anything.

A Bombay firm making automobile parts employs eighteen men, and is registered under the Factory Act which many firms of the same size evade (having less than twenty workers, the firm is not covered by Employees' State Insurance). Wages are comparable to those paid in some larger factories: unskilled workers get the legal minimum, others considerably more than the minimum for their grades. The owner attaches great importance to having a stable work force: he avoids taking on trained men, who are likely to leave, but tries to train and promote unskilled workers who will withstand the 'temptation' to leave unless they are offered a very high wage increase. Where other firms meet a sudden rise in demand by taking on temporary or contract labour, he prefers to stretch out the labour he has; and this flexibility is his strength – there is no clear line between one job and another as there is in a factory. Nothing stops a man from operating a different machine; since much of the work is repetitive, a man may be moved to another machine every week just to give him a change. There are no security staff, and no office staff except an accountant. An unskilled worker acts as peon (messenger and office helper) when one is needed.

Compare 'Naaraayan'a's' silk screen printing works, where everyone including the owner learns several trades and will do anything (pp. 98–9 above); or the tool and die maker who is proud that he and any of his ten workers can operate his full range of machines (p. 102). These men's chief assets are their own versatile skills and the flexibility of their workers.

Undoubtedly the small employers' main competitive advantage is cheap labour, though there are others, especially the greater degree of control over labour, which is not only of direct economic benefit to the employer, but makes his life simpler and bolsters his self-esteem. Higher wages – even the legal minimum wages in Bombay where these are relatively high – would cut the employers' profits severely and put some out of business, though they exaggerate this problem. I suspect, though I cannot prove it, that 'financier' entrepreneurs would switch their capital into commerce or into low-wage industries in the remote areas untouched by unions and the law. Entrepreneurs with a technical background – engineers or ex-factory workers whose assets are their skills and ideas – would still set up their own firms, employing about as many workers because they are not overmanned, and would find the extra wages by higher productivity and vigorous marketing.

Are small firms labour-intensive?

I suggest that the small firms' survival does not always depend on low wages but on other advantages as well, like flexibility and government help, which can outweigh the large firms' economies of scale and access to markets.

Low wages need not mean cheap labour. One could argue (with H. and V. Joshi, 1976a) that stronger policies to help small firms, and to remove constraints on them, would create much more employment and would be at least equally good for industrial growth. Labour costs could stay the same, but divided among more workers. Low wages, with or without security, would be the price workers pay for a better chance of a job.

The implication is that small firms are bound to use more labour-intensive methods than large firms, which have a built-in bias towards expensive modern machinery rather than employment creation, and are pushed further in the same direction by high wages, labour laws and unions. This is taken as an obvious general truth. Indeed the Joshis not only assume it as if it were beyond question ('Firms in the organized sector use mainly capital-intensive technology in contrast to the producers in the unorganized sector who use mainly a labour-intensive, indigenous technology' :45), but treat capital-intensity as part of the *definition* of the organized sector, more useful as a distinctive feature than other 'organized sector characteristics' like the number of workers, which they use in their statistics (:47).

Some official figures suggest large firms are much more capital-intensive. George Fernandes, Minister for Industries, told Parliament: 'While an investment of one lakh [Rs 100000] in heavy industry results in the creation of only four jobs, the same financial input can yield 25 or 26 jobs in small-scale industry and 60 to 70 jobs in rural industries' (*The Hindu*, 12 July 1977), implying that large-scale and 'heavy' industry are the same. I.C. Puri, Commissioner for Small-scale Industries, said:

> the small-scale sector had proved labour-intensive, employing on an average 27 persons per Rs 1 lakh of investment against only five to six jobs for similar investment in the *organized* sector [my italics]. However, even within the small-scale sector there were considerable variations in labour-intensity. His organization was now identifying the most labour-intensive of the small-scale industries, and would give maximum attention to these . . . Small units could not exist without large ones – they fed large units with ancillaries and in turn got machinery and intermediate goods from the organized sector. It was essential to reap economies of scale in the organized sector by setting up large plants, so that the cheaper equipment and raw materials could be supplied by them to small-scale and village units'.
>
> ('Employment-oriented growth') (*Times of India*, 12 May 1977)

A 1968 study showed that the fixed capital per worker was Rs 3170 in the small-scale sector and Rs 22 000 in large firms (S. Krishnakumar, n.d. 'Strategy for a massive effort for small industries in Kerala State'. Unpublished.)

Yet in chapter 1 (p. 16) I referred to studies which question this assumption that there is a close necessary link between unit size and capital-intensity, if one compares like with like (i.e. excluding traditional crafts); and sometimes it is doubtful whether the contrast between capital- and labour-intensity is of much practical use. 'To favour the cottage industries because they are "labour-intensive", comes, as Joan Robinson puts it, "perilously close to regarding inefficiency as a positive virtue"'.[6] Indeed there is some evidence that small firms are *more* capital-intensive than comparable large ones: comparisons are hard because of the problems of defining capital-intensity, limiting the universe of study and simply getting information. Dhar and Lydall (1961), discuss the question and its policy implications at some length, and theirs is still the best book on Indian small industries, though out of date. Sandesara (1969) argues persuasively that the modern small firms typical of Bombay are more capital-intensive than larger ones, but the evidence dates from 1953–8. Turnham (1971) and Gaiha and Mohammad (1975) are doubtful about the possibilities of substitution between capital and labour. Sutcliffe (1971) considers evidence from India, Pakistan,

---

[6] From Subrahmanian and Kashyap 1975:91, a paper which contains a useful short discussion of this question, and a good summary and bibliography of research on small-scale industries.

Japan and elsewhere for the assumption 'that labour-intensive operations tend to be small scale, and capital-intensive operations large scale': he concludes that there is little systematic evidence, that the assumption is false in some instances (partly because small industry is 'generally very working-capital intensive', :207) and at best 'a gross over-simplification' (:206), for example, because 'size of plant is being measured by the number of workers, and this begs the question: economies of scale relate to the size of output and not to the number of workers'.

In India there are wide variations between industries: thus the 1972 Census of small-scale industrial units showed that investment in fixed assets varied from Rs 5000 per worker in food products to Rs 12 500 in beverages, paper products and printing, and rubber and plastic products (table 3, p. 146 above). Even if the general impression is right, and there is a rough correlation between unit size and capital-intensity, the many important exceptions suggest that moving resources into small-scale industry may not be the best way to increase employment; though a policy to encourage industries and technologies with the greatest direct or indirect employment potential – without worrying too much whether the employment is in large or small firms – is likely to stimulate small firms in any case. Further expansion both of some large firms and some capital-intensive industries – which are not the same thing – will probably be necessary conditions for wider use of labour-intensive methods in linked industries.[7]

So the first ground for doubting the close link between size and capital-intensity is empirical. Not all large firms have high capital investment: some use old depreciated machinery (textiles, jute) or cheap fabricated copies of foreign machines, or use little or no machinery (bidi factories). Much more often, small firms use expensive Indian or imported machines, and save on labour, buildings and overheads (especially in precision engineering, chemicals and plastics).

---

[7] 'It is possible to make too much of the capital intensity/advanced technology bias in industrial development strategy. In particular the argument neglects the potential or actual importance of inter-industry linkages which could imply that labour intensive manufacturing is stimulated by capital-intensive input provider or output user industries' (Turnham 1971:98). This book, *The employment problem in less developed countries*, contains a general discussion and some material on India.

I described a small firm with eight workers in a congested part of Bombay, making 'precision components' for bigger firms (p. 123). The owner, whose relatives own much bigger engineering firms and are among his customers, has invested Rs 250 000 in automatic machines, which he bought from Germany and now gets from the same manufacturer's Indian subsidiary. The shed is so crammed that it is hard to squeeze between the machines and the wall: working conditions are worse than in small engineering firms in the suburbs. Wages are around the legal minimum, except for some fifteen of the workers' children who come in for casual work at about half the rate. Jobs that can be done more cheaply on hand operated machines are put out to men employing one or two low-paid workers.

A suburban firm (small, but in the organized sector: I think about twenty workers) makes precision components for one big electrical factory. Each automatic machine – from Switzerland, India or Czechoslovakia – costs about Rs 100 000 and produces parts sold for Rs 8000 a month (for the work only: the customer provides materials), of which the operator gets about Rs 400 (all figures from the union). This is slightly above the legal minimum: it was less until one of the two skilled men unionized the other workers. When I met them they were on strike for more, and organizing a march on the owner's head office with employees from his other firms.

Hein Streefkerk (1979) gives case studies of small-scale entrepreneurs in Bulsar – often from families with trading interests in Bombay and elsewhere – who have gone increasingly into synthetic textiles, chemicals and plastics, as the Indian and world economy turned from natural to synthetic materials: 'The production processes were either completely automatic, e.g. with plastic injectors, or not very complicated, as with chemicals; they required relatively few labourers and the average initial investment in equipment was not very high. Both types, including the textile looms, required no technical ingenuity or specific engineering skill on the part of the entrepreneur [who employed a skilled supervisor] . . . It was access to the supply, the administration and the market that was crucial' (:118). 'The plastic branch is characterized by a high degree of automation; they are at once capital intensive and labour saving' (:106).

But in plastics as in engineering there is some choice of technologies between automatic machines and simpler methods. In my experience and that of others who know the small firms, the owners spend as much as they can on automatic machines which any worker can quickly learn to use (as a toothbrush manufacturer said, it depends on your pocket – meaning that whoever can afford automatic machines will have them: his solution was to copy – see p. 96). Then they take on unskilled workers for finishing, shaping, assembling etc., with cheap machines or simple hand tools. Machines are more reliable than people. Skilled toolroom workers are already hard to find at wages these employers are prepared to pay; and though unskilled workers are plentiful, employers are afraid the spread of unions into small-scale industry will raise wages and cause trouble.

A marginal firm which cannot afford automatic machines, on a dirty run-down industrial estate in Bombay, makes eyedrop bottles and other plastic items for pharmaceutical firms. To operate each press, a man must push hard with both hands and feet: all the press operators, like most foundry workers, are immigrants from Uttar Pradesh who are believed to be specially suited to such hot heavy work. Girls finish the pieces in a loft, and small boys – some about ten years old – seal them in plastic bags.

The newly installed union was negotiating for the legal minimum wages, which would double the women's pay but not that of the men, who already earned about the legal minimum at piecework rates. The children earned a quarter of this: the union official was prepared to ignore their presence, since there was nothing else for them to do.

Chemical firms generally require the most expensive plant and not much labour: just some unskilled men to fetch, carry and pack, mix compounds and watch meters, apart from the chemists and super-visors. Yet some specialized processes, particularly in fine chemicals and pharmaceuticals, can be carried out on a small scale, requiring little labour apart from that of the owner and one or two others who, like him, are graduate chemists; and the simplest equipment, which can be bought or fabricated cheaply. 'Divaakar', who had built up such a firm in Bombay, said the business was 'neither capital-intensive nor labour-intensive but talent-intensive' (pp. 97–8). One could say the same of many firms which technicians have set up on a shoestring, like 'Naaraayan'a's' silk screen printing business (pp. 98–9).

In engineering, the fastest growing small firms appear to be relatively capital-intensive ones, making parts or sub-assemblies for sale to the big firms rather than assembling the finished product: big factories would generally prefer to keep the final stages of assembly under their own direct supervision, to be sure of a consistent high-quality product. They cope with the fluctuating demand for *parts* by ordering from small firms; they can control unskilled or semi-skilled *labour* more efficiently by varying the number of temporary or contract workers in the main factory. Moreover, assembly is often done by women, who will take lower wages and are much less militant. Thus it is sometimes economically rational to have a few skilled workers operating expensive machines in small workshops, while the labour-intensive jobs of hand assembly and inspection are carried on in much larger establishments.[8] In engineering as in other industries like chemicals and plastics it seems that the fastest-growing small firms have been the more capital-intensive ones, producing both for export (B. Bhattacharyya 1973) and the home market, whether this is a result of government and union policies, or of other economic and technical advantages which these firms have.

The evidence is thin and hard to interpret. I cannot disprove the theory that size and capital-intensity go together, but I can cast doubt on it. Even if as a general rule small firms *are* more labour-intensive, the balance is probably changing. In any case there is no reason why they must be: as I suggested in chapter 1 (p. 17) there are organizations in India, China and elsewhere which employ large numbers using cheap simple technology. In Indian conditions the assumption that large firms will inevitably be capital-intensive could be a self-fulfilling prophecy: thresholds for investment, employment and tax liability may keep firms which do use labour-intensive methods smaller than they would otherwise be, since they cannot afford to lose the advantages of recognized 'smallness'.

Lastly, the contrast between labour- and capital-intensity may itself be confusing and a hindrance to useful action, both because of the difficulties of definition and because it implies a choice which may not exist in practice.

Labour laws, unions and small firms

Does the small firms' survival depend on their freedom from labour laws, and from unions?

It is likely that many small firms are viable largely because wages are lower than in the organized sector. This could be because the

---

[8] A pamphlet by Hindustan Machine Tools, *How to lower production costs in small-scale industries*, says small-scale entrepreneurs used to consider only the cost of machine tools. Now they must think of the cost and time lost in maintenance, replacing components and training: 'The best way to play safe, as far as the ancillary manufacturer is concerned, is to select process-oriented, high-productive machine tools which minimize the risk of costly rejections, and also reduce, to some extent, the need for highly skilled machine operators.'

firms use labour-intensive methods (labour is not cheap but the wage bill is divided among more workers), or because they are inefficient or have marketing problems (low wages allow them to break even) or as efficient and capital-intensive as large firms but more profitable (the extra profits come from cheap labour) or for some combination of these reasons (e.g. labour-intensive technology, inefficiently used to supply uncertain markets, with very low wages). 'Wages' in this context includes labour costs like safety precautions and Employees' State Insurance.

The difference in wages and fringe benefits between the two sectors exists mainly because various labour laws are enforced, and unions are active, in large firms but seldom in small ones. Small-scale employers see the extension of these laws and union activities to their firms as a threat. It would cut their profits; it might put some of them out of business; and it may already have caused them to turn to capital-intensive methods in anticipation.[9]

Early factory legislation, dating from 1881 and gradually extended in the twentieth century, dealt mainly with child labour, working hours and safety, in the larger perennial (not seasonal) factories (pp. 50–2). The law gave no protection against dismissal, but by the 1930s the status of a 'regular' worker, with some *de facto* security, had become distinct from that of contract, temporary or badli (substitute) workers (pp. 53–4). Since Independence this distinction has been recognized in a whole body of new laws which give permanent workers – on paper, and often in practice – some security of employment, and the right to form unions.

A firm is liable to the most important of these laws when it reaches the threshold for registration under the Factories Act (ten workers if power is used, otherwise twenty: the threshold for some other laws is higher). Liability does not mean the laws are always obeyed or enforced; but the official criterion for the organized sector – registration under the Factories Act – is a useful shorthand for a whole package of legal obligations which very small firms are free of.

Indian labour law is complicated, it is often added to or amended, and some laws vary from state to state; so does enforcement. These are the main features:

The *Factories Act* regulates working conditions, health and safety, and hours of work. It gives workers a weekly day off and fourteen days'

---

[9] Or, as an Opposition peer said, opening his speech in the House of Lords, 'The Factory Act, as a matter of fact, is a most unsatisfactory Act' (Kingsley Amis, *New Statesman*, 20 Aug. 1976).

annual leave, bans child labour, and restricts the employment of young persons between the ages of 14 and 18. Each state must enforce the Act through a factory inspectorate, which is more effective in some states than in others but is always understaffed. In some states the Chief Inspector of Factories is also the Labour Commissioner (National Commission 1969:98). The *Mines Act* is similar. The *Shops and Commercial Establishments Act* contains similar provisions for smaller units, including industrial firms with less than ten workers (in some cases the provisions are more generous: e.g. twenty-one days' annual leave in Maharashtra). The difference is that this Act is enforced by local authorities, which usually means it is not enforced at all. However, Factory Inspectors are required to inspect unregistered workshops in certain conditions, for example if they have information that the work is dangerous.

The *Payment of Bonus Act* applies to firms covered by the Factories Act. A worker who does thirty days' work in a year is entitled to an annual bonus, which was originally intended as a form of profit sharing, and is now taken for granted by organized sector workers as 'a necessary adjunct of wages' (:256). The amount varies between 4 and 20 per cent of annual wages, according to a formula which is supposed to be related to the firm's profits but depends in practice on union–management negotiation, occasional arbitration and strikes. The National Commission on Labour was told that 'many employees

particularly those in the small establishments which employ less than 20 persons – who were getting bonus before the Payment of Bonus Act 1965 have now been deprived of that privilege' (:256). Since wages in bigger firms are higher in any case, and bonus is negotiated as part of the whole package, it is doubtful whether bonus adds much to employers' costs.

The *Minimum Wages Act*, on the other hand, applies to all firms, even the smallest, in designated industries. Yet:

> It is a common complaint that the benefits of labour legislation have not reached rural and unorganised labour. The Minimum Wages Act 1948 was the first attempt at statutory regulation of wages, and to some extent, working conditions of labour employed in the sweated trades. Labour engaged in these employments, being unorganised, had weak bargaining power and had been deprived of reasonable wage and working conditions. Apart from the ineffectively implemented Minimum Wages Act, they do not have any other legislative protection. The Factories Act, 1948 and the Industrial Disputes Act, 1947, which contain specific and detailed provisions for items within their purview, were not designed to meet the conditions of and requirements in unorganised industries and employments.
>
> (National Commission 1969:417–18)

State governments may set up Wage Boards to fix minimum wages, with differentials for skill and for different areas, in any industry (:230–8). In some states minimum wages for 'industrial' labour are below market rates. Where they are higher, as in Maharashtra, there is no effective official machinery to enforce them, but their very existence is a rallying-point and bargaining counter for unions, if there are unions. The small-scale employers' strong resistance to minimum wages suggests that the rates would cut sharply into their profits. Big firms pay more in any case.

The only real provision for unemployment or retirement is the *Provident Fund*. The Act applies to workers who have done 120 days' work in a year, in a firm with more than twenty workers. The employer and employee make equal compulsory contributions, which are invested in government securities and paid back with interest on retirement after the age of fifty; on death, disability or mass retrenchment; or on dismissal or resignation after fifteen years (with part refunds for shorter service). Workers often invest the lump sum in a shop or business; but they can face difficulty and delay in getting it, especially if they resign early, and this is a deterrent against changing jobs. Moreover, some employers delay payment of their contributions to the Fund, as well as workers' contributions already deducted from wages. A firm may close down without paying, leaving workers with no credit at all.

Employees' State Insurance (ESI) is supposed to cover all employees – including those engaged through contractors – up to a certain wage limit, in firms employing twenty workers or more. Like the Provident Fund, the scheme is financed by employers' and employees' contributions. An insured worker and his family are entitled to free medical treatment at ESI clinics and hospitals, sickness and disablement benefits for limited periods, and maternity benefits (:166–71; Holmström 1976:61). They lose their right to Workmen's Compensation from the employer in case of accident. Patients complain that they have to wait for hours for poor treatment, in understaffed poorly equipped ESI clinics and hospitals, sometimes in remote parts of the city: thus the ESI Subscribers Welfare Association in Bangalore described the scheme as 'a great bane and burden' to the working class, and asked the Health Minister for an opinion poll on its abolition ('ESIS, bane of workers', *Deccan Herald*, 8 Aug. 1977).

In Bombay 1800 ESI doctors refused to do paper work – though they said patients' treatment would not be affected – to press demands for a higher capitation fee, representation on the controlling bodies, and overhaul of the disentitlement procedure. Dr Shelat said: 'At present, a worker may continue to pay his contribution to the ESIS, yet he may be removed from the scheme because of the employer's failure to deposit the money along with his contribution to the corporation' ('ESIS doctors will intensify agitation', *Times of India*, Bombay, 30 Aug. 1977). He admitted the scheme was unpopular with workers: with proper representation, the doctors would make it popular.

Small-scale employers resent both Provident Fund and ESI, not just because of the direct cost of employers' contributions, but specially because of the extra paper work, which is a heavy burden to firms with few or no office staff.

The biggest fringe benefit of all is *security of employment*. Workers in small firms have none, except their scarcity value if they are skilled, otherwise the employer's good will and interest in keeping a stable work force: nothing in law (except in some states like Tamil Nadu). 'Permanent' workers in bigger firms have legal protection, which is more likely to amount to real protection if there is a strong union or the firm is very large.

The *Industrial Disputes Act* applies to workers who have completed 240 days' continuous work in firms with more than fifty employees. Workers are entitled to a fixed scale of compensation for lay-off or retrenchment (National Commission 1969:176), which is not itself a heavy burden on employers. However, other legislation requires employers in some states and industries to get official permission before dismissing workers.

The Act – taken together with other central and state Acts, and a growing body of case law – also allows workers in these firms to appeal against unfair dismissal to an industrial court or tribunal, which may order the employer to pay further compensation or to reinstate the worker:

> Tribunals normally do not sit in appeal over management's decision, but where want of *bonafides*, victimisation or unfair labour practices, a basic error of facts or a violation of a principle of natural justice, or a completely baseless or perverse finding on the material available, is established, tribunals have intervened to order reinstatement or award monetary compensation in lieu of reinstatement. Employers, for the sake of discipline, have insisted on compensation and workers on reinstatement. (:349)

A job is more important than cash in hand, which many employers would gladly pay to cut their work force or to get rid of 'trouble makers'. The bitterest and longest strikes are about dismissals, not pay.

This makes work for lawyers, both on the union side (many union officials have legal training) and representing managements. A worker has a chance of compensation or reinstatement only if he has the union behind him to fight the case in court and outside, through negotiation, the official machinery for settling disputes, and strikes. When a worker has to rely on the court's decision alone he may wait three years or much longer (in one case in Maharashtra, a group of workers sued for wrongful dismissal in 1965: their case was rejected in 1977, when one had been dead for five years). If the worker takes another job in the meantime (or rather, if the employer finds out), the claim lapses. The result, as an Indian economist told me, is that an employer can usually get rid of a worker, but only after 'some rigmarole'.

The rigmarole is expensive and produces bad blood. Employers go to great lengths to avoid it by keeping the firm small (with a nominal payroll of less than fifty workers, even if this means splitting the firm into fictitious units); laying workers off before they complete 240 days and then re-employing them; and careful selection of permanent employees, relying on trusted workers to introduce new candidates and to answer for their good behaviour. As a senior manager said, you can get a divorce from your wife but not from this fellow. According to a Bangalore personnel manager:

> When someone leaves, the firms ask: was his job necessary? When you recruit a man it means costs – you are taking him on 'for all time to come' (i.e. until *he* chooses to leave); and 'it isn't fair to recruit today and retrench tomorrow, because it affects the morale of the industry' (i.e. the union will make trouble).
> (Holmström 1976:47–8)

Workers in smaller firms, and some big ones, have little reason to trust in such a 'marriage'; but employers show by their deeds and words that they regard job security as one of the heaviest burdens the law imposes on them.

All these rights – especially job security – are effective only where there is a strong union to fight for them by legal and other means. *Union recognition* and *industrial disputes* are governed by the Industrial Relations Act and widely varying state laws (see National Commission 1969:319–51 for a full, though now out of date, account of the law and its working). The Industrial Disputes Act, applying to firms with fifty workers or more, provides for conciliation, voluntary arbitration and compulsory adjudication by tribunals and industrial courts; a period of delay and legal procedures to be gone through before a legal strike can be called; and state Labour Commissioners to administer the industrial relations machinery. It also lays down 'voluntary arrangements' for identifying the representative union in each firm, backed up in some states with laws on compulsory union recognition: for example the Maharashtra Recognition of Trade Unions and Prevention of Unfair Labour Practices Act, 1971, which most unions opposed on the grounds that it would not lead to genuine collective bargaining but to litigation on everything. In states like West Bengal and Tamil Nadu, the only provision for union recognition is an agreed voluntary 'Code of Discipline'.

In practice, unions and employers play a complicated game, each making tactical switches between legal procedures, the state conciliation machinery and informal contacts with officials, influence with central and state politicians, and direct industrial action (strikes, gheraos, lockouts, suspensions and dismissals): 'The formalities for starting a legal strike are so cumbersome that many strikes are technically "illegal", and a wise union leader knows how far illegal action can go without putting the union at a disadvantage in the legalistic process of negotiation' (Holmström 1976:66). Employers behave in a similar way. This legal shadow play is more or less confined to factories well above the fifty-worker threshold; in smaller firms the issues are settled by a direct trial of strength. What matters there is not whether the union is 'recognized' by the management, but that the law allows any group of workers (now seven) to form a union, which enjoys legal immunities and can take a worker's case to court.

This is not to say that the official machinery for enforcing labour laws is always ineffective or corrupt. Some state governments take a tougher line than others on enforcement, though there is a general policy that factory inspectors and government Labour Officers should persuade employers to improve working conditions, to pay minimum wages etc. rather than prosecuting. Some inspectors are corrupt; some side with employers or are equivocal (Streefkerk 1978:218–9).

One inspector told me workers are only dismissed for misconduct or perhaps union activities. Since rival unions are trying to establish themselves, they will persuade a dismissed worker to go to court. The workers' level of intelligence is so low that they are vulnerable to this kind of manipulation. The factories employ children for processes like assembling small components, where 'it is almost imperative to have them'. There are few prosecutions (probably none).

There are also dedicated inspectors who make surprise visits, listen to unions and use the threat of prosecution and contacts with the police and other government offices to put pressure on defaulting employers, but who are overwhelmed by an impossible work load and the employers' ingenuity.

The easiest way to evade the law is to ignore it. A very small workshop in a house or back yard need not be registered anywhere, for tax or any other purpose. A slightly bigger unit may accept the slight risk of prosecution for child labour, low wages or dangerous conditions: when the inspector comes, make the children or surplus workers disappear – in fact they may regard this as an exciting game of hide-and-seek and a break in the working day; or bribe the inspector if you can:

> Any brush with the authorities means that some official's palm has to be greased, and what is more, greased regularly. For instance, every year an employee of the factory inspectorate visits each plant to check whether industrial safety rules are being observed. Many inspectors do not bother to inspect anything; they merely come to collect their bribe. As one small manufacturer puts it: 'The factory inspector is a very nice man. He doesn't harass us; he only takes money. And if we give him enough he allows us to flout the inspectorate's regulations at will.' (G.S.G. Vohra 1975)

Since not all inspectors can be bought off, there are other ways to remain apparently within the law:

> One . . . finds many small scale employers who have made labour legislation the main target of attack in public and followed it up by non-observance or evasion in practice. They speak the language of a big employer, use the services of lawyers in the same manner as other employers do, and are prepared to face the wrath of union leaders, knowing well the weakness behind this wrath. Their method is crude splitting of larger units into smaller ones only in name. Signboards dividing a unit in two or more parts even within the same premises are not unusual, particularly in handloom and powerloom factories and small engineering units. (National Commission 1969:36)

This is like the fictitious division of land between relatives or front men to avoid the ceilings imposed by land reform laws.

A Bombay chemical factory is divided into three. One 'firm' makes a slurry which is 'sold' to another making chemicals for dyes and soaps under the same roof; the third seems to be completely fictitious. In other cases signboards hang in the middle of a shed where an integrated process is carried on, even over a large machine: each end is a 'firm' with its own register of employees, just below the ten- or fifty-worker threshold.

A Bangalore aluminium firm operated under three names. When the union complained to the Labour Officer, the owner quickly opened an office for each 'firm', with attendance records going back two months. The union pointed out that some names occurred in more than one register, and the owner settled with the union.

Another Bangalore engineering firm has sixty regular and forty temporary workers. It divided nominally into three firms, each with less than twenty regular workers because that was until recently the smallest number who could form a union. Workers who contacted a union leader got no overtime and are forbidden to talk together at work. The owner told them 'If you form a union, I've money in this hand, and I'll fight with the other hand.'

Records can be falsified. Workers getting less than the minimum wage, if they want to keep their jobs, may have to sign a book showing they have received the full rate. In one company workers sign in ink but the wages are pencilled in. A watchman, sacked after thirteen years, received Rs 120 in compensation and signed a receipt, which he said was altered to Rs 2120.

A common tactic is to sack them just before they complete the 240 days' continuous work which would entitle them to permanent status (with different qualifying periods for other fringe benefits): they are then taken on a few days or weeks later. 'The mill [in Coimbatore] was running an entire shift with temporary hands by resorting to the familiar device of laying off workers every three months and re-employing them after a few days' (E.A. Ramaswamy 1977:115). The shorter the period, the less the employer risks incurring obligations towards the worker. A Bombay pharmaceutical firm with thirty permanent workers (minimum pay Rs 350) and 130 'temporaries' (Rs 130) requires workers to sign this letter:

Temporary labour appointment letter

We have pleasure in appointing you as a Temporary Labourer to work in the _____ section from _____ due to temporary increase of work in the said section. Your appointment is purely temporary for a maximum period of two months . . . In case the work demands further employment, your services, as agreed under this letter may be continued for another period of two months or part thereof at the sole discretion of the Management, but, thereafter your services shall stand automatically terminated without assigning any reason, notice or notice pay. However, the Management reserve the right to terminate your service even before expiry of the agreed period of your employment, without assigning any reason and also without any notice or notice pay in lieu thereof.

One can remain a 'temporary' or casual worker at the same place for years, with short breaks; though some employers evidently find it safer to recruit new workers.

'The issue of the break system of temporary workmen shall be discussed and settled' – this was one of the chief points on the agenda for negotiations after a bitter strike at a Bombay plastic firm (twenty-five permanent workers, fifty temporaries getting half the minimum wage). Temporary workers from other firms, who are not union members, come into the same union's office to ask for help because they have been laid off just before they would have become 'permanent'.

Managements on one side, the more energetic unions, state governments and inspectors on the other, seek constantly to outwit each other at this game. Thus the Maharashtra Recognition of Trade Unions and Unfair Labour Practices Act, 1971, forbids managements: 'To employ employees as "*badlis*", casuals or temporaries and to continue them as such for years, with the object of depriving them of the status and privileges of permanent employees.' In 1977 the state government introduced new rules which – if enforced – would give permanent status to any worker, including casual and contract workers, who completes three months' service even with interruptions.

Harassed employers can turn to lawyers, or even union leaders, acting as 'labour consultants' or advisers ('G.R. Shah. Consultant. ESI and Provident Fund'), or they can buy books, like *Right procedure for dismissal*, which show how to make case law work in your favour. They can agitate for changes in the law: the printers of Karnataka appealed to the central and state governments to exempt small presses from the Factory Act, if they agreed to pay minimum wages ('In Karnataka, the majority of printing presses were in the small-scale sector, providing employment to over 50 000 persons. Strongly pleading for exempting the small printer from the provisions of the Factory Act, [their Vice-President] said they also suffered from the heavy burden of the Sales Tax' *Deccan Herald*, 27 June 1977). When the Maharashtra government raised minimum wages in 1974, small-scale employers first tried legal action (inspectors were told to 'persuade' employers but not to prosecute yet – 'Most employers are awaiting the decision of the Supreme Court and are not paying the prescribed rates', Office of the Commissioner of Labour 1976), then a campaign of deputations and mass demonstrations by employers threatening to retrench labour or to close firms ('According to small industrialists, the only advantage enjoyed about the competitiveness of their products had been taken away by the mandatory increase in minimum wages and had made their existence impossible' – 'Minimum wage echo: small units observe bandh', *Economic Times*, 8 Feb. 1975; cf. 'Small industries sore: minimum wages order', *Economic Times*, 8 Jan. 1977).

Simple evasion, evasion with bribery or legal chicanery, splitting firms or workers' periods of continuous employment: these are well-tried ways for an employer to keep clear of laws on working conditions, pay, unions and taxes – or perhaps, to be fair, to avoid spending all his time on paper work and fending off bureaucrats. Large firms use some of these methods too, and not all small firms. Many employers keep the law and make the best of it, either because unions or inspectors force them to do so, or for economic or ideological reasons – some find it a false economy to employ a low-paid shifting work force in poor conditions.

How seriously then should one take the complaint that extension of labour laws and unions would cut profits so sharply that the amount of industrial employment would fall? This has not been tested in practice, because employers have been able to move labour across the boundary, into the unorganized or unprotected sector, whenever they thought it necessary. For example, many firms threatened with the introduction of unions have closed down and reopened soon afterwards with non-union workers. This is often a panic reaction – employers see the unions as a personal affront, disrupting the close ties they fancy they have with workers, and violating 'management's right to manage' – rather than an economically rational decision, since in spite of their rhetoric the unions know there are limits to what they can get from an employer without bankrupting him. Where small firms have been made to pay the legal minimum wages, these are still much lower than the rates in big factories. In export markets all Indian firms have some competitive advantage, since the best Indian wages are very low by world standards. Even with slightly higher labour costs, the official concessions to small-scale industries – taxes, loans, assistance and reserved markets – still attract investors.

Labour laws are a constraint, but one the small employers can probably live with. For unions moving into the unorganized sector, enforcement of the labour laws is a rallying-point, something concrete to campaign for. Recent changes in central and state laws, introduced or under discussion, are designed to close the loopholes and to reduce disparities between organized and unorganized labour by giving some protection and security to workers in small units, to temporary and casual workers and even farm labour.

Contract labour

The employers' problem is this. Employing someone sets up lasting obligations: moral obligations which may not constrain employers much but mean something to them because they like to think they have a trusting paternal relation with their workers; and legal obligations, which the unions insist on and which are gradually extended to temporary workers and small firms. Employers operate in ruthless competitive markets for orders and capital, with some trust, mutual aid and patronage. It is convenient to turn employment into a short-term market relation as in nineteenth-century economic theory, where labour was a commodity bought and sold, the amount or duration and the price depending on supply and demand.

The solution is contract labour. In the early days of Indian industry, when even 'regular' workers had no security, employers found it simplest to manage much of their work force through labour contractors, who recruited, controlled and paid the workers. By the 1920s, with new technologies and trained managers, this practice was largely abandoned in factories, except for construction and genuinely temporary tasks. It has come back in the last twenty years, even for skilled full-time jobs, since directly employed workers expect security and will take industrial action to defend it.

According to employers:

> Payment by results, closer supervision by contractors, prompt penalty for staying below the output norms and high waste, and good work as the only basis of employment security, induced workers to produce more [except in certain skilled jobs] . . . But in most of the unskilled and other jobs, higher efficiency could be achieved by modifying the workers' employment relationship.
>
> (K.N. Vaid, 1966:21, *Contract labour in manufacturing industries*)

A Ludhiana firm making sewing-machine wheels raised the efficiency of its five workers by 75 per cent when it handed over the management to a contractor.

> To the argument that in these cases the contractor might be a better manager than the firm's manager, the employers replied that contractors were not subjected to the restrictive controls of laws and, therefore, could always get

more work from the operatives . . . The need to achieve higher efficiency compelled the establishments to substitute contract labour on jobs currently performed by regular workers. (:21–2)

Whether the management of the whole factory was given to a contractor, or only some of the work, contract labour cut the cost of fringe benefits, made it easier to shed labour, discouraged unions, 'made visits to my factory less attractive to government inspectors, and enlarged my sphere of influence in the local labour market' (:24). Vaid found that highly skilled engineering workers could sometimes earn more as contract labour; unskilled engineering workers earned about as much as regular workers, but without security or fringe benefits like leave; and textile workers earned half the regular wage or less (:6–7).

Since then the gap between permanent and contract labour seems to have widened. In some factories two workers stand side by side doing the same work, except that one is a regular worker earning two or three times as much as the other, a contract worker who cannot join a union, eat in the canteen or use the same lavatory. A union leader called it apartheid.

Big factories in the 'Thana–Belapur belt' pay their cleaners at least Rs 600 (1977 rates) to work with contract cleaners earning Rs 150–200. In the same area contract workers doing ordinary production jobs – mostly local people who lost their land to factories – get Rs 80–130; permanent production workers, at least Rs 650. A chemical factory here employs 400 permanent and 1200 contract or 'temporary' workers. In a big 'industrial house', with firms all over India, some 5 per cent of the work force are long-term 'casual' or 'temporary' workers; up to 10 per cent of the work force are contract labourers, who do loading, unloading, cleaning, building, salt pan work etc., at wages varying between one-half and one-sixth of the rate for comparable permanent workers. The proportion of contract workers is often much higher. The National Commission on Labour (1969:420–1) listed some jobs for which contract labour was used, like nickel polishing and electroplating in engineering firms, and observed that contract workers' pay was generally lower, working hours were irregular and longer without paid leave and 'There is no security of employment; the job ends with the contract.'[10]

---

[10] The Labour Bureau carried out surveys of contract labour, working conditions, and the jobs for which it was most used, in these industries: structural clay products; metal products except machinery and transport equipment; sugar; and edible oils. For a summary of the findings, with references to the original publications, see Labour Bureau 1978:207–10.

The amount of contract labour is hard to determine but is certainly growing, and higher than the few official figures show, because new legislation, and government and union pressure, give employers a motive to hide it. The National Commission (:419–20) found the proportion was as high as two-thirds in several industries (manganese and iron mining, jute pressing, tarpaulin etc.). A Maharashtra law, the Contract Labour (Regulation and Abolition) Act, 1970, requires firms employing twenty or more contract workers to register and regulates pay and working conditions. In an unpublished note of 1976 on the Act's working, the Office of the Commissioner of Labour estimated that at least 20 per cent of the work force were contract labour: especially construction workers, but: 'Almost all factories engage contract labour in one form or another.'

In the commonest form, the factory owner contracts with an outside entrepreneur who sees that labour is available to do some or all of the work in the factory (as in the Ludhiana firm described on p. 172). The employer has nothing to do with the workers and no direct responsibility for them, though state and national laws are edging towards a change. In principle this is like the 'labour jobs' where big firms or intermediaries lend materials, and sometimes dies or tools, to a small entrepreneur with his own premises, machinery and labour; except that contract labour is employed in the main employer's factory and on his machines, within sight of the regular employees – a detail which affects the way both contract and regular workers see their relationship: out of sight, out of mind. These contractors need little capital except contacts among workers and some management and technical skill: they include former skilled workers, and relatives of the factory owners. In some factories the contractor has his own machines, standing beside the factory owner's machines operated by regular workers.

These are ordinary production jobs. Certain jobs around the factory are regularly farmed out to contractors: in some cases because the labour requirement fluctuates, as in loading and unloading, and of course construction. Cleaners, watchmen and factory canteen staff often work for contractors: not always petty entrepreneurs, but also contractors who specialize in supplying these services to many firms, or a co-operative of the permanent employees who appoint one member to manage the canteen or cleaning workers.

Another kind of contract labour is home work: the contract – usually informal – may be between the main employer and the worker, but it is a contract to supply finished goods, not a contract of 'employment'. Almost all bidis or country cigarettes are now made at home, since labour laws have caused so many factories to close. Electronic assembly is often done at home by women and children: a Bombay factory owner claims that the women – often his former employees – can earn three times as much as in the factory; the advantage to him is that he has less liability, and if business falls off, 'I can shut it up'. Regular workers also take work home, like electric coils which they and their families can wind. A car component firm subcontracts urgent jobs to permanent workers, who choose one of their number as contractor and stay on after hours to finish the job, instead of doing overtime under the regular management. In many cases those who take work home have two or three employees of their own, working with simple tools or second-hand machines in houses and doorways, and this may become the nucleus of an independent workshop. Thus factory employees – who in any case may see themselves as members of joint families which employ farm labourers – are quite often small industrial employers as well.

There are chances, though not good ones, for contract workers to join the permanent staff in factories where they work. A few make personal contacts with workers and supervisors: thus an educated young man in Bangalore worked as a building labourer on a new factory, which took him on when it started production. New laws in states like Maharashtra and Kerala not only regulate conditions for contract labour, but are meant to phase it out by requiring employers to give permanent jobs to any temporary or contract workers employed continuously in their factories. A multinational with many plants has absorbed all its contract workers except those employed for genuinely temporary tasks. In some cases pressure to absorb contract labour comes from the union – permanent workers do not want their rates to be undercut, or the union activists have sympathy for the contract workers' plight. In one cement factory with 200 regular workers, 60 contract workers load trucks, print bags with tar etc., for piece rates paid by the three contractors: two ex-workers and a director's relative. In this factory, unusually, the contract workers are union members, and the union has persuaded the management to take six workers from each contractor on to the permanent staff as a step towards ending contract labour. In a Bombay firm making fire-fighting equipment, permanent workers supported the casual and contract workers who belonged to another section of their union, and forced a pay rise for contract workers to levels closer to those paid to permanent workers: the union insisted on negotiating directly with the company, not the contractors who were technically the men's employers.

Another Bombay firm, making aluminium utensils, closed down because of a raw material shortage, and paid the legal compensation to its own workers, but not to workers in a department managed by a contractor. The union went to court, where the contractor and the principal employer each said the other should pay. While the case was pending, the employer started the business again in another place.

Elsewhere employers have met the threat of legal action by laying off contract workers: Timir Basu (1977) claims that if the Contract Labour (Regulation and Abolition) Act were enforced in West Bengal, labourers with decades of service would have to seek other work: 'After the implementation of the Act in a Howrah-based industrial concern, contract labourers were dismissed. Sometimes companies resort to massive overtime schemes just to bribe the permanent workmen and to put them against the contract labourers' (:1042). In another cement factory, which kept a pool of casual but directly employed labourers to unload trucks, the casuals organized a successful gherao (confining management staff to their office) to prevent the firm from replacing them with contract labour.

Contract workers seldom get permanent jobs in the same factory. Much more often, employers turn regular workers into contract workers to cut costs and reduce their long-term liability to workers, to evade laws on working conditions or to break strikes and keep the unions out. This is one of a list of employers' bad habits specifically forbidden in Maharashtra ('To abolish the work of a regular nature being done by employees, and to give such work to contractors as a measure of breaking a strike.' Maharashtra Recognition of Trade Unions and Prevention of Unfair Labour Practices Act, 1971). The process has gone furthest in bidi manufacture. Where there is a need for machinery and teamwork, and therefore for factories, there are ways to keep some or all of the workers in the factory while ceasing to employ them directly.

In Bombay textile mills using man-made fibres – though not I think in cotton mills, where unions have stopped it – the owners lend money to a few favoured workers to buy looms from the company. The worker then becomes a contractor, employing his own men to operate three or four looms which are his property mortgaged to the employer. The looms stay where they were, bolted to the factory floor. In the Ludhiana hosiery industry, after a strike collapsed in 1970, whole factories were divided up in this way among worker–contractors, who employ the rest of the work force as piece-workers, buy wool from the owner and sell him the finished goods. In the West Bengal jute mills, the worker employs others but does not own the looms:

> The Bhagwala system, a kind of piece-rating, covers well over 40 per cent of the workforce in almost all the mills, it is alleged. A worker is asked to accept double the regular work norm in the carpet or hessian department and workmen are forced to hire outsiders, whom he (*sic*) pays out of his pocket, to fulfil the stipulated quota. These 'outsiders' are generally retrenched workers, sometimes of the same mill where they had once worked for years together, or women workers who happen to be wives of the respective workmen.
> (Basu 1979a:187; and see Basu 1980a)

With the steady advance of contract labour within factories, more and more employees have become employers on a very small scale, sometimes keeping the status of permanent employees themselves. The management of a Bombay electrical firm gave the profitable contract for cleaning the factory and running the canteen to a co-operative of the firm's employees, organized by the union representative, who brought in some cleaners but says he knows nothing about them because they are 'Scheduled Caste'. In another factory the canteen workers struck against the firm's workers who employed them, and the outsider union leader had to conciliate the two groups.

The situation where permanent workers, individually or as a co-operative, employ other workers within the factory but with no security and lower pay, is still not so common. But wherever directly employed and contract workers are found together in the same place, both groups are constantly reminded of the difference in their conditions – more so than if the employer sent some of the work out to contract somewhere else. Contract workers naturally envy permanent ones, who may rightly see contract labour as a threat to their jobs and pay: thus one man said he was dismissed for cleaning slotted angles more slowly than a contract worker. There are many examples of firms which went over to contract labour, leaving the employees with no security, harsher working conditions and often less pay. Although many people have crossed the boundary or may have to, it is here – in the split between directly employed and contract labour, rather than between large and small firms, or between permanent and temporary workers in the organized sector – that there seems to be some evidence that workers see themselves as forming two groups with divergent interests.

As I said, some permanent workers and their unions – often led by middle-class idealists who are outsiders or in junior supervisory posts – have tried to solve the problem, not by keeping contract workers out, but by putting pressure on the management to improve their conditions and to absorb them gradually into the permanent work force. On the other hand, some very large firms around Bombay employ roughly equal numbers of regular workers and of low-paid workers who, to avoid the Contract Labour Act, 'don't exist'. The unions, largely single-factory unions belonging to no federation, resent the presence of these 'black workers' (cf. 'black money') and make sure none of them get into the union. (I had this from a union leader, a fair-minded man of wide experience, and the one who compared the system to apartheid: another unionist said contract and regular workers were like two castes.) The general secretary of an important union said of contract workers, 'they are outsiders – we don't know who they are'.

One afternoon at a union office in North Bombay, a friend took me to see a gherao which had begun suddenly at a firm finishing road petrol tankers. The thirty regular workers were not satisfied with the details of a new bonus agreement, and were shouting slogans outside the office where the owner was confined with two of his staff. One man who tried to get out was warned to go back. Two union officials interceded but took care that the workers who had started the action should know what was going on: thus they insisted on negotiating publicly in Marathi and Hindi, not English. After three hours of shouting with breaks for negotiation and the owner's attempts to defuse the situation with jokes, the dispute was settled and the owner sat down to tea with the officials and with me.

All afternoon, while the regular workers shouted 'Workers' unity' and 'Workers are brothers' in chorus and sang a revolutionary song, a group of contract workers went on painting tankers a few yards away. Occasionally one of them would come over to see what was happening. None were union members, and no one paid any attention to them.

Live and let live; let everyone fight his own battle. But there is a real conflict of interest when permanent workers are dismissed and replaced with contract workers, either outsiders or ex-employees whom the employer still trusts.

A Bangalore firm making sugar-cane crushers laid off all 110 workers in 1966, and used only cheap contract labour for two years. The new contract workers joined a union, which forced the management to give all of them permanent jobs; meanwhile the same union took the dismissed workers' case to court. In 1972 the court accepted an agreement between the management and the majority of workers that the men should get their jobs back without back pay. A condition – not mentioned in court – was that they should resign from the union: thirty-two refused, and the union was still trying to get them reinstated five years later.

Another Bangalore firm makes bus bodies. When orders fell off in 1976 the firm laid off all fifty-two workers but continued with contract workers, the number varying between thirty and fifty. All the contractors, but only five or six of the contract workers, used to work there. The union complained to the Commissioner of Labour that this was 'an illegal lockout under guise of lay off' to harass the union and cut wages. 'The same number continue to work, but with new complements in place of retrenched workers': for example, four carpenters had been laid off 'on the plea of load of work', but the same work was being done by contract carpenters. The union demanded reinstatement with back pay. If it won, the vice-president said, the new contract workers would have to go.

In this case contract workers were regarded as blacklegs, stealing other men's jobs. In general, directly employed workers – including casual ones – and their unions resent the spread of contract labour, whether they blame the contract workers themselves or employers who use the system to avoid any long-term commitment to their workers: a moral obligation in workers' eyes, backed at least by the letter of the law, though employers claim they cannot fulfil it and stay in business.

Relations between firms and between workers

In this chapter I have qualified a view of the economy which is broadly true. Firms are links in chains of dependence, tempered by interdependence. The firms in the strongest position to extract profit from others are usually but not always the big ones. For an entrepreneur or a worker, the stronger his foothold in the big organized sector firms and the better his contacts there, the more control he will have over his own economic life and over other people.

About half the industrial work force are employed in the 'organized sector', though not all have permanent jobs. Most permanent workers have 'unorganized sector' workers as neighbours and relatives, but the converse is not true: in many areas and families, no one has a steady job.

Small firms, especially if they supply the newer industries, are not particularly labour-intensive. They save on labour costs rather than machinery, and cheap labour is their main competitive advantage. To keep it they resort to various ways of evading laws and union pressures which would force them to pay higher wages and to employ workers even when business is poor. These include keeping a pool of 'temporary' workers who are periodically laid off; fictitious division of factories into smaller firms; closing firms down; and, increasingly, the use of contract labour in place of directly employed labour. Many large firms also do these things.

This is the structure in which workers find jobs. Security, pay and prospects generally go together: only a few people are in a position to sacrifice one for another. The extent to which a worker enjoys all three depends mainly on how closely he approaches the status of a permanent employee in a big modern factory ('modern' refers to the technology, usually matched to the firm's age and style of management: it distinguishes the new kinds of engineering, electronics and so on from most cotton mills, all jute mills and some of Calcutta's heavy engineering). At the other extreme are tiny workshops which grub for orders on the fringe of the industrial economy, recycle waste products etc.: here workers have no security, and pay and conditions are worst. Between these two extremes, the divisions between the more and less fortunate workers are not very closely matched to relations of dependence between firms. Even some – not all – of the strongest firms rely heavily on the most insecure cheap labour they can get, which is contract labour.

5
Labour markets

How does one get a job? Which jobs are open to which people, for example people from different social origins? What happens to them afterwards: what are their chances of keeping the job or moving to a better one? And if people from certain backgrounds have an advantage in the competition for jobs, what are the other social consequences?

In the last chapter I showed how markets, linkages between firms, government policies and the law account for important differences in the terms of employment for industrial workers: permanent workers in large firms, workers in small firms with regular jobs but no legal security, 'temporary' or contract workers employed for continuous stretches and genuinely casual workers who are often out of work. The most secure jobs are generally the best paid, except for some skilled work like carpentry. Unions respond to this situation in various ways, but do not (I think) bring it about.

Workers in small workshops, or 'temporary' and contract workers in factories, often appear to do the same work as permanent factory workers, or very similar work, though they earn much less. In some cases (as factory managers claim) the same job title may conceal a wide difference in standards of skill and training and precision between factories and workshops. This need not mean factories get all the most able workers, only that they have the best machinery and training resources. But H. and V. Joshi are right when they say that a very wide range of skilled and enterprising people work for low wages in the unskilled sector (1976a: 56, quoted on p. 153 above).

This could not happen in a fully competitive labour market, where wages (and presumably security, if workers value it enough to sacrifice wages for it) would tend to be the same for similar occupations, or between occupations if workers have time and opportunity to retrain (Papola and Subrahmanian 1975:3–4); but 'even though markets for all commodities are imperfect, the labour market tends to be more imperfect everywhere' (:4). One reason is that information is not a free good, and getting jobs depends largely on contacts and influence. Of course a perfect labour market – if such a thing existed – need not reduce social inequalities, since it would favour those with education and with families to support them while they wait for the right job.

Owens and Nandy (1977:39) paint a picture of the Howrah small engineering industry which came close to an open competitive labour market. 'At the bottom is the worker who invests his own skill and energy in someone else's factory on a piecework basis.' Then there are all kinds of ways to work one's way up and become rich: 'The crucial point is that the cost of entry is very low economically.' Yet their own evidence shows that these opportunities are largely restricted to poor boys of Mahisya caste, which once ranked low but now dominates local industry and is respected. Other low castes lack contacts, and it is hard for the high-caste Kayasths and Brahmans to adapt themselves to this career. Owens and Nandy conclude: 'When formerly low-placed groups became involved in secondary industrialization the result is a wide transformation of the society in accordance with more egalitarian values' (:196); but a rearrangement of caste ranks is not equality.

This is a variant of the 'graduation hypothesis', which usually refers to migrants, since the move from village to slum is their point of entry into the urban labour market (see Joshi 1976a:132–5 for a brief discussion). The market is divided into compartments, but an energetic person can climb the fences and 'graduate' from casual to regular work, then to a good factory job or his own business.

The Joshis argue that very few workers 'graduate' from the unorganized to the organized sector, though they may improve their position within their own sector. It is unrealistic to talk of a single labour market, for there are two, each open to a different kind of people; and these correspond to the two halves of India's dual economy.

Lalit Deshpande (1970) asks which of two theories is more relevant to Bombay's labour market. One is the neoclassical theory of a single competitive labour market, where information is free and individuals maximize their money or 'psychic income' (:163). The other is the Segmented Labour Market (SLM) theory, like the Joshis' dualistic theory, which says that a person's social origins, and therefore his contacts, determine the segment of the labour market where he can compete for jobs: factories, small establishments or casual work. Once in a segment it is very hard to move into a better one. Several factors determine income from work, but 'a characteristic common to most of these factors is that an individual worker cannot change them by investing in himself' (:187).

The labour market is a large-scale aggregating notion. Labour market studies show how many from which origins get jobs, how many had friends or relatives to help them, changes in jobs and earnings over a lifetime and so on. From this information we can only guess at how people see the choices before them, and their motives. I shall try to match this statistical information to evidence of another kind: the experience and motives and values of people who have looked for jobs, according to the workers or unemployed people I have talked to; evidence from ethnographic studies, from trade unionists and journalists and others, and from what I have seen and heard in Indian cities (also Lalit Deshpande's conversation, since he is an acute and sympathetic observer).

The Bombay labour market

The best labour market study, and the only one which makes detailed comparisons between the organized and unorganized sectors, is Lalit Deshpande's 'Bombay labour market' (1979).[1] Bombay with its mixture of older industries (mainly cotton) and new technologies (engineering, chemicals, electronics) provides a good cross-section of the kinds of work found in other cities that have grown over the last twenty years, except perhaps in two respects: most industry is privately owned, while in places like Bangalore and Calcutta much of it is in the public sector; and Bombay has a very high proportion of rural migrants.

Deshpande and Papola, who began the study together, set out to collect information on Bombay's working population, migration, job finding, wages, family characteristics, careers; and to answer various questions. Is it true, as H. and V. Joshi argue (1976a), that the work force grew faster than organized sector employment between 1961 and 1971, leaving more people to find low-paid work in the unorganized or informal sector? (Deshpande's short answer is no.) If the labour market can be divded into three sectors – organized,

---

[1] Since it is not yet (1984) as accessible as it deserves to be, I give a long account of it here, with my own comments, and with the author's consent. I owe him a great deal besides.

unorganized and casual – how easy is it to improve one's earnings within a sector or to 'graduate' to another? How wide are the differences, not only in wages but in family living standards, between workers in different sectors? And how far is the stratification of labour determined by family background and social origin?

Using the 1971 Census as a frame, they chose three samples: factory workers (limited as in the Joshi's study to firms with over twenty-five workers, on which the state Directorate of Employment collects information); workers in small establishments registered under the Shops and Commercial Establishments Act (34 per cent were manufacturing workers); and 'a heterogeneous group . . . labelled Casual Sector for convenience' (Deshpande 1979:7). These casual workers were much harder to find, and the sample is less reliable:[2] again, 34 per cent work in manufacturing (household and non-household) as against 43 per cent of casual workers in the Census, which may under-represent construction. Investigators took questionnaires to 6000 workers, representing with their families a population of over 21 000.

The factory sample corresponds roughly to the industrial 'organized sector'. Most appear to have permanent jobs, since in each factory the investigators took a sample of employees (excluding supervisors and managers) reported to the chief inspector of factories. Some long-term 'temporaries' may be included, but not casuals (who might come into the casual sample if they wait at the factory gate for work) or contract workers.

Manufacturing workers in the small establishment sample represent the 'unorganized sector' workshops. They are distinguished from the non-manufacturing majority of the sample (shop and café workers etc.) in my own tables, which are based on the completed questionnaires Deshpande lent me, and indirectly in some of Deshpande's tables which refer to 'commercial establishments' (this does not mean shops) or particular occupations. Many small establishments were substitutes, because 'the proprietors did not allow the investigators to interview even half the numbers employed' (:15). Though the average 'commercial establishment' or workshop employs only six, I suspect many are bigger, but reported a number

---

[2] 'The investigators were instructed to go round the wards allotted to them and visually assess the number of workers collected at such sites as factory gates, rail and bus stations, wholesale and retail markets, construction sites etc. The quota was to be allocated to sites in proportion to the strength at each major site. Individual workers were selected randomly and interviewed after ascertaining the nature of work.' (Deshpande 1979:11)

below the Factory Act threshold or refused to answer. For example, only 1.14 per cent of small establishment workers (and 1.8 per cent of casuals) are children under fifteen (:76), though 12 per cent of all workers say they started work before that age (:149) and anyone can see that many children are still employed.[3] Bombay slum children (mostly aged from 12 to 15; 59 per cent Scheduled Caste or Harijan) showed that 70 per cent were employed, including 19 per cent in production units making plastic pens, sweets, shoes, bidis etc. (Pandhe 1979:112ff). Children were also widely employed in domestic work, in services and repairs, and the dangerous and unhealthy waste recycling industry which many production enterprises depend on.

Manufacturing workers in the casual sample, whether they find work in large or small firms, are part of my 'unorganized sector' work force; but it is likely that many other short-term or contract workers, who do not wait at the factory gate, did not come into any of the three samples.

This is such an important wide-ranging study that I shall have occasion to refer to it throughout this book, using Deshpande's findings as a check on my own observations. It is not only a labour market study, but a statistical profile of the Bombay working class or classes, with a discussion of 'dualism' and the prospects for industrial development. Here I concentrate on differences between workers in the three samples, with respect to their origins, search for jobs, and careers.

The great majority of Bombay workers are men: 94 per cent of the random factory sample, and the same proportion of small establishment workers (the casual sample is 82 per cent male, but here the investigators were given a quota of women to interview). Factory workers are older than the rest: their average age is thirty-seven, compared with twenty-nine for small establishment workers and twenty-eight for casuals. In each sample, three-quarters of the workers are from outside Bombay: factory workers, being older, are the only group of whom most lived in the city for over ten years. Other

---

[3] Deshpande suggests that child labour has fallen in Bombay over recent years, even in small firms, partly because the legal minimum wages are the same for all ages (1979:149–50): but how many small employers pay these wages? It is true that workers reported that only 0.54 per cent of their family members under 15 were 'working'; yet 21 per cent of the children of school age (9–14) were not at school – 50 per cent of the children in casual workers' families (:215–16) – and it is hard to believe these children make no contribution to the family income.

Table 4. *Worker' education, by sector, in Bombay*

	Factories	Small establishments	Casuals	Total
Literate (%)	79	86	68	80
Passed standard XI (i.e. completed secondary education (%)	20	24	4	18
Graduates (%)	2	4	?	2
Average years of schooling	6.0	6.7	4.0	5.9

Source: Based on Deshpande 1979:92–6

workers are not only younger, and more recent migrants, but they or their parents came from more distant places, especially South India: 71 per cent of factory workers are from Maharashtra State (Bombay is the capital), as against 54 per cent of casual workers and only 46 per cent in small establishments. A still smaller proportion of small establishment workers speak the local language, Marathi, as their mother tongue (39 per cent, cf. 54 per cent of casuals and 64 per cent of factory workers).

The biggest surprise is education. At every level (simple literacy, years of schooling, secondary education completed, even degrees) small establishment workers come out well ahead of the better-paid factory workers. Casual workers, as one would expect, come last (see table 4). There are no comparable studies of other cities, yet I am fairly sure that in places like Bangalore and Poona, educated workers get the pick of the best (i.e. factory) jobs, either because education is actually required or because they belong to well-connected families and make a good impression on factory officers. In Bangalore at least, educated middle-class people were already well entrenched in the factories when employment opportunities shrank.

In Bombay, factory workers are less educated than small establishment workers, more often Maharashtrian, and older. It is clear that earlier Maharashtrian migrants got into the factory sector and stayed there, not necessarily in the same factories. More recent migrants followed at a time when more people were being educated for longer but factory employment was stagnant, and when the few factory vacancies tended to be filled by relatives and friends of those already employed.

The investigators asked respondents their caste or religion, but the answers are hard to interpret partly because the same caste may have several names. The report shows only that 'the employment market does seem to discriminate against Buddhists', i.e. against Harijans or Untouchables: almost all Harijans in Maharashtra are converts to Dr Ambedkar's neo-Buddhism. Only 2 per cent of the sample are Buddhists (2 per cent of factory workers, 1 per cent in 'small establishments', 4 per cent of casuals) compared with 5 per cent of the city's population. However, 'small establishments' includes eating-houses which are reluctant to employ Harijans; and more small establishment workers than factory workers are from other states, therefore less likely to be Buddhist converts. My subsample of the questionnaires shows that about the same proportion of workers in factories and *manufacturing* small establishments, or workshops, are either Buddhists or Hindu Harijans: 6.5 per cent, which is much higher. The figure for casuals would certainly be more if Hindu Harijans were included. The proportions of Brahmans and high to middle castes are similar in factories and workshops, though the factories have more members of Maharashtrian castes.

Despande's account of job finding begins with migration. Migrants generally come from those families owning the least land: factory workers' families have the biggest holdings, while half the casual workers' families are landless. Factory workers have the highest proportion who worked on the family farm before migration (49 per cent); small-scale workers, the highest proportion who were students (36 per cent); 26 per cent of casuals were already casual labourers. Again, the big gap is not between those who go into factories and workshops, but between both and the casual workers:

> Rural-to-urban migration transforms the rural poor into urban poor and the rural rich into urban rich. This however does not mean that the rural poor are the worse off because of migration. On the contrary . . . they benefit substantially by migration but despite the gain, their relative ranking does not seem to change. (Deshpande 1979:116)

Deshpande estimates these gains from migration by comparing the migrants' first urban wages with their previous incomes (with a net gain of 391 per cent for casual workers) and the gains from changing jobs afterwards. Only a quarter have a job assured when they come to the city; a mere 0.4 per cent (2 per cent of the casuals) were brought by jobbers or labour contractors. Friends and especially relatives reduce the cost of migration and looking for work, by providing food, shelter, cash and information.

> Social institutions like the extended family, caste and village community play
> a substantial role in reducing the private cost of migration and ensure that the
> stream of migrants is determined by the existing stock.   (:145)

If his relatives work in factories or workshops, he starts looking there;
but a casual worker knows none of the right people:

> He migrates alone and has very few friends and relations to help him find a job
> and to support him till he finds one of his choice. These circumstances force
> him to take up any work he can find . . . The casual worker continues to be
> employed at the lowest rung of the socio-economic ladder in Bombay just as he
> was in the villages.   (:144)

So much depends on the first job – is it in a factory, in a workshop or
casual labour? – or, rather, on the network of relationships one
already belongs to, since this largely determines the sector and type of
industry where the first job will be. With effort, ability and luck it is
possible to get a better job within the same sector, and sometimes to
move into another sector.

Deshpande writes about migration because Bombay is a city of
migrants. The problems of finding a job, keeping it and moving to a
better one, are similar for people brought up in Bombay and in other
Indian cities. In Bombay only 8 per cent of 'regular' workers in
factories or small establishments began their working lives as casual
workers (or 13 per cent of those regular workers who had changed
jobs). Some of these may be educated people who received technical
training at private institutes: though more factory workers are
trained, 17 per cent of casuals are trained and for a longer average
period than factory workers: 'This may indicate that some trained
persons prefer low paying employment in the Casual Sector to
unemployment' (:105). But such people need to get out of the casual
sector fast. The typical uneducated casual worker has little chance of
a regular job, or even of a better casual job.

Though migrant casual workers earn much more than in the
villages, their real wages have remained almost unchanged (up 2 per
cent) since their first city job: in fact women's real wages fell by 11 per
cent. This is in contrast to the experience of workers in small
establishments (a rise of 45 per cent) and factories (155 per cent,
excluding yearly bonuses of 8–20 per cent; not adjusted for the higher
average age of factory workers, which goes with yearly increments).

> The rise in real wages of factory workers could be attributed to institutional
> factors but that in the Small Establishment Sector with 5 per cent of its workers
> reporting union membership, has to be attributed to a rise in the demand for

labour. We have shown that the demand for labour in the Organised Sector is likely to have increased faster than the supply of labour [:61;65-9, where Deshpande questions the figures in Joshi 1976a]. Hence the rise in the real wage of factory sector need not be attributed to institutional factors alone . . . Apart from lack of institutional protection, the Casual workers are exposed, as no other workers are, to the fierce competition from fresh migrants. (:181)

Respondents were asked how they heard of jobs (including previous jobs) and who helped them to get the jobs. Two-thirds heard about the jobs from relatives (44 per cent) or friends (24 per cent), often people from the same village. Twenty-four per cent found out by their own efforts, including 32 per cent of the casual workers who have to rely more on finding out for themselves, asking in the streets and on building sites. Only 1.5 per cent of workers found out by answering advertisements. Another 1.5 per cent (2.4 per cent of factory workers) heard of their jobs through government employment exchanges, which should legally be informed of all factory vacancies.

Having heard of a job, one needs help in getting it. Here too most regular workers have relatives or friends to help them (59 per cent of factory workers, 65 per cent in small establishment) but only 30 per cent of casuals, who have to rely on their own efforts (41 per cent of casuals cf. 27 per cent of regular workers) or on fellow workers (24 per cent). 'Very few [0.15 per cent of all workers] pay a commission to obtain a job; which fact shows that the rationing of jobs does not take place through price mechanism but is based entirely on family ties and friendships' (:169). This is an exaggeration but is largely true. One should allow for inaccurate or ambiguous answers: a worker may be ashamed to admit he paid a bribe or commission; it may be a point of pride that he got the job by his own efforts; 'help' could mean actually securing the job, recommending someone or some less specific service.

Clearly casual workers, with few exceptions, stay at the bottom, thought they may not get any poorer. Deshpande does not show whether the small establishment sector is as hard to escape from as the casual sector. Certainly it is possible for an energetic or lucky person to move up within a sector. Factory workers in particular can learn a skill and get promotion as well as annual increments within a firm: unions push hard for internal promotion to skilled and supervisory jobs, while managements prefer a free hand to recruit outsiders if necessary; but Deshpande suggests that a worker's best chance of improving his earnings is to change jobs.

The average regular worker has changed jobs once in his career, and a quarter have made at least two changes; though when the figures are adjusted for age or duration of residence in Bombay, it is clear that small establishment workers move more often (:153–9). Casual workers by definition are constantly changing employers: only 30 per cent have changed their 'activity'. Among both factory and small establishment workers, three-fifths of all job changes were voluntary: in most cases, because workers found their earnings inadequate, and it is likely (though the report does not say so) that they did not resign until they had found new jobs. Only 22 per cent of regular workers who moved for any reason say they were unemployed between jobs: 46 per cent of these people were still looking for work a year later, and 6 per cent were unemployed for five years or longer.

Most workers who leave jobs say the wages are too low. Are they right in thinking they can earn more elsewhere?

Deshpande claims to provide 'positive proof' that workers who changed jobs benefited substantially, especially in the factories (:165). A factory worker who moved four times had gained on average 25 times the amount he earned in his first job; a small establishment worker, three times. Those who never moved have gained only 12.5 times their first wages (in factories) or 1.5 times (in small establishments). These figures are not adjusted for inflation or age, and factory workers are older.

While one worker went from factory to factory in search of higher pay, his twin brother *might* have done as well by staying in one factory. Mobility may be profitable, but these figures do not prove it. Four per cent of all regular workers, mostly in small establishments, earn less than in their first jobs.

In the factories, jobs are finely differentiated. 'Rates are fixed for the job and not for the man. In the informal sector it is often the man who is rated and not the job. Absence of unions gives the managers, mostly proprietors, freedom to vary the reward according to the skill of the person employed' (:175). On paper the 'skilled' small establishment worker does not appear to earn much more than an 'unskilled' worker. In any case 'the differential paid to the same level of skill across sectors is wider than the differential paid to skill within each sector' (:176).

On average, 'a small establishment worker earns 63 per cent and a factory worker 181 per cent more every month than a casual worker' (:171). In other words, factory workers earn 72 per cent more than small establishment workers (who are younger). There are wide

Table 5. *Earnings, by skill and by sector in Bombay**

	Casual	Small establishments	Factories
Unskilled	100	144	240
Semi-skilled	126	184	314
Skilled	144	217	463

Note: Unskilled casual labour = 100 (Rs 144.50/month)
* For my own sample, I give medians and make this clear in the text. Elsewhere I use Deshpande's averages, which are means.
Source: Based on Deshpande 1979:175–6

variations in the premium which different occupations command in the factories, ranging from 184 per cent (above the small establishment rate) for mechanics and repairmen, and 119 per cent for 'coolies' or general labourers, to only 26 per cent for carpenters (who are well paid in small firms). My own tables, from a sample of the questionnaires, show that factory workers' median pay is twice that of workers in manufacturing small establishments (or 98 per cent more). The gap ranges from 13 per cent for printers to 159 per cent for 'other unskilled production process workers' and 236 per cent for furnacemen and moulders.

If a small establishment worker could double his income – with security as a bonus – by doing the same work in a factory, what prevents him?

Mainly, as we have seen, the same obstacles which prevent casual workers from getting regular jobs, though not to the same extent: lack of contacts, of friends and relatives who know of the jobs and would recommend him to the management. The few factory jobs which fall vacant are largely spoken for by present or retiring workers with relatives in search of steady jobs. If the jobs are skilled, the unions insist they should be filled by training and promotion within the firm. But this is not the whole story: managements can still bring in outsiders, especially but not only men with rare skills. New or suddenly expanding factories must be staffed all at once. The legal and statistical cut-off points which define the organized sector are not always in the places where further progress up the ladder becomes hard for men trained in small workshops, and the average incomes in the factory sector hide wide variations between the bigger modern firms and the rest.

Deshpande was not able to find out how many factory workers had worked in small establishments. 'Very few had been *casual* workers', but the evidence on the way in which placements are made leads him to doubt the 'graduation hypothesis' (:208). In spite of the rising demand for organized sector labour,

> recruitment from the Unorganised Sector would be very small indeed. Most of the new workers would then be selected from the better qualified among the unemployed and the fresh migrants . . . They [migrants] would include some with qualifications that would land them in the Organised Sector immediately. If they do not get a high paid job on arrival, they would rather be unemployed than take up an employment in the Unorganised Sector. The fresh migrants would also include others with lower qualifications. Some of them would be absorbed in the vacancies created by the small number who were promoted to the Organised Sector. Some may have enough support in the City to postpone entering Unorganised Sector. Those who would have none to support them would join the Casual and the Small Establishment Sector. (:183–4)

The information on workers' families also suggests that unemployment – or rather waiting for a job in the right sector – is a luxury only some can afford. Unemployment is highest in factory workers' families, 'showing that the families form a distinct group whose members would rather be unemployed than take up a job in the informal sector' (:249).

This part of the report, on families, contains surprises. Not about casual workers: their families are by far the worst off. Their wives and other family members are more likely to work, but for very low wages. Yet the gap between living standards in small establishment workers' families and factory workers' families is much narrower than the gap in individual workers' wages (table 6). Factory workers have bigger families; and although in both sectors about 70 per cent of families depend on one earner, the employed members of small establishment workers' families earn more than secondary earners in any other sector. The average factory worker earns 73 per cent more than a small establishment worker, but his family income per head is only 14 per cent higher, or 27 per cent higher per adult equivalent unit (counting a man as one consumption unit, a woman as 0.8 and a child under twelve as 0.5). In my subsample, factory workers' median earnings were 108 per cent higher than those of workers in manufacturing small establishments only, while family incomes per adult equivalent unit were only 79 per cent higher. In Deshpande's whole ˙sample, expenditure per head is actually highest in small

Table 6. *Average earnings, and family living standards, among Bombay workers in the three sectors*

		Casual	Small establishments	Factories	Factories, as a percentage of the figure for small establishments
Income per earner	Rs/month	181	280	479	171%
	Index (casual = 100)	100	155	264	
Income per principal earner	Rs	216	307	532	173%
	Index	100	142	246	
Income per secondary earner	Rs	123	243	341	140%
	Index	100	198	278	
Family income	Rs	267	429	664	155%
	Index	100	161	249	
Family income per head	Rs	93	147	168	114%
	Index	100	159	181	
Family income per adult equivalent unit	Rs	103	159	202	127%
	Index	100	154	195	
Family expenditure	Rs	207	348	423	122%
	Index	100	162	143	
Family expenditure per head	Rs	72	117	103	88%
	Index	100	162	143	
Family expenditure as a percentage of income[a]		78%	81%	64%	

[a] These figures seem unrealistically low: the gap may represent remittances to relatives. However the ratio between sectors may be accurate.

Source: Based on Deshpande 1979:233, 242, rounded to nearest rupee or 1%.

establishment workers' families. Given that these figures were collected in difficult conditions and will bear more than one interpretation, there are some grounds to doubt whether workers in small establishments are really as disadvantaged as Deshpande and especially the Joshis say they are.

Deshpande concludes that the Bombay labour market is segmented into three non-competing groups, and 'workers are confined to a segment because of some pre-labour market characteristics' (:254), mainly land ownership in their villages and the influence and connexions that go with it:

> The early risers from the 'haves' not only gather the crumbs in the city but help the late-comers of the same feather in a number of ways: they fix a job for them even before they migrate, bring them along to the city, support them while they search for a job and help them to get employment.   (:255)

Thus Deshpande agrees with the Joshis that Bombay's labour market discriminates against applicants with work experience in the unorganized sector, who are often skilled and trained, and better educated than the average factory worker, but lack the right connexions. Since the factories are capital intensive and enjoy state protection, workers earn high wages which they invest in education: 33 per cent of people aged from fifteen to fifty-nine in factory workers' families are students, as against 28 per cent – a little less – in small establishment workers' families and only 18 per cent for casuals. 'The better educated children take up new factory jobs created in the economy. Thus the class of factory workers tends to perpetuate itself' (:226).

But it is not true that the city's labour force has grown faster than organized sector employment over the previous ten years, as the Joshis say. This growth of factories allowed some movement out of the small establishments, though Deshpande was not able to find the extent of it. I suspect that once the line is drawn for legal and statistical purposes, it may come to seem more clear and substantial than it is. In any case Deshpande shows that the really high barrier is between casual and any regular employment, not (as the Joshis suggest) between the unorganized and organized sectors.

P. Ramachandran, *Some aspects of labour mobility in Bombay city* (1974), is useful, though the fieldwork was done long ago – in 1960 – and limited to organized sector workers in five industries: textiles, dockyards, engineering, BEST (which supplies Bombay's electricity and bus service) and the five departments of the Municipal

Corporation or city government (street cleaning, workshops etc.). Structured interview schedules were taken to 1893 workers, and the conclusions of this short study are based on a statistical analysis of their answers to questions about their careers and motives. Some kinds of work are dominated by particular ethnic groups: Hindus in the textile mills, Muslims in the dockyards, neo-Buddhists (ex-Harijans) in the Municipality. Most workers – especially skilled workers – had had several jobs, and three-quarters of job changes had been voluntary. The commonest way to hear of jobs was through friends and relatives: in particular, 'the early jobs were secured through friends and relatives, the middle jobs through their own efforts [except in the dockyards] and the later jobs [presumably with the same employers] through promotions' (:20). Ramachandran also discusses conditions and motives for entry into the labour market, and commitment to industrial employment; comparisons between agricultural and industrial jobs of ex-agricultural workers; and women workers' mobility. But in present conditions, motivations to enter the organized sector, and commitment to stay there, are no longer the problems they may have been when this information was collected.

To fill in the details on this map of opportunities, consider some studies of cities with similar industries. Some of these cities share a labour market with Bombay.

Other studies of labour markets

I mentioned (p. 66) T.S. Papola and K.K. Subrahmanian, *Wage structure and labour mobility in a local labour market: a study of Ahmedabad* (1975, summarized in Papola 1977 and criticized from a 'dualistic' point of view by Heather Joshi in the *Economic and Political Weekly*, 2 April 1977: 575–6). About a quarter of the city's workers are in factories, a quarter in public services, 35 per cent in small establishments, and 15 per cent are independent or casual wage earners (Papola 1977:142). The book is about factory workers only, in the textile mills which employ three-quarters of Ahmedabad's factory workers, and the smaller but growing engineering and other factories. In spite of this limitation, this is a good critical study of an imperfect labour market and the rationality of workers' choices, based on questionnaires and interviews with workers and managements. Temporary workers make up 30 per cent of the sample.

Papola and Subrahmanian's main argument is that even within

the factory sector there is not one labour market, but 'markets within market'. Workers' behaviour is rational if the market is seen as divided into homogeneous closed units or segments, each of which is a named occupation as carried on within one industry. An occupation tends to command a similar wage in all firms in the same industry. In textiles, wages are determined by centralized wage bargaining, and the employers' association has enough solidarity to resist the practice of pirating workers away with the lure of higher wages, which it considers immoral (Papola and Subrahmanian 1975:124). Wage levels depend partly on whether an industry is dominated by large units: these units pay best, for reasons of 'status' as much as economics, and this has a 'spill-over' effect on the rest of the industry (:122). Wages for the same skill can differ by up to 25 per cent between industries.

In a perfect labour market, rational workers would move to the best-paid jobs, retraining if necessary. Ahmedabad workers are not very mobile: the average worker has changed jobs only once, almost always voluntarily. When a worker does move, he is quite likely to go to a new occupation in a new industry, which suggests that many skills are not hard to learn. Low-paid or temporary workers in particular would like to move, but have few chances. Firms prefer to train their existing workers for skilled jobs, but even so promotion is slow. Yet the authors insist:

> One, the proverbial immobility of the Indian worker is a perfectly rational phenomenon. Secondly, the labour market seems to be in a state of highly stable equilibrium. A worker has a price, he cannot change it just by moving from one job to another . . . The lack of mobility in such a situation is not a hindrance in the way of an efficient allocation of labour resources, but a result of the rational behaviour of workers in the labour market. (:128)

Those who want to change jobs not only expect more pay, but in most cases greater security. The authors interpret this to mean not just a permanent job, but 'such job in better established units with better regularised procedures (e.g., in public sector dairy and transport understakings)' (:128).

A 'typical factory worker' lives with a family of six, including one other earner:

> With his family with him, with not too low an income and with a permanent job, he seems 'well-settled'. His method of increasing the family income seems not so much a search for the new job and frequent job changes, but getting a

job for another member of his family in the City. This situation provides a stable workforce and a constant and reasonably 'secure' source of labour supply to the factories. (:64)

He is in a good position to find employment for his relatives because of the way information travels and employers fill vacancies. 'The labour market information seems quite well spread, but the channels through which this information is disseminated are inherently discriminatory' (:133). This knowledge 'comes to some workers as a matter of routine and habit, and it may be with a worker who is not necessarily desiring a change' (:111). Workers who have changed jobs heard about the opportunities from 'friends, relatives and neighbours' in 69 per cent of cases, and from advertisements in 20 per cent of cases. Ten per cent of job-seekers register with the Employment Exchange, but less than 2 per cent of jobs were actually obtained in this way.

In recruiting workers, managements 'rely heavily on their existing employees. The latter naturally prefer their kith and kin, thus making the entry of anybody else difficult' (:114-7):

> Sixty-one per cent of the jobs were secured through 'other workers by introduction'. Formal application had to be made in only 24 per cent cases. Jobbers and contractors also seem to have gone into insignificance . . . A new entrant can find a job in a section, department or factory only when an influential worker there belongs to his family, caste or native place. In the 61 per cent cases where the job could be secured through another worker, the latter was a 'blood relation' in 35 per cent cases, 'belonged to the same caste' in another 44 per cent cases and to the same native place in still another 12 per cent cases. Friends helped in 7 per cent cases . . . The 'agent' did not charge fees for his services except in a little over one per cent of the cases. (:131)

Thus factory employment tends to become the possession of particular families or social groups. Unfortunately the book does not show which castes or groups these are, except that they are mostly people with some education from around Ahmedabad. The authors conclude that the system may not be *fair* – something which worries them, since they think an industrial system should serve broader social purposes – but it is *efficient*, it is as good a way as any to ensure that the few available jobs are filled by qualified people. A skilled work force can be built up by in-plant training or, as a last resort, by offering higher wages to a limited number of skilled outsiders – 'The inflow of workers has been insignificant' (:120).

Just as it is rational for these workers to maximize security first, then family or individual earnings, it is rational, profitable, simple and safe for these employers to prefer recruitment through the workers they already have – even leaving out of account the ties of obligation and patronage which bind workers to employers.

Even more than the Bombay study, this book emphasizes the informal system of recruitment within closed groups. One should allow for some local features. One industry – textiles – accounts for three-quarters of factory employment in Ahmedabad. It is an old stagnant industry, with an unusually united employers' association faced by one dominant centralized union, which is still under Mahatma Gandhi's shadow and steeped in gandhian ideology. Ahmedabad is the chief city of Gujarat, whose people have a reputation for being enterprising but socially conservative, with a strong moralizing and sectarian tradition. Employers and workers place a heavy stress on their moral obligations to each other, and this may make patron–client relations seem more natural and acceptable here than elsewhere. In other cities, especially where the dominant industries are technically advanced ones requiring many workers with new skills and often in the public sector, factory selection procedures are both more open and more formal. Of course it is possible to pull strings and use connexions to get a job, but the strings are decently hidden: those who take this way may have to protect themselves from resentment by pretending they got in on 'merit' (see Holmström 1976:42–51 on factory recruitment in Bangalore and the ideology of 'merit').

These studies of the factory labour market are relevant to the unorganized sector, because the factories' recruitment practices affect smaller firms all the way down the chain: partly by example, but mainly because the pool of labour available to small firms consists almost entirely of those who cannot get factory jobs. In their turn, those who cannot get regular unorganized sector jobs settle for casual work or self-employment. As Lubell (1973:28) says of Calcutta: 'The informal sector constitutes the residual labour market of last resort, which persons enter as self-employed, low-income producers of marginal goods and services for lack of any other means of earning a livelihood'; or as one Calcutta man said to me, the unorganized sector (including the self-employed 'informal sector') is a 'world apart' where pay and conditions are wretched, 'but they stick on because the world outside is worse'. We should see the labour market as a whole, and consider the various ways in which people climb into the organized sector, or are stopped on the way up.

Deshpande, Papola and Subrahmanian quite rightly explain workers' behaviour as rational, given the opportunities and costs which workers perceive. Their knowledge of these perceptions comes mainly, and inevitably, from the simple answers which large samples of workers gave to standard questions – for example which kinds of people (relatives etc.) first told you about your present job, and who if anyone helped you to get it? – and from wide personal knowledge of the classes of people they write about.

Workers say the critical factor in finding a job is access to 'contacts', to relatives or friends with 'influence', and the authors generally agree. But these blanket notions of 'contacts' and 'influence' will not take us far, except to set limits. Many are called but few are chosen. If we admit (for argument's sake, since it may not be so simple) that someone without contacts has little chance of a decent job, this is only a necessary condition, not sufficient. What makes some people's contacts effective?

There may be men whose influence with employers is so strong that they can guarantee a job to anyone but an idiot. In some firms a son has only to wait for his father's job (more on this later). But most serious job-hunters are between the two extremes, neither certain of a job nor hopeless, and the exact nature of their contacts matters very much. Who do you know? Why should he feel any obligation towards you? If he chooses to help, how likely is it that he can persuade someone to employ you? Who else has equal or stronger claims on this contact of yours? What price will he pay if he gets you the job, in lost opportunities to help others or in new obligations to his employer? There are some patterns and tendencies.

To find these out we need evidence of another kind: descriptive local studies supported by whatever quantitative evidence is relevant and available in sample surveys, answers to questionnaires and census publications. From the point of view of people who share a social background, the market for their labour will be divided into compartments, each with its own chances and rules for finding work; but these boundaries are not fixed, or the same for everyone, and the most important barriers may cut across 'sectors' and industries. We need studies of labour markets, and the divisions within labour markets, as job-hunters see them.

The best of these studies were made in 1970–2 by the Indo-Dutch Research Team in south Gujarat, in and around the town of Bulsar on the main line between Bombay and Ahmedabad (several publications in English: the most important are in Pillai and Baks

1979): particularly Klaas van der Veen's paper 'Urbanization, migration and primordial attachments' (1979) on job opportunities for people from Atgam village. Few families can live off the land or village crafts alone: some members must move away, permanently or seasonally, most often to the nearby urban agglomeration of Bulsar-Atul (44 per cent of migrants) or Bombay (21 per cent). One's chances of a job depend on 'primordial attachments' – close ties of mutual obligation with relatives and caste-mates already in work. Scarcity and insecurity, the system of partible inheritance and strong moral feelings force migrants to keep up their primordial relation-ships in the village. 'Economic exchanges imply kinship or friendship or neighbourliness' (:43), reinforced by social symbols and rules. As a factory worker said to N.R. Sheth (1968a:110): 'If your relatives and caste-fellows do not benefit from the authority you possess, what use are you to your society?': and it would be difficult to replace these attachments with less personal patterns of interaction.

Some primordial attachments are much more useful than others. First, 'there is a decisive difference between the seasonal migration of poor, uneducated and unskilled members of the lower castes and the semi-permanent migration of more educated and more skilled members of the middle and higher castes' (van der Veen 1979:44). The poor take casual work in saltpans or brick and stone factories; the better off go to workshops and small factories; or best of all, into government service, perhaps as teachers or postmen. Even these people need a village base and property to fall back on if they lose their jobs or earn too little: van der Veen (:56) agrees with Ashish Bose that: 'It [migration] seems a carefully calculated move and *retreat is an integral part of it*'.

There are several examples of caste groups or families from Atgam which have established bridgeheads in particular towns or factories. Not only from high castes however: Harijans from the village had worked in Bombay since the last century as house servants for Europeans or Parsis. Their sons were educated in Bombay and found better jobs there, but kept up their ties with relatives in the village and bought land.

> One Harijan went to Bombay in 1958, as the servant of a Parsi factory officer from a nearby village. The Parsi got his servant a job in the factory; and since the Harijan worked well and the Parsi liked to have Gujarati-speaking people around him, it was easy for the Harijan to bring in six more of his caste, some of whom got clerical and technical jobs.   (:56–7, my summary)

Two-thirds of the Atgam men working in Surat come from a single non-Harijan low caste, and mostly from the same falia or village ward. They work in weaving factories, or get jobs as drivers, office messengers etc. through friends in the weaving factories (:58). By the time van der Veen left, like the villagers he could often tell which caste and ward a migrant came from, if he knew the town or industry where the man was employed.

For people in government service, getting the right job is a two-stage process. First, to get in ('of course I took a job in teaching (or postal services) because so many of my relatives (or falia-members) are in that line.':62). But the government will post the new recruit too far away: he must wait until a relative or friends in a school or post office near the village tells him of a vacancy, so that he can apply for a transfer: 'So, in the long run most men manage to get work near their own village' (:62).

Van der Veen gives many examples of the ways people say they got their jobs: a relative, a neighbour from the same ward, another Muslim, put in a word in the right place. These stories are consistent with the concentrations of people from particular origins in the factories and occupations van der Veen investigated. His informants were 'absolutely without doubt' that laghvag, influence, was necessary; and although his own data shows no marked difference between high and low castes in the extent of personal mediation to get jobs, there is 'a striking disparity' in their perception of it (:66). The high castes admit freely that they got jobs through relatives and caste members; they are proud to be connected with such important people. The Anavil Brahmans have contacts in private firms and government service; the Banias take it for granted that they will go into their relatives' commercial firms. The middle and lower castes are cynical: they complain they have too few of their own men in important posts to profit from laghvag. These people's contacts are not with patrons, who can give jobs and favours directly, but with intermediates or brokers, men with 'strategic contacts' with those who control resources.

Brokerage is called laghvag only when the broker belongs to one of the high castes, who are traditionally thought of as patrons rather than brokers; but low-caste brokers act in the same way. Thus one educated Koli, with a good railway job, gave the names of ten men – including only three of his caste – for whom he had found jobs: 'My informant was not at all reluctant to state that he had given help and in several instances he could also indicate why he had done so. He was doing someone a favour because his family was so poor, or the man's health was bad, etc.' (:67): a broker may gradually become a patron, if he is in a position to select job applicants and pass them on to a trusting employer.

> It is a generally accepted policy among managers to accept labourers on recommendation and as groups. The managers of the above-mentioned factories could tell me how everyone of their workers (from 12 to 35 per factory) had been introduced. They really prefer to utilize these personal relationships, because it gives them a much stronger grip on their labourers. 'When one man misbehaves, I hold the one who introduced him responsible, and that man will keep the mischief-maker in check', said one manager.
>
> (:64–5)

Certainly this is a common employer's tactic. A Coimbatore mill worker said 'Since most of us have got jobs through recommendation they complain to our sponsors if we protest' (E.A. Ramaswamy 1977:44) or if a worker joins the wrong union. One man was called to the phone, with the supervisor standing over him, while his sponsor rang from the office and told him to leave the Textile Workers' Union – a 'traumatic' experience (:104). Enno Hommes and Nivedita Trivedi (1979:92) tell of a similar case in south Gujarat, where employers keep lists of their labourers together with the names of the people who brought them (but for these employers, any union is the wrong one). Apart from putting individual workers under an obligation, the practice of recruiting their relatives is a costless way of keeping the work force happy and avoiding labour trouble (Holmström 1976:44). In any case, as I suggested, employers find it simplest and safest to recruit through their present workers, when there are so many qualified applicants for most ordinary jobs.

Yet it is not all calculation. To some extent employers share the same values as their workers: this is how things ought to be done. They like to believe they have a personal relationship with their workers, and they have more respect and trust for workers who look after their own people.

On the other hand, both workers and employers are capable of appealing to impersonal notions of fairness: when it suits them, perhaps, as when managements want the best-qualified technical workers rather than the best connected, or when an applicant fails to get a job. I have merit, you have influence, he is corrupt. Van der Veen (1979:65) suggests that selection is more impersonal in the Atul chemical complex near Bulsar, because 'in such a large-scale organization opportunities for favouritism and particularism are of course more limited' (why 'of course'?). When applicants were called to interview for jobs at a new factory in Maharashtra, the executive engineer was away. A senior clerk said: 'Why should he be here? . . . the new employees have been chosen already'. This 'blatant acknowledgment' of laghvag led to a riot and the suspension of the engineer as well as the Employment Exchange chief (:78).

There would be no point in appealing to an ideal of fairness between individuals if it were not already there, as something people believe in, and an alternative to the dominant values of hierarchy and dependence. It is clear that many Indians do believe this, not just 'westernized' ones, and this is not something new to Indian culture. It is too simple to oppose a 'western' idea of equality to an entirely hierarchical 'Hindu ideology', as van der Veen does (:77).

The villagers of Atgam say influence is everything (not necessarily that it *should* be); but are they right? After all, many people have an interest in feeding this belief that no one gets work without a broker. A Harijan with political ambitions reads the 'Jobs vacant' columns daily and sends men to apply with his 'chith' or note of introduction:

> Such a note is no more than an acknowledgement that the man who sends it knows the applicant . . . The feeling that [laghvag] was necessary was so strong that people hardly dared to go ahead without some sort of an introduction . . . It is doubtful whether this 'laghvag' is really so effective. Important, however, is that people think it to be essential. (:68)

Deshpande's Bombay study, and my conversations with workers and managers of small and large firms, show that skill, luck and persistence are other ways to get jobs. Some workers never had an introduction. Some managers believe they can keep their freedom of action if relations with workers are impersonal: they do not want to be entangled in employees' family affairs.

Brokers and pseudo-brokers continue to flourish, as long as people are desperate for jobs. A 'job' in this context means regular work for one employer. The best kind is of course a permanent post in a factory or government service. Second best is when the worker has no legal security but can expect to come to work every day, for months or years together. Regular work looks like an enclosure, to which a limited number of people hold the keys; though this may not be as true as those holding the keys would have others believe.

One virtue claimed for the 'informal sector' is that entry is open, or at any rate easier than in the formal sector. If 'informal sector' means self-employment in services or manufacture, it may require markets, physical protection and often capital:

> The frequently heard view, that small-scale and non-institutionalised activities are capable of almost unlimited expansion and that newcomers can set themselves up as self-employed with almost no money or without too much trouble and with few tools, because those already present obligingly make room for them, is a dangerous and misplaced romanticisation of the hard fight for existence at the bottom of the urban economy.   (Breman 1976:1907)

If 'informal sector' means casual work for employers or contractors, this can sometimes be found by asking in the streets, in market places and on building sites, but here too contacts are a great advantage. Moreover the casual worker must cultivate his contacts because he has to use them again and again, perhaps every day. There could be networks of contacts among casual labourers, separate from but almost as elaborate and closed as among regular workers. This is largely conjecture, because casual labour markets have not been studied as systematically as those for regular employment.

Deshpande (1979:133) shows that almost all migrant casual workers had someone to help them come to Bombay, but it is not clear what this help amounted to. Nine per cent were helped by jobbers, and 10 per cent (presumably the same people) came with the firm assurance of a job. Forty-one per cent of casuals say they got their present jobs by their own efforts (cf. 28 per cent of other workers) but still most casual workers had someone to help (:169). Again, one should not read too much into these answers.

The best work on casual labour markets is Jan Breman's (1976, and 1979 specifically on south Gujarat). Breman points out that much 'informal sector' work, including illegal work like bootlegging, is not self-employment but irregular work done at the direction of an employer. It is contrasted with 'services', which offer not only security and higher pay but protection against the dependence and the 'humiliating and arbitrary treatment' which are always the lot of low castes and casual workers, generally the same people (1979:124). Higher castes prefer even long-term unemployment to 'the stigma of an unordered life', the insecurity and the low prestige of casual work. The low castes, for their part, manage only by spreading the risk among members of the household, most of whom do some paid work whenever they can, but who are sometimes willing to pass up the opportunity of a job with resignation, 'for seemingly irrational reasons' (:125); unlike people in 'service', for whom the loss of the single or main earner's job is a catastrophe.

Casual labourers are compelled to maintain 'a wide network of contacts':

> every single day [sometimes more than once] these odd-job men must look for new work and are directed in this by information they receive from their families, acquaintances, neighbours or during casual encounters along the road. (:126)

Early each morning, dozens of workers gather at the Tower, 'a labour market in the literal sense of the word' in Bulsar, where some have slept out. Employers come to ask for one or several men to work on a farm, or building site, to transport goods or pack bottles: for a day, perhaps a month. At first the workers bargain through a spokesman for a higher wage:

> M. tells me that many employers are very non-committal about payment and the duration of the work. When the work is done they give less than the vaguely agreed price. But also not too little, otherwise they would not be able to get anybody the next time. (:127)

Later in the day the remaining workers have to settle for less, with no argument. Some employers take workers they know, without negotiating.

> A man asks one worker to go with him but he says that he already has work for today. He has just come along for a chat. The man persists: 'I know you and I may require you again the whole of next week.' The worker still does not acquiesce but promises to send a friend whom he will vouch for. (:127)

In other towns I know of, there are 'labour mandis' (markets) for unskilled general labourers who offer their work individually or as a gang, or skilled men such as carpenters who carry the tools of their trade. Others wander about the streets: when a man gets the offer of a job, he must decide quickly whether to take the low wage or to hold out ('If I had not accepted and I had tried my luck elsewhere, I might also have lost that money.' :127). Yet casual workers are also sought after: employers need to be sure of reliable efficient manpower at times when there may be a sudden demand for labour:

> Semi-fixed relations thus arise between 'temporary' employers and temporary workers; the services of the latter are available on call. Similar loose relations exist between craftsmen [like masons or carpenters] and their assistants, called 'begari'. (:128)

A jobber or contractor may have 'a small core of steady workers', which he can expand by recruiting their families or acquaintances. Thus 'the decisive factor in getting employment in the informal sector is personal contact' (:129), and the mukadam or jobber – always an ex-casual worker – is the essential link between employers and gangs of workers. Those who get employment individually try to strengthen their personal ties with the employer – doing odd jobs in his house without pay, bowing and scraping – in the hope of future employment or even a permanent job (:133, quoted on p. 111 above). 'For this part of the urban population, work is not the basis for a more or less independent existence but the outcome of a comprehensive dependency relationship' (Breman 1976:1906).

But however many and strong your contacts with patrons or equals appear to be, this is a fiercely competitive world where you can seldom rely on anyone for long, except your immediate nuclear family. As in other poor countries, 'the inhabitants show growing disinclination to take relatives with a rural background into their homes and to help them find a place in the urban economy' (:1872). The casual work force is not homogeneous, but fragmented by differences in skill, social origin and contacts, and unlikely to unite politically:

> The fragmentation of the labour market is not combined with any form of poverty-sharing, but is more indicative of a search for security within limited group linkages. The necessity to fence off one's own domain and simultaneously to penetrate into other areas of work causes a rivalry which must detract from any common feelings of belonging to the same social class.
>
> (:1942)

Finding jobs: rivalry and solidarity

A man, Sir, should keep his friendship in constant repair.
Dr Johnson

Thane station in the outer suburbs is the junction for trains serving the Bombay peninsula, the industrial 'Thane–Belapur belt' and places further off. In the morning and evening rush hours, industrial workers coming from all directions change trains, or they walk or take the bus to and from the big factories nearby. Nowhere else around Bombay can one find such a gathering of workers of all kinds, skilled and· unskilled, educated and uneducated, of every language and caste, from the well-paid employees of multinationals like Pfizer and Philips to temporary employees in small workshops, who commute because of the prohibitive cost of housing in the peninsula and because in any case their next job may be in another suburb.

Waiting on the platform, these men and women meet friends and hear what workers with similar skills are currently earning: if the rates are much better elsewhere, they decide to look for a better job, or they hear of a union leader who has secured a big rise for his members in some other factory. They hear about factories which open, expand or close down, and about union activities throughout the city. They cultivate acquaintances who might pass on information about vacancies. Thane station is the best listening-post in Bombay for labour market intelligence. Here one can observe the workings of a labour market which is far more complex and dispersed than the 'labour mandis' where men wait patiently for some employer to offer casual work for a day or a month.[4]

Wednesday morning in a Bombay slum: a good slum as slums go, not too crowded or dirty. This is the day off for many local factories, so an industrial worker invited me home to meet his neighbours.

Govind, a young man from Poona, is now the main earner in his household, consisting of his father (a packer in a factory), his mother (an office cleaner) and three young brothers. Three years ago a friend introduced him to the owner of a plastic factory with twelve workers. The owner asked the friend two questions: 'Is he your man?' 'Will he do good work?' That was all. The owner tried him out as a helper, at Rs 5 for an ordinary eight-hour day, then Rs 7.50 for twelve hours. Now he is a regular unskilled worker, at Rs 8.50. He hopes to learn to operate a machine, and then to look for a job in a 'limited company'. A colleague sitting with us told a similar story: he learned to operate the machine as helper in another plastic factory, where someone in the office gave him an introduction to Govind's factory.

While we discussed careers, a Sindhi supervisor from the same firm came on a friendly call, with another worker. He kept three shops (in succession I think), all of which failed; so his relative who owns the plastic factory gave him a job. As a supervisor he cannot join the union, though the others discuss union affairs with him freely: they are demanding a bonus, which the supervisor says the firm cannot afford.

These sketches are not of Streefkerk's world, of helpless villagers at the mercy of cynical commercial-minded small-town entrepreneurs, a

---

[4] This account of Thane (or Thana) station is based on conversations with Kumar Ketkar, labour correspondent of the *Economic Times*, who talks and writes like an anthropologist.

world of cold calculation tempered by paternalistic dependence. These Bombay workers make their own way in a difficult insecure world, less cowed by employers and supervisors. Some genuine fellow-feeling and easy friendship, or simply an interest in new people and experiences, cuts across individual obligations and the divisions of status and caste.

Perhaps this is because Bombay is special: the Bombay man prides himself that he is independent and can make a living against the odds. In the words of a film song, ' My friend has come from Bombay: come and pay him your respects' (of course Bombay is where the films are made). Something more important than the Bombay air is that I have narrowed my scope to manufacturing industry, and the kinds of people who can hope to find jobs in it: the men on Thane station platform, not the drifting casual labourers I have seen living in their own filth in the lanes around Thane station, though the condition of such people and the horror of falling to their level must lie at the back of everyone's mind. What follows is a composite picture of manufacturing labour markets, not only in Bombay but in other industrial centres with both large and small factories and with prospects for growth. It is put together mainly from what workers, managers and union officials said to me.

All the studies I mentioned agree that the market for industrial labour is segmented. However the boundaries do not correspond in any clear simple way to the legal distinction between organized and unorganized firms. The labour market is multiple not dual; many individuals manage to cross the boundaries, and the boundaries are not fixed. Instead of static closed labour markets, think of Breman's more dynamic account of groups and shifting alliances between groups, each trying 'to fence off one's own domain and simultaneously to penetrate into other areas of work' (1976:1942), and individuals using group networks when it suits them but striking out on their own when they have the chance.

Questionnaire-based studies of individual career histories can miss this kind of information. When the answers are counted, comparisons have to be between clearly identified units, like the factory sector and small establishments. There has been a limited amount of movement across this boundary, from small firms to large; we know something about these workers' origins and who helped them. Yet there are other boundaries, other ways into factory employment – perhaps open to different kinds of people – and other obstacles.

Thus Deshpande (1979) and Papola and Subrahmanian (1975), in their studies of the Bombay and Ahmedabad labour markets, treat the 'factory sector' as a unit, more or less ignoring a distinction which is of great practical importance at least in the bigger factories: between permanent and 'temporary' employment (the quotation marks are necessary, as I explained, because many 'temporary' workers are nothing of the kind, but stay in the same factory for years together with short breaks to prevent them from achieving the legal status of a permanent worker). 'Temporary' workers in 'organized sector' firms, like the casual and contract workers, are themselves outside the 'organized sector', though some of them may have a chance of getting in. According to the 1971 Census, 43 per cent of Bombay's casual workers were employed in manufacturing (household or non-household). Only 34 per cent of Deshpande's casual sample are manufacturing workers, but the difference is probably accounted for by casual workers included in Deshpande's other two samples, since his investigators found them in factories or workshops, not waiting at the gate. If the unskilled work force is the factories' expandable 'reserve army of labour', then 'temporary' workers are that part of the army which is stationed at home, under the factories' direct command, while the rest is maintained more cheaply by client states, the small suppliers.

We can distinguish roughly between three kinds of manufacturing employment (cutting across Deshpande's samples): permanent factory jobs, which most people want; temporary, casual or contract labour employed in organized sector factories but not on organized sector terms; all employment in unorganized sector workshops. How are these three kinds of job found? Are there three or more separate closed labour markets, or many ways to move up the ladder gradually?

How the employers recruit labour

To begin near the top: I described (Holmström 1976:42–51) recruitment procedures which are typical of big modern factories all over India. These factories want a core of stable adaptable educated workers who can learn skills and move up the career ladder within the firm: not committed for life as in Japan, but workers who can usually stay with the firm if they want to, and will do so unless they get a better chance in a factory where pay and security are at least as good.

Generally these firms recruit young workers straight from school or from government Industrial Training Institutes, except for a few highly skilled men: it is important to get into some organized sector employment around the age of twenty, or you may miss your chance for ever. Half the workers in my sample of Bangalore factories had never changed jobs; half had been in their present jobs by the age of twenty-three, though their median age was thirty-one. New workers are taken on as temporaries, trainees or apprentices for a limited period, then permanently employed or sacked. This temporary employment is part of the selection process, not a reserve army of labour.

First there are formal procedures for recruitment and selection, which sometimes correspond to the reality. Jobs are advertised in the newspapers, sometimes in the English-language press only. The law requires firms to notify the Employment Exchange of all vacancies, and a few actually take applicants sent by the Exchange. A factory may ask the principal of a government or private training institute to recommend the best-qualified students; and many applicants simply write in to ask. Qualified applicants are interviewed, tested for aptitude and general knowledge, and medically examined. They should be educated, preferably with some technical training; and any special skills or qualifications needed for the job, like a knowledge of English, or the nimble fingers and capacity to withstand boredom which are said to fit women for small assembly work. The best qualified are given temporary appointments until they prove themselves.

This is called selection on merit. Workers and managers talk as if it is the morally superior way to find work: workers who got their jobs on 'merit' are proud of it, those who used influence are on the defensive. Thus 44 per cent of my Bangalore case study sample say they had no personal recommendation, while another 32 per cent say they did (:43). In some factories, workers say influence can get you an interview but only merit can get you the job: no personnel officer could see the vast number of apparently qualified applicants for most jobs. One may be appointed through influence but then promoted on merit.

'Merit' is an ideal standard against which to measure the other ways people get jobs. Merit is ambiguous, a mixture of innate qualities like 'intelligence' and acquired ones like education or the skills presently in demand on the labour market, but it always implies some element of achievement, as opposed to influence, connexions or luck. 'This ideology of merit is a way of moralizing the labour market, and it involves a conscious rejection of the dominant traditional justification for inequality: caste' (:50). More generally, it goes against the ideal of society as a system of hierarchical dependence and mutual obligation, while it justifies inequalities in pay and security.

There are other ways into factory employment. One can bypass some steps in the formal procedure for selection on merit, with someone's help – more neutral than 'influence'. 'Help' means anything from passing on information to personal introduction, recommendation (the commonest way, often thought to be essential) or nomination (when someone in a firm, or with influence there, can promise a job). The contact with the firm may be a worker, supervisor, manager, one of their relatives, a government labour officer, or a customer or business associate.

The personnel manager of a multinational electronic firm: most workers are semi-skilled women, and fairly well paid. Some of the women become supervisors. Women are better for this kind of work, because of their dexterity with their fingers and because they can stand the monotony of the production line.

Except in the toolroom (the only place where there are workers with experience gained in small units) the company prefers 'raw' workers, who can be 'moulded to our requirements'. They should be educated up to matriculation, pass or fail, and able to understand instructions and figures. In principle the company invites applicants from any source, including the Employment Exchange, and tests them all. But this took too long, so for the last three years there have been no tests and 'no consistent programme' of recruitment. The firm keeps a register of ex-workers who are at home or working in other companies, and calls them back when they are needed. New workers come with recommendations from existing workers, from other firms which pass on labour to each other, or from professional colleagues: a proportion are physically handicapped.

A worker's performance is assessed for a month. If it is satisfactory, she or he stays as a temporary for six months, after which most are laid off and a few made permanent. The union (he said) does nothing about this, because if the firm takes on too many permanent workers this will put the other permanent workers at risk. Unmarried women are best. Since a court case the firm can no longer lay off permanently employed women on marriage: there is a new and 'alarming' trend for women to insist on their right to return after maternity leave, when they are more likely to be absent from work.

The manager had reason to be alarmed. It is standard practice to take on a worker's male relatives as temporaries and to keep them waiting in the hope of permanent jobs, but even this might half commit the employer. In the past employers could safely take on extra women workers in busy times without running this risk: women would go when they were asked, they were seldom militant or actively involved with unions, and could be relied on as a moderating influence on their men. They were likely to leave in any case, on marriage or pregnancy, and could easily be replaced. They would do more monotonous work than men without complaint and for lower wages. Their main drawback was that by law they could not work night shifts. This comfortable situation has begun to change, at least in places like Bombay and Poona where a combination of economic need, education and a more militant spirit cause women, like men, to hang on to factory jobs for as long as they can.

Compare this firm's *ad hoc* recruitment procedures with the methods described by personnel officers in some Bangalore factories, where most jobs are permanent: advertisements, recommendations from workers and institutes etc. (Holmström 1976:46–8). The public sector factories give more emphasis to formal criteria, paper qualifications and quotas for Scheduled Castes: it is still possible to pull strings, but more discreetly.

Small units rely more exclusively on recommendations, for skilled and unskilled workers.

Streefkerk (1978:245, 260–2) writes of a tea-stall owner in Gundlav, south Gujarat, who is a broker between workers and small-scale entrepreneurs on a nearby industrial estate, with a foot in both camps. Though he helped form a union and led a strike, he is on good terms with entrepreneurs who rely on him to tell workers about vacancies and to recommend applicants. Unlike the jobbers, he makes no money out of this.

Small-scale entrepreneurs regularly pass on workers to one another. This cuts both ways: it is very useful to be able to find skilled workers at short notice, but it can also be a burden. An engineering employer with nine workers said applicants come uninvited but with the 'influence' of a colleague, and he has to employ them if he can. An engineer working in a Small Industries Service Institute said a small businessman will try to cut costs by employing as few as possible, but he has to oblige relatives and others by taking 'anyone who is dumped on him'. It may be necessary to oblige a customer or official in this way.

If I employ your relative or client, I am doing you a favour, creating or repaying an obligation (it is only if you send me a scarce skilled worker that you are doing me the favour). Other things being equal, like skill and qualifications, this is an efficient simple way to select workers. In large and small firms, most workers who come in with recommendations are relatives or friends of the present workers. The chance to bring in relatives is an important benefit of regular employment. It can be more than a chance – a firm expectation, or a right to keep at least one job in the worker's family. In big firms this is often made formal in written agreements with the unions, which lay down, for example, that on a worker's death or retirement his son or close relative will be employed if he is suitable; and in firms with no expansion – like the Calcutta jute mills – this may be the only way anyone ever gets a job.

A senior manager in a multinational chemical firm, with factories all over India, said they give preference to workers' close relatives: 25 per cent of recruits are employees' sons. This policy helped the company through the worst period of communist government in West Bengal, as older workers with sons were reluctant to join in strikes instigated by politicians. Another 25 per cent of recruits are specially qualified for their jobs: this kind of recruitment, to raise the level of the work force, is 'a totally different kettle of fish.'

The chief union in a large Calcutta textile mill claims to have a 'gentlemen's agreement', with this and other managements, that a retiring or dead worker's next-of-kin gets his job. This takes care of practically all recruitment, except for a few skilled men. The secretary of a major chemical workers' union in Bombay said his union has agreements or understandings with many managements that a retiring worker's son should succeed him: and workers in the big factories can put pressure on the factory officers to find jobs for other relatives, in their own factory or smaller firms where they have influence.

The union in a Bombay engineering factory insists that one dependant of a retiring worker should be employed, and almost all skilled jobs filled by internal promotion; there are no other ways for workers to bring in relatives or friends. A young man working in another union office is waiting to inherit his father's job in this factory in five years time. Another young man works in a small plastic factory, waiting for an unskilled job when his father, a plumber, retires from a car factory – otherwise he would have no chance of getting in, since he has no School Leaving Certificate or technical training. Others are not prepared to wait for a relative to go.

'There is an agreement in the Coimbatore textile industry to the effect that the heirs (*warisu*) of retired and retiring workers should be given preference in the matter of recruitment' (Uma Ramaswamy 1979:376). However 'Recommendation is necessary even for the recruitment of one's *warisu*' (:371), and since Harijans have less leverage with supervisors and unions they cannot count on jobs for their sons.

Even in the army:

> General T.N. Raina, Chief of the Army Staff, today conceded the demand of ex-Servicemen for recruitment of at least one son from each family in the Army on relaxed terms and conditions.   (*Times of India*, 23 Jan. 1977)

These are big organizations. Small employers may try to employ their workers' sons – as well as anyone 'dumped' on them, even relatives of workers in the big factories they supply – but they cannot offer the kind of security which factory workers may demand and occasionally get: not just a job for life, but one that can be inherited like land.

However a man with a job for life need not keep it for life, as he would in Japan. It is a possession to be improved, and if possible exchanged for a better one. Once a man has it he thinks of learning new skills and making contacts in other factories, as long as there is no risk to the job he has. At the same time he can invest in his children's education, giving them a chance of skilled work in his own factory or elsewhere. So the property is not a job in a particular factory, but rather a foothold or base in the organized sector, to add to any land or other property his family may own. And many 'permanent' jobs are not at all secure.

If a factory job is property, it should be possible to buy it; and of course many people assume this is how others got their jobs. Allegations of bribery are easy to make and very hard to check, not just because it is illegal but because it is much more widely disapproved of and condemned than 'influence'. You should repay a favour with another favour, not with cash. Workers will admit – not always in company – that they used influence to get their jobs; managers will explain how it works; but no one ever admitted to me that he sold or paid for a job. It is always someone else, and often some time ago: thus workers say officers in two Bangalore factories were notorious for taking bribes until a few were trapped by the police, and the practice stopped. People will tell you what is or was the going rate for a job in particular factories. One should be sceptical about these damaging allegations, although some are certainly true.

If it is not managers or supervisors who take bribes, it is the unions: again allegations are widespread – especially against rival unions –

and impossible to test. They arise in firms where the right to nominate replacements, or to recruit new workers, has been given to the recognized union, either instead of or in addition to the workers' right to nominate relatives: even if the union is occasionally in bitter conflict with the management, there are quiet intervals when both sides find it useful to oblige one another. In the Coimbatore textile mills the union's recommendation seems almost essential, and one has the best chance of getting it if one is both a union activist and a mill worker's son. In other places union leaders are alleged to take bribes, and again some of these allegations are probably true. An active unionist told me reluctantly that when an industry with many 'temporary' workers was nationalized, leaders of his own union joined personnel managers in the scramble to sell permanent jobs before some kind of control could be established: workers borrowed from moneylenders, and 'every union leader worth his salt' built a house with the profits.

As I suggested, the practice of taking workers' relatives and friends as replacements or new workers has led to clusters of people from particular castes or villages or language groups in the same occupation often throughout an industry. It is an accident of history that Bombay foundrymen and heat treatment workers are mostly Hindi-speakers from Uttar Pradesh and Bihar: when they were recruited in the 1940s, local Maharashtrians would not do this work, though they would be willing enough to take almost any job now. (It seems however that there were some local foundry workers in the 1920s and 1930s; after a strike they were sacked and replaced with Hindi-speakers, who brought in their compatriots when the industry expanded.)

Calcutta boiler makers are Muslims from Bangladesh, formerly East Pakistan. They were rounded up in the 1965 Indo-Pakistan war until the engineering employers made an urgent appeal to the military authorities to free them, since their internment had a devastating effect on the industry. The accident of history can be rationalized and justified. If a job can belong to a family, particular kinds of job could be the rightful property of people from one caste or place; but except in the case of jobs with an old caste tradition, such as sweeping, workers in big cities like Bombay do not often argue like this. Employers – they say – may be prejudiced, and appoint or promote workers just because of their caste; but it is hard enough for a worker to discharge his obligations to particular known people, his own cousins and neighbours, without worrying about the whole caste. 'Caste' solidarity is usually the solidarity of a much smaller group.

If there is a group with a rightful claim to jobs, it is larger still – the 'sons of the soil', people born and brought up in the same state and above all speaking the same language, who have a right to *all* the good jobs there. People from other states – or for that matter, people from the same state whose language is spoken by a majority somewhere else – should go and find jobs there. Language brings together many castes, from Brahmans to Harijans, in a powerful easily identified bloc; and this loyalty to a community of birth is easily rationalized as a kind of little patriotism or nationalism, a mystical bond between the land and all who belong to it. In Bombay the Shiv Sena has campaigned through its representatives in the state legislature and the corporation or Municipal Council, through harassment and intimidation, and through its unions, to keep jobs for Maharashtrians and specially to force south Indians out of the city: a campaign which reached its height in the mid-1970s and then receded. When police fired on striking Calcutta port workers, Timir Basu accused the pro-Janata Party union of

> stoking the provincialism of the workers. Most of the shore workers who had originally been recruited [from other areas] by Bird & Co. in 1948 are likely to retire *en masse* by 1984. So the question of employment of employees' dependents has long been a live issue. The fear has been systematically created among the illiterate workers that trade unionists belonging to West Bengal, irrespective of their political loyalty, would pursue a 'sons of the soil' policy and that as a result the present workers' dependents will not get jobs . . . The workers have been facing pay cuts while prices have been soaring. The principal bone of contention was, however, the question of future employment. (T. Basu, 1979c:1747)

That is the point: jobs for one's family, not a deep attachment to an ethnic group and its symbols. When there is cut-throat competition, all alliances are temporary and expedient except with one's closest kin.

This sort of populist language chauvinism appeals most strongly to unskilled workers in the older declining industries, to the unemployed or those with insecure jobs in small firms, rather than workers in the big factories who see themselves as modern, secular and broad-minded. Good jobs belong by right to those with merit, ability, a sense of responsibility, the values of the educated lower middle class – of clerks, officials, skilled workers, shopkeepers and big farmers – which many come from. Occasionally the argument is turned round: people from this background can be assumed to have the right qualities; they cannot take any labouring job, so they *deserve* permanent factory jobs or better (see Holmström 1976:50, 69, on 'the divine right of the middle class').[5] Those who have done well in their careers do not need this prop for their self-esteem; but factory workers and employers often share the assumption that the economy has its niche for people from every background. Several small employers told me they want workers with some education but not too much, because 'over-educated' workers will leave soon or stay and make trouble (which may be true).

As Deshpande showed in Bombay, small establishment workers may be *better* educated than factory workers: in this case because educated immigrants arrived when local families had already captured most factory jobs (p. 186 above). More generally, people often find their niche because of this kind of accident and the preconceptions people have about them rather than because they possess or lack specific skills and abilities.

The Brahman manager of a Bombay car component factory with 190 workers: most workers have reached school Standard VII or VIII, but any new applicant should be a matriculate from a good family background, with his father in a job and both parents living nearby: if the firm were to recruit workers from 'the lower strata of society', they would bring 'their own social problems'. Some of the toolroom workers however are recruited from small workshops: all of them come from 'three or four' castes of smiths who took to this work sixty years ago; and the six diemakers are relatives from 'one or two' castes.

The leader of a dock workers' union: certain jobs are for certain kinds of people. North Indians are used to working in ships, while people from the Ghat and Konkan regions prefer to work on shore. This is 'just like a hereditary job – it is in their blood that they can carry on the work'.

A state official concerned with manpower planning: some communities have special manual skills, like lifting heavy weights with a special jerk of the shoulders (he implied clearly: this is all they can do).

---

[5] The magazine *Blitz* (23 Oct. 1976) published a young man's photo under the headline 'He deserves a job.' He is 22 and handicapped, and writes 'I come from a respectable family. My father is a retired Major and one of my brothers is a Captain . . . Will any BLITZ reader come to my aid?' No other qualifications mentioned.

K. Lakkappa, a Congress Party member, introduced two bills into Parliament (or the state legislature?): one to 'abolish the caste system', another to pay an unemployment pension of Rs 100 a month to the uneducated, Rs 150 to the educated (*Sunday Standard*, 17 July 1977).

These assumptions about the likely performance of people from particular castes or classes or both have the character of self-fulfilling prophecies: only those who are expected to do well at a job are chosen for it. When employers speak of merit, the term does not have the strong moral tone which workers give it – personal achievement as against unfair influence. For employers, merit means demonstrated skill or any other qualifications – education, caste, family background – which employers believe are relevant to the job. When they insist on freedom to appoint or promote workers on merit – as in union agreements on the numbers to be promoted on seniority and merit – this means little more than the management's right to decide freely. In any case, abstractions like merit count only in the bureaucratic structures of the big factories, where there is sometimes a need to lay down and discuss general criteria. In a small firm each decision is *ad hoc*, the owner simply decides who he wants and can afford.

The bigger the factory, and the safer the jobs, the more bureaucratic and formal the selection procedures, and the more elaborately they have to be rationalized and justified (as selection on merit, the right to keep one job in the family etc.). There is no clear line between factories and workshops, but a gradation. Small workshops take those who cannot get into factories. Both in big firms and small, the social mix of employees tends to be perpetuated, because workers recommend relatives and friends and because of employers' caste and class prejudices. On the other hand, employers need skilled efficient workers from whatever origin: they cannot afford too many well-born incompetents. Yet opportunities to acquire skills may also be limited to people from certain backgrounds. We should look more closely at attitudes and practices with regard to recruitment, the pressures on employers, and the social origins and relationships of people doing similar jobs in factories and workshops.

Who you know and what you know: influence, skill and mobility

Consider the claim that employers recruit labour through those they employ already, not just because this is convenient and safe or because of pressure from workers and their unions, but as a way to make workers personally dependent on them; and that this is the reason for clusters of relatives, or people from the same caste or area, in each firm or a whole industry.

On p. 202 I quoted reports of factory managers in south Gujarat and Coimbatore who do this as a deliberate policy and a sanction against troublemakers, giving the employer a hold both over the recommender and the recruit. A worker can be held responsible for the good behaviour of anyone he has brought into the firm, while new workers will not want to antagonize the employer and lose the chance of bringing in their own people later, including members of their households; and this is often the only way to raise their own standard of living substantially. In West Bengal there is a further refinement: the elder brother is taken on as a permanent worker and his younger brother as a casual, with the promise of a permanent job in the future, giving the firm a hold over both brothers.

Narayan Sheth (1968a:77) says the management of the engineering factory he studied in Gujarat preferred every employee to have a link within the factory. The application form included the question 'Through whom has he come?'. As a workshop superintendent said, 'If we recruit a completely unknown man, he might misbehave . . . If we take a person coming through somebody we know, we are on safer grounds. For the person acting as a link would assume a moral responsibility for the man he brings in and would restrain him from negligence of work, misbehaviour, or trade-union activities.' On the other hand, the link gave the new worker someone to take his side in disputes with other workers or the management. 'As a worker said, "Since my brother is an old employee in Oriental, the management cannot turn me out though they often make it clear that they are not satisfied with my work." His supervisor endorsed his statement.' Managers and workers appear to play by the same rules and to share the same values of personal obligation and dependence.

The owner of a Bombay vehicle component factory with eighteen workers: above all, he wants a *stable* work force, people he has trained himself and who will resist the 'temptation' to leave. Most new recruits come through his existing workers, who would not like to send someone unacceptable for fear of spoiling their own reputation. Some bring in relatives, but he does not consider that when making appointments.

The owner of an electronic component factory employs seventy, including forty-five women: he used to take people who 'drift in' but found it dangerous. Now he asks the girls to recommend friends and relatives, generally fresh from school at fifteen or sixteen. He gets 'respectable' women, matriculates, even college graduates, and factory workers' wives, who would not work 'in normal circumstances' but who need the money and will work for him because he respects them.

Another small manufacturer of electronic components (twenty-two workers): for unskilled workers, 'we ask for relatives'. His neighbour, who
employs a fluctuating insecure work force of some forty men in a die casting
works, recruits unskilled men through a notice board outside the factory. If
workers suggest relatives, he will sometimes take them, but not if the
recommender is 'notorious'.

Some employers see clusters of kin or close friends as a danger, and
exclude relatives or ration each worker to one or two. Each worker
should depend on the employer directly, not through someone else.

The personnel officer of a plastic factory with 600 workers near Delhi:
getting into this factory is not difficult, but staying there is – only half the
recruits survive the 6–9 month assessment period. A few are recommended
by relatives, but the firm never employs brothers; and no two men from the
same village should work in a section, so that the place shall not become 'a
community club'. When a worker recommends someone, the firm must
'make positive or negative use' of that reference, otherwise the worker will
be loyal to the person who brought him in rather than to the management.
The relation between management and workers should be that of father and
son, as in Japan.

The owner of another plastic factory, with 140 workers in Bombay: all
applicants for unskilled jobs come in from the street, and most are very poor
– one was a beggar. He checks their police record (how?) and visits their
homes, then tries them out for ten days. He never takes a worker's relative or
nominee: relatives will take days off together, weddings for example. Any
trace of 'influence' disqualifies an applicant, because if a man gets in
through another worker's influence they will compare wages etc. There is no
union: he thinks of the workers as his relatives, visits their houses regularly
and helps them to get ration cards or electricity. He showed me round,
telling me all he had done for his workers and introducing some, which was
as embarrassing for them as for me.

The deputy manager of a Bombay chemical factory employing 200: most
new workers are related to old ones, but the firm is trying to break up family
clusters, and takes workers' friends rather than relatives: if a worker dies, at
least five relatives come for his job.

For various reasons, some employers prefer not to rely too much, or at
all, on networks of relatives and friends: whether it is because they
find tightly-knit groups of workers are likely to make demands and
join unions; or because they want a direct paternalistic relation with
their workers and are jealous of any attempt to take patronage out of
their own hands (those who talk most about the Japanese model know
little about it, and would never agree to anything like the Japanese

workers' lifetime security and strong unions: see Dore 1973).

Other employers find these networks useful as sources of unskilled labour, or people with enough basic education to learn semi-skilled jobs fast, but not for trained skilled workers. In engineering firms there are few openings for anyone else. If the firm has time to plan ahead, and only needs more men with the same skills, it can take workers' nominees and train them: in the factories, as trainees or apprentices on regular training programmes; in small workshops, as 'helpers' who learn by watching a skilled man, bringing him tea and materials and asking questions. Yet firms often need new skills quickly. Their own workers may be able to recommend someone: a relative belonging to a smith caste famous for its skill with metal, or a friend in a firm where a worker was employed before. More often the employer has to ask a business colleague, or try out men who answer advertisements or come in asking for work.

This gives a second chance of a factory job to some, not many, of the skilled workers in small units. Deshpande was not able to find out how many Bombay factory workers had worked in small establishments, but his evidence on recruitment practices made him doubt the 'graduation hypothesis' that workers learn a trade in the un-organized sector and move on to factory jobs (1979:208, see p. 192 above). H. and V. Joshi (1976a:134–5) came to a similar conclusion. In Coimbatore, John Harriss found that 'individuals do *not* move easily between sectors of the labour market'. In a sample of 123 organized sector engineering workers, only 26 per cent had previously been in any other sector, and only 16 per cent in 'unregulated workshops or foundries':

> Amongst the 826 households which we surveyed in 'slum' areas of Coimbatore, we could find only 39 clear cases of movement between sectors, and these were equally divided between instances of movement into the organised sector and those of movement out of it. (1982:996)

As I suggested, the big firms now prefer to take young men straight from school, or from a government Industrial Training Institute, and to train them up in the firm. They do not want to recruit outside, except for skills in which they lack training facilities. If they must go outside, they would rather recruit from other factories, perhaps smaller ones, but still inside the organized sector, because factory managers believe unorganized sector firms lack the modern machinery, planned training programmes, habits of work and quality control of the factories.

A manager of a very large company: only one of their many factories, in Poona, is recruiting. It does so by advertising locally for men with engineering skills, who should have either a training institute certificate or experience in another factory; but not an unorganized sector firm, since organized sector workers are 'more experienced' and you can get their previous history. There are so many factories in Poona that there is no need to look elsewhere.

Yet a union official said that in Poona a stay in a small unit is regarded as an apprenticeship, and there is more movement from small firms to factories than in Bombay. This is because the working class is more homogeneous than in Bombay, speaking one language and coming from the same area, generally educated, and organized in unions. With technological change, even small units require trained turners and fitters, and only a few 'helpers'.

Vacancies tend to occur in large numbers, all at once, when new factories are set up or embark on major expansion projects, attracting labour and setting off a chain reaction in smaller firms throughout a city.

Another thing that had unfrozen the job market just before my fieldwork was the exodus of skilled manual and clerical workers to well-paid jobs in the Persian Gulf: especially from Kerala, already one of the main sources of skilled migrant labour for the rest of India, but also from every industrial city. In Kerala masons, carpenters and even barbers became scarce, respectable and in demand on the marriage market (P. Aravindaksham and N.J. Abraham 1977). Skilled engineering workers and carpenters from Bombay and Calcutta joined the rush. Desperate or ambitious men paid thousands of rupees to confidence-tricksters who approached them at railway stations with the offer of a job in Dubai or Abu Dhabi, the price to include passage, passport and visa. A Bangalore milling machine operator told me he had narrowly missed the chance of a job in Utopia, which he believed to be a real country (it was Kuwait). Others thought twice even when offered a job in the Gulf, since they would have to leave their families behind.

When vacancies for skilled men occur in the Indian factories, applicants include men who already have permanent jobs in other factories, who will wait for the firm offer of a better job before resigning; men who learned the trade in small units and are now trying to move up; and victims of closures or layoffs in other big factories, since even a permanent job gives only relative security. Deshpande shows that in Bombay two-fifths of all job changes, both among factory and small establishment workers, were involuntary mostly because of dismissals or retrenchment; 5 per cent of all workers' job changes were the result of company closures (1979:164–5).

It used to be possible to start in a small workshop, learn a skill and move up. It still is, but only into the middle-sized firms without training facilities, not the big ones; though there are exceptions. Young men with a good general education, often supplemented by a spell in an Industrial Training Institute, come on to the labour market in increasing numbers. Older workers, who learned their trade before there was such a sharp division between the organized and unorganized sectors, say that nowadays employers want a certificate rather than genuine experience. In the small workshops one now finds a number of skilled men, all looking out for better jobs, who have some scarcity value at that price and whom the employer does not want to lose; and 'helpers' at very low wages, who are dispensable, and sometimes have the chance of picking up a skilled or semi-skilled trade by working with a skilled man. Yet even to get a 'helper's' job is difficult now.

This mobility for some skilled men exists especially in the engineering and allied trades – good tool and die makers are scarce (or were when my fieldwork was done) and there is a market for fitters, turners, drillers, millers, electricians, wiremen, moulders, carpenters and plumbers. To some extent it exists in the textile industry, which is not very buoyant but where some workers can acquire marketable skills; much less in industries like chemicals and pharmaceuticals, where the real skill is with graduate chemists and engineers – a worker's job is to fetch and carry, mix compounds, watch meters and do as he is told. These people know little about the process and have few chances to learn: indeed some managements discourage them from asking questions, because there are trade secrets. Consumer electronics requires a few skilled men and many assembly workers, mostly women, who can learn the job in days. However long you work in such a firm, you will never learn a skill you can take with you to another factory. If you move, you start from scratch: unlike an engineering worker whose experience has some market value – he might get a better job in a middle-sized organized sector factory, which pays much less than the big prestige firms.

I have described various ways to get a permanent factory job: through recommendations and influence; by nomination when one's father retires; by application on leaving school or a training institute; with luck, by learning a trade in small firms and moving up; or by some combination of these. Normally one will be offered a temporary or probationary post for a limited period, as part of the selection process. When one has passed that hurdle, one can hope to stay for life or until one gets a better offer from another factory.

There is another way: to join the factory's 'reserve army of labour' as a temporary, contract or casual worker, in the hope of getting a permanent job later. In some factories a temporary or casual job is in effect a place on a waiting-list for a permanent job, and this may be laid down in an agreement with the union. Thus a casual textile worker, registered as a *badli* or substitute, may wait from 3 to 7 years, coming to the mill gate every morning and living off relatives and whatever he can earn for a few days' work every month, but he is likely to get a permanent job in the end. In other factories temporary workers are in a similar position, except that they work full time and earn more. There may also be a fringe of temporary, casual or especially contract workers who have little or no hope of permanent employment. If these people are from different social origins and recruited over a different network, it may be possible to keep them out for ever; but where they are relatives and friends of the permanent workers, it is more likely that the union will press their claim for registration on an official or unofficial waiting list, and will try to speed up their absorption into the permanent work force; or if this is impossible, at least to improve their pay and conditions. Much more seldom, the union will recruit temporary workers as members.

A group of workers belonging to the communist union (AITUC) in a Calcutta textile mill: many of the mill's 10 000 workers go home in rotation to Bihar and Uttar Pradesh, for harvests, weddings and to see their families; especially between May and July when it is too hot to work comfortably in Calcutta. When a worker comes back, his job is secure. Meanwhile it is done by a badli taken from a standing list. The union succeeded in getting the management to offer permanent work to any badli with four months' (apparently continuous) work. One becomes a badli by knowing someone in the factory and getting the union's recommendation. Theirs is the recognized union, though there are two others.

Before the coal mines were nationalized, managers tried to keep their permanent workers happy by offering their relatives badli work. Badlis appear to have worked steadily with the usual short breaks, to deprive them of bonuses which would add 40 per cent to their wages; but after five years most of them were made permanent.

Some Bombay factories keep waiting-lists of men ready to replace absentees or to come in at busy periods. A man may be on several factories' lists: when he hears there is extra work at a factory he goes there, or the factory sends out someone to contact workers. Unlike the old jobbers, these men seldom take money for the information. Most factory managers have abandoned 'one-day recruitment' of casual workers waiting outside the gate. It is more convenient to take workers on as temporaries for short continuous periods; but once there is a substantial temporary work force they are likely to ask for permanent status and to look for allies among the permanent workers who can put pressure on the management.

The secretary of a Bombay chemical workers' union (already quoted on p. 213): a pharmaceutical firm had many low-paid temporary workers, mostly women (probably other workers' wives). The union got a wage increase; and after a long expensive legal battle, a court order that all temporaries should become permanent. The company changed its name and started up, ostensibly as a new company, with the same workers making the same product in the same place: so the union has to start all over again. In larger firms, this union has reached agreements with the employers that there should be a pool of temporaries, who succeed to permanent jobs by seniority. Now workers try to get their children and relatives a place on these waiting-lists.

One company owns a group of Bombay engineering factories, and most of their workers belong to one militant union. Temporary workers 'pestered' the union for an assurance about their future. The union fought a long battle with the management, which finally agreed to draw up three lists of temporary workers. The first group were made permanent. The second were to continue to work intermittently, especially in holiday seasons or when permanent workers went on leave, and they could be sent to work for the company elsewhere: they were to be given preference when there were permanent vacancies. The third group would never become permanent.

The second list included many relatives of the older permanent workers, who refused to work overtime until everyone on that list had been absorbed. This raised the hopes of the third group, mostly immigrants from Uttar Pradesh who lived in all-male households and waited at the factory gate for any casual work. The union was sympathetic; so nearly six years after the agitation began, almost all these men had become permanent as well. The union is still agitating on behalf of the rest.

The union insists that when a worker retires, one dependant should be employed: otherwise the family would be left with no support, and usually in debt. A worker cannot nominate anyone else for a job: the very few new jobs are filled by advertisement. Only some of the older workers came from unorganized sector workshops. Once in the company, an unskilled man can rise to any level of skill, because the union also insists on internal training and promotion, but one's chances of promotion (according to the union Secretary) depend largely on the 'influence' of the firm's officers – not the union, which wants nothing to do with selection (I have reasons to believe this is true). Each department tends to have a majority of one language or ethnic group, depending largely on who the first workers were (e.g. north Indians in heat treatment), who was the first man in charge (Gujaratis in accounts), or state government pressure to take 'sons of the soil' (Maharashtrians).

A small Bombay firm makes wooden shuttles for textile mills. There was no distinction between permanent and temporary workers until 1975, when a young worker persuaded the others to join a union, and the management agreed that those who had worked longest should become permanent. Now there are fifteen permanent workers, and eight temporaries who are not in the union.

Contract workers employed within a factory sometimes move into a permanent job with the main employer, either through personal contacts they make there, or because of a sympathetic union, state laws designed to phase out contract labour, or company policy (see pp. 175–6 above). This is rare: much more often, employers turn regular workers into contract labour, technically employed by someone else.

Thus a temporary or similar job in a big factory may amount to a virtual promise of a permanent job later, a reasonable expectation of such a job if one has connexions, a hope against hope, or a strictly temporary job with no chance of a permanent one. One gets on to the waiting list largely in the way one gets a permanent factory job, using the same networks of kinship, friendship and influence. Moreover, if people on the waiting list are only employed intermittently or on very low wages, they may need outside resources to tide them over the long waiting period: like unemployment, this may be an investment in the future. Both these factors would tend to limit the waiting list to the groups which predominate in permanent employment. On the other hand workers' personal histories show that this can be a way into the big factories for some people who would have had little chance otherwise: skilled men coming from the unorganized sector, or simply people who are lucky. One reason why temporary work provides these byways into factory employment is its unpredictability: employers keep a semi-permanent fringe of 'temporaries', but they may also have to take on large numbers suddenly to meet some crisis or surge of demand, and this gives the cunning outsider his chance.

At this level there is still a wall to climb, from temporary to permanent; but not when one comes to the middle-to-small firms, even in the organized sector, where even regular workers with legal security of employment have no way of enforcing it without a strong union. In smaller firms the difference between skilled and unskilled is more important: your skill is your only security.

Work for women

I mentioned (p. 211) the alarm felt by one factory manager because his women workers were beginning to insist on their right to return after maternity leave: that is (though he did not say so) to behave like men, who will fight for job security before anything else, even wages. The few women in a position to stand on their rights, and prepared to do so, are not only behaving like men but competing for men's jobs. Clerical work has already fallen to them: there are still plenty of male typists and office workers, in many places a majority, but mixed departments are more and more common. It is true that employers believe women are best suited to the most boring assembly jobs, but enough men would do the same work if they could get it.

> When a certain job requires, in the employer's eyes, delicate handling, or when the work is time-consuming and tedious, women are called upon to do it. Thus, women are favoured in the electronics industry, for jobs which require tiny parts to be handled gently and carefully, and where fine wires have to be twisted and wound. In the textile industry, women have traditionally been employed as menders, spinners, winders, reelers, folders and cottonwaste pickers. In the pharmaceutical industry, women are generally employed as packers. (Jyoti Punjwani 1976)

In factories there is equal pay for equal work, but in India as elsewhere women's skills are rated separately and paid less.

The owner of a Bombay factory with eighty workers, making packing materials, battery containers etc. from cardboard and tinplate: unskilled men take home Rs 150 a month, skilled about Rs 350, a few up to Rs 900. The twenty 'girls' are also 'skilled', in labelling, packing and inspection – they are not like skilled men, and they earn about Rs 200. Most are married, often to the men who work here.

Women factory workers are very often the wives or unmarried daughters of men working in the same or other factories (though only

6 per cent of Bombay factory workers' wives, and 8 per cent of women
in their families, are 'economically active': Deshpande 1979:220).
Several employers told me they prefer to recruit respectable women,
well settled, belonging to known families living near the factory: some
employers insist that women should leave on marriage. Increasingly,
middle-class women – the wives and daughters of clerks, teachers and
officials, for example the educated Bengali middle class in Calcutta –
are looking for factory work (Nirmala Banerjee, in conversation);
though according to Jyoti Punjwani:

> Women from both the upper middle-class and the middle class are not
> considered suitable for recruitment. Top executives feel that economic
> security tends to make the former 'casual and indifferent' towards their work,
> while the latter are 'too bound down by tradition' to continue with their jobs.
> 'It is women from the working-class who are the most stable and conscientious,
> because they have no economic security', said a factory manager.
>
> (Punjwani 1976)

Some factories hesitate to employ women because of the cost of
providing a crèche (required wherever thirty married women are
employed), lavatories etc., and specially because women are not
allowed to work night shifts. A textile mill labour officer told Jyoti
Punjwani that the winding department had stopped recruiting
women because the men objected to working on the night shift only.
E.A. Ramaswamy (1977:100) says that when there was widespread
redundancy of women in the Coimbatore textile mills, it was hard to
absorb them in departments working night shifts: 'Nor would the
unions allow the surplus hands to be dismissed. Where the TWU is
powerful it has forced the millowners to distribute the available work
among all the women although this entails periodic lay-offs of even
the most senior workers.' In any case unskilled women have been
forced out of the cotton mills by automatic machinery: in the Bombay
mills, unskilled women's employment fell by 40 per cent between
1961 and 1971, while female employment rose in 'industries'
requiring mainly educated women: teaching, public administration,
medicine and nursing, commerce and banking, pharmaceuticals
(mainly packers), and post and communications (telephone operators) (Joshi H. and V. 1976a:67, 69). The Employers' Federation of
India (1969, summarized in Labour Bureau 1978:68) found that
although women made up only 5–6 per cent of Bombay's industrial
work force in 1962–4, the proportion was much higher in chemicals
(about 32 per cent) and cigarettes (about 25 per cent). Since then one
should add electronics to the list.

Far more women work in the unorganized sector, especially if we include home workers and 'temporary' factory workers. Deshpande (1979:74) found the same proportion of women (6 per cent) in Bombay small establishments and factories, but the factory sample included temporaries. In my subsample of his questionnaires, 5 per cent of factory workers (including temporaries) were women, mostly winders and textile workers; and 13 per cent of *manufacturing* small establishment workers, especially plastic product workers, general workers and packers. With Deshpande's sampling method it was not possible to find out the proportion in the casual work force: his estimate was 18 per cent.

In all sectors, women's average earnings are below those of men. In Bombay, Deshpande (:171) found that women earned 27 per cent less than men in the factories, 9 per cent less in small establishments, and 56 per cent less in the casual sector. The gap of only 9 per cent in the small establishments is surprising: Rohini Banaji (1978), in a small survey of Bombay working-class families, found the same gap (27 per cent) between men's and women's earnings in factories, but a gap of 57 per cent between the average earnings of all men and women wage earners (whether in factories or elsewhere). Comparing the mean earnings of women in my subsample with those of men in Deshpande's sample, I found a gap of 15 per cent in factories and 31 per cent in manufacturing small establishments.[6] This is a rough and ready comparison, but I am fairly sure that the earnings gap between the sexes is at least as large in small workshops as in factories, and probably larger. Women are strongly represented in units with very low pay and bad conditions: making garments, for example, or cleaning and sorting broken glass.

Apart from these women who are more or less regularly employed in factories and workshops, I know of no reliable estimate of the number who work at home, on electrical or electronic assembly, sewing on buttons, embroidery, making agarbathis or incense sticks and innumerable other tasks. Employers say they rely largely on home work. Visiting working-class homes, again and again one sees women doing this work. Yet, with the partial exception of bidi workers, they disappear from most surveys and statistics.

The picture of women's employment is generally one of low pay,

[6] It would of course be better to compare the mean earnings of women in my subsample with those of men in the same subsample, but this would have been laborious given the level of intermediate technology I had to work with: handwritten hand-sorted cards and a calculator. The women's sample was small and easy to sort.

insecurity and boredom, and usually poor physical conditions of work; yet the women who take this work are by no means from the poorest or most disadvantaged families. As I suggested, the wives and daughters not only of factory workers, but of teachers and officials, want paid work to supplement the family income, and if they cannot get factory jobs they will consider small firms or home work. It is true that only a minority of women in these families (varying from city to city) go out to work, but their number is large in relation to the jobs available; and the proportion who would look for work if there were a better chance of finding it is probably growing. These women are educated, in some cases to a high standard. Hilary Standing (research project, 1978) found that women industrial workers in Calcutta, though appallingly paid, had on average from four to nine years of schooling and some were graduates. The effect must be to close this job market to uneducated women from poorer families: Deshpande (1979:218) found that 8 per cent of women of working age (15–59) in Bombay factory workers' families were 'economically active', and 10 per cent in small establishment workers' families. The figure rises to 35 per cent for women in casual workers' families, and it is clear that these women must be doing the heaviest and worst-paid casual work, such as building labour. On any building site one sees them, carrying head loads in baskets for long hours in the heat, while their babies lie wrapped in cloth on the ground.

There is little evidence on how women find jobs in factories and workshops, except impressions from talking to the men and to employers. It is hard for a male research worker to interview women at length. Hilary Standing (ibid.) who studied a small non-random sample of women in Calcutta, mostly in the smaller organized sector firms, found that employers often ask for written applications: 'Kinship links played a negligible role in the acquisition of jobs, nor did they often characterize relations between workers.' But more generally – at least in places like Bombay and Bangalore – it seems that men bring their wives to work for their own employers, and women already employed recommend neighbours and friends.

Heather Joshi (1976b) stresses the close links between the labour markets for the two 'sectors', points out that the percentage of women in the urban population is rising and argues against a policy of reserving jobs for men. The promotion of organized sector employ-ment for women should be part of a package to raise living standards, reduce fertility and enhance the status of the urban unorganized sector which already employs many women. Elsewhere (Joshi 1980) she argues that we should consider the dynamic relationships, not between two sectors, but three: formal, informal and domestic. Only the first two kinds of work are 'economic' in Amartya Sen's sense: paid, and regarded by the performer and others as 'work' and 'worthwhile'. 'When there is not enough work in the economic sphere, women retreat into the domestic 'sphere' (:640); this coincides with other developments which mean there is less useful work for women to do in the domestic sphere: they become mere dependants, and lose their autonomy.

Most women workers live in households where the main earner is a man, and although women tend to work in separate departments or occupations, the networks through which they find jobs are extensions of the men's networks. Where more than one household member does paid work, these networks are quite likely to extend into both the organized and unorganized sectors, since even where members of a household are not working in different 'sectors' they may have done so in the past and will have friends and contacts in different firms. It is hard to disentangle the two 'sectors' of the job market when one looks at them, not from the point of view of individual careers, but from that of households and wider groups of kin who depend on one another for economic help and information about jobs.

Job-finding networks and their limits

I have described the methods employers use to find labour; then the strategies which job-hunters follow in the search for industrial employment and, when they have it, for safer better-paid jobs in bigger factories. The point is to show how recruitment practices affect people of different social origin – different castes, classes, people from different areas etc. – and whether these recruitment practices form new groups with their own interests and loyalties.

There are partly closed labour markets for the three main sorts of industrial work – permanent factory jobs in the organized sector, temporary or casual or contract work in factories, jobs in unorganized sector workshops – and limited movement across these boundaries. Recruitment to each kind of job depends partly on skill and luck, but largely on contacts, especially networks of kin or of friends from the same village or area, who often belong to the same caste or range of castes if they are not relatives. Thus one finds clusters of people from similar social origins in a firm, sometimes in a trade or an industry.

Occasionally there is a link between a caste's traditional work and their industrial jobs. In other cases this is a rationalization of something that came about for different reasons, historical accident or lack of alternatives.

'Social origin' is deliberately vague: it could mean caste, economic class, region or religion or language, but that does not matter too much, since these distinctions often coincide in rural areas as well as towns, and the instances where they do not (poor Brahmans, low-caste landlords or businessmen) may disguise the fact. It is not too misleading to think simply of those who are or have been at the top, in the middle and at the bottom, and to ask if they are likely to remain there.

Is *permanent factory employment* – either generally or in certain industries – the more or less exclusive property of groups, at least in the same city? If so is this because they were already advantaged (high caste, middle class, educated) before industrialization or migration, or because of local accidents (so that whatever advantage factory workers now have came afterwards)? Similarly, does *industrial employment of any kind* tend to be the property of groups, and if so why?

If we find people from similar origins working both in the organized and unorganized sectors of the same industry, or following the same trade in both sectors, then it is likely that the same job-finding networks extend into both sectors, and there is one labour market not two in this industry or trade. Employment in the whole industry or trade may even be a group's property.

Imagine a map of industry. Horizontal lines separate permanent factory work and the other two types, and the bottom line separates people with and without any industrial employment. Below that line one can fall to any depth. The vertical lines are between industries (such as textiles and engineering) or between trades (fitters, weavers): this is like the notion of vertical linkages, but in relation to labour markets not markets for products. Are people from similar origins concentrated in the layers (types of employment) or columns (industries or trades) or rectangles (e.g. permanent textile workers only)? Which groups if any are below the bottom line, that is, seldom get industrial work at all, even casually?

Until recently most studies of industrial labour were of factory workers only. Each industry – textiles, jute, steel – had its own sources of labour, usually migrants and sometimes from the lower castes, recruited through jobbers (see pp. 39–44 above). In some cases this gave communities a foothold or a monopoly in particular lines of work. In other cases, like the Bombay cotton mills, all castes and communities were mixed together, with specific exceptions like the exclusion of Untouchables from weaving sheds. The newer factories, especially engineering factories set up after the war, wanted a more educated work force who could be trained in new skills (see pp. 71–5 above). This led to an influx of applicants from the middle ranks of society, both in caste and class, including the urban lower middle classes, the sons of prosperous peasants, and in places like Bangalore where industry had a new image, Brahmans and other high castes as well. This is why one finds middle-class Bengalis in the Calcutta engineering factories, beside jute and cotton mills manned by Hindi-speaking migrant labourers.

Until Independence there were no really 'permanent' factory jobs, but there was a distinction between regular workers and the large fringe of temporary or casual or badli (substitute) workers. Writings on the early work force suggest that these workers were usually recruited by the same methods and over the same networks as regular workers: through jobbers, recommendations from regular workers and managers etc., and that many temporary workers eventually got regular jobs. As I have shown, this still happens, and managements are sometimes forced to make workers permanent when they had no intention of doing so. This risk is one reason why employers have turned again to contract labour, which can more easily be prevented from any joint action with the permanent work force. When contract workers do different jobs from the permanent workers – especially construction, cleaning, and menial or heavy labour – they are generally from different origins and often the lowest castes: not however when employers replace ordinary production workers with contract labour, even turning permanent workers into contract workers technically self-employed or employed by someone else (see pp. 172–9 above). Not much has been written on the recruitment of contract labour in factories (Vaid 1966 is the fullest study but says little about who is recruited and how); and since the work force is so mixed and unstable, I have to rely on impressions and conversations.

Because of the ways in which temporary factory workers are recruited, and permanent workers largely from their ranks, it seems likely that permanent and temporary workers in most factories come from the same origins, except where only the few skilled workers are permanent and all the rest are 'temporary', however long they stay. Temporary workers tend to be the permanent workers' sons, other relatives or friends; and now increasingly their wives and daughters.

Contract workers are likely to be from different social origins, and may have little to do with the permanent workers at work or outside: except where ordinary production workers have been replaced by contract labour.

In other words, where many people from the same origins are found in an industry – especially if they have the same skill or trade – this cluster is likely to extend to both sides of the shadowy line between permanent and 'temporary' employment. This cannot yet be shown statistically, because figures for factory work forces do not distinguish consistently between permanent and temporary workers.

There is a sharper distinction between terms of employment in the typical factory and the typical unorganized sector workshop, even if there is a grey area where the Factory Act is evaded and unions are weak. Are there two separate work forces from different origins in each industry or trade, and two labour markets?

Before the war, the entrepreneurs who set up small engineering workshops in each city or region tended to come from a few castes, usually with a background in crafts or trade but sometimes, like the Mahisyas of Howrah, in agriculture. If the caste had a tradition of manual work, they employed their own relatives and craftsmen first, and often helped them to set up independent businesses later. However it seems that men from very diverse origins were able to get some industrial experience in these small firms. When the factories had vacancies, they were willing to take men trained in small firms because there was no one else. Few men had paper qualifications in technical trades, and it was not thought necessary for a workman to have much education, beyond literacy perhaps. The opportunity was there and some people took it, establishing a bridgehead for their community in factory employment. Others, like the Mahisyas, were less interested in working for big firms owned by outsiders (in their area, the British) but preferred to work for their own castemen in firms of any size until they could become their own masters. The more technically advanced factories set up after Independence, especially in the 1960s, took some older skilled men who had worked their way up, but they were looking mainly for educated young men, largely from different classes and castes who had not considered industrial employment before.

However, in some places like Bombay the people of the region had already established a bridgehead in the factories, and firms came under increasing political pressure to employ 'sons of the soil' (in practice, those whose mother tongue is the regional language). This ruled out otherwise well-qualified people from other areas. It segmented the labour market further, giving an advantage in the scramble for factory jobs to well-educated local people, generally of middle to high caste but including the small class of educated Harijans; and forcing on to the labour market a very large number of equally or better-educated people, often with industrial experience, who spoke other languages even if they were born locally. This is why Bombay's small establishment workers appear to be better educated than factory workers.

To find out the occupations in which people from similar origins are concentrated, and whether the same groups are concentrated in factories and workshops, I took two subsamples of the completed questionnaires for Deshpande's Bombay labour market study: one of factory workers (including some temporary workers), the other of workshops, i.e. *industrial* small establishments only. I combined some of the original occupation codes into new classes and groups of occupations.

Tables 7 and 8 show that the cotton textile mills – Bombay's oldest industry – are still dominated by the Marathi-speaking Hindus, especially from the Maraatha farming castes, who first took employment there. No one else can break in, because the industry is stagnant. The newer industries and occupations, especially engineering, have a mixed work force both in factories and workshops, more representative of this cosmopolitan city's population. There is no clear pattern in the figures to confirm or disprove the hypothesis that people find jobs through caste or community networks extending into both sectors, though they do show that there are certain kinds of work where immigrants and non-Hindus have generally a better chance, whether this is because of their contacts, their special skills, the time of their immigration or other reasons.

The figures have not much bearing on the other question, whether certain groups (identified by caste or otherwise) are excluded from all industrial employment. Locally born Harijans, and educated Hindus, are quite well represented; though it is clear from other evidence that large groups, like the Telugu-speaking low-caste or Harijan migrants from south India who make up much of the casual building labour force, are hardly ever in a position to get regular work. Their chances of casual work depend largely on factory building and the health of the city's industrial economy.

Table 7. *Occupation and language: Bombay factory workers (including temporaries) and workers in industrial small establishments*

Occupation, groups and classes		Marathi	Hindi/Urdu	Gujarati	Southern languages[a]	Other languages	No. in sample
		First language (%)					
	F[b]						
10 Fitters, assemblers and machine erectors	F	50	30	4	6	9	70
	S	60	15	10	15	—	20
11 Furnacemen and moulders	F	(29)[c]	(43)	—	(29)	—	7
	S	(86)	(14)	—	—	—	7
12 Turners	F	60	12	24	—	—	25
	S	(100)	—	—	—	—	1
13 Millers and pounders	F	60	30	—	10	—	10
	S	—	(100)	—	—	—	1
14 Welders and flame cutters	F	(78)	—	—	(22)	—	9
	S	—	—	—	(100)	—	4
15 Other skilled engineering and metal workers	F	60	20	7	7	7	15
	S	(20)	(40)	(20)	(20)	—	5
1 *Engineering and metal workers*	F	54	24	7	7	7	136
	S	53	16	11	21	—	38
20 Weavers	F	71	13	3	11	—	62
	S	—	—	—	—	—	—

No.	Category							Total
21	Doffer-boys	F	91	9	—	—	—	23
		S	—	—	—	—	—	—
22	Other textile workers	F	71	20	2	6	2	123
		S	(33)	(33)	(33)	—	1	3
2	*Textile workers*	F	73	17	2	7	—	208
		S	(33)	(33)	(33)	—	—	3
30	Printers	F	(71)	(29)	—	—	—	7
		S	52	4	4	26	13	23
31	Compositors and typesetting machine operators	F	(67)	(17)	(17)	33	—	6
		S	40	6	6	—	—	15
32	Other printing workers	F	—	—	—	—	—	—
		S	(100)	—	—	33	—	9
33	Bookbinders	F	(67)	(33)	6	23	—	3
		S	80	—	4	15	—	10
3	*Printing and books*	F	59	25	6	23	—	16
		S	61	4	4	—	—	57
40	Tailors etc.	F	(67)	(33)	—	—	—	3
		S	70	15	9	—	—	33
41	Leather workers	F	(50)	(50)	—	—	—	2
		S	93	7	—	8	—	14
42	Jewellery engravers	F	(100)	—	—	—	—	1
		S	68	36	1	—	32	19
43	Carpenters	F	55	—	—	—	—	11
		S	—	—	—	—	—	1
44	Painters, decorators etc.	F	(78)	(33)	4	8	(22)	9
		S	(67)	23	1	6	9	3
4	*Traditional and similar crafts*	F	65	13	4	—	—	26
		S	73	—	1	—	—	70

Table 7. (cont.)

Occupation, groups and classes		First language (%)					No. in sample
		Marathi	Hindi/Urdu	Gujarati	Southern languages[a]	Other languages	
50 Machine operators	F	55	21	7	9	7	85
	S	68	12	11	4	5	57
51 Mechanics and repairmen	F	88	6	6	—	—	16
	S	(38)	(13)	—	—	(50)	8
52 Winders	F	85	8	4	—	4	26
	S	—	—	—	—	—	—
53 Electricians and wiremen	F	(83)	(17)	—	—	—	6
	S	(50)	(25)	—	—	(25)	4
54 Jobbers	F	67	24	—	5	5	21
	S	—	—	—	—	—	—
55 Plastic product workers	F	—	—	—	—	—	—
	S	83	10	3	—	3	29
56 Checkers, testers and examiners	F	71	7	7	7	7	14
	S	—	—	—	—	—	—
57 Other semi-skilled production process workers	F	63	21	4	8	4	157
	S	69	21	4	6	—	72
58 Other unskilled production process workers	F	79	14	7	—	—	14
	S	(40)	(40)	—	—	(20)	5
Other manufacturing workers	F	65	19	5	6	4	339

Occupation							Total
60 Typists and stenographers	F	52	6	16	17	9	81
	S	19	—	19	31	31	16
61 Accounts	F	(50)	—	—	(50)	—	2
	S	40	—	20	20	20	15
62 Unskilled office workers	F	(67)	—	(17)	—	(17)	6
	S	(88)	—	—	—	(11)	9
63 Other clerical and office workers	F	(56)	—	(33)	(11)	—	9
	S	45	15	10	15	15	20
64 Supervisors, foremen and technicians	F	(100)	—	—	—	—	2
	S	38	21	25	8	8	24
6 *Clerical and supervisory*	F	54	6	17	16	7	100
	S	42	15	13	14	15	84
7 *Services: cooking, catering etc.*	F	62	23	8	8	—	13
	S	36	36	—	21	7	14
80 General workers, packers and deliverymen	F	67	11	—	—	22	18
	S	76	13	2	2	7	45
81 Watchmen	F	45	45	—	—	9	11
	S	(100)	—	—	—	—	1
82 Sweepers and cleaners	F	69	15	8	8	—	13
	S	—	—	—	—	—	—
83 'Coolies' and khalasis	F	80	—	—	20	—	10
	S	(100)	—	—	—	—	2
8 *General workers*	F	65	17	2	6	10	52
	S	71	19	2	2	6	48
9 *Miscellaneous*	F	64	9	6	10	11	89
	S	(29)	(14)	—	(43)	(14)	7
Total	F	60	20	6	8	5	979
	S	61	13	6	10	8	496

[a] Southern languages are Tamil, Malayalam, Kannada and Telugu.

[b] F(actories) and S(mall industrial establishments).

[c] Percentages in brackets where the whole sample is less than 10.

Source: Based on a sample of questionnaires completed for Deshpande's bombay labour market study (1979).

Table 8. *Occupation and community (caste or religion): Bombay factory workers (including temporaries) and workers in industrial small establishments*

Occupation groups and classes			Community (%)											No. in sample
			Hindus & Buddhists[a]						Christian	Muslim	Sikh	Other, or not known		
			Maraatha	'Ks'atriya'[b]	Brahman	'Vaishya'	Harijan, 'Shuudra' or Buddhist	Other Hindu castes						
10	Fitters, assemblers and machine erectors	F[c]	26	16	4	3	3	16	10	19	—	6		70
		S	42	—	5	11	—	11	11	11	—	11		19
11	Furnacemen and moulders	F	(43)	(14)[d]	—	—	(14)	(14)	—	—	—	(14)		7
		S	—	(14)	(14)	—	—	(43)	—	(14)	—	(14)		7
12	Turners	F	16	20	8	—	16	32	—	—	—	8		25
		S	(100)	—	—	—	—	—	—	—	—	—		1
13	Millers and pounders	F	10	10	10	10	—	30	20	—	—	10		10
		S	—	—	—	—	—	—	—	—	—	—		—
14	Welders and flame cutters	F	(22)	(22)	—	—	(33)	—	(11)	—	—	(11)		9
		S	—	(25)	—	—	—	—	—	(25)	—	(50)		4
15	Other skilled engineering and metal workers	F	20	27	—	—	7	27	7	13	—	—		15
		S	(20)	—	—	(20)	(20)	—	(20)	—	(20)	—		5
1	*Engineering and metal workers*	F	21	18	4	2	4	21	10	14	—	7		136
		S	37	6	6	9	—	11	6	11	3	14		36

Workers in this class (based on several occupation codes used in Deshpande's tables 1979) are mainly factory workers: most workers in engineering small establishments have been classified under less specific codes (esp. in class 5 below). The factory sample shows higher proportions of 'Ks'atriyas' (my spelling), 'other castes' (very mixed) and Christians. The language table shows a high proportion of southerners (21 per cent) in the small establishments but there are no specifically southern caste names in the sample; so these southerners are probably Christians, Brahmans, Muslims or Harijans.

20	Weavers	F	45	16	3	3	5	18	2	5	—	3	62
		S	—	—	—	—	—	—	—	—	—	—	0
21	Doffer-boys	F	48	22	4	—	4	13	4	—	—	4	23
		S	—	—	—	—	—	—	—	—	—	—	—
22	Other textile workers	F	38	17	6	2	10	16	3	2	—	6	123
		S	(33)	—	—	—	—	(33)	—	—	—	(33)	3
2	*Textile workers*	F	41	17	5	2	8	16	3	3	—	1	208
		S	(33)	—	—	—	—	(33)	—	—	—	(33)	3

None of the many small-scale textile establishments appear to have come into this sample, though three 'other textile workers' slipped in. In the mills, weavers and doffer-boys are overwhelmingly Hindu and mostly Maraathas or 'Ks'atriyas' (and Marathi-speaking). Eleven per cent of weavers are of the Padmashaii caste. 'Other textile workers' are a little more mixed, including several from low castes.

30	Printers	F	(14)	(29)	—	—	—	—	(14)	(29)	(14)	—	7
		S	9	9	4	4	9	22	17	4	—	22	23
31	Compositors and typesetting machine operators	F	(17)	—	(33)	7	(17)	13	(17)	7	—	7	6
		S	27	7	7	7	—	—	20	7	—	7	15
32	Other printing workers	F	(44)	(11)	—	—	(22)	(22)	20	—	—	—	9
		S	—	(67)	—	—	(33)	(33)	10	10	—	—	3
33	Bookbinders	F	30	30	—	10	10	20	20	—	—	—	10
		S	30	30	—	10	10	20	20	—	—	—	10
3	*Printing and books*	F	13	25	13	13	—	6	—	13	6	—	16
		S	23	12	4	5	9	19	12	4	—	12	57

Most printing shops are small. No caste predominates.

Table 8 (cont.)

| Occupation groups and classes | | Community (%) Hindus & Buddhists[a] | | | | | | Christian | Muslim | Sikh | Other, or not known | No. in sample |
		Maraatha	'Ks'atriya'[b]	Brahman	'Vaishya'	Harijan, 'Shuudra' or Buddhist	Other Hindu castes					
40	Tailors etc.	F	(33)	(33)	—	—	—	—	—	(33)	—	—	3
		S	24	9	12	—	3	9	3	18	—	21	33
41	Leather workers	F	—	—	—	—	(50)	—	—	(50)	—	—	2
		S	—	29	7	—	57	—	—	—	—	7	14
42	Jewellery engravers	F	—	—	—	—	—	(100)	—	—	—	—	1
		S	5	5	—	5	16	63	—	5	—	—	19
43	Carpenters	F	18	—	—	9	9	36	18	9	—	—	11
		S	—	—	—	—	(100)	—	—	—	—	—	1
44	Painters, decorators etc.	F	(22)	—	(11)	—	—	(33)	(22)	(11)	—	—	9
		S	(33)	(33)	—	—	(33)	—	—	—	—	—	3
4	*Traditional and similar crafts*	F	19	4	4	4	7	31	15	15	—	—	26
		S	14	13	6	3	19	21	1	10	—	11	70

Again, most of these craftsmen work for small employers (except perhaps carpenters, who are self-employed). As one would expect, there are clusters of people practising their traditional caste occupation or one allied to it (about half the jewellery engravers are of the Sonar or Goldsmith caste). Very few high castes. A fairly high proportion of Harijans.

No.	Occupation		1	2	3	4	5	6	7	8	9	10	Total
50	Machine operators	F	25	9	9	4	4	25	15	7	—	2	85
		S	30	12	11	4	7	18	5	5	2	7	57
51	Mechanics and repairmen	F	31	25	6	13	13	—	13	—	—	—	16
		S	(13)	(13)	—	—	(38)	(25)	(13)	—	—	2	8
52	Winders	F	38	15	8	4	4	23	4	—	—	4	26
		S	(13)	—	—	—	—	—	(13)	—	—	—	—
53	Electricians and wiremen	F	(67)	(17)	—	—	(17)	—	—	—	—	—	6
		S	(25)	—	—	—	—	—	(25)	(25)	(25)	—	—
54	Jobbers	F	33	19	14	—	5	19	5	5	—	—	4
		S	—	—	—	—	—	—	—	—	—	—	21
55	Plastic product workers	F	—	—	—	—	—	—	—	—	—	—	—
		S	—	—	—	—	—	—	—	—	—	—	—
56	Checkers, testers and examiners	F	32	11	4	7	11	29	—	4	—	4	28
		S	21	29	—	7	7	21	7	7	—	7	14
57	Other semi-skilled production process workers	F	27	21	2	4	9	16	2	10	1	3	157
		S	29	15	7	6	7	15	4	—	11	6	72
58	Other unskilled production process workers	F	21	14	7	7	7	36	7	7	—	—	14
		S	(20)	—	—	—	—	—	(60)	—	(20)	—	5
5	*Other manufacturing workers*	F	28	18	5	4	7	19	6	7	1	4	339
		S	29	13	7	5	7	19	5	5	6	5	174
60	Typists and stenographers	F	27	15	15	4	6	20	6	2	—	5	81
		S	6	6	19	—	—	13	25	—	—	—	16
61	Accounts	F	—	(50)	(50)	—	—	—	—	—	—	—	2
		S	(50)	7	33	—	13	13	—	13	—	7	15
62	Unskilled office workers	F	7	7	—	(17)	(22)	(50)	(11)	—	—	—	6
		S	(67)	—	—	—	—	—	(11)	—	—	—	9

'Other manufacturing workers' is a residual class. The origins of workers in both sectors are as diverse as their occupations: a high proportion of non-Maharashtrians (i.e. non-Marathi-speaking) and non-Maraathas (by caste). Harijans, Christians, Muslims and southerners probably in about the same proportions as in the general population. Sikhs in the small establishments (though the sample is small). No marked differences in caste distribution between the sectors: the names of some 'other castes' (Kunbi, Patel) appear once or twice in both samples for some occupations, but not often enough to suggest a network.

Table 8 (cont.)

Occupation groups and classes		Community (%) Hindus & Buddhists[a]										No. in sample
		Maraatha	'Ks'atriya'[b]	Brahman	'Vaishya'	Harijan, 'Shuudra' or Buddhist	Other Hindu castes	Christian	Muslim	Sikh	Other, or not known	
63 Other clerical and office workers	F	27	9	9	9	9	27	—	—	—	9	11
	S	15	5	10	—	—	15	10	15	30	—	20
64 Supervisors, foremen and technicians	F	—	—	—	8	—	(100)	—	—	—	—	2
	S	4	17	8	8	—	17	4	25	13	4	24
6 *Clerical and supervisory*	F	26	14	14	5	6	24	5	2	—	5	102
	S	14	8	14	2	4	13	10	13	5	18	84

The sample of 'factory workers' includes few clerical or supervisory workers except typists or stenographers: Brahmans in both sectors, more Christians in the small establishments. Supervisors etc. in the small establishments include Brahmans, Christians and Sikhs. The whole class has a high proportion of southerners (almost certainly Brahmans or Christians) and Gujaratis.

		Maraatha	'Ks'atriya'[b]	Brahman	'Vaishya'	Harijan, 'Shuudra' or Buddhist	Other Hindu castes	Christian	Muslim	Sikh	Other, or not known	No. in sample
7 *Services:* cooking, catering etc.	F	31	23	8	—	—	23	—	15	—	—	13
	S	14	—	14	7	—	14	—	7	14	29	14

Small sample

		Maraatha	'Ks'atriya'[b]	Brahman	'Vaishya'	Harijan, 'Shuudra' or Buddhist	Other Hindu castes	Christian	Muslim	Sikh	Other, or not known	No. in sample
80 General workers, packers and deliverymen	F	17	6	6	—	6	17	33	11	—	7	18
	S	40	7	9	4	4	20	7	7	—	4	45

81 watchmen	F	27	18	18	9	—	9	—	—	9	11
	S	7	31	—	7	23	(100)	—	—	7	1
82 Sweepers and cleaners	F	—	—	—	—	23	—	—	—	—	13
	S	30	10	10	30	20	—	10	3	10	10
83 'Coolies' and khalasis	F	30	10	10	—	30	10	—	—	—	10
	S	—	—	—	—	—	(100)	—	—	—	2

Comparisons between sectors are difficult. Sweepers (mostly Harijans) and 'coolies' are certainly under-represented, probably because these jobs are often done by contract labour. In both samples, general workers are overwhelmingly Marathi- or Hindi-speaking.

8 *General workers*	F	19	15	6	4	13	17	13	9	6	52
	S	38	6	8	4	2	19	6	20	4	48

No indication of what these people do.

9 *Miscellaneous*	F	22	9	16	4	9	20	3	9	6	89
	S	10	10	10	10	—	40	10	20	—	10
Totals	F	28	16	7	8	19	7	0+	7	5	981
	S	24	10	8	4	18	6	3	8	10	496

More Maraathas and 'Ks'atriyas' (probably Maraathas) in the factories. Similar proportions of Brahmans, Harijans, Christians and Muslims in both samples. Almost all the Sikhs are in small establishments.

Notes: in the original questionnaire, enumerators were asked to write down the caste given by the informant. In some cases they were not able to do so, and simply ticked one of four boxes, marked B(rahman), K(s'atriya: probably Maraathas), V(aishya: merchant castes) and S(huudra: in Maharashtra, this means Harijan).

The 74 Harijans in the F sample include 14 Buddhists. In the S sample, 36 Harijans include 7 Buddhists.

'Other Hindu castes' include some that are hard to identify, and a few that are probably Scheduled Caste or Harijan. In the F sample, they include (spelled as written down): 25 Bhandari, 12 Yadav, 12 Kunbi, 8 Padmashali, 7 Agri, 7 C.K.P. (Chandraseniya Kayastha Prabhu), 6 Koli, 6 Teli, 5 Jaiswar, 4 Patel, 4 Sindhi, 3 Carpenter, 3 Erzava, 3 Lohar, 3 Mali, 3 Nayar or Nair, 3 Rajput, 3 Singh, 3 Sonar or Goldsmith, 3 Wani, 2 Bhahiya, 2 Fishermen, 2 Mistry, 2 Thakur; and one each from 37 castes (including 'Cowboy'). In the S sample: 12 Bhandari, 11 Vani, 7 Kunbi, 5 Sonar, 3 Patel, 2 Barber or Naie, 2 Nayar, 2 Rathod, 2 Shimpe; and one each from 20 castes.

'Other, or not known' includes, in the F sample: 36 Hindus of unknown caste, 4 Parsis, 3 Jains, and 4 whose religion is not known. In the S sample: 41 Hindus of unknown caste, 3 Parsis, 3 Jains, and 5 of unknown religion.

a All Maharashtrian Buddhists are Harijan converts to Dr Ambedkar's neo-Buddhism.
b 'Ks'atriya' (Warrior) is a title claimed by many castes all over India, often locally dominant peasant castes. Most 'Ks'atriyas' are probably Maraathas.
c F(actories) and S(mall establishments).
d Percentages in brackets where the whole sample is less than 10.

Of course Bombay has special features – waves of migration from different areas when different industries were set up, booms and slumps – and these things leave their traces in the composition of the work force long afterwards. The towns of the Punjab show the effects of a very different pattern of growth, where an agricultural boom came first, then small industries, then large ones, and where industrial employers have to compete with farmers for labour. Most of the big industrial cities, like Calcutta, Bombay and Bangalore, have important ethnic minorities, with pockets of employment for this or that group which can only be explained by fits and starts in industrial development and migration. In cities where industrial workers have been recruited mainly from the settled urban population and from surrounding districts, like Poona (Lambert 1963) or Coimbatore (Harriss 1982) organized sector workers are more likely to be high caste educated people of the region, usually landowners or artisans. Those who came later to take employment in small industries were from lower down the local social scale.

Other things being equal, people from the middle or upper ranks of the regional society have a headstart, and are likely to keep it by bringing in their own people when more factory jobs fall vacant. But in the bigger cities, and the places where industry has grown fastest, other things are not equal: both the employers and workers in small industries are often educated skilled people from other regions and speaking other languages, and the factories too have to draw on these people to fill gaps in their skilled work force. The division between the labour markets for factories and workshops is often, not always, the result of local historical accidents as much as any systematic discrimination in favour of the rich, educated and high caste. There is only a loose fit between the inequalities in the industrial labour market and the older forms of social hierarchy.

The biggest barrier is not between regular workers in factories and small workshops, but between all of these and another 'unorganized sector' altogether, the mass of casual labourers who may be neither urban nor rural but nomadic, and who are often left out of statistics and reports. Even in the slums one may forget them, since so many sleep out in the streets or stations or on patches of open ground. They come from the bottom of the social pile and have few chances to move up: only a few are lucky or clever enough to find some regular employment. These people at the bottom are diverse, fragmented, and often in competition with each other. They have little in common but their poverty, and little sense of a class interest:

Those who join the lower ranks of the urban economy generally remain there, and even horizontal mobility is limited. Shortage of work and limited chances to accumulate capital or to invest in any formal education, can lead to a position of defensiveness in which one's accustomed sphere of activity is protected as much as possible and entrance to it is restricted to those who can appeal to particularistic loyalties – although the success in doing so may vary.

(Breman 1976:1907)

The habit of closing off one's domain to people not on the right network may run through society, but is often strongest among the poorest and most insecure: those who make their living in the 'informal sector', which is supposed to provide so many opportunities for new entrants to the work force.

6

Who are the 'working class'?

People commonly refer to industrial workers, and sometimes other kinds of wage-earners and self-employed workers, as the 'working class'. Usually this means a group who share a similar economic situation, which distinguishes them from others, like property-owners, employers and managers. It suggests common interests and a shared consciousness of these interests. When left-wing people (not just marxists) use the term, it implies that the working class work not for themselves, but for those who control the means of production and live off other people's labour.

Alternatively one could argue that it is misleading to lump together, as 'working class', people who share few interests and are not conscious of any; and that there is an important class line to draw between organized and unorganized sector industrial workers (Joshi 1976a, see p. 17 above), or between an urban class, which includes all industrial workers, and the mass of rural poor (Lipton 1977, see p. 19 above). In either case, well-paid organized sector workers are allied with the privileged or exploiting class, though the sections of this class fight among themselves for the spoils. That is what trade unions are for.

Are organized and unorganized sector industrial workers two classes with different or conflicting interests? On the face of it they seem to be, and I half implied that they were in *South Indian factory workers* (Holmström 1976): those inside the citadel of permanent employment, together with their close relatives; and those outside trying to get in, with little chance of success.

Do these two kinds of worker think and act as if they were classes with distinct interests, either in their everyday lives at work and at home, or when they become involved in joint action organized by unions or parties or more short-lived movements? And if they are sometimes aware of common interests, do these cut them off from other people like casual general labourers, the self-employed and small peasants?

As I suggested in chapter 1, these are aspects of the same problem, the relations between two kinds of workers seen from outside, and seen from inside (by workers): questions about people's economic situations and life chances, and their assessment of their own situation – how they experience it, judge it and act.

This chapter matches objective evidence – working and living conditions, careers, family economies – to what I know about workers' experience and thinking, according to what they told me or others – unionists, sociologists and journalists: workers' mental maps of society, built up from their experience of everyday problems.

In the end, everyone has her or his view of the world, which we may hope to understand but cannot reduce to a mere expression of self-interest, or to 'culture', values and perceptions which each person learns without question. People's motives and thoughts are more complex. But members of a group share ideas and assumptions, which reflect their common experience without being determined by it. How far do these workers see society as divided into those inside and outside the citadel? To the extent that there really is a citadel wall and people perceive it, how much movement takes place across the wall, and what links remain between people on opposite sides of it? Do organized and unorganized sector workers live in separate social worlds? What links are there between all industrial workers and other people, especially peasants: for example, is there really an alliance between industrial workers and rich farmers which bolsters 'urban bias' in Indian planning and politics?

Wages

To start with the most obvious difference: big firms usually pay much more than small ones, at least to permanent employees. The bigger the firm the higher the pay, especially within the same industry (thus a 1973 settlement between engineering employers and unions in West Bengal laid down different minimum wages for firms employing over 50, 250 and 1000; firms with under 50 workers to be dealt with separately). Whether a small firm is technically in the organized sector does not seem to make much difference, though the presence of a union does: for many firms near the borderline, laws on bonus and overtime payments are a dead letter. Where there is a legal minimum wage it applies in theory to all local firms in an industry.

Some of the reasons why big firms pay best are clear: the law, the unions, economies of scale; often they take their pick of the skilled workers; many small employers are marginal and cannot afford to pay more, while the others take advantage of workers' weak bargaining position.

In a small union office in north Bombay, I talked to a welder who works in a firm with thirty employees. He earned Rs 7 a day until the union came, now (1976–7) Rs 14.85. In a big factory he would get Rs 40, while welders in small firms were still getting Rs 7. Why the difference? Look at that strip light: it burns as much electricity if there is one person sitting here, or several (i.e. economies of scale).

A turner works for a Bangalore firm which employs over 100, in two factories making sugar cane crushers (p. 179). He joined the factory seventeen years ago and worked there ever since, except for seven years when the owners tried to break the union by laying off the registered workers and employing temporaries.

Now he gets Rs 350 a month: far less than turners in a big car component factory. Why? Their work is quite different from his: sugar cane crushers do not have to be so precisely made, but the car component workers have to make exact measurements and to use instruments like micrometers. They must be educated, and learn the skill while they are young. (Compare workers on the other side of the line, at the 'Oriental' engineering factory: 'Once when the workshop superintendent was trying to convince some workers that in terms of wages they were far better off than their counterparts in other factories, their spokesman at once replied, "You cannot compare the work we do with the work in other factories. Our work involves millimetre-precision. They do not even mind the discrepancy of an inch."' Sheth 1968a:117–8)

Another worker: of course the big firms pay more – they are 'limited companies'.

However there are glaring exceptions to the rule that big firms pay best. I mentioned a Faridabad engineering factory where the minimum unskilled wage was Rs 600 a month, and a bigger one where it was Rs 230 (p. 152). (These figures for 1976–7 include Dearness Allowance, added to a national basic wage in large firms: the distinction no longer matters except as a bargaining counter. In one Bombay factory the minimum basic wage is Rs 40, + Rs 460 as DA!) Multinationals generally pay best, private firms better than the public sector; so communist workers and union officials prefer the firms and managements which are ideologically the most suspect. Some small firms pay factory wages – without the security – to get skilled labour.

Assume the average factory worker earns twice as much as an unorganized sector manufacturing worker (pp. 153, 191 above). This average conceals wide variations in some trades and industries, wider than those shown in official statistics based on information from employers. Thus in Bombay the legal minimum wage in 1975 was Rs 8.50 a day for unskilled workers (or Rs 221 for a 26-day month), Rs 9.60 (Rs 250) for semi-skilled workers including anyone who handles machinery, Rs 11 (Rs 286) for skilled workers and Rs 13.80 (Rs 259) for the highly skilled.[1] By 1977 an allowance brought the unskilled minimum up to Rs 10.

The better small or middle-sized firms paid around this rate, or more for men with rare skills. Other workshops on back streets or multi-storied 'industrial estates' paid Rs 3.50–8 (Rs 91–208 a month). Where employers agreed to pay the legal minimum, under pressure from unions or government Labour Officers, machine operators got only the unskilled rate, or the rate for an eight-hour day when they worked for twelve, or single not double rates for overtime. Established workers were classified as 'apprentices' or made to sign for more than they received.

Most big factories pay well above the minimum: in the old Bombay textile mills, Rs 500 a month upwards (as against Rs 200 for powerloom workers in small firms, or Rs 50–65 for children): in the biggest engineering or pharmaceutical factories, Rs 800 or more. Some car workers take home Rs 1200–1500 including overtime. The rates do not include the bonus, which varies between 8 and 20 per cent and is seldom paid in small firms. In some cases temporary workers get the same rates as permanent ones doing the same work, without the security or chance of promotion. Otherwise temporary, casual or contract workers earn less, sometimes a fraction: Rs 150 for contract cleaners, working beside factory cleaners who earn Rs 600 (p. 173).

The legal minimum varies between industries, but this does not make much difference in practice. Thus in Bombay the minimum for plastic workers is lower than in engineering, but unskilled workers in small firms get about the same, though with far less chance of learning a skill and raising their market value: the same in pharmaceuticals. The legal minimum can however serve as a rallying-point or target in

[1] Some wages are normally expressed as daily rates, some (esp. in larger firms) as monthly salaries. I have not standardized them all. In some factories the distinction between 'daily-rated' and 'monthly-rated' employees is important, for status and security.

campaigns to raise wages. I mentioned (p. 160) a Bombay plastic firm where an agreement to pay the legal minimum would raise the women's daily wage from Rs 4 to Rs 8.60: the men already earned as much at piecework rates, and though the union was against piecework it had to go slowly.

In Bangalore, on the other hand, the legal minimum is below the market rate for most kinds of work, and the wages gap is even wider than in Bombay. Workshops employ labourers at Rs 3 a day (Rs 78 a month) upwards and semi-skilled workers from Rs 4 (Rs 104), while wages in the big factories are as high as in Bombay.

One of two partners, ex-factory workers, starting a Bangalore engineering workshop (pp. 99–100): they employ two men, and hope for ten when they get a bank loan to buy new (expensive) machines. They cannot pay more than Rs 150; but for young local men with a high school education, Rs 100 is 'more than enough' – just pocket money, since they live with their fathers who are government officers or factory workers. Men from villages would need more – you cannot live on less than Rs 200–300 in Bangalore.

A Bangalore man making aluminium furniture with simple tools: his five full-time workers earn Rs 8–10 a day, even when he has no work for them – otherwise he would lose them. He employs 'helpers' – even graduates – when he needs them, paying Rs 3 until they learn the job, then Rs 5. However 'this labour mentality is very difficult': when one worker gets more pay, the others want it.

Has the earnings gap become wider or narrower over the last thirty years? The National Commission on Labour (1969:28) found that: 'Since 1956, real wages have been showing a downward trend' in the organized sector. H. and V. Joshi think that in Bombay, organized sector workers' real wages were roughly level through the 1950s and 1960s, while 'it is very likely' that unorganized sector workers fell behind (1976a:108). In the inflationary seventies, while organized sector real wages fell slightly, 'the groups which have been hardest hit are the urban unorganized workers', and the earnings differential was 'almost certainly' wider; while 'Owner-cultivators (though not necessarily landless labourers) in agriculture have, to some extent, been insulated from the effects of inflation' (:111–2). However Deshpande (1979:178–81, see pp. 188–9 above) found that Bombay factory workers' real incomes have risen substantially over their working lives, because of an increasing demand for labour and a general rise in wages as well as individual gains from job changes and promotion. Real wages in small establishments have risen but less fast; casual workers' real wages have fallen.

In the main cities it seems that real wages, and the wage gap between the two sectors of industry, have not changed much for many years, except for workers employed in a few multinationals and other firms which pay very well. Living standards have been affected less by wage rates for particular jobs than by chances of movement between jobs and sectors, employment for other family members, and moonlighting or a secondary source of income for the main earners.

Working conditions and the experience of work

Some people work in safer, more pleasant conditions, with less accidents, discomfort, fatigue, noise and monotony; more space, shorter hours, bearable or even pleasant work rhythm and personal relations, freedom from harassment or close control; interesting varied work with a chance to learn something that could lead to a better career.

Some of these things are easy to observe, like safety measured by accident rates, or work space, canteens, crèches, lavatories and washrooms. Other are more subjective: their importance depends on workers' own preferences and other things in their lives outside work.

At a meeting of skilled building workers in Ahmedabad, one man said they had built most houses in the city, yet they did not own them and could not rent them out: everyone laughed. No doubt this is alienation, which however is cloudy and hard to pin down, and sometimes an intellectuals' gloss which distorts the importance of things for those who do the work ('If I did that sort of work, I would be alienated from my true nature'; or see Clayre 1974, esp. p. 58). I am not talking about alienation, but the experiences and opinions and feelings which workers express. Some things come up again and again, others less often.

How closely do these differences in working conditions go with other differences in terms of employment, between organized and unorganized sector workers, or between large and small firms? Do the best paid (and most secure?) work in the best conditions? Is there little relation, or even a trade-off, as there is for many English working-class people who, unlike the middle class, face 'the dilemma . . . of having to *choose between* work which offers variety, scope for initiative and relative autonomy, and work which, for any skill level, affords the highest going rate of economic return' (Goldthorpe *et al.* 1969:64)?

Conditions in many small workshops are appalling by any standards: the cramped dirty rooms on the private multi-storey 'industrial estates' of Bombay, or worse conditions in many slum or back street workshops. There is no trade-off here: people work here only because they cannot get anything better, though they might get something worse – casual building work; making bidis at home until their fingers are too numb to continue; or the walled and guarded stone quarries outside Bangalore:

> Thirty-five families, all in debt to the contractor, worked in a quarry. A mother of five who escaped to another quarry was hunted down, brought back and branded on the breast. At one quarry, whole families were never allowed out together, in case they should escape.
>
> (Based on *Indian Express*, 7 Nov. 1975)

In city workshops the problem is not atrocities on this scale (apart from the occasional use of goondas or thugs to deal with unrest) but rather the blatant disregard of safety precautions, required by law in small firms as well as large, and the resulting accidents and occupational diseases. In Bangalore, men earning Rs 4 a day are in danger from the belts connecting their lathes to one overhead drive shaft, which saves electricity and the cost of separate motors. Presses, polishing wheels and machines to cut out tin cans have no guards. Welders and lathe operators work without goggles; men handle hot metal without protective clothing. Workers with burns, lost or injured fingers or splinters in the eye complain they have been sacked, or laid off without compensation until their injuries heal. Men working with chemicals complain of acid burns, weakness, pain and long-term illness. Yet several small employers told me they paid all medical bills for workers and their families, who were better served than they would be by Employees' State Insurance.

Conditions are just as bad in many larger factories. The Factories Act, including the safety and health provisions, is enforced by the grossly understaffed and overworked Factory Inspectorate. In most states it is the policy to avoid prosecution wherever possible, and to persuade factory owners to put right any violations. The owners have nothing to lose by waiting until an inspector puts in an adverse report, which is unlikely. Very unpleasant conditions may be legal and unavoidable: the intense heat of foundries and heat treatment sheds, especially in hot weather; the dust in a cement factory, even with extractor fans; the deafening noise in a weaving shed or bicycle factory. Some managements, large and small, try to improve conditions because they think it is wrong to employ sweated labour, and a false economy; but the best enforcement agency is a strong union, which can protest about conditions and press the claims of sick or injured workers for compensation. Though unions care very much about working conditions, they are bound to put job security and wages first.

A Bombay firm with twelve workers, a subsidiary of one of India's biggest companies, makes wooden shuttles (p. 226 above). Two men stand on opposite sides of an unguarded mechanical plane. One pushes a wooden block in one direction: then the other pushes it back, which could be dangerous. A visiting union official discussed the matter with workers. The manager said there is no danger if the men are careful: this is the general practice – when other firms stop it, so will he.

Another Bombay firm, with fifty workers, makes aluminium cooking vessels and buckets in an old building: recently the roof fell in. Workers with tongs take hot slabs from the annealing furnace and put them through rollers: they have to judge the temperature by eye, since there are no temperature controls. Men sit on the ground polishing, dusting and shaping the vessels, which rotate fast on machines. Aluminium filings and dust fly everywhere. One man turns the vessels into buckets; another taps the sides of cooking vessels with a hammer to give them a traditional hand-made look. The vessels are washed in caustic soda, then in diluted hydrochloric acid: the men in this shed look pale and ill, and complain of fumes and acid burns on their hands. The union has obtained a milk allowance (against TB) in other firms doing similar work, and is trying to arrange a study of health hazards in a bigger factory where aluminium is washed; but in this firm the union is more concerned about a new agreement on wages, which are only Rs 6–16 a day.

Even in the bigger factories, where physical conditions are generally – not always – better and safer, workers complain of monotonous dead-end jobs and overbearing supervisors.

K.N. Saxena (1965) asked Kanpur cotton mill workers what they liked and disliked about their work. Those who enjoyed their jobs found the work easy and familiar, and got on well with others in the mill ('I know my job from A to Z. It is a simple job, and the supervisor does not have any occasion to come and tell me how to do my work.' 'I have been working in this mill for the last thirty-five years. Some of my pals have become supervisors, but still to me they are all friends and equals. I enjoy the respect and affection of all my fellow-workers. This is why I like my job'). They complained of discomfort, monotony and humiliating treatment ('Is this a machine or a calamity? The faster I put in the bobbin, the faster it comes back for more. It is really back-breaking, too fast for me.' 'You never know when you will be charge-sheeted and turned out.' 'Factory work is degrading. It is a dog's life. A man works like a dog, is treated worse than a dog, and dies the death of a dog'). Most were resigned to the work ('Sahib, what else can I do? I will go on doing what I have been doing so far.' 'As long as the . . . Organization exists, my bread is destined to be earned in this place'), though some hoped to become peons or messengers with safe easy government jobs, or small shopkeepers.

One man left school at twelve to work in a Bangalore engineering factory, as his father had once worked with the owner. He became a skilled turner; but in his twenties he was still earning only Rs 300, not enough to keep his family and educate his four children, and he was horribly depressed by conditions in the factory. So he took casual leave and wandered all over the city looking for any work – he would even have done 'coolie' work, loading coal at the station, if they had offered more than Rs 7 a day. He could not bring himself to return to the factory, until his father and others told him to think of his responsibility to his family. Very reluctantly he asked the owner to take him back.

I mentioned the small assembly tasks that are given to women in electronic factories, since managers say women can stand the monotony better than men (meaning they have few alternatives and seldom complain). In a big radio factory at least they sit comfortably, in well lit and ventilated conditions, instead of sitting in cramped rows under the watchful eye of a woman supervisor, in a room too low to stand up in. Skilled workers say they enjoy their jobs even if they grumble about pay and conditions: the work is varied and interesting, they are not closely supervised, and are always learning something new and useful (cf. Holmström 1976:62–4). Others want such jobs, to improve their pay and prospects and because the work itself is interesting.

Yet there are other satisfactions even in boring work done in bad conditions: the pleasure of company, of jokes and friendship, of solidarity, or simply the pleasure of defying the system in a group, turning unpleasant tasks into a game or a challenge, sometimes co-operating with supervisors and managers, sometimes dodging their demands and making fools of them.

> Satisfaction with work – even with work that might seem extraordinarily unattractive to commentators from a distance – could be found existing side by side with dislike even in factory industry today; indeed it may well be that the peculiar nature of satisfaction with work can only be understood when both

the enjoyment and the dislike are considered together . . . Highly complex
attitudes to work – dislike, and also satisfaction despite or even in some way
because of the intrinsic hardness of the tasks – can be found in different areas of
industry and agriculture both before and after the industrial revolution . . .
Many people seemed to be more interested in the social aspects of working life,
in the kindness, cruelty or justice of those they dealt with at work, in family life
and in elements of 'play' both in and out of work, than in the intrinsic nature of
the tasks involved in their labour.   (Clayre 1974:223–4)

People can and do turn necessity into freedom and laugh at their
oppressors. An 'instrumentalist' attitude to work – working only for
money to spend on one's family and free time – may be a healthy
assertion of freedom and one's own priorities. Foundry workers,
whose work is exhausting and dangerous and also hard to exchange
for some easier job, are as proud of their ability to stand heat as a
toolmaker is of his skill. The National Commission on Labour
(1969:35) was only half wrong when it observed that: 'It is a part of
the worker's make-up that he does not generally mind the nature of
work that falls to his lot . . . When, however, it comes to a question of
conveniences outside the workplace, the worker is certainly anxious
to work for a measure of equality.'

One should not romanticize small industries – small employers
have an obvious interest in the theory that labour relations are closer,
more personal and relaxed than in factories – but it is *sometimes* true
that physical conditions in small firms are at least as good as in
factories, the pace of work is easier and relations between the
employer and his workers are based on trust and long familiarity.
Workers have security as long as the firm stays in business: only the
pay is low. Naaraayan'a's silk screen printing works (p. 98) seems to
be such a firm. Any of his workers would probably leave if they found
well-paid factory jobs, but this is unlikely.

Working conditions – health and safety precautions, space,
ventilation, working hours, leave and weekly rest days, access to
medical care for the worker, are all regulated by laws which apply to
factories, not small workshops. Conditions in some big modern
factories are better than those required by law. Whether the law is
observed elsewhere depends on the factory inspectors' zeal, employers' attitudes – 'modern management', old-fashioned paternalism or cold calculation – and especially the strength of the unions;
also the importance workers attach to working conditions, and how
far they are prepared to go in demanding better conditions rather
than, for example, higher wages or security.

Jobs, careers and security

A permanent factory worker not only has a job, but a career. His working life is not just a list of things that happened to him – jobs he got and lost – but a line leading somewhere. When he tells the story of his life, it has a plot – each stage led to the next in some rational intelligible way; and although job finding and promotion depend largely on luck, his actions affected the outcome, even if it was only the negative action of hanging on to his job, never moving forward without a secure base to fall back on.

His career extends into the future. Assuming he keeps his job, he may plan to improve it by learning a skill and getting promotion; to change it for a better one; to improve pay and conditions through union action; to start his own workshop; to earn his long-service gratuity and then to farm or keep a shop; or simply to use his steady income to support and educate his family.

I described (Holmström 1976) the ways in which some Bangalore workers see the relation between their jobs and careers and other things in their lives, and how they make sense of past experience and plan for the future. My experience of workers in big modern factories in other cities suggests they have similar career patterns and expectations.

Ideally a permanent job is secure. A worker can look forward to gradual promotion, more or less reflecting skill and experience: or at the least, yearly pay rises until he reaches the top of his grade. Job changes are voluntary: he moves from one safe job straight into another. In the end he retires comfortably.

In practice, factories close down or lay off workers in bad times. Workers are dismissed for bad work or making trouble. They fall ill, their sick leave and Employees' State Insurance run out, and they lose their jobs. They resign for personal reasons, perhaps because they cannot bear the work any longer. These are the accidents in the plot, which one has to allow for. One plans one's life on the assumption that these things will never happen.

When the disaster strikes, it can hit very hard, because it is unexpected and the worker has long-term commitments, like children to educate:

The Labour Bureau (1971b, summarized in Labour Bureau 1978:123–4) shows that the great majority of retrenched industrial workers in the sample had no other earner in the family: they borrowed from shopkeepers, relatives and friends, took their children out of school, gradually lost hope and spoke of their fear of destitution. 'The shopkeeper, however, refused to give him goods on credit when he came to know about his lay off. Had not the shopkeeper been merciful and promised to help him in his hard days, he would have joined the rank of beggars. Shri Ganga Ram, however, was constantly under fear lest the shopkeeper change his mind and withdraw the help' (:4, 'Profiles of hard cases'). Those interviewed were not yet destitute, unlike ex-factory workers who join the pavement-dwellers of Calcutta.

A Bangalore worker, struggling to establish a union in his engineering factory, said that uneducated workers are the most easily intimidated by the management because they are terrified of losing their jobs. A highly skilled or well-connected worker may know he has a good chance of finding a new job quickly; yet some skills, though hard to learn, are over-supplied or too specialized.

> The most prized possession of the Coimbatore mill worker is his job. Considering the level of skill there is almost no other employment around which would pay him as well. Nor is there much chance of his being able to shift from one mill to another . . . It is only by remaining in his employment that the worker can hope to maintain a valued standard of living. The mill worker is in much the same position as the craftsman who jealously restricts entry into the trade to protect the conditions of his employment. His job is to the worker what the craft is to the craftsman. The important difference between the two is that the mill worker is unskilled and cannot hope to find an alternative job with comparable pay whereas the craftsman is so highly skilled that he does not want to incur the cost of giving up his trade and moving to another. (E.A. Ramaswamy 1977:69)

One man told me his skill would only be useful in a foam rubber factory: there are few in Bangalore, none as good as his present place. Some skills are specific to one firm, for example in the telephone industry.

Office workers, supervisors and managers, who may have savings or property but whose relatives expect them to keep up a middle-class life-style, may feel the blow worst of all.

'Officers' or management staff cannot join a union protected by the Industrial Disputes Act. At one very large Bombay engineering factory, they formed an Officers' Guild instead, and the four leaders were dismissed at once without any charge – something that could not happen to a union member there. The same night they went to the house of the 'insider' union leader (who told me the story): they were desperate and did not expect much help from the union. One who was soon to be married talked of suicide.

The next day the union leader persuaded his reluctant union committee that the officers too were employees and deserved help. The committee took up the officers' case, even threatening to strike, and after three months they were taken back. The union leader says that when a worker loses his job, even if he is in utter misery, 'he is able to pull on' in the knowledge that the union is behind him: an officer feels everything has gone. This incident showed the officers that their only protection was to make common cause with the union.

I suspect that ordinary workers are more inclined to keep their panic fear of unemployment to themselves: they would hardly agree with another union leader, fighting to save jobs in a threatened factory, who told me the workers were not born to factory jobs, and if they lost their jobs in the end they could work for themselves, sell vegetables by the roadside or start small businesses.

This rational fear of unemployment explains why factory workers look to their union, first, to protect jobs; then, if possible, to protect or raise real wages. In Coimbatore 'the corner-stone of the TWU's industrial relations policy is that no worker at all should be fired' (E.A. Ramaswamy 1977:100), even if this means periodic layoffs of even senior workers to avoid redundancies among women workers who cannot work night shifts. 'Some of the bitterest strikes in the [textile] industry have been over dismissals', and although the unions will not say so openly, there are almost no grounds they would accept to justify dismissing anyone (E.A. Ramaswamy 1978:23). Most Indian unions act in the same way if they are strong enough: 'Many of the employees are not fighting for wage-increases. In at least forty establishments the workers have gone on strike to demand reinstatement of the victimised or retrenched workers' (Kumar Ketkar 1977): the exceptions given are of firms with 200 or more workers – in small firms the strikes were for the legal minimum wage. Officials of a Bombay general union told me the union will strike over dismissals: demands for pay and allowances are kept alive for tactical reasons, so that the union will have something to give in exchange for reinstatement. Even workers dismissed for good reason are sometimes taken back, since ultimately most managements need union co-operation. A worker who is dismissed, especially for union activity, may be employed in the union itself: this union's treasurer had been waiting five years for a decision on his case. Every employee of one Coimbatore union is in the same position. Yet these tactics are signs of union weakness. The unions can make managements hesitate before dismissing workers; once it is done, few unions are strong enough to insist on reinstatement.

The point is that 'permanent' workers in big factories assume they have, or ought to have, jobs for life or until they choose to leave. They see this security as a necessary condition for the chance to make plans and advance their careers. The search for security explains both immobility (when workers think they have security) and mobility (when they move to get it). Thus Papola and Subrahmanian (1975:128, cf. p. 196 above) say that while the Indian worker's 'proverbial immobility' is rational, 60 per cent of Ahmedabad factory workers wanting to change jobs give security as a reason: this is more than the proportion of temporaries, and includes permanent workers who think their jobs would be safer with some other employer. A Bombay man of fifty, who could earn Rs 20 a day as a freelance plumber, preferred to work as a company watchman for Rs 120 a month until he was laid off (though some skilled craftsmen, like carpenters, feel so certain of well-paid casual work that they will not work in a factory). At a Bombay factory making aluminium containers, I asked a group of workers: when someone looks for a job, which is more important, pay or security? Security of course, but beggars can't be choosers.

A common but exhausting way to maximize both security and income is 'moonlighting' – taking an extra job in the evenings and at weekends. Engineering factory workers make or finish small parts with their own tools or second-hand lathes, or help in someone else's workshop. Others add to their wages by driving autorickshaws, doing repair work, setting type, bookbinding or sewing. Their families help, or make bidis or incense sticks at home.

Temporary workers have at least some chance of permanent jobs: in some factories, a good chance. Casual or contract workers, and those in small workshops, do not expect this kind of security, guaranteed by law and insisted on by unions. Their only security is a paternalistic employer's good will, a scarce skill or land (a Bombay worker asked whether I had a farm or land in England). If you have any of these assets you can plan a career. Only the first ties you to one work place. If you have only skill or land, or no security, it is rational to maximize income wherever you can.

Yet in fact these people are not constantly on the move looking for new jobs, either from necessity or choice. Though Bombay small establishment workers change jobs more often than factory workers, the average worker in both sectors has moved only once (factory workers being older), and in both sectors more than half the changes were voluntary (Deshpande 1979:153–9, see p. 190 above). Workers have stayed with the same small employer for thirty years or more. Deshpande tells me that when the unorganized sector workers interviewed in his survey were asked about their problems at work, 'they just don't mention insecurity at all'. In my experience they would all like secure well-paid factory jobs if they had the chance; but as long as they are in small firms they complain about low pay, less often about danger and bad working conditions, and *unfair* dismissals, for example of men laid off without compensation when they are injured or sick, or for union activities. When workers try to bring a union into a small firm, this can provoke a strong emotional reaction from the owner, who sees the union not only as a threat to his profits but to a close paternal relation with 'his' workers. If sacking the ringleaders is not enough, some owners would rather close the firm than reach a working agreement with the union as their more cool-headed colleagues do.

But the main threat to security in small firms is from factors beyond the employers' control: falling orders, seasonal demand, or the end of a single large contract, which force the employer to close the firm or lay off workers (if they are only laid off, the employer may keep in touch until he needs them again). If orders fall, workers – and their unions, if any – know there is little they can do, except wait for better times. The strike and gherao at a Bombay engineering firm with thirty workers (p. 178) was about bonus, not the reinstatement of twelve men – the last in – who had recently been laid off for lack of work. The owners had turned down the union's proposal for work sharing, and that was that.

If orders can fall abruptly, they can rise. Big factories have a core of skilled labour which they can expand by taking on temporaries or putting out work to small firms. The small firms are much more vulnerable to sudden shortages, not only of skilled workers like toolmakers, but even semi-skilled workers used to particular machines: they may not take very long to train, but the employer must start on the new order at once if he is not to lose it. While factory managements complain, frequently, that their work force is too stable, too secure, small employers have to entice workers to stay; building up close personal relations if they can, offering loans to workers in times of need, turning a blind eye to absence and spoilt work, sometimes even paying factory wages without factory security.

The large modern factories have a formal promotion structure. Movement up the ladder depends on skill, years of service, managers' assessment of individuals, and union pressures. Some men enter the factory already trained and skilled. The others either learn a skill over time, or are likely to be promoted to a 'skilled' grade in recognition of long service, rationalized as experience. In factories of an older type, there is security but little promotion. In small firms, there is no formal classification of skills: the wide variations in pay reflect the manager's present need for each worker. In workshops, much more than in factories, there is a wide gap in wages and prospects between workers with a skill in real demand, and the rest, the 'helpers', who may pick up a marketable skill if they are lucky.

Some of these 'helpers' and unskilled labourers are always moving from job to job, with periods of unemployment when they depend on relatives. Others are on good terms with an employer whose business is stable, and this gives them enough security to rent two rooms, keep their families in the city and send their children to school. They are the more fortunate part of the mass of urban poor that Breman writes about: 'The poor try to increase their security within the urban system by entering into dependency relations with social superiors' – employers or brokers; 'For this part of the urban population, work is not the basis for a more or less independent existence, but the outcome of a comprehensive dependency relationship' (1976:1906). But an important minority of unorganized sector workers have real bargaining power. Unemployment has costs for them, but no terrors. If you can acquire a marketable skill in the unorganized sector, it is unlikely to get you into a big factory, but it frees you to a large extent from personal dependence on employers, brokers and contracts. It allows you to plan some kind of career strategy for yourself and, if you choose, to call in a union to help you and your fellow workers.

Let me modify my simple image of the organized sector as a citadel. A small number of workers have real security: almost, not quite, jobs for life if they choose. All their other projects depend on this, whether these concern their career, family life, friendships, political and religious activities, or anything else. The thought of losing this security is terrifying.

Then there is a much larger group of factory workers who know that no job is safe, and plan accordingly. Security comes before income or good conditions: unions sometimes have to make this choice, but individuals seldom do when job hunting, because the safest jobs are generally the best paid.

In the smaller factories as well as the whole unorganized sector, the ideal of job security becomes more and more unrealistic. A job saved may not be saved for long. Unions will fight dismissals, but as part of a strategy to win the best immediate advantages for their members: workers will talk of a strike for higher wages as a success, although it meant sacrificing a few jobs. These people do not *expect* security, but they work hard to get it, through relations with employers which can be seen sometimes as one-way dependence, sometimes as mutual need; by keeping their friendships in good repair; or for those who have the chance, by learning a skill and keeping it up to date.

Families

I have been writing about individuals who work in large and small firms, their wages, careers, motives and so forth. Their families cannot so easily be placed in one 'sector' or another. Even in cities where most workers live only with their wives and children – apart from temporary arrangements to accommodate relatives – each worker is not the sole support of his nuclear family and no one else. Other members including women earn money, and money goes out to relatives. The units that spend and plan are households and networks of households often many miles apart.

To call any of these units 'joint families' begs too many questions: for example, do members of a 'nuclear' household regard it as the start of a potential joint family in a new place, or do they expect to separate? Is it the city outpost of a family with a home and land elsewhere, whose members expect accommodation and help with finding jobs in town? In an excellent discussion of joint families and urbanization, I.P. Desai writes 'the present complex of different types of the family is more an adjustment of an old ideal and norm to new environments rather than the result of any new ideology' (1964:56–7); but it can also happen the other way round, when an extended household is meant as a temporary arrangement to solve housing or child-minding problems, among people who have come to regard nuclear families, separate budgets and privacy as normal, with mutual aid rather than sharing between related households. Just as morality can point in more than one direction, so can advantage: sometimes it makes sense for brothers to live together with shared incomes, sometimes apart.

Deshpande (1979:210) shows that Bombay factory workers' families are larger than those of small establishment workers but smaller

than the Bombay average, because most factory workers are immigrants but they arrived before the small establishment workers. In
Poona, factory workers had on average more dependants than the
whole city population, and their wives (as in Bombay) were less often
employed (Lambert 1963:39–43). This could mean either that
factory workers can more easily afford to live in the traditionally
approved way, in joint families; or just that they cannot avoid the
obligation to support unemployed or low-earning relatives. In either
case, well-paid factory workers are not necessarily in a class by
themselves, though they could be if the effect is to limit opportunities
to a narrow circle of workers' relatives, caste and friends.

First consider a kind of family whose careers, aspirations and life
style appear to place them clearly on one side of the boundary, in a
relatively closed social world where permanent factory workers know
and help only each other. These are not just the educated middle-
class factory workers I described among others (Holmström 1976),
but often people of peasant origin who have arrived in the organized
sector and expect that they and their children and friends will stay
there.

'Shankar' is a semi-skilled press operator at a pharmaceutical factory with
eighty workers outside Bombay. He came to Bombay from a village near
Goa, and stayed with his sister until he found this job in 1961. His wife, from
a neighbouring village, works in the same department, and their total
monthly earnings must be around Rs 1000 (I have not the exact figure).
After each of their three children was born, she took maternity leave and
went back to work, leaving the children in the daytime with a domestic help
who gets Rs 60 and her keep. Since the journey to work, on two buses and
two trains, takes two hours each way, and women cannot work night shifts,
when Shankar is on the night shift they meet only on their weekly day off.

He invited me home to an excellent lunch: a shellfish curry, little fried fish,
an omelette. An easy relaxed family on their day off. All five and the
domestic help live in one room with kitchen, bathroom and the end of the
passageway outside, on the top floor of a municipal block: cramped but airy
and pleasant, with a ceiling fan, a big television set, and carefully tended pots
of flowers.

His friends came round – mostly semi-skilled men from other companies,
and a chargehand from a machine tool factory – and we talked about jobs.
All came from villages to stay with relatives in Bombay. Usually they got into
factories as temporary workers – one started as tea-boy, then bottle-washer,
before learning to operate the machines. Once they become permanent, they
stayed for years, since there were generally no chances to learn a skill and

move to a better-paid job. Nowadays, Shankar said, only young who have a School Leaving Certificate and know English had any chance of a first job in a factory: a less educated man, like Shankar, could only start in a small workshop and would never get into a bigger firm.

They talked a lot about education. The boy is thirteen: Shankar will try to get him into an Industrial Training Institute. The two girls must finish school and then get married – that is apparently their career, whether they go out to work like their mother or not, since technical training (he says) is only for boys except in a few skills like typing.

We discussed housing. Their friends who are not lucky enough to win a subsidized municipal flat like Shankar's (or a bigger one if their income is higher) all live in chawls or tenements, *not* in the slums or hutments (jopadpatti). These are not for 'industrial workers' but only for casual labourers, even 'beggars', and are infested with goondas or thugs.

Shankar and his friends have a lifestyle and aspirations for their children like those of office workers or educated skilled workers, the people called 'middle class'. They know little about unorganized sector workers and do not want to know: they are in another world. For that matter they seem to know little about the hutted slums of Bombay, where some factory workers live, and which vary enormously in cleanliness, amenity and safety.

Shankar and his wife can afford to live like this because both have permanent jobs, though not very well-paid ones. Skilled workers in the bigger modern factories, like the multinationals, can even hope to pay a deposit and own a flat in five years time, and to join what Kumar Ketkar calls 'the co-operative housing society culture', the segregated world of the new middle-class commuters in north Bombay. Other unionists say: 'When Glaxo workers go on a morcha [demonstration], they take a taxi', which was originally meant as a joke.

Talking to people like this and seeing how they live, one has the impression of a wide social gulf between factory workers' families and families that depend on temporary work or small workshops. This would perpetuate old social divisions, if well-off educated high-caste people moved into factory work from the start; or create a new class, if poor or peasant families were able to climb up and then to kick away the ladder, because of historical accidents unlikely to be repeated now that the job market is so tight.

These families have come up the ladder and can expect their children to go further. One might distinguish factory workers of another kind, also with 'permanent' jobs, but in vulnerable industries, often as well paid, but with little hope of upward mobility. In Calcutta, for example, there is a wide gap between educated Bengalis from landowning or middle-class families, who work in the engineering factories and live in town with their families, and the uneducated mainly Hindi-speaking workers who leave their families in remote villages while they work in the city's cotton and jute mills; both groups being distinct from the mixed labour force in the engineering workshops of Howrah across the river. Here residential segregation is reinforced by differences in language and class origin; there are three almost closed social worlds, for local historical reasons. Workers at the 'Oriental' engineering factory to Gujarat put a distance between themselves and uneducated workers in other factories:

> A worker, for instance, advised me: 'If you go to textile mills, you will get to know a lot more about factory workers than you will learn here. There, workers are all gamblers and drunkards and heavily in debt; they are dirty and quarrelsome.' This distinctiveness of status attached by Oriental workers to themselves became evident when a quarrel occurred between two workers and they used obscene language to each other. A third worker, who was watching the quarrel, remarked. 'What! have we turned millhands? If *we* use such obscene language, what is the difference between mill workers and us?'
>
> Work in Oriental was considered superior to work in other factories, because the management had introduced some of the latest machinery and techniques of production. Both engineers and skilled workers thought that the experience gained in Oriental was very valuable for their future prospects.
>
> (Sheth 1968a:117)

Of course these workers may exaggerate their own advantage; and workers in the mills – or in other old stagnant industries – may not fit the stereotype; but in places like Bombay where recent industrial growth has been fast, there is no such rigid line between the two social worlds, because workers in new and old factories come largely from the same Maharashtrian peasant-caste origins. More mill workers were able to bring up their families in Bombay, and their sons learned skilled trades and moved into better factory jobs in advance of educated migrants from the south and other parts of India.

Throughout India, workers with well-paid really safe jobs and good promotion prospects are a minority of 'permanent' factory workers. They shade into employees in small or middle-sized firms, or firms with older technologies like textiles and some kinds of engineering, where wages are lower and jobs much less secure. Factory workers at either extreme could still have very different interests, but all of them share an interest in laws guaranteeing job security, and in unions which try to protect jobs and living standards. One could still argue that all factory workers form an aristocracy of labour, using their unions' power and connexions to keep their advantage: but not if there are strong links of family obligation reaching across the organized/unorganized boundary to benefit many kinds of people who have few other advantages, and some boundary-crossing by workers.

As I showed in the last chapter, workers already in industrial employment have a good chance of moving one step up, but they are not likely to get much further. They go from casual employment into a badly paid but fairly regular job in a workshop; or from a workshop into 'permanent' employment that is not really permanent, in a small factory: from a small to a middle-sized factory, or occasionally from a middle-sized factory to a big one. Much of this movement is possible because of family contacts and influence, though some of it reflects individual effort, initiative, skill and luck.

The same family, and sometimes the same household, includes people employed on very different conditions. This is why the gap between living standards in small establishment workers' families in Bombay is much narrower than the gap in individuals' wages (see pp. 192–4 above). Deshpande found that the average factory worker earns 73 per cent more than a small establishment worker; his family income is 55 per cent higher; income per family member is only 14 per cent higher, or 27 per cent higher for each adult equivalent unit; and family expenditure per head is actually 14 per cent *higher* in small establishment workers' families. In my own subsample, factory workers' median earnings are 108 per cent above those of employees in workshops (manufacturing small establishments), while family incomes per adult equivalent unit are only 79 per cent higher. This is because workshop employees are much less likely to be the only earners in their households, and are more likely than factory workers to be secondary earners; also because more workshop employees live in one-member households, so that their earnings are not divided (though many must support relatives elsewhere).

Deshpande's own figures (1979:218–20) show that the proportion of family members of working age (15–59), including the respondent, who are economically active is lowest in factory workers' families (32

Table 9. *Other earners and dependants, in households of workers in Bombay factories and manufacturing small establishments*

		Factories	Manufacturing small establishments
(a)	Respondent the only earner in household but not the only member	43%	28%
(b)	The principal earner but not the only earner	19%	11%
(c)	Principal earner (a + b)	61%	39%
(d)	Secondary earner (someone else earns more)	12%	26%
(e)	Lives alone, counted as a one-member household	27%	35%
	Number in sample	984	494

Source: My subsample of Deshpande's completed questionnaires (1979)

per cent), higher for small establishment workers (39 per cent), and much higher for casual workers (61 per cent). There are even greater differences between the participation rates for females (8 per cent in factory workers' families, 10 per cent for small establishments, 35 per cent for casual workers) and wives (6 per cent of factory workers' wives, 30 per cent for casual workers, no figures for small establishments). It is clear that factory workers in particular can afford to keep their wives at home. However, in all sectors taken together, the proportion of earning women was quite high (11 per cent) among illiterate wives, probably those of casual workers; much lower (4 per cent) among wives with from 1 to 10 years' education; and by far the highest (22 per cent) among wives with 11 or more years of education. 'Among educated wives the activity rate is higher, the higher the level of education' (:222). In Bombay, small establishment workers are better educated than factory workers and so, almost certainly, are their wives. Here education, the need for money and opportunities in factories and offices all work against the male conservatism that would keep women at home.

In one way or another, small establishment workers in Bombay at least seem to manage rather well:

> Being better educated, the worker in the Small Establishment tries to maintain a higher standard of living despite his lower family income and expenditure.

The fact that the families of respondents in this sector are relatively smaller
explains how even with a lower family expenditure they are able to spend more
per capita.   (:243)

Twenty per cent of the people in factory workers' families lived below
the 'poverty line' (enough expenditure for calories to live on), as
against only 16 per cent in the families of small establishment workers
and 64 per cent in those of casual workers.

In Poona, Lambert (1963:42) found that factory workers earned
considerably more than most workers but had bigger families, so that
average incomes per head were the same.

In view of the uniformity of per capita income levels at a figure below the
poverty line and the widely different family structures which all come to
roughly the same average, one is tempted to wonder whether the household
expands to the point where subsistence balance is reached and remains at that
point.   (Lambert 1963:53)

This levelling down of living standards – even in nuclear family
households – is partly the result of workers' own choices, to keep their
wives at home and their children at school; but the main reason is the
moral pressure on well-paid workers to feed and accommodate
relatives who earn little or nothing. Some of these are dependants like
aged parents or, in Bangalore, school children or students from
country families who stay with city relatives in term time. The rest are
migrants who come to live with relatives in town, expect their help in
finding a job and often have to stay with them afterwards until they
can afford a place of their own (this is probably one reason why
permanent workers sometimes agitate to have temporary workers in
their firms made permanent: they have found their relatives temporary work, but only permanent jobs will get these relatives out of
the house). 'A few principal earners in each sector bear a dis-
proportionately large burden of dependents . . . It is the older
principal earner who is the good Samaritan' (Deshpande 1979:228)
and he is often less educated than the secondary earners.

It is the younger skilled workers who want to avoid getting into the
same position, yet their high wages and contacts attract job-seekers
who cannot easily be put off. Not always, by any means: I know
families where the fulfilment of family obligations is a pleasure and a
source of pride for people whose ambition is to live with their brothers
and brothers' families and to be well thought of by all their kin – what
else does one earn good money for? Besides: 'Given a strong tradition
of partible inheritance . . . it is of crucial importance for migrants to

safeguard their interests in the village and that implies keeping up relations with their joint-family' (van der Veen 1979:68). Others want privacy and their own money to spend, and say brothers get on better if they live apart. The tension between self-interest and moral obligation in these unwilling joint families, especially in the slums, can lead to seething resentment as a well-paid worker and his wife try to find a way out into a place of their own, without letting down their kinsmen too blatantly. People like Shankar aspire to a middle-class life style; a longer, more expensive, education for their children; a room in a chawl or tenement with shared washing facilities, or even a municipal or company flat. They tend to see less and less of the workers in small workshops, including relatives who fell behind in the race. In Coimbatore, John Harriss found not only that few people move between sectors (p. 221 above), but that 'It is . . . quite unusual to find *households* with members both in permanent wage work in the organized sector and in other sectors of the labour market' (1982:996), and half of these were households of mill workers with working wives or with sons waiting for the fathers' jobs:

> Amongst the 123 workers in permanent jobs in the engineering industry only 10 of them (8 per cent) have workers from other sectors of the labour force residing in their households; but as many as 21 of the short-term wage workers (25 per cent) come from households in which there are also members working in organised sector units (13 of them are boys or young men whose fathers are mill workers or workers in large engineering companies. (:997)

Only 27 per cent of workers in any branch of organized sector industry said they had 'relations' in another sector of the work force.

Jan Breman, drawing on his experience in Gujarat, but writing about Indian urban workers generally, says:

> Members of a household – and this is the unit of analysis, not an individual – may function in different modes of production, thus thwarting any attempt to classify according to life-style as an indication of social class . . . Such inconsistencies are usually cancelled out in course of time when members leave the household and set up on their own, forming a new household.
> (Breman 1976:1941)

When this happens, it is often not a once-for-all break but part of a cycle, as relatives who move out are replaced by new ones, or by sons and daughters who leave school but cannot find steady jobs. Some workers escape the burden; but the statistical evidence suggests that factory workers' high earnings are often spread thin among casual or temporary workers or unemployed relatives within the household.

The quicker the turnover of dependent relatives, provided they are replaced, the more people benefit at a critical point in their careers. This is consistent with my impressions: perhaps a fifth or a quarter of factory workers' families share their homes with relatives of working age who earn less or nothing, but a much higher proportion have stayed with employed relatives until they themselves had steady jobs.

Add the burden of remittances to relatives living elsewhere. These are large, but there is no reliable way to find out how large, because the amount fluctuates, and in any case many people are unwilling to name a sum; like the migrants in Bulsar, who 'stressed that they sent money to their relatives when it was "needed", while they themselves could ask for help at any time . . . They all denied that they send a fixed monthly amount to their relatives in the village, as this would imply a "business-like" relationship' (van der Veen 1979:70). Nor can one find out the total indirectly, for example from money orders sold and cashed, because much consists of money and gifts handed over on visits. The Ambekar Institute's survey of indebtedness among Bombay textile workers showed that even second generation mill workers continued to visit their village homes regularly, that many workers had village dependants and that 'A network of socio-economic obligation and need makes extraordinary demands on their meagre resources' (Amrita Abraham 1978:1761). Fifteen per cent were in debt because of expenses incurred in their 'native place' (ibid.).

I have been describing a social world where workers live in town with their wives and children, or expect to live like this when they are settled and can afford it. In both 'sectors' there is still a large work force of the older kind: men who leave their wives (if they have wives) in villages far away, and move to town to live by themselves or with other men, going home once a year or at longer intervals.

About a third of Bombay industrial workers are men living alone (table 9, p. 269 above) and some other households consist only of men. The worker's real home, and the household that spends much of his wages, is somewhere else. These figures, not adjusted for age, do not show how many workers regard this as normal, and how many expect to have their wives and children with them later. There is a very marked difference in the expectations of people from different regions or language groups. Since the nineteenth century, south Indians have tended to migrate as families, so that the sex ratios in southern cities have shown a smaller excess of males than in the north

(p. 68 above). The gap has narrowed as more educated skilled workers in northern cities have become less willing to tolerate long separation from their families, especially if their wives also have education and earning power. Such workers, whether from north or south, speak of family separation as a temporary hardship forced on them by high city rents or immigration restrictions in the Persian Gulf, not as a normal way of life.

This difference between the living habits of ethnic groups, corresponding largely with their levels of education and their place in the urban economy, is most glaring in Calcutta (pp. 60–2 above), where two-thirds of married engineering workers (mostly Bengalis) live with their wives, compared with only 39 per cent of married jute workers (mostly Hindi or Urdu speakers), a figure which would certainly be still lower for the many Hindi-speaking migrants without steady jobs in the jute mills.

Workers from the same Hindi-speaking areas in Uttar Pradesh and Bihar go in the opposite direction to Bombay, where again they tend to work together in trades like foundry work in which they have a semi-monopoly, and to live in clusters. 'A very significant difference between Hindi and non-Hindi migrants [to Bombay] is that in the former case over 44 per cent of those who are married have left their wives behind in the village home; the Tamil and Marathi migrants usually take their wives with them. Only 21 per cent of the married Tamils and 22 per cent of the married Marathi migrants have left their wives behind in the parental home' (Gore 1970:56).

'Mohan', now twenty-six, came eight years ago from a village in Uttar Pradesh where his family has a little land. A friend helped him to find work as a fitter and welder. After he was laid off three years ago, he took his present job as one of a group of hand press operators – all from the same area – in a small 'organized sector' plastics factory. His wife and son live with his parents: he sends what he can, but not every month because he only earns Rs 10 a day, and he last saw them two years ago.

He and a friend share one of a row of corrugated iron shacks, belonging to a foreman ('mistrii') from UP, and all occupied by men from the same area. In the next row, a few yards away, all the people are Maharashtrian or Marathi, and (he says) solid supporters of Shiv Sena (an anti-immigrant populist movement) which has its local office in a small house nearby. There are constant quarrels and tensions between the two communities. Maharashtrians always bring their wives and children to the city, and often send them out to work. He knows none of them personally. He goes to the cinema occasionally and uses the union office as a club house, but he has hardly ever made the half-hour train journey to central Bombay and speaks of it as of a foreign country.

A 65-year-old Hindi-speaking watchman lives among Maharashtrian neighbours. He came to Bombay in 1942 and was a textile printer, then organized an illegal matka gambling ring. His family never came to join him; his wife is dead, his son is a farmer and his daughter married a farmer. Every year he can just manage the fare home for the Diivaalii festival.

For most industrial workers, the earning and spending unit is the nuclear family settled in the city, depending on one main earner, which expands to take relatives in need and then goes back to its normal size; linked to relatives elsewhere by bonds of duty and sentiment which are sometimes expensive. The duty to support relatives, either in one's own home or by sending money, is like a progressive tax on factory workers' higher incomes, which some can avoid. A worker in a small firm is a less obvious target for relatives, and his household are more likely to earn something. These workers' employers do not want a constantly changing work force: the nominal job security at the bottom end of the organized sector is not worth more than this. There is a very large overlap, where the families of unorganized sector workers, especially skilled men, enjoy standards of living and even security comparable to those of permanent employees in small to middle-sized factories.

There is a sharper line between families where someone has more or less regular work, at least in a small firm, and those which depend on whatever casual earnings any family member can pick up. Individuals can sometimes cross this line by their own effort or luck. They leave behind a very large mass of people without contacts, skill or education, generally low-caste migrant labourers who may have to move between the town and the country in search of seasonal work. People in this class have much less chance to benefit from the kinds of family help – accommodation, gifts, finding jobs – which blur the boundary of the organized sector.

Neighbours

Family obligations cut across 'sectors', making a neat classification of workers impossible, though some workers have better-placed relatives and a better chance on the job market. What about neighbours?

How mixed are working-class neighbourhoods; and when people employed on different terms live side by side, do they help and support each other, or just selected friends, or are their relations those of patron and client?

A few skilled men live in comfortable houses with their middle-class relatives, or in middle-class areas like Bombay's co-operative flats. 'Shankar's' municipal flat (p. 265) is airy and pleasant, though small for his family and isolated in a remote suburb. These flats form a one-class enclave, allocated by lot to workers whose factory managements take part in the scheme. Elsewhere in Bombay the same authority builds larger flats for middle-class groups like journalists.

Factory townships are segregated in the same way: rows of identical small houses built, rented out and policed by factory managements on the outskirts of towns like Ranchi, Bhopal and Bangalore, or around rural factories (Kapadia and Pillai 1972 is about such a township). If you are promoted, you move to a bigger house in another part of the township. The biggest houses are for managers. No commuting: each township has its school, cinema, some shops and a sports club: only shopping and boredom drive people out on their days off. Generally only a minority of employees get a subsidized township house.

Settlement patterns differ between cities. Calcutta has ethnic clusters of people who came to fill niches in the economy and stayed where they were as the economy stagnated, to be joined by waves of refugees from persecution in East Pakistan or agricultural distress in India. Calcutta's overcrowding is the result of extreme poverty and insecurity. Bombay neighbourhoods are more mixed but almost as crowded, because land values on the narrow peninsula are so high. Towns like Delhi and Poona had more room to expand. Especially in southern cities, where there has been a tradition of family migration since the nineteenth century, farmers in surrounding villages built small houses for anyone who could pay the rent: factory workers, employees of small businesses, high castes and low. The farmers became building contractors or traders, their sons often skilled factory workers. As the space between villages was built over, these villages kept a strong self-conscious identity as centres of social, political and religious life for a population of commuters, with the more successful men of the old peasant families acting as landlords, patrons or brokers, employers of casual labour and friends to some of the factory workers. I wrote about one such village in Bangalore

(Holmström 1971, 1972) and the political influence of its 'big men' extending outside the village (1969).

The villages round Coimbatore are strongholds of rival textile unions, which used to be organized in local branches where the workers live; this is unusual, and the local branches have lost much of their importance to mill-based branches (E.A. Ramaswamy 1977:36, 50).

Kunj Patel (1963:80; cf. p. 56 above) describes conditions in the crowded 'chawls' of Bombay, typical of older working-class neigh-bourhoods around the big textile mills. A chawl is a block of small tenements with shared lavatories and washing places, built by private landlords, mill managements or the pre-war Bombay Development Department. Some are tolerable; many, being old, are rat-infested, filthy and dilapidated. From time to time they burn down or collapse, killing whole families.

These mill workers come mainly from certain districts of Mahar-ashtra. Although they visit their villages and keep up links with relatives there: 'Labour is no longer migratory, but has become semi-permanent in Bombay . . . in which state workers like to live with their families in the city' (:103). A worker's widow will take a mill job rather than go back to the village (:83).

At one time these areas were dominated by the mills. Apart from a few shopkeepers and others, everyone worked there, if not as a permanent employee then as a badli or casual worker, who stayed with relatives or friends from his village until he got a permanent job, as he usually did. All shared similar experiences of work and conflict: this was the scene of the heroic union struggles between the wars. The jobber was employment agent, patron and protector, sometimes a tyrant or class enemy, occasionally a strike leader. His control over 'his' workers depended entirely on his position in the mill.

Now the mills have declined, and the old solidarity has gone. The mill workers' own sons and daughters cannot count on mill jobs. Since they are educated in the city and know more people there than the immigrants do, some have gone into the suburban factories, others into small firms. The area supports a diverse economy of small to middle-sized businesses – shops, cafés, services, printing presses, engineering, food, plastic or garment factories. Like the mill towns of northern England, such areas in Bombay or Calcutta or Ahmedabad or Kanpur still give many Indians and foreigners their stereotype of a unified working-class neighbourhood and culture.

There is another stereotype, just as misleading: the 'slum' or shanty town, on the edge of the city, where workers in the new factories and workshops are believed to live in squalor and insecurity. This includes everything from the rows of small brick and tile houses round stone-paved courtyards in Bangalore, or lines of ugly but solid corrugated iron houses with cement floors in areas cleaned up under Bombay's 'slum improvement scheme', to the 'bastis' which spring up on any space between buildings in Calcutta; the vast areas of Bombay or Calcutta where people put up makeshift shelters of wood and corrugated iron or plastic sheeting, with communal lavatories too filthy to use, polluted water and stinking lanes which flood in the monsoon; or settlements of migrant casual workers in tents of sticks and sacking around railway stations, or in big concrete pipes left beside the road until they are laid. 'Slums', like 'unemployment', covers too much, from tolerable conditions to the worst.

The great majority of industrial employees, even in small workshops, live in rented permanent structures, or at least a friend's room. In places like Bombay where the housing shortage is acute, you get a house or room by paying a deposit of several thousand rupees, after which the rent is light. The first time you may have to borrow; but the money is an investment linked to the rising price of housing. When you leave, you take a deposit at the going rate from the next tenant; you may tell the landlord you will now collect his rent from your 'relative'.

In 1972, a tenant paid a 'pugree' ('turban' or deposit) of Rs 4000, or sixty-six years' rent in advance, without receipt, for a room in a chawl. 'But the irony of it is that the tenant himself is not entirely unhappy: he feels that if he moves out he can collect Rs 8000 as *his* price for vacating the room!'

(Taken from *Times of India*, 6 Jan. 1976)

When unauthorized hutments on public land in Bombay were demolished, 'many "owners" of the tenements pleaded with the municipal authorities not to demolish their "homes" as they had "bought" them with hard-earned money' (*Times of India*, 6 Aug. 1977).

In 1980 some 3 million of Bombay's 8 million people lived in hutments, where 42 per cent of the working population were in manufacturing employment. A 'slumlord' and a contractor would build new hutments over a weekend, and charge tenants a deposit of Rs 5000–25 000. 'In a vast majority of the cases the slumlord or structure owner has constructed the slum without the permission of the landlord by relying on his muscle and/or political power. In fact, as a political worker . . . half jestingly remarked, the question of ownership of slums in Bombay has become as complex as the agrarian question with a many-tiered structure comprising the landlord, main lessor, sub-lessor, end-lessors and finally the structure owner and then the tenant.'

(Taken from Chithelen 1980: 1171)

Some of the links in these chains are industrial employees who may also be small employers, subcontracting small jobs from their factories or workshops to people who work at home.

One should distinguish industrial working-class areas – where most or very many have regular outside employment and the talk is all of factories and workshops and unions – from the really poor hutment areas like parts of Dharavi in Bombay (p. 135) where only a minority have any regular employment and fewer still have permanent jobs.

Buddhanagar is another Bombay slum occupied entirely by neo-Buddhists or Harijans. Some are sweepers, permanent or casual municipal employees; others do low-paid casual work when they can get it. A group of neighbours live by polishing furniture, either at home or on temporary employers' premises. A very few have permanent industrial jobs, like a fitter working in a technical college: these are the men who are active in clubs for people speaking the same language, or the rival 'welfare' associations with political links. The others tell me no one can get a factory job unless he knows a factory officer, or has a brother working there.

In such areas, the few men with good permanent jobs are the ones who lend money at interest to their neighbours, help them to find work or at least pass on information, and sometimes know the political party workers or municipal officials who can take up complaints about amenities and harassment. These areas are largely, not entirely, for casual and home workers belonging to the lower castes, often subdivided into areas for each language or caste group. It is something to have a roof, a padlock and neighbours to give some protection; unlike the wandering families of labourers who sleep in lean-to shelters or on pavements.

There are no typical working-class neighbourhoods. In some places a neighbourhood has a strong identity and social life of its own, perhaps because it is an old village, or has a thriving local economy of small businesses, or it contains a cohesive ethnic or occupational group with shared problems who are drawn into political movements (see Lynch 1977, 'Political mobilisation and ethnicity among Adi-Dravidas in a Bombay slum'). Other neighbourhoods have only a name, shadowy boundaries and no local loyalties, only small clusters of people who arrived together. People move in and out constantly. In a community of small houses where there is little privacy, life is lived largely on the streets, and most people are fairly poor, each family depends on a few close neighbours not just for company but for services like child-minding, occasional help with finding jobs, arranging funerals, small loans, news and information.

Organized and unorganized sector industrial workers are not segregated, except for those factory workers who live in company townships or in flats specially built for industrial workers. The rest live in mixed areas, though generally not in the same streets as the mass of casual workers. In the poorer slum areas, especially where the lowest castes live, the few permanent workers, like the independent local businessmen, may become all-purpose patrons or brokers, the only channel of information about jobs and opportunities, or even small employers themselves, moneylenders, and link men with the authorities and political parties. These patron–client relations are between permanent workers on the one hand, and casual labourers rather than other industrial workers. Again the important contrast – though not always a clear line – is between regular workers who work in the same place for months or years even without legal security; and casual workers who take any work when they can get it and need powerful protectors all the time, particularly those casuals who, for lack of education and contacts and social esteem, have little chance of finding regular employment.

Social worlds

I began with a simple dualistic image of Indian society, at least in towns (taken from Holmström 1976): those with safe well-paid jobs inside the organized sector citadel, and those outside trying to get in. Whether this was true or not, I suggested it was at the back of everyone's mind and explained much of their behaviour.

That was too simple. The labour market appears to separate people into at least three groups, or perhaps to continue and reinforce a separation which existed already, before these people came into industrial work. These three kinds of people have different chances in the job market, different earnings and working conditions, often live in different places and have different friends; though kinship and friendship can cut across these boundaries.

First there are permanent organized sector workers, including factory workers as well as government and office employees; though there is an enormous gap between the best factories and the worst. This group shades into workers with fairly regular employment unprotected by law, including all workers in small firms and 'temporaries' etc. in large ones. A sharper line separates both kinds of regular workers from unskilled casual labourers.

That covers most people whose living depends on manufacturing industry, though there is also a fourth group: the self-employed, ranging from those depending on one or a few customers who can dictate terms, to independent craftsmen like carpenters who have a real market for their work.

Writing about a similar problem – whether there are separate labour markets and social worlds in Coimbatore – John Harriss says:

> Whereas they [Bromley and Gerry 1979:5] distinguish between 'permanent wage workers', 'short term wage workers', 'disguised wage workers', 'dependent workers', and finally those who are 'truly self employed', we distinguish *permanent wage workers* (in factories and workshops registered under the Factories Act); *short term wage workers* by which term we refer to casual and temporary workers, and to contract workers in the same registered factories and workshops, and also to those who are 'permanently' employed in small workshops which are unregistered and whose jobs are thus unsecured by protective legislation; *casual wage workers*, those who are employed outside manufacturing or service establishments, like construction workers, 'Kalasi' workers (load carriers, porters), and pullers of hand-carts, and *dependent and self-employed workers*, more or less independent producers and traders. We have found the differences that exist within Bromley and Gerry's category of 'short-term wage workers' to be rather important, and believe that it is useful to distinguish between those who are employed in manufacturing or service establishments, and those who are employed outside them like construction workers and porters. In part the difference here is that between those who are often at least semi-skilled and who may in fact enjoy a good degree of permanency and stability of employment – in small workshops which are often run on paternalistic lines – and those whose employment is intrinsically restricted to short term contracts for which they must search almost continuously. (Harriss 1982:993)

There is no point in classifying for the sake of classifying, but these distinctions refer to important differences in people's situation and perhaps to conflicts of interest, which they may or may not be aware of. How separate are these groups, both in reality and in people's minds, and what relations cut across the dividing lines? There are really three sorts of questions: about real differences in economic conditions and life chances, which depend on large-scale economic forces and the job market; about social maps – the differences and alignments that people think are important; and about the social worlds they live in – whatever they think or say, who do they spend their time with, depend on, and help or oppose or avoid?

Evidence from the labour market, from families and from areas where industrial workers live is sometimes contradictory, especially about the relations between 'organized sector' and other regularly employed workers. There are instances of solidarity and mutual aid; of dependence, where factory workers profit in one way or another from acting as patrons or brokers to their less fortunate neighbours; of movement across the line by able or lucky individuals, who may or may not help their relatives to follow; separation into different groups with their own kinship and job-finding networks, living apart and not aware of any common interests; and sometimes, tension and open hostility.

I mentioned (p. 271) John Harriss' finding that few Coimbatore workers have relatives employed in another sector. He concludes that:

> the labour market in Coimbatore is strongly segmented, and current trends in factory employment may be strengthening this segmentation even further. We refer to systematic exclusion of people from low cast backgrounds from employment in some of the big mills. (1982:999)

Now that labour is abundant, the dominant caste millowners exclude low-caste people where they can.

> Employment in workshops is not necessarily a route into factory employment, and . . . petty commodity producers and traders are generally from different backgrounds than casual workers, or factory and workshop employees . . . Connections between 'sectors' or parts of the labour market – within families or even within wider circles of kin – are not much developed. The principal exception to the general picture of separation is that of the PCPs [petty commodity producers] in 'new' activities who are often people who have had experience of employment in workshops or factories.
>
> The historical existence of a strong relationship between certain occupations and membership in particular communities of caste or kin has provided an ideological context for this strong differentiation within the labour market; and the way in which large numbers of people are continually deprived of access to means of earning their livelihoods now supplies a firm basis for the persistence of caste identities – when these identities constitute one of the few 'resources' that many people possess. (:999)

In other words, there are almost separate social worlds, from the top to the bottom of the social scale, and an ideology of difference which keeps each little world closed to outsiders. This is truer in Coimbatore, or for example in Calcutta, than in places like Bombay and Bangalore where there are better chances to move up and less rigid ideological barriers to movement, and to some extent one can put the difference down to local cultural factors and historical accident.

Things are just as bad at the bottom, for the 'informal sector' which provides some sort of a living is not the bottom. The foulest most dangerous badly paid work may be hard to break into. There is no reason to think the lines between factory and workshop employees, or between both and casual workers like building labourers, are any sharper than these divisions among the very poor, and a good deal of evidence – for example, in Deshpande's 'Bombay labour market' – to suggest the opposite: that people at the bottom live in little closed boxes, competing fiercely with very poor people in other closed boxes. Once you break out and gain a foothold, however insecure, in small industry where you can get experience with machines and make useful friends, your chances of better-paid regular work improve gradually. The first step is the hardest.

Everywhere it seems that those at the bottom generally stay there. Migration to town may make them less poor and blunt the edge of prejudice and discrimination, but they occupy roughly the same space on other people's social maps.

Now the first social category of 'traditional' India – as everyone knows – is caste. The social world consists of interdependent castes, none of them complete without the religious and economic services of the others, and social maps are maps of castes.

But in Indian cities there is only a loose fit between caste ranking and present differences. Even if most casual labourers are Harijan or low caste, the converse is no longer true. There are Harijans in almost every kind of work, largely because of positive discrimination in education and government employment which has helped a new self-confident Harijan middle class. Job-finding networks are sometimes confined to castes, sometimes not; when they are, for historical reasons the best jobs may not go to the highest castes. Industrial workers' neighbours and friends may or may not be of similar caste; again, the line between Harijans and others is the most resistant, but it is often disregarded all the same in places where Harijans live openly among higher-caste neighbours who say that old rules no longer count here – they are more concerned about the differences between workers and employers or supervisors, or between language groups.

It is not simply a matter of class (or partly achieved status) 'replacing' caste (or ascribed status), or modern urban values replacing traditional rural ones. What is happening to Indian society now is a tilting of balances that were never stable, between values of hierarchy and equality, or between fixed roles and competitive individualism; and the changes have many causes besides industrialism. Even 'traditional' caste was not matched closely to occupation, except for those like priests and barbers and sweepers whose work was closely bound up with ideas of purity and impurity. Agriculture and trade, the sources of wealth and the occupations of the large majority, were almost always open in practice to anyone with the means to engage in them, whether or not he also had a caste monopoly to fall back on (Pocock 1962; see p. 34 above) and factory work was just one more open occupation.

The caste system – in the days when one could still speak of such a thing – was more adaptable than it seemed, or than people admitted: not so much a constraint on social mobility (except sometimes for the minority in the lowest castes) but rather a way of explaining and justifying the lack of mobility which had other causes; and also legitimizing group mobility when it happened (see pp. 35–6 above). There were well established ways, like 'sanskritization', to translate gains in wealth, power and local inflation into higher caste status: if not for individuals, then for upwardly mobile splinter groups which exploited the ambiguities about caste or subcaste names and boundaries to get their claim recognized, and even to marry into what had previously been regarded as separate and higher castes.

Thus caste was always a code for economic class differences to some extent, and changed with changes in the wealth and power of groups one might call classes. This no longer happens: economic success is its own justification, and there is less need to turn it into caste rank, even if there were still the conditions for getting local agreement about a caste's new status.

To generalize, leaving aside the differences between regional cultures, and between patterns of industrial growth and settlement and political movements in particular cities: industrial workers, like other Indians, think of themselves as members of castes, and generally marry their children within the boundaries of recognized (sub)castes, or religious minorities, like Muslims and Catholics, which are sometimes divided into caste-like groups. Especially not only in the industrial towns, castes exist, but no longer within a caste system of interdependent ranked groups: a caste is no longer a united group –

certainly not a corporate one – but rather a network of links with particular people on whom one has a claim, but who are also pulled in other directions by obligations and loyalties and interests that have nothing to do with caste (see chapter 5 on the various kinds of pull which operate in the labour market, and the limited extent to which job-finding networks are confined to named castes).

'In the job market, a caste tie is a kin tie at best and an extension of the logic of kinship ties to a wider circle at the least' (Gould 1961:38). You have a moral obligation to help relatives, who are bound to be of your caste if (sub)castes are endogamous, and there is a good chance that they will help you when the time comes. But the 'logic of kinship ties' becomes less compelling when you approach someone who is only potential kin, or who could not be your relative because he belongs to a different subcaste of Brahmans or Rajputs. It is worth trying: in a fiercely competitive uncertain world, it is just possible that someone will give you preference in the search for jobs or a place to live because he trusts a person brought up with the same values, or he shares a feeling that caste members must stand together or no one else will help them; but the same logic can, and often does, apply to people from the same village, or much bigger groups like those who come from the same state and speak the language. People say they got a job through an uncle or gave one to a nephew: someone from the same village helped them, or they prefer not to employ Tamils. The *caste* that comes between these two extremes – particularly kin, and a wider community of residence or language – comes to mean little more than a division of society into three blocks: one big block containing all the middle castes and most religious minorities, and two smaller groups whose caste is very visible: Brahmans at the top, Harijans at the bottom, paradoxically both suffering from some prejudice and discrimination and enjoying some special advantages, occasionally even seeing each other as natural political allies (Holmström 1976:88). Brahmans are by no means always in the best jobs or Harijans in the worst.

Caste becomes 'casteism' – a modern Indian–English word for a new thing, blind loyalty to one's caste in open competition with others, with no sense of hierarchy left. '"Casteism" is very much a part of urban life in India. Caste in the urban situation, like ethnicity in America or tribalism in the African city, may be viewed as a categorical relationship, operating to simplify or codify behavior in otherwise "unstructured" situations' (Hardgrave 1970:47). Perhaps it always was, but it was better disguised as natural hierarchy and interdependence, where a caste's position is justified only by its relation to others, and privileges imply responsibilities: an idea that can be carried over into factory life, but not easily.

In a Madras factory, workers belonging to the high KoNTaikaTTi VeLaLar (or KV: Barnett's spelling) caste met to discuss the line they should take over a possible strike:

> One man suggested KV workers oppose the strike: 'After all, most of us own some land [village land] and have PaRaiyan workers there so that we are bosses as well as workers. What if those PaRaiyans decided to strike?' Another countered, 'It is our custom to own paddy land, but what is KV factory custom? We should lead the strike and lead other workers just as we lead other castes in the village.' A third said, 'How can we lead others if we ourselves are being commanded by the factory foreman at the same time? We are simply workers like other workers. Maybe we can use our caste to contact KVs who know the factory owner, but those KVs have nothing in common with us anyway' . . . Unanimity could not be reached, however, and at the end of the meeting a young KV said in disgust, 'Being a KV is like being fat: you can recognize other fat people, but the only thing you have in common is eating. All we have in common is a name; either we are workers or scabs, nothing else.'
> (Barnett 1977:405–6)

Once caste becomes 'casteism' it can be put to different uses, as a pull in the job market, a political pressure group to defend sectional interests and sometimes (not often) the prospect of a bloc vote to tempt politicians, or a new rationalization for old inequalities: Harijans do dirty low-paid jobs because they are uneducated and still have dirty habits, though Harijans with clean habits are all right. Among Coimbatore textile workers:

> emphasis is now shifting from considering the Harijans as polluting, to considering them as unclean. Those who are willing to socially interact with Harijans as well as those who are unwilling for such interaction stress hygiene as a crucial determinant. However for the unwilling category, the stress on cleanliness is merely a smokescreen to justify their reluctance. That they need such justification instead of simply defining the Harijans as polluting is itself a major change.   (Uma Ramaswamy 1979:371)

Thus 'casteism' becomes just one variety of 'communalism', loyalty to a community of birth with common interests to defend, some cultural symbols, with or without a racist 'biological' rationalization. 'Communialism' can take the form of closing ranks against a religious minority like Muslims, or against Harijans with their job quotas. It can also cut across caste lines, in movements to reserve jobs and privileges for 'sons of the soil' – people from the same state and speaking the same language, whatever their caste, their religion (sometimes), and the kind of work they do: Maharashtrians – high castes and low, businessmen, factory workers and the unemployed – should unite against the threat from south Indians in Bombay, who themselves are of all castes and classes. The further this process goes, the more obvious it becomes – sometimes to the people themselves – that the moral solidarity which holds each 'community' together is easily manufactured for the sake of short-term expediency, often by opportunistic leaders. Tomorrow a different alliance might be more advantageous: thus the Tamil DMK stopped its anti-Brahman campaign and the Hindu-nationalist Jan Sangh put on a show of secularism and sought Muslim support.

'Communalism' exploits powerful emotions of fear and loyalty. It is strongest among the unemployed and insecure, because it explains failure and promises better things once the scapegoats are driven out (Holmström 1976:37). It can also appear to be the only possible rallying point for oppressed groups, as in the Jharkhand movement in 'tribal' Bihar or language associations among southern migrants in the Bombay slums: so that left-wing people speculate about the chances of steering such movements away from the false consciousness of ethnicity towards class struggle (Nirmal Sengupta 1981).

'Communalism' – including caste in its new form, as loyalty to a group in open competition with others – provides many people with a handy weapon to fight particular threats, especially when they feel they have no other defence; but it does not generally provide a clear consistent theory they will use to explain all the main differences in wealth and opportunity in society. There are too many obvious discrepancies, at least in most industrial towns. Even to the extent that those working in different 'sectors' also live in separate social worlds – among neighbours with similar jobs, and in close touch only with relatives in a similar position – the boundaries of these worlds do not coincide clearly or consistently with 'community' or caste and are not usually explained in these terms. Skill and hard work and useful friends are a better explanation; except among the poorest and most insecure people, especially Harijan casual labourers who see that their caste counts against them, as well as their lack of education and contacts. Factory workers with secure jobs do not need this weapon and do not often use it.

'Caste', like ethnic labels, is a language that can be put to different uses, not a simple unambiguous classification of people and their duties. Probably it never was: among other things it was a code for class differences. To ask whether class is replacing caste is to compare unlike things, even if the people are now more ready to recognize openly that society is divided into classes determined by luck and the market, without the need to disguise these differences behind caste and ethnic labels. Ideas of respectable behaviour, a decent neigh-bourhood to live in and suitable friends are linked closely and visibly to success in the job market, and a career: skill, promotion and income which can be taken as a sign of hard work and intelligence. One marries one's children into similarly placed families within the caste, extending the boundaries of the caste where necessary, sometimes contracting a marriage which is openly out of caste or even letting the partners choose for themselves (on 'love marriage', meaning inter-caste, see Holmström 1976:81–4).

The people at the bottom – casual labourers and the uneducated unemployed – are cut off not only from those more fortunate than them, but from each other. They are the ones most likely to stay in separate closed compartments, jealous of each other but more or less equally miserable and hopeless. They are the most likely to believe that what keeps them in their own little boxes is caste or ethnic discrimination; and sometimes – especially if they are Untouchables – they are right.

The unions and the 'working class'

The industrial work force includes people in large and small firms, permanent and temporary factory workers, casual and contract workers, high castes and low, skilled and unskilled, educated and uneducated, with and without land. When all these people are called or call themselves 'workers' or 'working class' (Hindi *mazduur varg* etc.) is this mere rhetoric, or does it mean they share and know they share important common interests?

I have shown that boundaries between permanent factory work and other employment – and between the social worlds that factory workers' families live in – are less clear-cut than the legal distinction of organized and unorganized sectors, for several reasons. For example, many have legal security of employment without the means of enforcing it, while some have real security without legal protection; if there is a boundary, individuals cross it in their careers; families contain people employed on different terms.

The line between more or less regular daily employment – even in small workshops – and casual labour is sharpest, especially because most casual labourers are uneducated and low caste; but this line too can be crossed and divides families.

One could argue that this blurring of lines makes people less aware of the reality, which is that a minority of secure well-paid workers, with their relatives and clients, are privileged at the expense of the rest: in marxist language, that unorganized and especially casual workers form a class in itself but not for itself, because they are fragmented and cannot see who is exploiting them or how to stop it; and moreover (a conclusion only a few Indian marxists would draw) that some factory workers are an 'aristocracy of labour' on the exploiters' side. Thus the stratification of the work force is a zero-sum game, where factory workers' gains are the unorganized sector's losses; or even negative-sum, if total production and wages would be more without these artificial barriers.

Alternatively, thinking in 'sectors' may obscure another reality: a single labour market where some people manage to build temporary defences round their positions, in ways that sometimes reward those already ahead in the race – well-connected educated high-caste workers – but can have the opposite effect because of historical accidents of migration or factory building, or individual skill and determination. An open competitive labour market, without legal protection for some employees, would give similar results in practice. This argument too can be given a marxist slant (workers' rivalries distract attention from the real class struggle) or a free enterprise one (large and small firms are complementary; so are workers and employers – limited conflict over wages and conditions may be normal, but if both sides co-operate there will be a bigger 'cake' for everyone, and more jobs).

'Working class' is a term with political overtones, used especially by union members. Unions are there to defend the working class against employers, the rich, the bourgeoisie, often the government. But there are rival unions, linked to parties, sometimes in the same factory. Cleavages between skilled and unskilled workers, those with and without land, or from different ethnic groups, lead to rivalries within unions. Above all, a vast number of workers in small firms, and temporary workers in large ones, who ought in theory to belong to the working class, are generally outside unions. What use are unions to such workers, and what help can these people expect from the 'organized' working class?

First consider the more typical organized sector unions. Most Indian unions are for employees of a single factory or employer, though a factory may contain rival unions belonging to national or regional federations ('centres') each linked to a political party but not (as some allege) controlled by it: the relation is more often a transaction between the membership and a politician known as a good negotiator (see Holmström 1976:65–72 on Bangalore unions), except where the union is kept going by a core of politically committed activists (E.A. Ramaswamy 1977:139–63). In some towns there are also industrial unions, like the textile, engineering and chemical unions in Bombay, which usually recruit only permanent factory workers, competing with rival industrial or factory unions. Craft unions of the British kind are rare, unless one counts the growing white-collar and staff associations which sometimes call themselves trade unions.

Indian labour law is so complicated – with procedures for union recognition, compulsory arbitration, conditions for calling a legal strike, and labour courts to hear cases of unfair dismissal – that even a factory union with 'insider' leadership needs an outsider leader or adviser with legal knowledge and political influence to guide it through negotiations, fight cases and advise it when to risk an 'illegal' strike.

Each union has its style. Especially in unions belonging to the rival communist federations AITUC and CITU, leaders and activists talk of working-class unity, of solidarity between members of different unions, rural people and the poor, and these activists are often sincere dedicated idealists who mean what they say. Other unions do without the rhetoric. In either case, most workers join a union for specific services and protection; sometimes more than one for double protection, since the dues are low.

Many unions are overwhelmingly defensive. They are there to protect jobs first, then the real value of wages against inflation, with safety and working conditions a poor third, rather than to win more than the members have already. They know their bargaining power is weak; noisy militant demands for more are a tactic to hold the line, something to be bargained away when vital interests are threatened. The union has a hard enough job protecting its own members without worrying about outsiders.

A union can be a racket, run for profit by outsiders and a clique of privileged workers, with or without the employer's help. Unions say this about their rivals, and those who hate unions say it about all of them; nevertheless it is sometimes true, especially where both permanent and other workers are employed. Truck drivers' unions in West Bengal take advantage of 'coolie' contract labourers desperate for a job:

> Drivers are reluctant for industrywide unionism because they are allowed opportunities for corruption by the management in a limited way which sets them apart from the other workers. Contract labourers are totally dependent on the *babus* [educated men, or clerks] who are the go-betweens and also have the effective leadership in all trade unions . . . The *babus* bargained with contractual labourers as pawns, and finally deserted the workers in the latest agitation. (Basu 1980b:1609)

In unionized small firms in South Gujarat: 'If a union leader is on good terms with management it means that he has access to a scarce good which is critical for workers – *viz.* alternative or better jobs . . . Once an organiser is established in a firm, he begins to act as an advocate for *individual* workers; thus the promotion of general worker interest increasingly assumes the character of largesse distributed on an individual basis' (Streefkerk 1981:776). 'A number of bosses told me, independently of each other, that the requirement for forging a compromise boiled down to negotiating basically only one of the BDIEU [union] secretary's demands, *viz.* the size of his bribe' (:770).

The most notorious example is the gang warfare between union mafias in the nationalized Dhanbad coalfield, where 'the [labour] contractors are also trade union leaders, [state] legislators or political leaders, social "reformers", moneylenders, underworld operators and musclemen' (Ketkar 1979). Workers must pay them to get or keep a job, and borrow from them at high interest. 'The so-called union-rivalry in the Dhanbad coalfields is therefore a business rivalry over contracts. And with the growing list of contracts, the bloodshed is also growing with vengeance.' After at least 400 murders in fourteen months, the government intervened and arrested some of the leading politicians and racketeers.

Cases like this give ammunition to the enemies of trade unions, but most unions are not rackets. Much more often the union gives workers what they join it for, as much protection for their shared interests as it is possible to get. The transactions are between workers held together by a strong ethic of solidarity within the group, leaders they trust for the time being and outsiders, like politicians, who give help and protection to the whole group rather than to favoured individuals.

A commonly heard argument is this: the union federations are just the industrial wing of parties, organized nationally or sometimes at state level. Individual unions need educated leaders who can cope with the legal and paper work, and who know English. This gives an opening to law graduates and others to make a career as union leaders, and then to move into full-time politics if they make a success of it. The ordinary members, being simple folk, believe what they are told and vote according to their leaders' instructions. Therefore Indian unions, instead of putting their members first, are manipulated by parties and career politicians whose interests are not those of the workers. The solution is non-political unions with insider leaders only, which would care for their own members' interests and also the national interest. This is called 'responsible unionism'.

But there is plenty of evidence (e.g. E.A. Ramaswamy 1977) that if there is manipulation, it is more often the other way round: industrial workers know very well what their interests are, and can use their leaders' political connexions to put pressure on national and specially state governments to protect these interests. They may not succeed: they may pull the wrong strings, back a party without enough influence in the right places, and in any case there are stronger pulls from other interest groups on most parties. Union leaders and officials, whether they are careerists or not, are caught in the middle; and since there are rival unions in most industries, workers may not hesitate to desert a leader who has not delivered and to take their custom elsewhere; either when individuals join a rival union in the same factory, or when a factory union transfers its loyalty to another federation with a full-time leader known as a strong negotiator.

Workers at a north Bombay electroplating works transferred their allegiance from the militant left-wing Sarva Shramik Sangh to the federation linked to the Maharashtrian-chauvinist Shiv Sena, then back again when the Shiv Sena union failed to get any wage rises. The non-Maharashtrian (Tamil and Hindi-speaking) minority agreed to both changes: the Shiv Sena party may threaten them, but its union federation was just an instrument.

This is a transaction: specialized union services in exchange for higher membership figures and subscriptions. It is not even an ideological market place, because you can buy the service without paying the price of a vote. Thus M.S. Krishnan, communist leader of the AITUC federation in Karnataka, has a high reputation as a union leader and negotiator, honest, effective, backed by a dedicated team;

but although he belonged to the state Assembly he did very badly in a parliamentary election for the Bangalore constituency, because the members of his many unions gave him their warm respect but not their vote. They saw no advantage in it; or if they had a political loyalty, it lay somewhere else.

Some unions have hard-fought internal elections; in others the elections are seldom or never contested, not because workers do not care who leads them but because they can exercise their choice by shopping around rather than voting. Union activists commonly deplore this shopping around as something that weakens the working-class movement and limits it to selfish 'economistic' demands;[2] though one can make a case for it as the only way to put effective power in the hands of workers, rather than self-perpetuating union leaderships.[3]

At the time of writing, the best buy for many Bombay workers is the astonishing Dr Datta Samant, whose Association of Engineering Workers grew fast after a bloody and successful confrontation at the Godrej factory in 1973. Samant established a reputation for quick decisive action without much regard for legal forms or ideologies. Javed sees the 'Samant phenomenon' as:

> a transitional phase of the working class movement in Bombay, between a working class badly in need of a leadership to act on its behalf (textiles typically) and a new workforce sufficiently educated, urbanised and cultured, possessing the ability, aspiration and will to act in its own name. The years of Samant's rise to prominence are also the years which saw the emergence of independent plant-level unions in the more modern precision engineering, chemicals, petrochemical plants, within which the status of the union president is more of an 'advisor', 'consultant', 'expert' rather than a leader in the former sense of the word. For a fee the workers are prepared to buy a service, and no nonsense here. It is not accidental that within such plants, with a relatively stabler industrial relations climate, Samant is neither necessary,

[2] 'Trade union leaders have by and large tended to relate to workers as professionals providing services to a poor, insecure, numerous clientele. Not surprisingly then, workers in turn have reciprocated by developing an instrumental, consumeristic attitude to their unions. The net result has been a weak trade union movement with a tenuous relationship to its members: witness the unusually high turnover of membership in Indian trade unions' (Panjwani 1980:7).

[3] 'Workers view themselves as consumers of the service provided by the union in return for the support they lend from time to time. Naturally, the more suppliers there are the more choices the consumer has for obtaining the needed services' (B.R. Sharma 1978:1237). 'This arrangement [outside leadership] apparently suits the worker for, beside saving him time and effort, it minimises the risk of victimisation at the hands of employers. To ensure that the unions dominated by outsiders do in fact safeguard the occupational interests of the workers, the latter wield the ultimate power, which they often use, of leaving one union and joining another' (:1239).

nor adequate, nor present in any significant way . . . The work of Samant's
union represents widespread pressure on management to rationalise their
industrial relations, and therefore, their industrial management practices. The
extent to which he succeeds in this task, is the extent to which he makes himself
redundant. (Javad 1981)

M.S. Krishnan saw this new educated and skilled work force as a
'problem' in Bangalore:

These men were many times anarchistic in their behaviour and they had
aggressive tendencies. They would create 'spontaneous' strikes without telling
the leadership. But this new type of worker did have its possibilities for the
development of unionism as well as its dangers. The middle class educated
worker was uprooted from his moorings and he had to face new situations. The
slightest insult from a foreman and he was up in arms. He would cause trouble
and strike and he was prepared for collective action.
(Quoted in Reindorp 1971:204)

One of Krishnan's own unions, at the MICO car component factory,
proved the point in 1979 by joining another federation and going on
an eighty-day strike in protest against his failure to resist the transfer
of one department to Nasik, which would have left Bangalore workers
to be shunted around between departments, with less chance of
promotion. Dilip Subramanian (1980:M–68) says the MICO strike
shows that trade union bureaucracies, used to fighting for higher
wages, cannot meet the expectations of this educated working class:
'The struggles instead increasingly gravitate towards the shop-floor,
around issues related to productivity and the utilisation of skills – in
brief over the organisation and content of work.'

One should not assume that these educated workers will always
look after their own interests and put a distance between themselves
and other factory or unorganized sector workers. They are often
politically radical, articulate and active in wider union affairs. If only
a minority of them take the rhetoric of equality seriously and will
sacrifice time, money and even career prospects for a cause, they are
enough to provide a stiffening of dedicated organizers both to their
own factory unions and to allied unions among poorly paid and
insecure workers. Krishnan saw this, and I know from personal
experience that it is true of his unions in Bangalore.

Nor should one assume too easily that the relation between less
educated workers and their leaders is a transaction and nothing else.
People's motives are more complex.

The one book which gives a detailed description of a union's
everyday activities and what it means to its members is E.A.

Ramaswamy's *The Worker and his union* (1977), about the Textile Workers' Union (TWU) in Coimbatore (and see an article on leaders and workers in an industrial suburb of Coimbatore by his wife Uma Ramaswamy (1979), also an anthropologist). The textile mills date back as far as 1890, so the Textile Workers' Union and its rivals have their heroic histories in books and oral tradition, their martyrs, their classic struggles with employers and each other and memories of appalling conditions and management brutality in the old days. Two-thirds of the mill workers commute from the surrounding villages. They are not well educated like the engineering workers. If they have skills these are not easy to transfer out of the textile industry, so they cling to their mill jobs as their only resource, which a man can pass on to at least one son. Apart from wildcat strikes which flare up and die down without union blessing until afterwards, or strikes that are rites of passage by which a union proves to managements and rival unions that it is here to stay, the long bitter strikes are always about threats to job security.

The TWU appeals to members or consumers, first, because it offers a service – mainly job protection – in the face of competition from other suppliers, especially the pro-Congress National Textile Workers' Union. But the leaders are not well-paid political careerists; and the union at branch level is kept alive by a stiffening of activists, committed to an ideal of social equality cutting across caste lines, and to the socialist party (or rather, to various forms of the party as it splits and reunites from time to time). The details of the social and economic changes which would make a classless society possible are not spelled out or perhaps very realistic; but this ideology is different enough to be a real challenge and alternative to the ideology of caste and the defence of narrow sectional interest among workers.

These men seldom get much material benefit from union activities, just the respect of fellow workers and whatever satisfaction is to be had from belonging to a closely-knit group with high morale, in the neighbourhoods and suburban villages where mill workers are concentrated. I know from my own experience that this picture is probably true, and that alongside the corruption and hypocrisy of much union politics one finds astonishing examples of self-sacrifice and dedication. The Ramaswamys describe in detail – with sketches of individuals and their life histories and thoughts – a world of the union activists as distinctive as the catholic and communist 'worlds' in Italy (Kertzer 1980), held together by an ideology of working-class solidarity cutting across barriers of caste and employment. By their personal example, they carry along the mass of ordinary workers who are moderately apathetic about wider issues, but still loyal enough to strike, demonstrate and perhaps vote when asked by those they respect. The union provides a service when needed; in return it sometimes asks for sacrifice and enthusiasm.

This union 'world' has its ritual, myths, martyrs and festivals, and a permanent visible base in branch offices and reading rooms. Until recently – when branches based on the mills had become more important – the main unit of participation was the local branch in a mill workers' neighbourhood, bringing together all members of this industrial union employed in any mill; and around these local branches there grew up a culture of the activists, devoted union men their neighbours looked to for guidance. In the early days these men were known as tyagi, those who had sacrificed, because of the sacrifices they had made not only for the union but also for Independence; and this ideal of what a leader should be lingers on. This is significant, because it suggests that ordinary members see themselves, not just as members for convenience, but as people too weak and selfish to aspire to the saintly single-mindedness they admire in a leader.[4] Not all unions have such examples before them, but some have.

Unions here are like religious sects: as the lines of doctrine and organization between unions hardened, so within the union the activists did what they could and dared, to break down caste segregation, caste loyalty and sometimes even caste endogamy which is always the last rule to go. Unions even became partly endogamous, so that at one time there could be no marriage between families active in different unions; even now, at any activist's wedding, a top union leader blesses the couple (Uma Ramaswamy 1979:368). These active members, if they are sometimes naïve about politics, are at least passionately concerned about political reforms not just in their interest.

Without this core of people who have a commitment beyond the

---

[4] Compare the meaning of Easter gifts among the Sarakatsani of northern Greece: 'The union of men in Christ is reflected at the level of social relations in an expression of ideal solidarity which for a moment breaks down the barriers which isolate family from family and community from community. At other times, the notion that all the ills of the world derive from the view that every man is concerned only for his own family is constantly asserted, and as often deplored. There is always a yearning for unity and goodwill in the community, but it is a yearning accompanied by the knowledge that it can never be' (Campbell 1964:350).

union, the union could not be as effective as it has been in defending wages and job security, which is what ordinary members join it for. Members buy at least some of the ideology as part of the package. Going beyond what Ramaswamy says: recent political developments in India, and especially the direction the unions have taken in some newer industries with an educated well-paid work force, suggest that union membership often has a strong ideological content: a naïve but real longing for a new moral community, with universalistic norms and a demand for economic changes to make these effective. The moral argument has a logic of its own. Sometimes at least these people notice the possible contradiction between the rhetoric of working-class solidarity used to defend permanent workers' jobs and rights, and the interests of others, like unorganized workers and agricultural labourers.

It may seem that I am making these factory workers out to be more idealistic and intellectual than they probably are. The point is to bring out one side of reality which hard-nosed cynical anthropologists and others regard as beneath their notice. Yet this – the beginnings of serious ideological debate, distorted by naïve ignorance and private interests – is the motive force behind radical movements which appear to have sprung from nowhere only if one refuses to take ideas seriously, but only as symptoms of something else like social needs. The naïve devoted union activists may have the last word, because what they have started may help to transform Indian society after all.

The general rule is: each union for itself.

Workers at a Bangalore factory found the gates locked, and a notice saying the management had closed the firm because of falling production and strikes. Some had worked there for eighteen years. I went with them the same day to the small office of their union leader, an ex-lawyer turned 'social worker', to see whether he could get the factory reopened, perhaps by using his political influence. None were optimistic. They expected no support from workers in the owner's other factory, where there was a different (AITUC) union. One man said: everyone looks after his own family (meaning his union), he can't expect others to help.

A union decides to support or oppose a strike, or to be neutral, depending on how it affects its own members. Strikes over suspensions and dismissals which involve the members of just one union are least likely to be joint . . . The easiest form of co-operation [between unions] is for the leaders to join hands in industrywide negotiations since local animosities have no chance of raising their head at this level. But the moment a common demand has to be pressed through a strike thorny problems arise . . . Generally one union or the other backs out after the initial enthusiasm is over.

(E.A. Ramaswamy 1977:110)

Of course there is even less mutual aid between unions in the same factory:

> The four unions are competitors for the loyalty of the same workforce and no union, including the TWU, would generally co-operate with another except in its own interests. This is well understood and TWU members do not expect gratuitous fraternal assistance from the rivals, and would indeed view any such assistance with circumspection . . . Commitments to one's union and hostility to the rivals are merely two sides of the same coin. (:176)

To the extent that members' relation to their union is a transaction, it involves no obligations except to other members: not to rival unions, nor to 'unorganized sector' workers (meaning workers not covered by the Factories Act: it does not mean they are outside unions, though most of them are). I described a strike about bonus at a Bombay petrol tanker factory, where workers shouting revolutionary slogans besieged the management in the office, paying no attention to the contract workers who went on painting tankers a few yards away (p. 178 above); when I asked a union activist about the contract workers, he said he had invited them to join the union but they were afraid.

There is plenty of evidence to support the view that union membership is just a transaction. Workers and leaders often appear indifferent both to the fate of temporaries in their own factories and to appeals from other unionists to help workers in small units, or construction or farm labourers. When a Bombay union leader asked others to support a campaign to get the legal minimum wage paid to workers in small units, the leader from a synthetic fibre factory said: we are not concerned – my members get much more than the minimum, and a 20 per cent bonus. Jan Breman (1978:1356) describes a strike by workers belonging to the Red Flag union at a co-operative sugar factory in Gujarat: they took no interest in the casual cane-cutters, who asked Breman to help them form a union.

Not just indifferent, but suspicious or hostile: temporary or unorganized workers may be seen as a threat, as competitors. At best they would dilute the advantages of permanent employment. A Calcutta union leader said 'we generally discourage' unionization of temporary workers; after 240 days the law gives them the privileges of permanent employment – 'then we sometimes allow them to become members'. In south Gujarat, 'the Dharampur Majur Mahajan union, when concluding an agreement with the owner of a large tannery . . . insisted on including a clause to the effect that the annual bonus should only be paid to those employed on a permanent basis' (Breman 1979:164). At the worst, contract workers are seen as strike-breakers, as in the Bangalore bus body firm where the union demanded that all dismissed workers should be reinstated and the contract workers who had replaced them should go (p. 179 above).

There can be an even sharper conflict of interest when union members have their own employees, separately if they run private businesses or subcontract for the employer, or even collectively, as in the case of the canteen workers who struck against the factory workers' co-operative which employed them (p. 177). Their families may have casual farm labourers or tenants: B.T. Ranadive, a leader of the CITU marxist union federation, said the union movement had been a silent spectator of repression and exploitation elsewhere, and had failed to come to terms with the fact that 'maybe 50 per cent of the workers have land' (Waterman 1980a:3).

A union activist, who said he had been dismissed for forming a union, introduced workers from small factories on a Bangalore industrial estate, and spoke eloquently of the bad conditions in factories without unions. He also complained of the tenancy laws which prevent his family from getting a tenant off their land near Mysore, where they want to plant a commercial crop.

A radical Bombay union was trying to enlist support for farm labourers' unions. I discussed the plan with workers from a small factory, all active in this union. One was in favour. The others agreed, conventionally, that the labourers are exploited and get a poor deal, but said there was no need for unions, because the labourers are only needed for part of the time, the farmers give them three meals a day and do not treat them badly, and anyway the farmers are poor and cannot afford more.

Differences between workers with and without land can split the work force and unions, especially in places like south Gujarat where many households depend both on agriculture and industrial work (Streef-kerk 1981). Workers with land are more independent, and used to commanding others; for this reason, some employers prefer landless workers, and the wages of the two groups are almost the same. However 'The mutual distrust between landholding and landless labourers is based on a combination of social and economic differences and inequalities' (:723), especially caste rank, rather than landownership alone.

All this evidence suggests there are few links of solidarity between organized and unorganized sector workers, and organized sector workers themselves are split into hostile factions in different unions or from different social origins. Yet it is not so simple. To begin with, there are many cases where permanent workers and their unions have helped temporary or contract workers in the same firm, if possible to get them permanent status, otherwise to improve their pay and conditions (pp. 224–6 above). In 1978 the communist AITUC led a strike of permanent workers at the TELCO factory in Jamshedpur, to demand permanent status for the casual and contract workers, mostly tribals and/or women (Waterman 1980:13–14).

An American multinational has a pharmaceutical factory in Bombay, with 1100 permanent workers. To meet extra overseas demand, and to break a strike, the company took on 507 temporary workers, whose service was broken every 89 or 119 days (because the company would be liable for Provident Fund payments after 90 days, and other benefits including job security after 120). The permanent workers' union encouraged the temporary workers to form their own union.

When the temporaries struck to press a list of demands, and prevented raw material from going into the factory, the permanent workers gave them moral and financial support but continued to report for work. The union insisted that none of the permanent workers should be laid off, becuase it was not their fault that production was paralysed. (Information from Kumar Ketkar)

One reason why permanent workers' unions show this concern for the temporary or contract workers is that many of them are relatives or friends of the permanent workers, who got them their temporary jobs and still feel an obligation towards them: if the temporary still lives in his relative's household, there may be an extra incentive to find him a steady job which will get him out of the house. In some factories there are two kinds of temporary workers: those with a place on the waiting-list for permanent jobs, and those without patrons who may still benefit from union action on the temporary workers' behalf: as in a group of Bombay engineering factories, where the union forced the management to absorb some temporaries, to put others on a waiting-list, with a third group (mainly north Indian immigrants) who would 'never' become permanent, but who persuaded the union to help them too and have mostly been made permanent (p. 225 above). Another reason which union officials mention is that a pool of low-paid labour weakens the union's bargaining position and threatens the permanent workers' jobs and wages.

When a permanent workers' union presents a charter of demands to the management, this very often includes an improvement in temporary workers' conditions, which is usually but not always the first item to go when serious negotiations begin: the sympathy may be genuine, but workers care first about their own security and wages.

Timir Basu has reported twice (1979b, 1981) on the condition of casual railway workers:

> There are three kinds of railway workers: permanent, casual, and 'Open Line' ('temporary' but with effective job security, paid leave, and travel passes). The casual workers formed their own union, but for years they got no help from the permanent workers' union. In 1980 the All-India Railwaymen's Federation called the first Project and Construction Casual Labour Conference, to press a 30-point charter of demands – mainly 'Open Line' status for all casuals – but 'so long as permanent railway workers remain passive towards the just demands of casual employees the railway authorities will not have much difficulty in pursuing their present practices' (Basu 1981:230), and Basu doubted whether the AIRF would pursue the cause with tenacity.

Individual or group self-interest explains a lot, but not everything: sympathy for particular relatives or friends without secure jobs can extend to temporary or unemployed workers generally, in a society where people are often cynical but a pure cynicism is almost unthinkable. Like the Coimbatore textile workers, other workers will sometimes make sacrifices demanded by the few union leaders whose dedication they admire, not just on their own behalf but to help others.

So talk of working-class unity must sometimes be taken seriously, not only because of genuine idealism, but because it is in organized sector workers' interest not to allow managements to play one group of workers off against another, to keep wages down or even to turn permanent workers into contract workers. Unorganized sector workers have some bargaining power after all, and are sometimes in a position to force the pace.

Permanent workers and their unions are most ready to give sympathy and practical help to temporary workers in the same factory, whom they see every day and may have brought into the factory in the first place. Workers in smaller firms – whether or not these are in the 'unorganized sector' – are in no position to form strong unions of their own, and have no other protection except the employer's good will and a scarce skill if they are lucky. To form or join unions, they need help from the established union federations of organized skilled workers, and they have only recently started to get it.

In the early 1970s, rival union federations began to move into the smaller organized sector factories before the others could get there. But the smaller the unit the more the problems, and the harder it was to get concessions from employers who were operating on small margins; or if they were not, were determined either to keep unions out, or to bring in tame unions they could control. So in Bombay, for example, factories with 60 or 100 workers were organized into branches of general workers' unions like the competing engineering or chemical workers' unions, attached to the main federations and organized by full-time union workers from the head offices. But charters of demands, strikes, gheraos and negotiations only come up from time to time: the everyday time-consuming work of a union is legal business, taking up individual workers' grievances – especially about dismissals – with managements, government labour officers and the courts. Union leaders say frankly that they cannot afford the time or money, from low union subscriptions, to cope with the smaller units' problems. One leader said it took as much time and effort to unionize a small firm as a large one, 'and obviously I can't do it on my membership fee from 15 workers'; besides, he said, more political unions thought such workers had little to contribute to the class movement – a strike by Kamani's 4000 workers brought immediate results, while a strike by the same number of workers divided among small units would have a negligible effect. The leader of a union which recruits in the smaller chemical firms said other unions did not want members in small factories finding them, 'from a commercial point of view, uneconomical'. The result, according to an anonymous writer, is 'a vicious circle: the only unions that can afford to unionise these workers are those which have many large units; and the unions with large units feel no need to organise these workers'. Moreover 'too much of involvement with the smaller units is considered to adversely affect the "status" of the union; it might even permanently relegate the union to a small-factory field of operation' (*Econ. and Pol. Weekly* 1977:497).

However some smaller and newer unions have no choice. Usually these are groups which break away from the main federations because of political differences or personal clashes between the leaders:

> Were a 'charismatic' leader to break away from a large union and set up a new one with nothing but his personality as its capital and credential, he is soon rudely shocked into the realisation that his 'charisma' has suddenly got diluted. The worker is not naive; he is as tough a 'salesman' as any in the labour market . . . The result is that the only units the newer unions can capture are the smaller ones. These become their point of entry into the trade union field.   (:497–8)

Nor is it just a matter of identifying an untapped market. The same writer gives the example of the Bombay Labour Union set up by the railwaymen's leader George Fernandes:

> There were two reasons which prompted the BLU to get involved in this [small] sector; one, that it was a late starter and did not have the tradition or prestige of the giants; another lay in its ideology, though it would never be declared in so many words, which identified the poorest sections as the key sector and had a vague distrust for the working classes, especially the large, organised sector.   (:498)

Unions of the conventional kind are not adapted to the needs of workers in the small firms – including the 'unorganized sector' – even when these workers want unions and the leaders and members of established unions want to help them. But before asking what forms of organization might suit workers in smaller firms, consider what if anything these workers stand to gain from union action (apart from the uncertain prospect of a big social change in the long term).

In factories, a union's first function is to protect jobs. In small firms this is usually quite unrealistic: even employers who prefer a stable work force supply wildly fluctuating markets. They cannot afford to lose skilled or experienced workers, but if they want to shed labour they can do so easily, and their firms are seldom overmanned. It is still more unrealistic to hope to improve working conditions or safety, though these are not always bad in small firms. Almost the only thing workers can hope to achieve by joint action is to raise wages and bonuses, at least as fast as inflation. Industrial action is dangerous, but it can bring results if the employers cannot afford a break in production and are not prepared to close down.

In states where there is a legal minimum wage for certain industries – and where this is above the market rate – government inspectors may not be able to enforce the law but its very existence is a rallying-point for forms of organization modelled more or less closely on the unions in bigger factories. Workers in isolated units are at risk: some kind of joint action is essential, involving workers in the same branch of industry, or the same small area, or both. The initiative can only come from the workers themselves, who are often poorly educated and vulnerable; or from idealists, either middle-class union leaders and sympathizers or workers in the big factories. If there are self-interested 'agitators' in the union movement, there are few pickings for them here.

The first serious attempt to develop joint action among un-organized sector workers was the Bombay minimum wage move-ment, which began in 1973–4 at a time of rapid inflation and great distress (on the background see *Econ. and Pol. Weekly* 1975a, 1975b, 1977, *Econ. Times* 1975, 1977; I observed the last stages). Left-wing groups had agitated for an extension of minimum wages for years; and in 1972 the Sarva Shramik Sangh ('all workers' union', originally active in textiles) and Kamani [engineering factory] Employees' Union, both sympathetic to the dissident communist Lal Nishan Party, held a conference of 5000 workers to demand minimum wages and unemployment benefits. This was followed by a series of short strikes by organized and unorganized workers and famine relief workers throughout Maharashtra. Whether or not as a direct result, in 1974 the state government fixed minimum wages for agriculture (unenforceable in practice) and engineering, and later for other industries like plastics. The small employers claimed that the new wages – often double the going rate – would put them out of business. They petitioned the government, organized demonstrations and two short 'employers' strikes', and refused to pay.

A number of radical union leaders and activists, from different federations and parties, started a new kind of movement to enforce the law, with further conferences, demonstrations and one-day strikes: the Trade Union Joint Action Committee, representing most union federations except the Congress and Communist Party of India federations which supported the government, gave its official sup-port. The initiative for the new movement came from these leaders; from well-paid workers with a history of successful struggle in a few large factories, living in areas surrounded by small-scale units; and a minority of unorganized sector workers, often the skilled men the employers cannot afford to lose, whose factory worker friends had told them something about unions and who came into suburban union offices to ask if the unions could help them. Some wanted advice on organizing their fellow workers to demand higher wages; others came with their own problems, like dismissal or accident compensation. Member or non-member, no one was turned away. For a time I spent my evenings in one of these small offices ('lent' for an indefinite period, with the typewriter and duplicating machine, by a sympathetic union in a nearby factory), which was a centre for organizing strikes and demonstrations at a few hours notice, a club house for members and friends to meet and talk, and a clinic for unattached workers needing advice and help.

The conventional form of union organization – a fixed member-ship, paying regular subscriptions and organized into branches – was often out of the question with a vulnerable floating population of temporary workers. The leaders of the campaign tried instead to form *ad hoc* committees, bringing together workers from small firms in the same areas – especially the multi-storied industrial estates – and activists from rival unions; with financial support from factory and office workers whose leaders appealed to them to give for the sake of working-class solidarity. A wave of strikes and demonstrations in the small firms forced some employers to pay the minimum wages, but also led to dismissals and lockouts. The movement ended abruptly when the Emergency was imposed in 1975 and (as someone told me then): 'Strikes are not illegal, just immoral' – but in any case dangerous. It began again when the Emergency was lifted before the 1977 election, with another inter-union conference held inside the Kamani factory at its union's invitation, forced a few more employers to pay the minimum wage and to recognize unions, then subsided largely because supporters in the big factories paid more attention to their own demands.

When the minimum wage became law – and again, after the Emergency – the Sarva Shramik Sangh and its sympathizers in other unions selected a few industrial suburbs where unions were weak, and especially the industrial estates where large numbers were employed in small firms making all kind of products. Here news travels fast; it is easy to catch workers' attention with posters, gate meetings and processions shouting slogans around the buildings and even in the corridors, defying the estate watchmen as well as the goondas or thugs some employers use to beat up trouble-makers. Posters and speakers gave the addresses of local union offices and said even a single worker could join: a few came to the offices to enquire, and were enrolled into informal committees to take the campaign a stage further, with more meetings and short sudden strikes in individual units.

Some employers talked to the full-time union officials and agreed to pay the minimum wage. In many cases they paid only the unskilled rate to men working with machinery, who by law should receive the semi-skilled rate; or the rate for eight hours when the working day was longer; or the same rate for overtime, when the law required double. Yet the union saw this as a victory of sorts. The *ad hoc* committees broke up, leaving each union based outside the estate with its own core of support in a few units, and an uneasy peace with the employers there. The idealistic leaders – middle class outsiders, or skilled factory workers – blame themselves for their failure either to lay the foundations for self-reliant autonomous unions on the industrial estates or to get factory workers to go beyond vague sympathy and to give sustained practical and financial support. Meanwhile the more theoretical marxists keep aloof from workers who lack the correct political consciousness and education (see the anonymous writer's comments on middle-class left organizations in *Econ. and Pol. Weekly* 1975b:613).

Nominally revolutionary leaders, in private conversation and in speeches to industrial estate workers, stress that they are only trying to get the law enforced: workers must claim their legal rights. The Sarva Shramik Sangh distributed a Marathi booklet setting out the important points of law, and reminding them that a Supreme Court judge had ruled in 1957 that a company which could not pay the legal minimum wage had no right to exist. Most union work is concerned with getting labour laws enforced, fighting court cases over dismissals and so forth. For union officials as for ordinary workers, it is a moral asset and a source of strength – though by no means essential – to have the law on one's side. Even a gherao, the forcible confinement of managers to their offices, is made to seem morally legitimate because it is an illegal way to enforce the law.

The fate of the minimum wage movement showed the strengths and limits of solidarity between organized and unorganized sector workers, and the different attitudes among organized sector workers: on the one hand, those – especially from among the skilled educated workers and clerical staff – who gave practical support to striking unorganized sector workers, and who would say when asked that factory workers must be the spearhead of the common struggle; on the other hand, those workers and union leaders who took the view that it was none of their business, every group of workers must look after themselves; just as striking or dismissed workers belonging to one union federation cannot expect another federation's support, except in rare cases. You pay your subscriptions and get the protection you pay for, though there are also times when sympathy and solidarity are more than rhetoric.

Notice also the direction some of the leaders tried to give the movement by linking it with movements to unionize agricultural labour in Maharashtra and to enforce the agricultural minimum wage: they managed at least to raise a good deal of money for the purpose. Yet industrial workers in either sector are ambiguous in their support for militant farm labour, since so many are from country families which employ labourers – often of low caste – constantly or from time to time. There is an uncomfortable gap between the rhetoric of working-class solidarity which moves them, and their attitudes towards their families' farm labourers or tenants.

Temporary or contract workers look to the main factory union for help, and sometimes get it. Workers from small firms go to union offices for advice, and a few radical unions meet them halfway. Skilled construction workers recruited in Bombay unionize casual labourers on the Ganga dam in Bihar, to the dismay of the contractors who could not find skilled labour elsewhere. Yet working-class solidarity can work in both directions: unorganized sector workers do not always look to permanent employees for support. A Bombay union official said it was easier to get temporary factory workers to join a strike that would chiefly benefit the permanent workers than vice versa; and I have visited unionized small firms with an official of the same union, who asked the managers to give workers time off to demonstrate in support of a strike at a big engineering factory. If it is difficult to form unions in small firms, the demand is there, especially from educated articulate workers who see little chance of moving out of the unorganized sector (in Bombay the standard of education is higher in small firms than in factories: p. 186 above) and from ex-factory workers who end up in small firms: sometimes men who say they were sacked for union activities. The people who need union protection most – unskilled casual labourers – are least able to support unions of their own.

To fight the union–contractor–moneylender mafia which preys on casual and contract labour in the nationalized Dhanbad coal mines

(Ketkar 1979, see p. 290 above), the marxist A.K. Roy started the Bihar Colliery Kamgar (workers) Union, which Prem Pradeep and Arvind Das see as the 'organization of the future' (1979; also Waterman 1980; Das, Rojas and Waterman 1981; 'A.S.' 1980). The work force consists largely of Adivasis (tribal people) and Harijans, poorly educated and suspicious of incomers who have taken the best jobs. The BCKU is meant to be a new kind of union, open to permanent and casual labour and anyone else in the area; linked to other radical movements like the Jharkhand Mukti Morcha, which demands autonomy for this tribal region; without bureaucracy or hierarchy; run cheaply and simply, unlike other unions with their well-equipped offices; depending on voluntary subscriptions only; organized from the bottom up – the branches where members, whether they pay or not, can decide their own priorities and action, are loosely co-ordinated by a central committee of delegates in constant touch with members.

By 1979 the union had some 60 000 members, of whom less than half paid the ten-rupee yearly subscription. Each branch is largely autonomous: 'it often happens that unplanned action takes place at different levels which has a bad consequence for the organisation in the short run. (A recent example of this is the beating up of a few managerial employees at Amlabad Colliery without the approval or even the knowledge of the central leadership' (Pradeep and Das 1979:252). Elections for union and branch officials are held yearly, 'in the presence of some "observers" of the Central Union Executive Committee. Although the modalities of the elections are by raising of hands or by ballot there is in some cases a somewhat informal cooption of the candidate in which the observer from the centre plays a significant role. No set procedures and role descriptions and definitions have been specified and considerable discretion is exercised at the local level itself' (:250).

The union is so closely linked with other organizations, like those of tribal people, peasants or transport workers, that 'it is sometimes difficult to say where one organisation ends and the other one starts' (:252). 'Whenever instantaneous collective intervention of the tribals is required, and this is not limited to the central office but is also done in the collieries, the nearest tribal village is informed in person. Thereafter, each village informs the next village by beating drums, using coded drum beats to convey the message. The result is the immediate mobilisation of a vast surrounding area of villages. The tribals, with their traditional weaponry of bows and arrows, are able to collect in huge numbers on remarkably short notice' (:251). However it is not clear whether the writers observed such a gathering of the tribals, or took what may have been an exaggerated account on trust.

The theory is that only a cheap flexible decentralized anti-hierarchical organization can unite permanent and casual workers, peasants, tribal people and incomers in a movement to redistribute wealth and power in the region. Yet the union depends largely on one intellectual's inspiration, and has grown fast precisely because he was seen to refuse the role of a union boss like Datta Samant, who takes all the decisions. Officials are supposed to be equal and interchangeable, so whoever is in the tiny office can deal with any matter at once. 'However an informal hierarchy *does* exist and this is determined by the nature and extent of personal sacrifice made by different people. Thus a hierarchy of different levels of asceticism has emerged and this is perpetuated by the examples set by A.K. Roy himself' (:252). This harsh self-discipline keeps out some sympathizers, especially from the middle class; Pradeep and Das say this may be no bad thing in the long run, but it leaves the union without a proper secretariat or staff for its newspapers.

The BKCU may be a pointer to the 'organization of the future' but its time has not yet come. It has achieved little beyond arousing the militant enthusiasm of workers who were helpless before, giving them confidence and experience of discussion and industrial action. The union is supposed to be decentralized and participatory, yet everything revolves around one charismatic leader against his own wishes. It has organized strikes for the abolition of contract labour, for bonus and employment of local people, and against mechanization which costs jobs: apparently with little success. A.K. Roy proclaimed a 'single-point manifesto of "struggle against goonda [gangster] terror"' ('A.S.' 1980) yet the murders and beatings continued; indeed 'A.S.' says the union's loose form of organization has allowed 'moneylenders and extortionists' to take over some colliery branches, as they did in the old discredited unions. The union and its ally the Jharkhand Mukti Morcha have failed to unite all the poor of the region, since activists claim that the 'local people' who should benefit from industrialization are only the Adivasis or tribals, not the people of plains origin even if their families have lived in Dhanbad for generations. Das, Rojas and Waterman (1981:18) conclude that although such loosely structured movements – like the Bombay minimum wage movement – are open to a wide range of working people, and 'flexible in responding to new moods and demands', 'they tend to decline with the wave of militancy which brings them into existence'. They lack a developed long-term strategy and the necessary national or international linkages which would allow them 'to gell into a permanent *movement*'.

Previous attempts to find new forms of organization, uniting workers from different 'sectors' for effective action, have been short-lived and dependent on educated articulate people, mostly graduates or skilled workers who are also to be found in smaller firms but only in small numbers. One can point to plenty of examples of permanent factory workers and their leaders who do not want to know, and who appear to be moved only by narrow self-interest or group interest. Yet to reduce all motives to interest is to explain nothing, to make the notion of self-interest useless. People interpret their interest in different ways, they draw different boundaries around the group with a common interest, and sometimes they deliberately act in ways which go against their own interests. There are strong pressures of self-interest (to protect jobs and wages), ideology and sympathy for individual relatives and friends, which lead factory workers and their unions to give practical help and money, and even to strike or demonstrate, in order to get security and better wages for temporary workers, to check the worst abuses of contract labour, and to encourage any stirrings of independent unionism among workers in small firms, casual employment and agriculture. This help is a necessary but not sufficient condition for any sustained movement to improve conditions for unorganized sector workers, or even to get what is legally theirs already. E.A. Ramaswamy (1976:1818) was right when he said: 'Industrial workers have been the only section of the downtrodden to be able to take care of their own interests to some extent, and it is very much in the national interest that they be allowed to continue to do so.'

7

A dual economy and society?

I began with three kinds of question (pp. 7–8) which can now be reduced to two: more objective questions about people's real economic situation; and questions more accessible to the methods of social anthropology, about their thinking and how this explains their actions.

First, since most organized sector workers are clearly better off than most unorganized sector industrial workers, how sharp are the boundaries and how easy to cross, who share the benefits of organized sector employment and who are excluded? Is it true that the Indian industrial economy is a dual economy, where the whole organized sector – owners, managements, workers and unions – form a privileged enclave or élite, at the expense of the whole unorganized sector – owners and workers alike – which is prevented from realizing its potential for employment and production; and these unorganized sector workers, like peasants and others outside industry, get the backwash of industrialization not the benefits? Should we say organized sector workers are well off *and* the others are badly off, or *because* the others are badly off?

Secondly, the same problems seen from inside by the people themselves. Do organized and unorganized sector workers think and act is if it were a dual or multiple economy? For example, do they see themselves as two or more classes with separate or even conflicting interests? Do they live in different social and mental worlds, meeting and helping only their own kind? Are they right in their assessment of their situation, or which of them are right? Where they appear to be wrong, why do they hold mistaken views, and which view explains the facts better?

We should take the actors' opinions seriously but critically, without explaining them away as mere ideology or false consciousness, or falling into the opposite trap of relativism, where to understand all is not just to forgive but to assent.

310

If industrial workers are divided between two worlds, these seem at first sight to match the official distinction between organized and unorganized sector employment. The 'organized sector' means firms with ten or more workers (or twenty without power) which should be -registered and inspected under the Factories Act. The smaller unorganized sector firms come under another Act which is enforced, if at all, by local authorities. 'Informal sector' is used in much of the literature, as in other countries, to cover a wide range of ways to make a living. 'Small-scale industries', defined in India as those below a certain investment limit, are entitled to advantages like easy loans and reserved product lines. Thus many small industries are in the organized sector, and more would be if the law were enforced. Ownership is something else: many small firms are owned or controlled by men with multiple interests, who switch their capital from one use to another, or sometimes by very big companies. There is a wide grey area, of firms which should legally be 'organized' but in fact are not.

The big modern factories look like modern factories anywhere, but less automated. Chemical or cement plants are fairly self-contained, though they put out engineering and maintenance work to small firms; but the main engineering, automobile, electrical and electronic factories are assembly plants, using components made or worked up by smaller firms.

The organized sector consists of *firms*. Many people work in these firms without enjoying the benefits of organized sector employment, because they are temporary or casual or contract workers: it is not possible to say what proportion of the work force, because there are no reliable figures. A temporary worker is entitled to permanent status after 240 days continuous work, so some firms employ a large 'temporary' work force who are regularly laid off and taken back. An increasing amount of work is done by contract labour: construction almost always, often cleaning and canteen work, sometimes maintenance and ordinary production. Workers employed on different terms may do identical jobs in the factory: two cleaners, one with a permanent job and twice the wages of the other, who works for a contractor. Even when temporaries get the same wage as permanent workers, they are seldom allowed to join unions, they are not covered by the Provident Fund or Employees' State Insurance, they get no annual leave and so on. Workers can be turned into contractors, as when a textile mill owner lends money to a few workers to buy the looms and employ their own labour inside the factory. Firms put out jobs for their own workers to do at home, with the help of their families and sometimes hired labour. There are many variations.

The commonest way to evade the laws which apply where over ten workers are employed is fictitious division of the company into several firms, each with its own name and signboard inside the building, and a register to show that not more than ten are employed, no children under age etc.

Even the big factories, the multinationals and other good payers, are often engaged in assembling, finishing and marketing products of smaller units further down the chain. The next link consists of middle-sized factories, still with fairly strong unions, a largely permanent labour force paid quite well, but in closer touch with the small suppliers. Below these suppliers are still smaller firms which cannot afford a shed on an industrial estate, accommodated in back streets all over the city: tiny rooms where a few men with worn-out machinery do whatever work they can get, or rooms where women assemble tiny parts.

However not all small workshops are marginal firms using worn-out machines, simple technology and unskilled workers to save the big firms' wage costs. Many very small units have expensive foreign machinery; or they are run by engineers or skilled workers who modify existing designs or make new ones, copy or improve on machinery and work out new ingenious solutions to technical problems. The small firms – whether or not they are also 'capital-intensive' – work hard to develop their own markets; they try not only to sell to more than one big firm but to market their own finished products. And although the chain reaches down from the big prestige firms to small back street firms, there is an intricate network of links between the small firms themselves. Not only does one small firm put out work to another, but sometimes a small firm gives work to a larger one which has the machine for a specialized job.

So I was wrong when I implied (Holmström 1976) that there was one clear boundary between organized and unorganized sector firms. There are several thresholds for legal, fiscal and practical purposes. For workers, the big difference is between having a permanent organized sector job and not having one; but this too is not a clear-cut distinction, there are degrees in it. Generally the bigger the firm the better the pay and the security: there is not often a trade-off between pay and security. Small firms are more likely to close down or to lay workers off because of market fluctuations, and less likely to have strong unions without which no amount of legislation or minimum wages and job security will work. If you start in a small firm, you can try to move up gradually into bigger firms which pay better; though with rising standards of education this is much harder than in the past. But for the temporary or casual worker in a big firm, there is still a single quantum jump to be made, into permanent employment. How then does one get a job?

The real economy expands very slowly. Jobs are desperately short, and the pool of people qualified to do any job fairly well is large: except for certain special skills which are in short supply, especially because the skilled men are going to the Persian Gulf. A shortage of any skill is unlikely to last long, since desperate young men will find some way to learn it.

The commonest way to get jobs is through recommendations: either from influential people (thus a small firm's customer can sometimes force the employer to take someone he does not want) or more often through workers already in the firm. This last method gives the employer a useful hold, both over the recruit and the recommender. Big firms also use formal procedures – advertising, and calling applicants for test and interview; and a few take workers from Employment Exchanges. There are distinct labour markets for the larger organized sector firms and the unorganized sector, with some overlap in the middle.

To get any kind of job, you generally need a sympathetic contact inside. Someone from the same village, a friend or neighbour may help. People without jobs or with bad jobs cultivate the acquaintance of someone in a good factory; and since such a worker is under pressure from many people and the number he can bring into his firm is rationed to perhaps one or two, he has to make the selection himself. He must not offend the employer by bringing in someone who is incompetent or a trouble maker. Other things being equal, first preference goes to relatives: in big firms this is sometimes formalized in union agreements, which lay down that on death or retirement a worker's son or other close relative gets a job, and in firms with no expansion this may be the only way anyone ever gets a job. In some cases a young man is content to do any work while he waits for his father to retire. Each factory or line of work tends to be reserved for a group – people from certain villages or castes or regions, whose fathers first got these jobs when conditions were different.

Almost everyone wants a permanent job in a big factory. Second best is a temporary job with the prospect of permanency: in some factories a temporary or casual job is in effect a place on a waiting-list, and again this may be laid down in a union agreement. But there may also be a fringe of temporary, casual or contract workers who have little or no hope of permanent employment. Especially if these people are from different social origins and recruited through another network, it may be possible to keep them out for ever; but where they are the permanent workers' relatives or friends or clients, it is more likely that the union will press their claim for registration on a waiting-list, and will try to speed up their absorption in the permanent labour force; or if that is impossible, to improve their pay and conditions.

When a firm establishes an official or *de facto* waiting-list of temporary workers, because of union or other pressures, the boundary of the organized sector has been pushed further out, to take in people who can expect a good job in the future if not yet. But the new boundary is as clear as the old one: as some medieval cities rebuilt their walls to enclose new suburbs.

At this level there is still a wall; but not when one comes to middle-to-small firms, even in the organized sector. These firms may keep a reserve of temporary or casual workers who are just that, perhaps with a better chance of permanent jobs but nothing more, no waiting-list. The permanent employees have legal security of employment, but this is hard to enforce without a strong union. In smaller firms, the difference between skilled and unskilled workers is more important.

The big firms now tend to take bright young men straight from school, or from a government industrial training institute, and to train them in the firm. They do not want to recruit outside, except for skills for which they lack training facilities. Managements prefer to take young men, and unions want to safeguard their members' promotion prospects. If you have a School Leaving Certificate, you have a chance of employment in a big factory; if not, little chance unless your father works there. It used to be possible to start in a small workshop, learn a skill and then move up: it still is, but usually only into the middle-sized firms without training facilities. In small workshops one finds a limited number of skilled men, all looking out for better jobs; and 'helpers' at very low wages, who sometimes get the chance to pick up a skilled or semi-skilled trade by working with a skilled man.

This mobility for some skilled men exists especially in the

engineering trades; to some extent in textiles; much less in industries like chemicals and pharmaceuticals, where the real skill is with chemists and engineers.

I do not think workers experience the organized/unorganized division as a sharp line: even a small change for the better is difficult when so many compete for the same prizes. A change for the better means pay *and* security: it was hard to test my theory that security is more important, either by asking directly or by inferring the answers from people's actions and comments, because it is usually a matter of having both or neither. But it is not (as I had thought) just a matter of having or not having the pay-and-security package, but of having more pay and security or less, a difference of degree.

A continuum has poles. There is a vast difference between a couple of small peasant origin (Shankar and his wife, p. 265 above) who both work in the same pharmaceutical factory, living in a municipal flat with television and taking great trouble over their children's education; and workers who go around the suburban streets asking for helpers' jobs in small workshops, who are lucky if they can stay in one place for months, and who are also lucky if they can share, with a relative in permanent employment, a one-room corrugated iron shack on a lane three feet wide in the Bombay slums. These people again are very different from the uneducated migrant casual labourers who sleep in the streets or camp with their families on building sites; or the real lumpenproletariat, people who never go to work regularly but make what they can on the fringes of the underworld – gambling, illicit distilling, theft and prostitution; or below them, the beggars and ragpickers. I am talking about those whose living comes from industry: is there really one working class with common interests and a common fate?

I cannot give a simple answer, though the answer is probably yes. But the differences between cities are striking. In Calcutta there are several watertight groups even in the big factories: educated Bengalis in the big engineering works, uneducated people from Bihar and Uttar Pradesh in the depressed textile and jute mills who have some security; and a large mixed population in the small engineering workshops of Howrah over the river, working in appalling conditions, with little chance of a factory job. In Ludhiana there is an astonishing growth of small engineering firms, which are recruiting grounds for the large ones. In this area, the Punjab, the gradient in pay and conditions appears to be less steep, just as this is the one part of India where agricultural work is well enough paid to be a serious alternative to an industrial job. But the big industrial centres like Bombay, Bangalore and Poona are more typical. In such places, are workers in large and small firms one class with shared interests?

Just as the economic linkages between large and small firms are close and complex, there are links of residence, kinship, friendship and obligation between workers in large and small factories, and between people living in the city and often distant villages. To get any job one needs a network of friends or relatives or contacts. Which networks are most effective depends partly on the group's influence and wealth, partly on historical accidents which may give otherwise depressed groups a niche in the industrial economy. Often the same network extends into the organized and unorganized sectors of an industry. Caste is not the only thing that binds a network together, but it is a useful indicator of social origins; and in many industries and trades, the distribution of castes is similar in the two sectors, especially where a skill is related to a caste's traditional work. However, in industries where there is a marked difference in the caste distribution in the two sectors, this may or may not be because high castes work in the better-paid jobs: the most significant difference may not be caste rank but language, if all the factory jobs were already taken by local people of mixed castes before immigrants from other states arrived to work in the new smaller firms.

In Bombay the difference between earnings of workers doing similar jobs in the two sectors is much greater than the difference in their family income per consumer, which means that organized sector workers' higher pay is spread either among more dependants or among low-paid workers who live with them: my own observations, in Bombay and elsewhere, tend to confirm this. Migrants come to live with employed relatives in the town, expect their help in finding a job and often stay with them afterwards because they cannot afford their own place. The tension between self-interest and moral obligation in these unwilling joint families can lead to seething resentment, as a better-paid worker and his wife try to find a way out into a place of their own, without letting down their kinsmen too blatantly. Well-paid workers aspire to a middle-class life style; a more expensive education for their children; a room in a chawl or tenement with shared washing facilities or even a municipal or council flat. They tend to escape from the slums and to see less and less of the workers in small workshops. So although organized and unorganized sector workers may come from similar backgrounds, the gap has grown wider over the last few years.

Take Bombay: the city always had a widely based commercial and industrial economy, based largely – unlike Calcutta – on Indian capital. The big industry was textiles, now stagnant. After Independence, especially in 1957–60, there was a rapid growth in new engineering and other industries, followed in the 1960s by a new influx of foreign capital. This is when the gap became wider: before then, workers in factories and workshops drew similar wages, and it was not too hard to move from one sector to the other. The foreign companies paid more because their workers had efficient unions and because the companies could no longer repatriate profits on the same scale as before. After 1960, 'small-scale industries' emerged as a separate growing sector. Wages in the multinationals rose sharply; other organized sector wages rose but not as fast; unorganized sector wages rose a little and then levelled out. The living standard of the unemployed – mostly depending on relatives – remained level or went down.

Generally a worker in a big modern factory earns two or three times as much as a worker with the same title, like a turner, in a small organized sector factory or a workshop; and he has security and fringe benefits. Some of this difference reflects skill, and experience on machines which only the big factories have. I asked low-paid workers why there was this difference. The usual explanation was simply that big factories naturally paid more, they were 'limited companies', there were economies of scale and stronger unions. They did not imply that these high wages were at their own expense, they just wanted to get into the same situation themselves: either individually (by getting a better job) or collectively, by forcing their employers to give higher pay and security. To do either of these things, they need the better-paid workers' help: to get a job, one needs friends in the firms where the jobs are; to organize effectively, the help of unions based in large firms, which are only now beginning to take an interest in the smaller companies and workshops. Since it is now clear to unorganized sector workers that the old avenues of upward mobility are closed except for a few with special skills, the low-paid workers on both sides of the organized/unorganized boundary now see their best chance in militant union action, though they do not appear to see this as a confrontation with the better-paid workers.

Until recently, most unions were organized in single firms and belonged to rival federations, each linked to a political party but not (as some allege) controlled by it. A union looked after its own members, the permanent employees. Its leaders, whether factory workers or outsiders, expressed sympathy for temporary and unorganized sector workers, but that was all. They first went beyond this defensive role to press the demands of temporary and casual workers: for permanency if possible, otherwise for better pay and conditions. There were two main reasons: one was that the temporaries came from the same social background as permanent workers, might even be relatives they had recommended for jobs and lived with, and they felt sympathy for them. The other reason was that a pool of low-paid labour weakened the unions' bargaining position and threatened the permanent workers' jobs. Often, a charter of demands included an improvement in temporary workers' conditions, which was the first item to go when serious negotiations began. But not always: this is how many factories came to have a waiting-list of temporaries who could expect permanent jobs.

In the early 1970s, rival union federations began to move into the smaller more exploited organized sector firms; but the smaller the firm the more serious the problems, and these workers made the greatest call on the unions' time and money. Conventional unions, with a fixed paid-up membership and permanent officials engaged mainly in legal business, were of little use in the unorganized sector, where a vulnerable floating work force had no legal protection except the unenforceable minimum wage. In the last chapter I described the limited success of attempts to find other forms of union organization useful both to workers in small firms, and to casual and contract workers in bigger ones; in a loose alliance with permanent organized sector workers – whose help was essential – and with agricultural labourers, who were even worse off than unorganized industrial workers. In particular, the Bihar Colliery Kamgar Union with its allied political and labour organizations, still heavily dependent on the example and inspiration of one leader who has tried consistently to encourage poorly educated workers to act for themselves in autonomous local branches, with support from a genuinely democratic central organization; and the Bombay minimum wage movement, where mainly skilled unorganized sector workers, with support from middle-class idealists and union activists in some large factories, formed *ad hoc* strike committees in the industrial estates and other suburban areas where small firms are concentrated. I described the extent and limits of solidarity between organized and un-organized sector workers, and also between industrial workers in either sector and the agricultural labourers they were asked to help.

One could argue that, if unorganized sector workers are at last getting organized and winning concessions, this simply has the effect of moving the boundary of the protected sector further out, rebuilding the wall; that it may leave the majority outside industrial employment worse off than before, because the newly protected work force will price itself out of markets and there will be less new jobs; that unions in developing countries inevitably lead to an aristocracy of labour, because the masses, especially in rural areas, can never win the same advantages for themselves. However, this is only likely to happen if the boundaries – between the protected and unprotected sectors, or between industrial and rural labour – can be clearly defined, fortified and made stable, which is unlikely because of continuous political pressures from groups just outside any boundary that might be drawn: pressures of ideology, sympathy and family loyalty from some of those inside, rapid changes in technology and labour requirements (as in electronics) and the discovery of new sources of labour. An effective move to develop new forms of union organization and to raise wages in the small units could not, politically, stop there: it is likely to lead to more far-reaching changes, the organization of landless rural labour (which has already begun, especially, in Kerala), and eventually to a redistribution of wealth and power, and production for mass markets without any need for artificial aids to small units, reserved products, or 'appropriate technology' as a thing in itself.

My image of the 'citadel' was too simple. The organized/unorganized boundary is not a wall but a steep slope. Indian society is like a mountain, with the very rich at the top, lush Alpine pastures where skilled workers in the biggest modern industries graze, a gradual slope down through smaller firms where pay and conditions are worse and the legal security of employment means less, a steep slope around the area where the Factories Act ceases to apply (where my wall stood), a plateau where custom and the market give poorly paid unorganized sector workers some minimal security, then a long slope down through casual migrant labour and petty services to destitution. There are well-defined paths up and down these slopes, which are easiest for certain kinds of people. Chapter 5 provides a map.

Whether the boundary is a wall or a slope, the important question is whether the whole organized sector exploits the unorganized. Michael Lipton (1977; see p. 19 above) believes there is a Grand Alliance of industrial owners and workers, unions, big farmers and intellectuals, who maintain 'urban bias' in planning (though it is not always clear whether he is writing about urban–rural differences or differences between rich and poor). Heather and Vijay Joshi (1976a; p. 17 above) show some sympathy for the argument that the whole organized sector – workers, unions, owners, managers and related interests – form a privileged upper class, making luxury goods for an upper-class market: we should revise our view of the unorganized sector as riffraff without productive potential. However the trend is now to go to the opposite extreme: to subsidize small firms because they are small and assumed to be labour-intensive, and to develop 'appropriate' technology as if suitable technologies were not available already for any economic strategy worth choosing.

Those who are sceptical about 'the philosophy of small-scale industries' are on the defensive. A good counter-attack is in Jan Breman's article (1977), where he argues that it is a mistake to think of the 'informal sector' as a thing in itself, a separate economic compartment or labour situation. There are no separate markets, no dual economy, and the informal or unorganized sector has little growth potential of its own. The different criteria for distinguishing between waged and self-employed, formal and informal, organized and unorganized, security and insecurity etc. do not add up to any clear stratification. I implied that they did (Holmström 1976), and I was wrong.

The organized sector depends on the unorganized in many ways: for parts, components, processing, and sometimes maintenance which it would be uneconomic for a large firm to do for itself; or because the large firm needs temporary access to specialized skills or machines, which may be expensive – not 'intermediate technology' at all; or because unions and labour laws prevent large firms from expanding or reducing their work force quickly, to cope with fluctuations in demand (thus Hind Motors in Calcutta reacted to falling demand for its cars by concentrating production in the factory and cutting orders to small firms); and especially because large firms take advantage of low wages and bad conditions, rather than cheap machinery, in the unorganized sector. Also because wages from unorganized sector employment, though very low and unstable, when added to family incomes make it possible for present or potential organized sector workers to maintain themselves somehow in expensive cities like Bombay – costs which would otherwise have to be borne by a welfare state, or by paternalistic managements on the Japanese model.

Small firms also market their own finished products, and make some mass consumption goods which bigger firms are not interested in making, but not to the extent that is sometimes suggested. Where there is official discrimination, on balance it works more in favour of small firms than against them: markets protected against competition from large firms, technical aid and cheap credit. Some small firms flourish on this diet. What holds the others back is partly lack of access to markets where the big firms have contacts and a name, but much more the big firms' ability to make better, more consistent and up-to-date goods more cheaply, often by methods which are no more capital-intensive than those the small firms use. Small may sometimes be beautiful, but there are still economies of scale. There is a viable and even thriving part of the unorganized sector, which complements the organized sector without being an alternative to it. Traditional cottage industries and handicrafts have a future in sophisticated urban and export markets; but much of the really independent unorganized sector has been a failure, in economic and human terms, and probably will continue to be.[1] To talk of two sectors existing 'side by side', as McNamara does (p. 1 above), is misleading: this is a complex industrial economy, which can be divided in various ways for analysis. To emphasize this one line – between large and small firms – turns attention away from other important cleavages in Indian society: like the lines between those who own or control large parts of the economy, those who own or control small parts of it, those who are able to sell their labour and those who cannot even do that. In the same way Lipton confuses the class difference between rich and poor with the choice between urban and rural development, which is another problem, or perhaps no problem.

As for the question of scales of industrial organization and alternative technologies (now much discussed), several issues are being confused. It is taken for granted that there are two contrasting

---

[1] Nirmala Banerjee ('Is small beautiful?', 1981) demolishes one by one the arguments used to justify a policy of uncritical support for small industries: that they are labour-intensive, create more employment (or that more employment at any human cost is necessarily good), spread ownership and wealth, and have greater growth potential.

packages. One contains large units with largely imported technology, using capital-intensive methods to make luxury goods; well-paid workers with secure jobs, legal safeguards, unions and some personal autonomy; geographical concentration and concentration of owner-ship. The other package (now more in favour) contains small decentralized units, unprotected labour or at any rate fewer labour laws to impede enterprise, innovative labour-intensive technology, geographical dispersal and dispersal of ownership. If the present informal sector is not providing the full package, something or someone is to blame.

The studies that have been made, and my own fieldwork, make it possible to unpack the packages and to show that these things need not and do not go together: in particular, unit size and capital intensity. Small firms sometimes use expensive imported machinery; must cluster round large units to survive; are often owned or controlled by people with wide industrial and commercial interests; and often exist only as devices to get raw material quotas or to evade the Factories Act or taxes. Even if large firms are in general more capital-intensive, there is no reason why this must be so.

I have spoken in metaphors, about demolishing the citadel wall, making maps of mountains and unpacking packages. However, the evidence I have collected – at first hand from industrial workers, and at second hand through those who know them, as well as evidence from reports and statistics, suggest these answers to my two composite questions.

There is no dual economy. The relatively well-paid are not privileged at the expense of the unorganized sector, and there is no way that making factory workers poorer could help the others.

Secondly I argue – though with many qualifications – that organized and unorganized sector workers do not think of themselves and act as separate classes with conflicting interests, and the reason is that they are not separate classes. There is no clear boundary between the two social worlds. Organized sector factory workers often recognize heavy obligations to particular unorganized sector or unemployed workers. Even if their unions have not always shown much concern for the unorganized sector, they are doing so now, for reasons both of competitive self-interest and of ideology. Now that it is harder than before for individuals to find factory jobs, unorganized sector workers turn increasingly to collective self-help, that is, unions of some sort. Any major change that would benefit workers in one sector would also benefit the others, so their interests do not conflict, and they see this. The short answer to both questions is no.

References

'A.S.' 1980. 'Dhanbad: new aspects of coalfield politics'. *Econ. and Pol. Weekly*, 6 Dec. 1980, 2046.

Abraham, Amrita. 1978. 'Conditions of Bombay's textile workers'. *Econ. and Pol. Weekly*, 21 Oct. 1978, 1761–2.

1979. 'Violence in a Bombay slum'. *Econ. and Pol. Weekly*, 3 Nov. 1979, 1789–91.

Aravindaksham, P. and Abraham, N.J. 1977. 'Anatomy of Kerala Gulfward exodus'. *Indian Express*, 22 Aug. 1977.

Avachat, Anil. 1978. 'Bidi workers of Nipani'. *Econ. and Pol. Weekly*, 22 and 29 July 1978, 1176–80 and 1203–5.

Bagchi, A.K. 1972. *Private investment in India 1900–1939*. Cambridge University Press and Madras: Orient Longman 1975.

Baldwin, George B. 1959. *Industrial growth in south India*. New York: Free Press.

Banaji, Rohini. 1978. 'Working class women and working class families in Bombay: report of a survey'. *Econ. and Pol. Weekly*, 22 July 1978, 1169–73.

Banerjee, Nirmala. 1981. 'Is small beautiful?' in A.K. Bagchi and N. Banerjee (eds.), *Change and choice in Indian industry*, pp. 277–95. Calcutta: K.P. Bagchi for Centre for Studies in Social Sciences.

Barnett, Steve. 1977. 'Identity choice and caste ideology in contemporary south India' in Kenneth David (ed.), *The new wind: changing identities in south Asia*, pp. 393–414. The Hague: Mouton.

Basu, Timir. 1977. 'Futility of Contract Labour Act'. *Econ. and Pol. Weekly*, 2 July 1977, 1041–2.

1979a. 'Jute workers' struggle'. *Econ. and Pol. Weekly*, 3 Feb. 1979, 186–7.

1979b. 'Plight of casual workers in railways'. *Econ. and Pol. Weekly*, 7 July 1979, 1115–16.

1979c. 'Workers as pawns in parliamentary politics'. *Econ. and Pol. Weekly*, 27 Oct. 1979, 1747–9.

1980a. 'Whose ideas of work norms?' *Econ. and Pol. Weekly*, 29 Mar. 1980, 626–7.

1980b. 'West Bengal: "Road kings" win'. *Econ. and Pol. Weekly*, 27 Sept. 1980, 1609–10.

1981. 'Plight of railway casual construction labour', *Econ. and Pol. Weekly*, 14 Feb. 1981, 229–30.

Béteille, André. 1969. 'Ideas and interests'. *International Social Science Journal* 21, 2, 219–35.

1970a. 'Peasant associations and the agrarian class structure'. *Contributions to Indian Sociology*, N.S. 4, 136–39.

1970b. 'Clerks and skilled manual workers: some considerations for research on Calcutta'. *J. Ind. Anthrop. Soc.* 5, 79–86.

Bhagwati, Jagdish N. and Desai, Padma. 1970. *India: planning for industrialization*. London: Oxford University Press.

324

Bhattacharya, Nikhilesh and Chatterjee, A.K. 1973. 'A sample survey of jute industry workers in Greater Calcutta'. Mimeo. Research and Training School, Indian Statistical Institute, Calcutta.

1974. 'Some characteristics of jute and engineering industry workers in Greater Calcutta'. Mimeo. Research and Training School, Indian Statistical Institute, Calcutta.

Bhattacharyya, B. 1973. 'Labour intensity of engineering export industries'. *Econ. Times* (Bom.), 7 July 1973.

Biswas, A., Chatterjee, P. and Chaube, S. 1976. 'The ethnic composition of Calcutta and the residential pattern of minorities'. *Geographical Review of India* 38, 2, 140–66.

Bose, Ashish. 1970. *Urbanization in India: an inventory of source materials.* Bombay: Academic Books. See esp. 'The analysis of urbanization and research problems', pp. 62ff.

1973. *Studies in India's urbanization, 1901–1971.* Bombay: Tata-McGraw Hill.

ose, A.N. 1978. *Calcutta and rural Bengal: small sector symbiosis.* Calcutta: Minerva Associates for ILO.

se, Nirmal Kumar. 1965. 'Calcutta – a premature metropolis'. *Scientific American* 213, 3 (Sept. 1976), 91–102.

1968. *Calcutta: 1964. A social survey.* Bombay: Lalvani.

Bouglé, C. 1971. *Essays on the caste system by Célestin Bouglé.* Translated with an introduction by D.F. Pocock, Cambridge: University Press.

Breman, Jan. 1976. 'A dualistic labour system? A critique of the "informal sector" concept'. *Econ. and Pol. Weekly,* 27 Nov., 4 Dec. and 11 Dec. 1976, 1870–6, 1905–8, 1939–44.

1978. 'Seasonal migration and co-operative capitalism: the crushing of cane and of labour by sugar factories of Bardoli'. *Econ. and Pol. Weekly,* special no., Aug. 1978, 1317–60.

1979. 'The market for non-agrarian labour: the formal versus informal sector' in S.D. Pillai and C. Baks, (eds.) *Winners and losers: styles of development in an Indian region,* pp. 122–66. Bombay: Popular Prakashan.

Bromley, Ray and Gerry, Chris (eds.) 1979. *Casual work and poverty in third world cities.* Chichester and New York: Wiley.

Broughton, G.M. 1924. *Labour in Indian industries.* Bombay: Oxford University Press.

Burnett-Hurst, A.R. 1925. *Labour and housing in Bombay.* London: P.S. King.

Campbell, J.K. 1964. *Honour, family, and patronage: a study of institutions and moral values in a Greek mountain community.* Oxford: University Press.

Census of India. 1971. *Paper I of 1971: Provisional population totals.* New Delhi: Census of India.

See Natarajan, D. 1971 (?). *Changes in sex ratio.*

Chithelen, Ignatius. 1980. 'Bombay: reprieve but no protection'. *Econ. and Pol. Weekly,* 12 July 1980, 1171–3.

Chopra, K.A. and U. 1974a. 'Pattern for industrial estates of future: a Rajasthan case study'. *Econ. Times* (Bom.), 27 Mar. 1974.

1974b. 'Industrial estates in Rajasthan'. *Econ. Times,* 21 Aug. 1974.

Clayre, Alasdair. 1974. *Work and play: ideas and experience of work and leisure.* London: Weidenfeld and Nicolson.

Das, Arvind N., Rojas, F. and Waterman, P. 1981. 'The labour movement and labouring people: notes towards a research proposal'. *Human Futures* (New Delhi), 4, 4, 3–24.

Das Gupta, Ranajit. 1976. 'Factory labour in eastern India: sources of supply, 1855–1946'. *Ind. Econ. and Soc. Hist. Review* xiii, 3, 277–329.

Davis, Kingsley. 1951. *The population of India and Pakistan*. New York: Russell & Russell.

Desai, A.R. and Pillai, S. Devadas. 1972. *Profile of an Indian slum*. University of Bombay.

Desai, I.P. 1964. *Some aspects of family in Mahuva: a sociological study of jointness in a small town*. Bombay: Asia.

Desai, P.B., Grossack, I.M. and Sharma, K.N. (eds.) 1969. *Regional perspective of industrial and urban growth: the case of Kanpur*. Bombay: Macmillan.

Deshpande, Lalit K. 1970. 'Competition and labour markets in India' in J.C. Sandesara and L.K. Deshpande (eds.), *Wage policy and wage determination in India*, pp. 281–6. University of Bombay.

1979. 'The Bombay labour market'. Mimeo. Department of Economics, University of Bombay.

De Souza, Alfred (ed.) 1978. *The Indian city: poverty, ecology and urban development*. New Delhi: Manohar.

Devanandan, P.D. and Thomas, M.M. 1958. *Community development in India's industrial urban areas*. Bangalore: Committee for Literature on Social Concerns.

Development Commissioner, Small Scale Industries. 1974. *Small-scale industries in India*. New Delhi: Ministry of Industry.

1977. *Report on census of small scale industrial units*. New Delhi: Ministry of Industry.

Dhar, P.N. and Lydall, H.F. 1961. *The role of small enterprises in Indian economic development*. Bombay: Asia.

Dore, Ronald. 1973. *British factory – Japanese factory: the origins of national diversity in industrial relations*. London: Allen & Unwin.

Doshi, Harish C. 1968. 'Industrialization and neighbourhood communities in a western Indian city – challenge and response'. *Sociological Bulletin* 17, 1, 19–34.

1974. *Traditional neighbourhood in a modern city*. New Delhi: Abhinav.

Dumont, Louis. 1970. *Homo hierarchicus: the caste system and its implications*. London: Weidenfeld & Nicolson.

Economic and Political Weekly. 1975a. 'Battle of minimum wages'. 15 Mar. 1975, 467–8.

1975b. 'Engineering workers: struggle for minimum wages'. 12 Apr. 1975, 612–13.

1977. 'Working-class in small sector'. 19 May 1977, 496–8.

1977. 'New economic policy: shibboleth or programme of action?' 30 July 1977, 1236–42.

Economic Times (Bombay): anonymous articles. 1975. 'Minimum wage echo: small units observe bandh' and 'Minimum wages tangle: talks only way out'. 8 Feb. 1975.

1977. 'Small industries sore: minimum wages order'. 8 Jan. 1977.

Employers' Federation of India 1969. *Absenteeism in industries in Bombay – a survey*. Bombay: Employers' Federation of India.

Engels, Friedrich. In Marx and Engels 1962, *Selected works*, vol. i. Moscow: Foreign Languages Publishing House.

Ford Foundation. 1954. *Report on small industries in India*. Delhi: Ministry of Commerce and Industry.

Fox, Richard G. (ed.) 1970. *Urban India: society, space and image*. Durham, N. Carolina: Duke University.

Frank, André Gunder. 1969. *Capitalism and underdevelopment in Latin America*. New York: Monthly Review Press.

Frykenberg, Robert E. 1965. *Guntur District, 1788–1848: a history of local influence and central authority in south India*. Oxford: University Press.

Gadgil, D.R. 1971. *The industrial evolution of India in recent times, 1860–1939.* Bombay: Oxford University Press, 5th edn.

Gaiha, Raghav and Mohammad, Sharif. 1975. 'Employment implications of India's fifth five-year plan'. *Demography India* iv, 2 (1975), 365.

Gandhi, M.K. 1948. *Cent per cent swadeshi, or the economy of village industries.* 3rd edn. Ahmedabad: Navajivan.

Gerschenkron, A. 1966. 'The modernization of entrepreneurship' in M. Weiner (ed.), *Modernization,* pp. 246–57. New York: Basic Books.

Gillion, Kenneth L. 1968. *Ahmedabad: a study in Indian urban history.* Berkeley: University of California Press.

Goldthorpe, J.H., Lockwood, D., Bechhofer, F. and Platt, J. 1969. *The affluent worker in the class structure.* Cambridge: University Press.

Gordon, A.D.D. 1978. *Businessmen and politics: rising nationalism and a modernising economy in Bombay, 1918–1933.* New Delhi: Manohar.

Gore, M.S. 1970. *Immigrants and neighbourhoods.* Bombay: Tata Institute of Social Sciences.

Gould, Harold A. 1961. 'Some preliminary observations concerning the anthropology of industrialization'. *Eastern Anthropologist* 14, 1 (Jan.–Apr. 1961), 30–47.

Gupta, P.S. 1974. 'Notes on the origin and structuring of the industrial labour force in India 1880 to 1920' in R.S. Sharma (ed.), *Indian society: historical probings.* New Delhi: People's Publishing House, pp. 414ff.

Habbakuk, H.J. 1955. 'The historical experience on the basic conditions of economic progress' in L.H. Dupriez (ed.), *Economic progress,* pp. 149–69. Papers and Proceedings of a Round Table held by the International Economic Association. Louvain: Institut de Recherches Economiques et Sociales.

Hafner, Annemarie. 1978. 'Some factors shaping the Indian trade union movement after World War I, shown through the example of the Madras Labour Union, founded in 1918'. Paper presented to the Sixth European Conference on Modern South Asian Studies, Paris, July 1978.

Hardgrave, R.L. 1970. 'Urbanization and the structure of caste' in R.G. Fox (ed.), *Urban India: society, space and image,* pp. 39–50. Durham, N. Carolina: Duke University.

Harriss, John. 1981. 'Two theses on small industry: notes from a study in Coimbatore, south India'. Paper presented to the Seventh European Conference on Modern South Asian Studies, London, 7–11 July 1981.

1982. 'Character of an urban economy: "small-scale" production and labour markets in Coimbatore'. *Econ. and Pol. Weekly,* 5 and 12 June 1982, 945–54 and 993–1002.

Holmström, Mark. 1969. 'Action-sets and ideology: a municipal election in south India'. *Contributions to Indian Sociology,* N.S. 3, 76–93.

1971. 'Religious change in an industrial city of south India'. *J. Roy. Asiatic Soc.* (1971), no. 1, 76–93.

1972. 'Caste and status in an Indian city'. *Econ. and Pol. Weekly,* 8 Apr. 1972, 769–74.

1976. *South Indian factory workers: their life and their world.* Cambridge: University Press; and 1978, New Delhi: Allied.

Hommes, Enno and Trivedi, Nivedita. 1979. 'Functioning of the labour-market for local graduates' in S.D. Pillai and C. Baks (eds.), *Winners and losers: styles of development in an Indian region,* pp. 81–99. Bombay: Popular Prakashan.

Hone, Angus. 1974. 'The employment potential of appropriate technologies and export-based industrialization in South Asia: analysis and policies.' Mimeo. Oxford. Summarized in H. and V. Joshi, 1976a, *Surplus labour and the city,* p. 179.

Indian Council of Social Science Research. 1974. *A survey of research in sociology and social anthropology*, vol. i. Intro. by M.S.A. Rao. Bombay: Popular Prakashan. 1975. *A survey of research in economics*, vol. v. *Industry*. New Delhi: Allied.

International Labour Office. 1972. *Employment, incomes and equality: a strategy for increasing productive employment in Kenya*. Geneva: ILO.

Jakobson, Leo and Prakash, Ved. 1967. 'Urbanization and regional planning in India'. *Urban Affairs Quarterly* 2, 3 (1967), 36. Beverley Hills: Sage Publications.

Javed. 1981. 'The personality cult'. *Econ. Times* (Bom.), May Day supplement. 2 May 1981.

Johri, C.K. 1967. *Unionism in a developing economy: a study of the interaction between trade unionism and government policy in India, 1950–1965*. Bombay: Asia.

Jolly, Richard (ed.) 1973. *Third world employment: problems and strategy*. Harmondsworth: Penguin Education.

Joshi, Heather and Vijay. 1976a. *Surplus labour and the city: a study of Bombay*. Delhi: Oxford University Press.

Joshi, Heather. 1976b. 'Prospects and case for employment of women in Indian cities'. *Econ. and Pol. Weekly*, special no., Aug. 1976, 1303–8.

1977. Review, 'Market for labour', *Economic and Political Weekly*, 2 Apr. 1977, 575–6.

1980. 'The informal urban economy and its boundaries'. *Econ. and Pol. Weekly*, 29 Mar. 1980, 638–44.

Kannappan, Subbiah (ed.) 1977. *Studies of urban labour market behaviour in developing areas*. Geneva: International Institute for Labour Studies.

Kapadia, K.M. and Pillai, S. Decadas. 1972. *Industrialization and rural society: a study of Atul-Bulsar region*. Bombay: Popular Prakashan.

Kapp, K.W. 1963. *Hindu culture, economic development and economic planning*. Bombay: Asia.

Kelman, Janet Harvey. 1923. *Labour in India: a study of the conditions of Indian women in modern industry*. London: Allen & Unwin, New York: Doran.

Kertzer, David I. 1980. *Comrades and Christians: religion and political struggle in communist Italy*. Cambridge: University Press.

Ketkar, Kumar. 1977. 'Bombay workers up in arms', *Econ. Times* 26 May 1977. 1979. 'Gangsterism in Dhanbad: an anatomy of the trouble'. *Econ. Times* (Bom.), 5 Mar. 1979.

Kumar, Dharma. 1965. *Land and caste in south India*. Cambridge: University Press.

Kurien, C.T. 1978. 'Small sector in new industrial policy'. *Econ. and Pol. Weekly*, 4 Apr. 1978, 455–61.

Labour Bureau. 1971a. *Report of survey on living conditions in bidi factories in India (1965–66)*. Delhi: Labour Bureau, Ministry of Labour.

1971b. *Survey as to how workers support themselves during retrenchment, lay-off, closure and strikes and collection of data regarding indebtedness*. Simla: Labour Bureau. Summarized in Labour Bureau 1978: 123–4.

1974. *Second digest of Indian labour research (1962–1967)*. Delhi: Labour Bureau, Ministry of Labour.

1976. *Indian labour statistics*. Chandigarh: Labour Bureau, Ministry of Labour.

1978. *Third digest of Indian labour research (1968–1972)*. Chandigarh and Simla: Labour Bureau, Ministry of Labour.

Lakdawala, D.T. and Sandesara, J.C. 1960. *Small industry in a big city: a study of Bombay*. University of Bombay series in economics, no. 10.

Lakshman, T.K. 1966. *Cottage and small-scale industries in Mysore*. Mysore: Rao and Raghavan.

Lambert, Richard D. 1963. *Workers, factories, and social change in India*. Princeton: University Press, and Bombay: Asia.

Leach, E.R. (ed.) and intro. 1962. *Aspects of caste.* Cambridge: University Press.

Leibenstein, Harvey. 1957. *Economic backwardness and economic growth.* New York: Science Editions.

Leys, Colin. 1975. *Underdevelopment in Kenya: the political economy of neo-colonialism, 1964–1971.* London: Heinemann.

Lipton, Michael. 1968. 'Strategy for agriculture: urban bias and rural planning' in P. Streeten and M. Lipton (eds.), *The crisis of Indian planning,* pp. 83–147. London: Oxford University Press.

  1977. *Why poor people stay poor: a study of urban bias in world development.* London: Temple Smith.

Lubell, Harold. 1973. 'Urban development and employment in Calcutta.' *International Labour Review* 109, 1 (July 1973), 25–42.

  1974. *Urban development and employment: the prospects for Calcutta.* Geneva: ILO.

Lynch, Owen M. 1969. *The politics of untouchability: social mobility and social change in a city of India.* New York: Columbia University Press.

  1977. 'Political mobilisation and ethnicity among Adi-Dravidas in a Bombay slum'. *Econ. and Pol. Weekly,* 28 Sept. 1977, 1657–68.

MacNamara, Robert, 1975. *Address to the Board of Governors.* Washington: International Bank for Reconstruction and Development.

Mars, Zoë. 1973. 'The manufacture of manufacturers: small industry in Kerala'. Mimeo. Institute of Development Studies, University of Sussex.

Marsden, K. 1973. 'Progressive technologies for developing countries' in R. Jolly (ed.), *Third world employment,* pp. 319–40. Harmondsworth: Penguin Education.

Marx, Karl. 1959. 'The British rule in India', *New York Tribune,* 25 June 1853; in L.S. Feuer (ed.), *Marx and Engels: basic writings and philosophy,* pp. 474–81. Garden City, N.Y.: Doubleday.

  and Engels, Friedrich. 1962. *Selected works,* vol. i. Moscow: Foreign Languages Publishing House.

Mazumdar, H.K. and Nag, A. 1977. 'Survey of mortality of smallscale industries in south India: summary of report'. Mimeo. Hyderabad: Indian Institute of Economics.

McClelland, David C. 1963. 'The achievement motive in economic growth' in B.F. Hoselitz and W.E. Moore (eds.), *Industrialization and society,* pp. 74–96. Paris: Unesco and Mouton.

  1966. 'The impulse to modernization' in M. Weiner (ed.), *Modernization,* pp. 28–39. New York: Basic Books.

Meadows, D.H. *et al.* 1972. *Limits to growth: a report for the Club of Rome's project on the predicament of mankind.* London: Earth Island.

Mehta, M.M. 1968. *Industrialization and employment, with special reference to countries of ECAFE region.* Bangkok: Asian Institute for Economic Development and Planning.

Meillassoux, Claude. 1973. 'Are there castes in India?' *Economy and Society* 2, 89.

Mishra, V. 1962. *Hinduism and economic growth.* New Delhi: Oxford University Press.

Moffatt, Michael. 1975. 'Untouchables and the caste system'. *Contributions to Indian Sociology,* N.S. 9, 1, 111.

  1979. *An Untouchable community in south India.* Princeton: University Press.

Moore, Wilbert E. and Feldman, Arnold S. (eds.) 1960. *Labor commitment and social change in developing areas.* New York: Social Science Research Council.

Morris, M.D. 1960a. 'The labor market in India' in W.E. Moore and A.S. Feldman (eds.), *Labor commitment and social change in developing areas.* New York: Social Science Research Council, pp. 173–200.

  1960b. 'Caste and the evolution of the industrial workforce in India'. *Proceedings of the American Philosophical Society,* Apr. 1960, pt 2, 124–33.

1965. *The emergence of an industrial labor force in India: a study of the Bombay cotton mills, 1854–1947*. Berkeley: University of California Press.

1979. 'Modern business organisation and labour administration: specific adaptations to Indian conditions of risk and uncertainty, 1850–1947'. *Econ. and Pol. Weekly*, 6 Oct. 1979, 1680–7.

Mukerjee, Radhakamal. 1951. *The Indian working class*. Bombay: Hind Kitabs. 3rd edn.

Mukherjee, Sudhendu. 1975. 'Under the shadow of the metropolis – they are citizens too: a report on the survey of 10 000 pavement dwellers in Calcutta'. Mimeo. Calcutta Metropolitan Development Authority.

Munshi, Surendra. 1977. 'Industrial labour in developing economies: a critique of labour commitment theory'. *Econ. and Pol. Weekly*, Review of Management, 27 Aug. 1977, pp. M–74ff.

Myers, Charles A. 1958. *Labor problems in the industrialization of India*. Cambridge, Mass.: Harvard University Press.

Nambiar, K.K.G. 1977. 'Should small-scale units be propped up?' *Indian Express*, 15 June 1977.

Natarajan, D. 1971 (?). *Changes in sex ratio*. New Delhi: Census of India, 1971. Census centenary monograph no. 6.

National Commission on Labour. 1969. *Report*. New Delhi: Government of India, Ministry of Labour and Employment and Rehabilitation.

National Sample Survey Organization. 1976. *Tables with notes on small-scale manufacturing in urban and rural areas*. New Delhi: Ministry of Planning.

Nehru, Jawaharlal. 1956. *The discovery of India*. London: Meridian.

Niehoff, Arthur. 1959. *Factory workers in India*. Milwaukee: Milwaukee Public Museum Publications in Anthropology.

Ornati, O.A. 1955. *Jobs and workers in India*. Ithaca: Cornell University Press.

Owens, Raymond L. 1973. 'Peasant entrepreneurs in an industrial city' in Milton Singer (ed.), *Entrepreneurship and modernization of traditional cultures in south Asia*, pp. 133ff. Durham, N. Carolina: Duke University.

and Nandy, Ashis. 1975. 'Organizational growth and organizational participation: voluntary associations in a West Bengal city'. *Contributions to Indian Sociology*, N.S. 9, 1, 19.

and Nandy, Ashis. 1977. *The new Vaisyas*. Bombay: Allied.

Pandhe, M.K. (ed.) 1979. *Child labour in India*. Calcutta: Indian Book Exchange.

Panini, M.N. 1977. 'Networks and styles: a study of Faridabad industrial entrepreneurs'. *Contributions to Indian Sociology*, N.S. 11, 1, 91–115. This issue was reprinted as S. Saberwal (ed.), *Process and institution in urban India: sociological studies*. New Delhi: Vikas, 1978.

Panjwani, Narendra. 1980. 'Workers first'. *Econ. Times* (Bom.) 10 Aug. 1980, 5–7.

Papola, T.S. 1977. 'Mobility and wage structure in an urban labour market: a study in Ahmedabad (India)' in S. Kannappan (ed.), *Studies of urban labour market behaviour in developing areas*, p. 142–56. Geneva: International Institute for Labour Studies.

and Subrahmanian, K.K. 1975. *Wage structure and labour mobility in a local labour market: a study in Ahmedabad*. Ahmedabad: Sardar Patel Institute of Social and Economic Research. Distributed by Popular Prakashan, Bombay. (And see Heather Joshi's review in *Econ. and Pol. Weekly*, 2 Apr. 1977, 575–6).

Parthasarathy, V.S. 1958. 'Caste in a south Indian textile mill'. *Econ. and Pol. Weekly*, 16 Aug. 1958, 1083–66.

Patel, Kunj. 1963. *Rural labour in industrial Bombay*. Bombay: Popular Prakashan.

Perlin, Enid. 1979. 'Ragi, rice and four-yard dhoties: Indian mill workers as historical sources' in *Asie du sud: traditions et changements*, 451–7. Colloques

Internationaux du Centre National de la Recherche Scientifique (intro. M. Gaborieau and A. Thorner). Paris: Editions du CNRS.

Philips, C.H. 1963. *Politics and society in India*. London: Allen & Unwin.

Pillai, S. Devadas and Baks, Chris (eds.). 1979. *Winners and losers: styles of development in an Indian region*. Bombay: Popular Prakashan.

Pocock, D.F. 1955. 'The movement of castes'. *Man* 55, 71–2.

  1958. 'Notes on the interaction of English and Indian thought in the nineteenth century'. *Cahiers d'histoire mondiale* 4, 833–48.

  1960. 'Sociologies: urban and rural'. *Contributions to Indian Sociology* iv, 63–81. Reprinted in M.S.A. Rao (ed.), *Urban sociology in India*. New Delhi: Orient Longman, 1974, pp. 18–39.

  1962. 'Notes on jajmani relationships'. *Contributions to Indian Sociology* vi, 78–95.

  1968. 'Social anthropology: its contribution to planning' in P. Streeten and M. Lipton (eds.), *The crisis of Indian planning*, pp. 271–89. London: Oxford University Press.

  1972. *Kanbi and Patidar: a study of the Patidar community of Gujarat*. Oxford: University Press.

Pradeep, Prem and Das, Arvind. 1979. 'Organisation of the future? A case study of the Bihar Colliery Kamgar Union'. *Human Futures* (New Delhi), 2, 3, 240–55.

Prakasa Rao, V.L.S. and Tewari, V.K. 1979. *The structure of an Indian metropolis: a study of Bangalore*. New Delhi: Allied.

Punjwani, Jyoti. 1976. 'Women workers – deep-seated prejudices'. *Times of India*, 10 Oct. 1976.

Ramachandran, P. 1974. *Some aspects of labour mobility in Bombay city*. Bombay: Somaiya.

Ramaswamy, E.A. 1974. 'The role of the trade union leader in India'. *Human Organization* 33, 2, 163–72.

  1976. 'Trade unions for what?' *Econ. and Pol. Weekly*, 20 Nov. 1976, 1817–18.

  1977. *The worker and his union: a study in south India*. New Delhi: Allied.

  (ed.) 1978. *Industrial relations in India: a sociological perspective*. Delhi: Macmillan. Includes E.A. Ramaswamy, 'The meaning of the strike', pp. 14–40.

  and Ramaswamy, Uma. 1981. *Industry and labour: an introduction*. New Delhi: Oxford University Press.

Ramaswamy, Uma. 1979. 'Tradition and change among industrial workers'. *Econ. and Pol. Weekly*, annual no. (1979) 367–76.

Ranson, C.W. 1938. *A city in transition: studies in the social life of Madras*. Madras: Christian Literature Society for India.

Rao, B. Shiva. See Shiva.

Rao, M.S.A. (ed.) 1974. *Urban sociology in India*. New Delhi: Orient Longman.

Ray, Rajat K. 1979. *Industrialization in India: growth and conflict in the private corporate sector, 1914–47*. New Delhi: Oxford University Press.

Read, Margaret. 1927. *From field to factory: an introductory study of the Indian peasant turned factory hand*. London: S.C.M.

Reindorp, Julian. 1971. *Leaders and leadership in the trade unions in Bangalore*. Madras: Christian Literature Society.

Reserve Bank of India. 1964. *Survey of small engineering units in Howrah*. Report of a survey undertaken by the Jadavpur University under the auspices of the Reserve Bank of India. Bombay: Reserve Bank of India.

Revri, Chamanlal. 1972. *The Indian trade union movement*. New Delhi: Orient Longman.

Rizvi, S.M. Akram. 1976. 'Kinship and industry among the Muslim Karkhanedars in Delhi' in Imtiaz Ahmad (ed.), *Family, kinship and marriage among Muslims in India*, pp. 27–48. New Delhi: Manohar.

Royal Commission on Labour in India. 1931a. *Report*. Calcutta: Govt of India, Central Publication Branch.

1931b. *Evidence*, vol. I, *Bombay Presidency (including Sind)*, pt 1, London: HMSO.

1931c. *Evidence*, vol. I, *Bombay Presidency (including Sind)*, pt 2. London: HMSO.

1931d. *Evidence*, vol. V, *Bengal*, pt 1. London: HMSO.

1931e. *Evidence*, vol. V, *Bengal*, pt 2. London: HMSO.

1931f. *Evidence*, vol. XI, *Supplementary* (contains short life-histories of workers). London: HMSO.

Saberwal, Satish. 1976. *Mobile men: limits to social change in urban Punjab*. New Delhi: Vikas.

Sandesara, J.C. 1969. *Size and capital intensity in Indian industry*. Univ. of Bombay.

and Deshpande, L.K. (ed.) 1970. *Wage policy and wage determination in India*. University of Bombay.

Saxena, K.N. 1965. 'Workers' attitudes towards their jobs'. *Indian Journal of Labour Economics* viii, 2–3 (July–Oct. 1965), 177–98.

Schumacher, E.F. 1974. *Small is beautiful: a study of economics as if people mattered*. London: Abacus.

Sengupta, Nirmal. 1981. '"Sons of the soil" in particular, ethnic upsurges in general'. *Human Futures* (New Delhi), 4, 4, 34–44.

Sharma, Baldev Raj. 1974. *The Indian industrial worker*. Delhi: Vikas.

1978. 'Union involvement revisited'. *Econ. and Pol. Weekly*, 29 July 1978, 1233–40.

Sharma, K.L. and Singh, Harnek. 1976. 'Entrepreneurial growth and industrial development programmes in Punjab and U.P.: a comparative study of small entrepreneurs'. Mimeo. Ludhiana: Dept of Economics and Sociology, Punjab Agricultural University.

Sheth, N.R. 1968a. *The social framework of an Indian factory*. Manchester: University Press.

1968b. 'Workers, leaders and politics: a case study'. *Indian Journal of Industrial Relations* 3, 3, 286–99.

Shiva, Rao, B. 1939. *The industrial worker in India*. London: Allen & Unwin.

SIET Institute. 1976. 'Sick units'. SENDOC Bulletin, pt 3. Management and behavioural sciences, 4, 3 (March 1976), pp. D1–D6. Hyderabad: Small Industry Extension Training Institute.

Silverberg, James (ed.) 1968. *Social mobility in the caste system*. The Hague: Mouton.

Singer, Milton. 1960. 'Changing craft traditions in India' in W.E. Moore and A.S. Feldman (eds.), *Labor commitment and social change in developing areas*. New York: Social Science Research Council, pp. 258ff.

1972. *When a great tradition modernizes*. New York: Praeger.

1973. (ed.) *Entrepreneurship and modernization of traditional cultures in south Asia*. Durham, N. Carolina: Duke University.

Singh, V.B. 1969. 'Industrial relations climate in Kanpur' in P.B. Desai, *et al.* (eds.), *Regional perspective of industrial and urban growth: the case of Kanpur*, pp. 105–13. Bombay: Macmillan.

Sinha, J.N. 1969. 'Occupational structure of the three major textile centres of India' in P.B. Desai *et al.* (eds.), *Regional perspective of industrial and urban growth: the case of Kanpur*, pp. 114–26. Bombay: Macmillan.

Sovani, N.V. 1966. *Urbanization and urban India*. Bombay: Asia.

Srinivas, M.N. 1952. *Religion and society among the Coorgs of south India*. Oxford: University Press.

1962. *Caste in modern India, and other essays*. Bombay: Asia.

1966. *Social change in modern India*. Berkeley: University of California Press.

Srinivasulu, S.J. 1977. 'Tasks before the small sector', *Times of India*, 25 June 1977.

Streefkerk, Hein. 1978. *Lichte industrie in een kleine indiase stad: ondernemers en arbeiders in Zuid-Gujarat sinds 1900.* (Light industry in a small Indian town: entrepreneurs and workers in South Gujarat since 1900. With an english summary.) Amsterdam University: Anthropologisch-sociologisch centrum, Vakgroep Zuid-en Zuidoost Azie, Sarphatistr. 106a. Publicatie nr. 27. (Publisher's name not given.) Printed by Rob Stolk. ISBN 90 9000075 5.

    1979. 'Small entrepreneurs – agents in underdevelopment?' in S.D. Pillai and C. Baks (eds.), *Winners and losers: styles of development in an Indian region*, pp. 100–21. Bombay: Popular Prakashan.

    1981. 'Too little to live on, too much to die on: employment in small scale industries in rural south Gujarat'. *Econ. and Pol. Weekly*, 11, 18 and 25 Apr. 1981, pp. 659–68, 721–8, 769–80.

Streeten, Paul and Lipton, Michael (eds.) 1968. *The crisis of Indian planning: economic planning in the 1960s.* London: Oxford University Press.

Subrahmanian, K.K. and Kashyap, S.P. 1975. 'Small-scale industries' in Indian Council for Social Science Research, *A survey of research in economics*, vol. v: *Industry*, 75–112. New Delhi: Allied.

Subramanian, Dilip. 'The MICO strike: a retrospective.' *Econ. and Pol. Weekly*, Review of Management, 31 May 1980, pp. M–59 to M–68.

Sutcliffe, R.B. 1971. *Industry and underdevelopment.* London and Reading, Mass: Addison-Wesley.

Thorner, Daniel. 1966. 'Marx on India and the Asiatic mode of production'. *Contributions to Indian Sociology*, ix, 33–66.

Thorner, Daniel and Alice. 1962. *Land and labour in India.* Bombay: Asia.

Tinker, Hugh. 1963. 'Tradition and experiment in forms of government' in C.H. Philips (ed.), *Politics and society in India*, pp. 155ff. London: Allen & Unwin.

Turner, Roy (ed.) 1962. *India's urban future.* Berkeley: University of California Press.

Turnham, David. 1971. *The employment problem in less developed countries.* OECD Development Centre Studies, Employment series 1. Paris: OECD.

Vaid, K.N. 1966. *Contract labour in manufacturing industries.* New Delhi: Shriram Centre for Industrial Relations.

    1968. *The new worker.* Bombay: Asia.

Vakil, C.N., *et al.* 1931. *Growth of trade and industry in India.* Calcutta: Longmans Green.

van der Veen, Klaas. 1979. 'Urbanization, migration and primordial attachments' in S.D. Pillai and C. Baks, (eds.), *Winners and losers: styles of development in an Indian region*, pp. 43–80. Bombay: Popular Prakashan.

Vohra, G.S.G. 1975. 'Woes of small industries'. *Times of India*, 23 Aug. 1975.

Waterman, Peter. 1980. 'Reflections on unions and popular movements in India'. The Hague: Institute of Social Studies, for restricted circulation.

Weber, Max. 1930. *The protestant ethic and the spirit of capitalism.* London: Allen & Unwin.

    1958. *The religion of India.* New York: Free Press.

Wiebe, Paul. 1978. 'Interdependence not duality: slum perspectives' in A. de Souza (ed.), *The Indian city: poverty, ecology and urban development*, pp. 17ff. New Delhi: Manohar.

Wiser, W.H. 1922. 'Welfare work for Indian employees', series of articles in *British Indian Crafts* (Calcutta), Jan.–Aug. 1922. Quoted in Kelman 1923, *Labour in India*.

    1936. *The Hindu jajmani system.* Lucknow Publishing House. Reprinted 1958.

Index

334